THE MEDIEVAL WORLD
AN ILLUSTRATED ATLAS

NATIONAL GEOGRAPHIC

WASHINGTON, D.C.

CONTENTS

Page 1: Jerusalem sits at the center of this 13th-century *mappa mundi,* or map of the world. Many animals, real and fantastical, populate the continents.
Page 2: Christ sits enthroned, surrounded by four angels, on the illuminated opening page of the Gospel of Matthew in the 9th-century Irish masterpiece, the *Book of Kells.*

FROM THE EDITOR

In *The Medieval World: An Illustrated Atlas,* the National Geographic Society presents the vast array of people, places, and events through 1,000 years of world history, combining maps, time lines, illustrations, and text—both central narrative and sidebars—into a tapestry as complex and fascinating as the world was then.

The book is divided into 12 chapters, the first an overview and introduction to the worldview of the times. Each of the remaining chapters represents one century in the span most broadly defined as the medieval period, from the 5th to the 15th century. Even though the geographical frame of the book is confined to the world of the Mediterranean, many cultures, peoples, and vicinities coexisted in those times, and so often the focus of one chapter will move from one corner of the map to the other, the counterpoint indicative of the many things happening all at once during these ages that were anything but dark. And even though the temporal frame of a chapter is set at 100 years, the narrative must at times gaze back or forward in time, since human events do not necessarily pace themselves according to the arbitrary numbers of a calendar, and history does not start or stop with the turn of the century.

Our authors have chosen to include a mix of the familiar and the unfamiliar, exploring and explaining those things that we customarily associate with the Middle Ages—castles and knights, Beowulf and the Crusades—but also including glimpses into people, places, and things that have not made it into everybody's view of history: queens who ruled with iron wills, theological arguments that drove military actions, and everyday items such as shoes or farming tools. As much as possible, images from the Middle Ages illustrate these pages, but now and then a later interpretation of the times reminds us how the stories of this millennium have resonated with meaning through every generation since.

We begin each chapter with a time line of that period, highlighting the events that shaped the world in those days. Beyond that, though, we hope that the maps, illustrations, quotations, and narrative help fill in between the landmark moments of history, infusing life into this period of world history at once so foreign and so familiar to us today.

NARRATIVE AND SIDEBARS

Each chapter tells the story of a century. Some words are defined in glossary boxes below, and these definitions appear in the back of the book as well. Quotations from medieval documents have been translated into modern English. Sidebars highlight five aspects of medieval life: **Personae:** people; **Locus:** geography; **Edifices:** types of buildings; **Innovations:** technological advances; **Arts and Letters:** cultural landmarks.

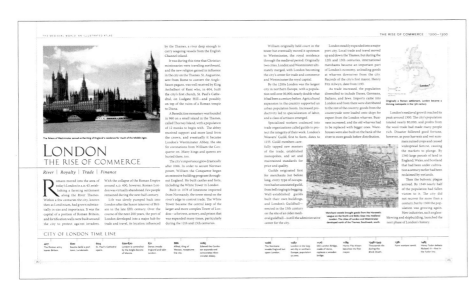
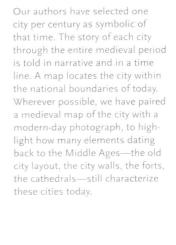

CITY OF THE CENTURY

Our authors have selected one city per century as symbolic of that time. The story of each city through the entire medieval period is told in narrative and in a time line. A map locates the city within the national boundaries of today. Wherever possible, we have paired a medieval map of the city with a modern-day photograph, to highlight how many elements dating back to the Middle Ages—the old city layout, the city walls, the forts, the cathedrals—still characterize these cities today.

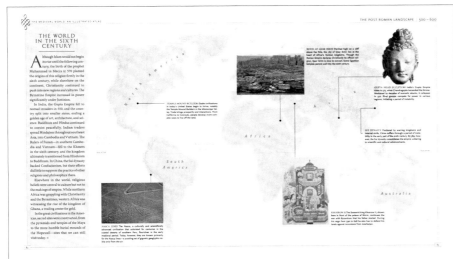

WORLD MAP

Traditionally, the history of the Middle Ages is the history of the Mediterranean world, and yet wars were fought, civilizations were built, and great art and architecture was created elsewhere in the world during this same period of time. For that reason, Chapters 2 through 12 include world maps signaling a few of the advances, changes, and developments happening on every continent of the world in the 11 centuries between A.D. 400 and 1500.

MEDIEVAL THEMES

Every chapter concludes with a visual gallery of artifacts that help bring the medieval world to life by showing the very things that people made, used, and touched—clothing, animals, dishware, books, and games, for example. Culling from the archives of libraries and museums throughout the world, we display a number of objects dating from the Middle Ages that give a sense of the texture of daily life in those times.

THE MEDIEVAL WORLD

The events that we call the Middle Ages all happened within the geographical frame defined by the Mediterranean Sea. Influences on this world arrived from all directions—Vikings from Scandinavia, tribesmen such as the Huns from Central Asia, Berbers from North Africa. But the royal courts, the imperial capitals, the religious centers, and even the far-flung monasteries—the sum total of what then would have been called the known world—all were located in Europe, the Middle East, and North Africa.

By and large the cities that were important to the medieval world are still important today: Paris, Rome, Constantinople, Jerusalem. A few, such as Antioch or Palermo, may have faded some with time. Most are situated near water, whether along rivers or on the seacoast itself. Daunting mountain ranges divide the terrain, particularly the Pyrenees and the Alps, making long-distance travel between many medieval centers of culture actually swifter and easier over water than over land.

Access to water allowed settlements to grow and prosper as the centers of trade and activity. Certain land and water features, whether a calm harbor or a high point of land with good visibility, offered protection from weather and invasions. Other features offered conveniences for travelers, such as oases or mountain passes. To tell the story of these lands is to shed new light on the Middle Ages—as this illustrated atlas is designed to do. ◾

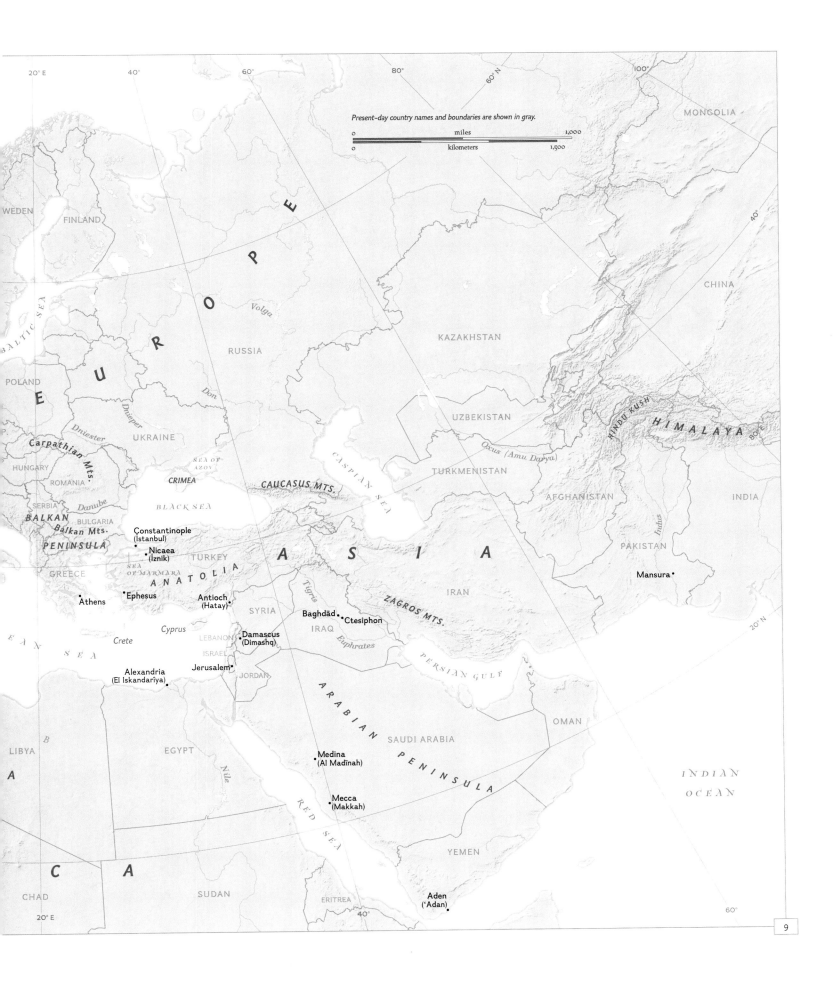

Present-day country names and boundaries are shown in gray.

miles
0   1,000
kilometers
0   1,500

SWEDEN
FINLAND
E U R O P E
Volga
BALTIC SEA
RUSSIA
POLAND
Don
Dnieper
UKRAINE
Dniester
Carpathian Mts.
HUNGARY
ROMANIA
Danube
SERBIA
BALKAN
BULGARIA
Balkan Mts.
PENINSULA
GREECE
SEA OF AZOV
CRIMEA
BLACK SEA
Constantinople
(Istanbul)
Nicaea
(Iznik)
TURKEY
SEA OF MARMARA
ANATOLIA
A S I A
Athens
Ephesus
Antioch
(Hatay)
SYRIA
Tigris
Cyprus
Crete
LEBANON
Damascus
(Dimashq)
IRAQ
Euphrates
ISRAEL
Baghdād
Ctesiphon
ZAGROS MTS.
IRAN
Alexandria
(El Iskandarîya)
Jerusalem
JORDAN
CAUCASUS MTS.
CASPIAN SEA
KAZAKHSTAN
UZBEKISTAN
TURKMENISTAN
Oxus (Amu Darya)
AFGHANISTAN
HINDU KUSH
HIMALAYA
MONGOLIA
CHINA
INDIA
PAKISTAN
Indus
Mansura
MEDITERRANEAN SEA
LIBYA
EGYPT
Nile
ARABIAN PENINSULA
SAUDI ARABIA
Medina
(Al Madīnah)
OMAN
PERSIAN GULF
RED SEA
Mecca
(Makkah)
AFRICA
CHAD
SUDAN
ERITREA
YEMEN
Aden
('Adan)
INDIAN OCEAN

20° E
40°
60°
80°
60° N
100°
40°
80° E
20° N
40°
60°
20° E
40°
60°

9

Liber Magistri Hugonis Sancti Victoris (The Book of Hugh of St. Victor), *circa 1130*

The Medieval Worldview
400 – 1500

Knights in glistening armor. Colorful banners emblazoned with fleur-de-lis and lions. Swords and shields, marked with symbols of family legacies, wealth, and power. Castles and dragons, unicorns and magicians. Vikings and barbarians, troubadours and minstrels. Serfs in coarse-woven clothing and rough wooden shoes tilling the soil. Popes and emperors, caliphs and kings, queens and saints, hermits and heretics. Crowns heavy with gems and gold, gowns draped in silk and velvet. Charlemagne. Joan of Arc. The Crusades. The Inquisition. The Plague. The Battle of Hastings. The Magna Carta. Say the words "Middle Ages" and a fully populated landscape of benchmark events, larger-than-life characters, myths and stories, colors and images comes to mind. We have heard these stories from childhood—Robin Hood and his Merry Men, King Arthur and the sword in the stone. We guffaw at satires of those times in Monty Python movies; we patronize theme parks dedicated to medieval times. It's a world that we carry in our shared imagination, as if we knew it, as if we once lived there, as if we would love to go back in time. While many of our fantasies about the medieval world may not match historic fact, all can be traced back in some way to actual human experiences during that remarkable era, those thousand years that stretch between the times we call ancient and those we deem modern—between the Roman Imperial era and the Renaissance. In this book we spread out that rich and sumptuous tableau, offering an array of the most interesting stories, the most significant events, the most meaningful accomplishments, and the most influential personalities. Here we present the full, rich, complex, and amazing span of history that we call the Middle Ages.

We begin by defining the medieval world in time and place. The words "medieval" and "middle" are linguistically related, and the idea that this period came in the middle, between two other eras that stood tall and significant, is a Renaissance concept steeped in self-importance that persists today. Renaissance thinkers prided themselves on rediscovering the art and philosophy of the ancient Greeks and Romans in a way that they believed their forebears of centuries past had not done. However, as the coming chapters reveal, many medieval scholars had found wisdom in the classics, and many worked hard to bring that wisdom—and the classics themselves—to light.

A similar disdain for medieval thought and culture is echoed in the term "Dark Ages," a term that did not enter the

Britain sits in the center, invaded by seafaring barbarians from all around—or at least that was how one 12th-century artist portrayed his country's 9th-century history.
preceding pages: Brothers, sons, and cousins fought one another for land and title; here Fulk IV and Geoffrey the Bearded battle over 11th-century Anjou, France.

English language until the 18th century, according to the *Oxford English Dictionary*. The phrase usually refers to the first half of the period generally considered the Middle Ages—the centuries from which we have the least historical and cultural evidence, because writing and record keeping were more primitive.

Technologies were also simpler in those five or six centuries after the fall of the Roman Empire. In the last few centuries of the Middle Ages, agriculture, architecture, city planning and infrastructure, and money systems, for example, all seem to have evolved more swiftly and into closer correspondence with what we know today. Those early centuries weren't necessarily dark, although a moonless night in this time before many cities had developed—and thus before much manmade light after sundown—must have presented a shade of pitch-black that we moderns cannot even imagine.

Roughly speaking, the time represented in this book spans one thousand years. Many historians regard the Middle Ages as extending from the fall of the Roman Empire, in A.D. 476, to the fall of the Byzantine Empire as it was overtaken by the Ottomans in A.D. 1453. For simplicity's sake, this book defines the Middle Ages as the fifth to the sixteenth century—from A.D. 400 to A.D. 1500—and thus redefines the endpoint of the period as the time of the first influential transatlantic voyages of discovery. This definition of the period makes sense within the geographical frame of events in the book.

Well into the 20th century, standard history books considered western Europe to be the center of power and activity in the medieval world. The advance of

This iron-and-bronze helmet from a seventh-century ship burial reveals the wealth of the Anglo-Saxon kings of England.

THE MIDDLE AGES

455
The Vandals capture Rome.

570
Muhammad is born.

733
Charles Martel defeats the Moors at Tours.

800
Pope Leo III crowns Charlemagne emperor.

836
Vikings sack London.

962
Otto I becomes first Holy Roman Emperor.

1097
First Crusade arrives in Constantinople.

1191
Richard the Lionheart defeats Saladin.

1215
The Magna Carta is signed.

1337
The Hundred Years War begins.

1492
Christopher Columbus sails west.

Islam across North Africa into Spain and through Turkey into Eastern Europe was considered an invasion; the Crusades were considered a series of holy wars mounted by Christians against infidels of a foreign culture. For generations, the standard story of the Middle Ages in the Western world was delivered as explicitly and exclusively European history.

Today, in the 21st century, the historical worldview in the Western world has broadened, and curiosity about and respect for the rise of Islam as a force of history equals interest in the influences of Christianity. With that shift, the frame for mapping the medieval world broadens slightly. The Mediterranean Sea still sits at the center of the map, but events that were taking place in the Middle East and in North Africa, as well as in Islamic Spain, are brought into the tableau as we now recognize how important they have been, and continue to be, within the political, religious, and cultural heritage of the entire world.

It is the place of the National Geographic Society to look around the world even farther, though—and in this book we do, thanks to specially created maps in every chapter that highlight important moments of history occurring in every part of the world during each century of the Middle Ages. Rather than focusing just on western Europe, or just on the lands skirting the Mediterranean Sea, this book opens to a wider world. It includes landmark events that were taking place on other continents as well: the dynasties of China, the insight and architecture of India and Southeast Asia, the rise and fall of great Mesoamerican civilizations. All of these may have been vaguely known, or not known at all, by the people whose lives we are tracing in our narrative about the medieval world, and yet such grand events must be part of the picture of the world during these key centuries.

Even those people who were only barely aware of other realms beyond their own towns reaped the benefits of inventions and trade from the far corners of the known world. They knew of silks and brocades, paper and porcelain from China; pearls from the Indian Ocean; incense and spices from Arabia; and ivory from Africa. All such valued goods amount to clear evidence of how closely interconnected cities, kingdoms, and continents were, even then.

This book covers a large part of the world and a long period of time. For that reason, many of the stories told here can only be painted with broad brushstrokes. We know more about the leaders—the kings and emperors, popes and caliphs—than we do about the common man. (And we know more about the common man than we do the common woman and child.) Historical documents; artworks from the time, as well as historic evocations from times since; the great medieval buildings still standing at the center of many cities; and the findings of ongoing archaeology, both artifacts and sites—all provide the materials needed to weave a complex tapestry of the daily lives and the history-making people and events of the medieval world.

A Story of Three Civilizations

This book surveys history from the declining years of the Roman Empire, in the 5th century A.D., to the European voyages of discovery at the end of the 15th century, narrating the events of 11 centuries in 11 chapters. To tell this part of world history, we must trace the parallel, but divergent, stories of three civilizations—western European Christendom, eastern European Byzantium, and Middle Eastern Islam—from their shared origins in late antiquity and the early Middle Ages through their diverse fates in subsequent centuries. Throughout this saga, the stories of these three cultures often intersect.

Of these three civilizations, only one, the Byzantine, existed at the outset of our narrative—and, as it happened, while the civilizations of both Islam and western Christendom had grown strong by 1500, the Byzantine Empire had by that date ceased to exist.

The civilization of the Byzantines grew directly out of the traditions of the Roman Empire of antiquity. The Byzantine Empire was centered in Constantinople, the capital city of the eastern portion of the Roman Empire, established by Emperor Constantine in the fourth century. Constantinople prospered in the ensuing centuries, and it came to be regarded as "the new Rome"—while Rome itself, so long deemed the Eternal City,

Medieval monarchs, such as Hugh Capet (seated), whose descendants ruled much of France for three centuries, established regional dynasties through warfare, marriage, and the obligations of vassalage.

withered from the onslaught of foreign invasions and indeed almost died, only to be reborn as the spiritual capital of western Christianity.

The Byzantine state endured vicissitudes for more than a thousand years, becoming the stronghold of Eastern Orthodox Christianity. In 1453 invaders from Turkey conquered Byzantium and ultimately established an Islamic successor state, the Ottoman Empire. They gave the ancient city of Constantinople a new name: Istanbul.

Both western Europe and the Arabian Peninsula were inhabited by peoples whom the ancient Romans had described dismissively as barbarians. In the fifth century there was little to indicate that these barbarian peoples would eventually build impressive civilizations of their own on the ruins of the Roman Empire—but that is just what they did.

Both of the civilizations built up over the course of the medieval centuries were founded and driven by something more important to them than it had ever been to the Romans: religion. At least, one could say, religion had a role in the medieval civilizations of Christendom and Islam that was distinctly different from the role it played in ancient Roman society, and the difference was not merely one of degree: It was a difference in kind.

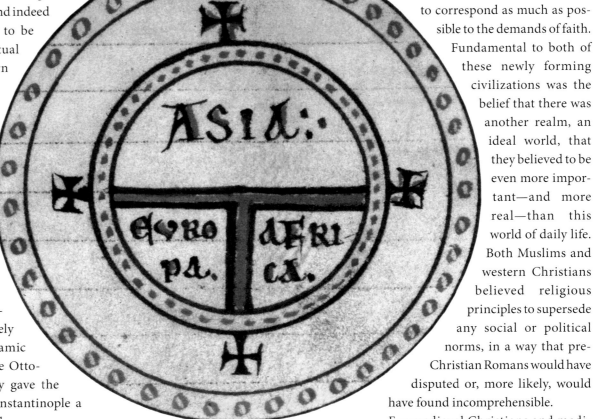

The worldview of medieval Europe consisted of three continents, Asia, Europe, and Africa, all surrounded and divided by ocean, as depicted in this diagram inspired by seventh-century encyclopedist Isidore of Sevilla.

CULTURES OF RELIGION

For the ancient Romans, and to a large extent for their Byzantine heirs, religion was essentially a department of the state and a convenient means of lending legitimacy to existing conditions. By contrast, for the medieval civilizations of both the Islamic world and western Christendom, religion provided the spiritual foundation for any civic structures. Medieval Muslims and Christians both came to understand religious belief and practice as the ideal and true touchstone for all economic, political, and social principles. Religious and civic leaders alike believed that these principles ought to correspond as much as possible to the demands of faith.

Fundamental to both of these newly forming civilizations was the belief that there was another realm, an ideal world, that they believed to be even more important—and more real—than this world of daily life. Both Muslims and western Christians believed religious principles to supersede any social or political norms, in a way that pre-Christian Romans would have disputed or, more likely, would have found incomprehensible.

For medieval Christians and medieval Muslims, religion provided the basis and the context for whatever economic, political, and social norms human beings were supposed to adhere to, and whatever economic, political, and social goals they could expect to achieve in this world. In the crassest of situations, as with the Romans, religion would be used to legitimize worldly conditions. Ideally, however, religion would show the way to a better life in every realm.

For these reasons, it is accurate to describe the civilization of medieval Europe as "Christian," and to characterize medieval Arab civilization as "Islamic." A well-balanced history of the medieval world must chronicle the origins, birth, and growth of both of these great world cultures.

This history tracks the development of medieval Europe—Christendom—from its early years in the 5th century to the beginnings of its disintegration, on the threshold of the Protestant Reformation of the 16th century. In the 5th century, all that the Romans had labored for centuries to build and maintain was decaying and falling into ruin. Successive waves of so-called barbarians with seemingly little interest in what the Romans had been doing, and even less understanding of it, sought to use pieces of this crumbling civilization to build a new one.

FROM THE RISING OF THE SUN, TO THE SHORE OF THE SEA WHERE IT GOES DOWN AGAIN, ALL HEARTS ARE FULL OF GRIEF . . . O CHRIST, TAKE THE PIOUS EMPEROR INTO YOUR HOLY DWELLING PLACE AMONG YOUR APOSTLES.

From an elegy for Charlemagne by an Irish monk
Italy, circa 814

Building upon the ruins of the ancient city of Rome, a culture emerged that represented the unifying force of medieval Europe: the Roman Catholic Church. One of the ironies of medieval history is that the civilization that was then the most insecure and the least accomplished—the culture developing out of Christianity, centered in the city of Rome—emerged to become the most self-assured and powerful social force in modern history.

This book likewise tracks the development of medieval Islamic civilization,

The medieval castle of Turegano, Spain, still reveals inner and outer curtain walls, designed to protect nearby villagers in times of siege. The defensive fortifications of medieval castle walls were continually improved and strengthened in response to innovations in weaponry.

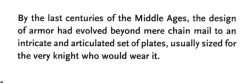

By the last centuries of the Middle Ages, the design of armor had evolved beyond mere chain mail to an intricate and articulated set of plates, usually sized for the very knight who would wear it.

from its seemingly obscure origins among desert tribesmen in the Arabian Peninsula of the 6th century, through its remarkable rise and spread, and ultimately to its manifestation as a political power, seen first in the succession of Muslim dynasties through the Middle Ages and culminating in the Ottoman Empire of the 15th century. By that time Islam, like Christianity, had become a universal religion—a religion whose call and appeal was not limited to the members of any particular region, race, or tribe, but was offered, implicitly or explicitly, to all human beings.

At the close of the 15th century, the moment in time when this book ends, Christianity and Islam were both poised to contend for dominance not only over one another but indeed over the entire world. The next few centuries would witness continuing rivalry between these two civilizations. By the 18th century, the civilization of Islam was in retreat, while the civilization of western Europe, having become more secular, was dominating the world— so much so that scholars, writing of the 19th and 20th centuries, often used the terms "westernization" and "modernization" as if they were synonymous.

ELEVEN CENTURIES OF CHANGE

This book is organized so that each chapter tells the story of one century of medieval history. It is an artificial and arbitrary division in some respects, although the turn of each century was regarded as a watershed, just as today the turn of the century or the arrival of the new millennium is regarded as momentous, marking time and history. Often the narrative must cast a glance back to decades or even centuries previous, but the story and the characters in it stand for each hundred years of time.

Chapter 2 describes the cultural, political, and social structure of the Roman Empire in its final days, during the fifth century, A.D. 400-500. By this time in history, the Roman state had existed, first as a republic and then later as an empire, for approximately one thousand years—a long time by any standard.

But by the early fifth century, the empire was falling prey to both internal decay and external attack. For centuries, Roman society had found ways to assimilate successive waves of outsiders—some conquered, some seeking to conquer, and some simply seeking new land on which to survive. As the Roman Empire began to lose its supremacy, roving bands of peoples from outside the bounds of the empire moved in. Their influences reshaped the map, conceptually and geographically, of what had long represented the height of human cultural, political, and social potential.

As the fifth century approached, however, Roman society was losing the capacity to assimilate foreign peoples without weakening itself in the process,

MEDIEVAL Referring to the time between the fall of the Roman Empire and the age of discovery, roughly 450 to 1500. From the Latin for "middle," the term was coined by Renaissance historians who saw the period as an interim between the classical age and their own.

and so it was losing its luster as the ultimate human social order. Also during this time, the Roman Empire had begun abandoning outlying provinces, such as Britain. Indeed, the empire was proving incapable of protecting even its center, its core regions—including the Eternal City itself—from humiliating attack. Looking for explanations for its weakness, some wistful pagan intellectuals blamed the decline of Roman power and civilization on the increasing popularity of a new religion, Christianity, which, in their view, undermined traditional Roman values.

Augustine of Hippo, the most eloquent spokesman for early Christianity, countered the claim by arguing that in fact Rome was falling apart because of its peoples' continued adherence to traditional Roman values. It was because of Christianity, argued Augustine, and because of the benevolence of the Christian God, that Roman civilization continued to exist at all.

In the sixth century, A.D. 500-600, the known world was emerging from the shadow of Rome, and so Chapter 3 surveys the post-Roman world of the 500s. This century was once commonly described as the beginning of the Dark Ages, when the lights of civilization and culture allegedly went out, not to be relit until the advent of the Italian Renaissance of the 14th century. The fall of Rome did not amount to the end of the world, or the end of light, or the end of intellect, however, even though Augustine's pagan opponents thought that it might; nor was early medieval European culture and civilization as dark and dreary as later historians were to imagine.

During the sixth century, building in part on the deteriorating foundations

PERSONAE

SOCIAL CLASSES

From Farm to Feudal to Market Economy

Never a static phenomenon, the old social order fell apart along with the Roman Empire, replaced by a decentralized agrarian economy that was a blending of Mediterranean culture and Germanic customs. Land was the basis of wealth, and landowners pursued the increase of wealth through the acquisition of more land. This left small-scale farmers vulnerable to rampant violence, so contracts of vassalage became common. Lords provided their retainers military protection in exchange for the toil of the earth.

Thus three classes of society were born: those who worked, those who fought, and those who prayed. Military protection included the construction of walled cities, where a fourth class was created, the merchants or bourgeoisie. This class struggled against abuse and taxation to claim a large stake in society. By the high Middle Ages, a gradual shift to a money economy gave birth to market capitalism and a new Europe. ▪

In the feudal system, peasants raised food in exchange for military protection.

of the legacy of Rome, a Germanic tribe called the Franks began to establish a semblance of order in and control over western Europe. In isolated monasteries in Britain and Ireland, monks labored with remarkable success to preserve the learning of the ancient world. On the European continent as well, the Benedictine Rule—an ethic of prayer, good works, and divine service—served as the foundation for monasteries as centers of learning, piety, and obedience.

Out of this tradition emerged one of the greatest leaders in the history of Christendom, Pope Gregory I, whose sixth-century ideas would guide the Christian church and, in effect, the whole of Christendom, for centuries to come. Gregory the Great strove with remarkable success to take the norms guiding and inspiring Benedictine monks and make them the norms that guide and inspire all people of western Europe—especially the leaders. During the sixth century, an alliance was established between the sword-wielding Franks and the spiritually authoritative institutions of the papacy and the monasteries. This alliance was to drive the course of western European cultural history through the remainder of the medieval age. Meanwhile, the eastern part of the Roman Empire, founded by the Emperor Constantine in the fourth century and centered in Constantinople, flourished as well.

Chapter 4 covers the seventh century, A.D. 600-700, when the world witnessed the birth of a new religion. Islam (which means submission to God) originated in Arabia and then spread throughout the southern and eastern reaches of the former Roman Empire by winning converts from paganism.

At the same time, in western Europe, a dynasty known as the Merovingians was securing a place as the ruling line of Frankish kings—if only to set the stage for their own successors, known as the Carolingians. In eastern Europe, the Byzantines were battling the Sassanids of Persia, a traditional imperial foe. In the process, both empires were growing weaker, even before the coming incursions from Arabia, which neither as yet recognized.

Next, Chapter 5 tells the interwoven stories of the eighth century, A.D. 700-800, when the world of ancient Rome began to give way in earnest to the civilizations rising anew in the medieval world, in and around Europe. In this century, the three major cultures—Byzantine, western European, and Islamic—began to take the shapes that would endure for centuries to come, formed as much by conflict between one another as by creation from within.

Western Europe faced grave danger throughout the eighth and ninth centuries, both from the aggressive Islamic civilization and from aggressive northern and eastern neighbors who plundered new lands to compensate for poverty at home. In the process, newcomers pressed into European territory, at first to acquire easy riches and eventually

The fourth-century Theodosian Code—named for Roman Emperor Theodosius II—established Christianity as the religion of the Roman Empire.

to claim land for settlement. The victory of Christendom over these outside threats is symbolized in the reign of the Frankish emperor Charlemagne, who defended western Europe from its various foes, at the same time constructing the administrative, economic, legal, military, religious, social, and even cultural and artistic bases of a new civilization. Quite consciously, this new Christian leader formed a vision of a world order, an amalgam of Roman, Germanic, and Christian traditions.

Of the three cultures dominant in the eighth century, the Byzantine Empire most overtly continued the traditions

of ancient Rome. Both the western European and the Islamic civilizations were built on Rome's ruins as well, and they had grown up, for the most part, in lands that had once been part of the old Roman orbit, centered on the Mediterranean Sea—which the Romans had once called "our lake."

Despite struggles with the Persians, despite a growing awareness of the Muslims as a threat, and despite a looming tension with western Christendom, the chief threat to the Byzantine empire of the eighth century was internal, and almost psychological in nature: It was the iconoclast controversy, a deeply divisive debate over whether religious practice should include physical representations of sacred beings, like Christ, the Virgin Mary, and the saints. Ironically, this controversy among Christians was very likely influenced by Islam's strict rules against any artistic renderings of the sacred, particularly the Prophet Muhammad. In the Byzantine culture, the debate became a political touchstone, however—a defining issue in conflicts within the Byzantine Empire of the eighth century.

Western Christians owed a debt to contemporary Rome not shared by the Muslims or even the Byzantines of the eighth century. Christians everywhere were coming to rely more and more on

ECUMENE Derived from the Greek, this word means the entire inhabited world. It can also mean worldwide followers of a specified religion: the Islamic ecumene, for example. From this word derives the concept of an ecumenical, or worldwide, church council.

the Church of Rome for spiritual guidance and administrative manpower, and as an institutional model of organization. At the same time, western Europe faced a growing threat from the spread of Islam, whose forces had quickly swept west through North Africa and into the Iberian Peninsula. The Muslims now seemed on the verge of conquering Europe as they pushed into Frankish territory until they were defeated by the army of the warrior Charles Martel in the Battle of Tours in 732.

As much as we tell their history through political and military actions, each of these three civilizations depended on its religious core for cultural unity; both Christianity and Islam offered their adherents a medium of personal and collective identity of greater significance than tribe, clan, or locale. Even so, factions and rivalries began to create splits within each civilization, as is evident in the transition of power from the Umayyads to the Abbasids within Islam and the growth of a new, cosmopolitan capital in Baghdad, to replace the old Arab-centered capital of Damascus.

Chapter 6 narrates the tensions between unity and factionalism during the ninth century, A.D. 800-900. Less threatened by external foes, the civilizations of Islam and of Byzantium began thriving periods of cultural growth, emanating from their respective urban centers of Baghdad and Constantinople. Late in the ninth century, the emerging state of Anglo-Saxon England proved able, under the leadership of Alfred the Great, to establish and maintain itself despite successive Viking attempts first to harass, and ultimately to take over, the island realm.

Chapter 7, representing the tenth century, A.D. 900-1000, approaches the end of the first millennium. This century witnessed the division of Islamic civilization into rival centers of political power—rivalries that persist today in the conflicts between Sunni and Shiite Muslims. Despite divisions, the cultural unity

Pious even in death, Eleanor of Aquitaine, queen consort of two successive kings, participated in the unsuccessful Second Crusade to the holy land. She and her husband Henry II still rest in effigy atop their tombs in Fontevraud Abbey in Anjou, France.

of the Islamic ecumene remained intact and thrived through the tenth century.

In northern Europe, the Vikings began to leave off plundering and established settlements in England and France. Despite the influence of the Danelaw, England continued developing its own social and political structure, based on the system of administration and defense set up by Alfred the Great.

As the kingdoms of continental Europe began to develop into feudal societies, three social orders came to be recognized, distinguishing those who work, those who fight, and those who pray. The German King Otto I defeated the marauding Magyars decisively and restored vigor to the Holy Roman Empire when, following Charlemagne's example, he was crowned emperor by the pope. His coronation also signaled the increasing moral authority of the papacy and the church in western Christendom.

The events of the 11th century, A.D. 1000-1100, described in Chapter 8, turned out to be decisive for the future course of history. Two events, late in the century, were of major significance.

One was the Investiture Controversy, a struggle between the papacy and the Holy Roman Emperor over which one wielded the ultimate authority in the Christian world. The outcome was that while power (called *potestas* by medieval philosophers) resides in the sword of the state, true authority *(auctoritas)* resides in the offices of the church. This controversy and its outcome articulated the principle of the separation of church and state and determined that the church, deriving its authority directly from God, could never be a mere department of the state—which is what the Emperor Henry IV was trying to make it.

The other big event of the late 11th century was the Christian response to the continuing spread of Islamic powers: the Crusades. Jerusalem was a city with sacred ties to each of the three Mosaic religions: Judaism, Christianity, and Islam. Ostensibly, the Crusades were pilgrimages made by Europeans to the Middle East in order to wrest the city back from

> YOU SHOULD NOT TRY TO DEVISE NECESSARY ARGUMENTS ON BEHALF OF FAITH, SINCE THIS WOULD DEROGATE FROM THE SUBLIMITY OF FAITH, WHOSE TRUTH EXCEEDS THE CAPACITY NOT ONLY OF HUMAN BUT ALSO OF ANGELIC MINDS.
>
> ———
>
> THOMAS AQUINAS
> *DE RATIONIBUS FIDEI*
> *(ON THE REASONS FOR FAITH)*
> *Circa 1260*

the Muslims—but such huge social movements always have many layers of meaning, implication, and actual effect.

The Crusades represented a chance to reunify the Eastern and Western churches—the Byzantine and the Holy Roman Empires—which had split decisively in 1054. As it turned out, that mission failed miserably. Once underway, the Crusades came to be controlled by, and of interest chiefly to, western Christian powers, not eastern. Not only did the Crusades appear to Western church leaders

as an opportunity to perform seemingly holy deeds; they also represented a field of battle beyond the borders of Christendom for bellicose feudal lords. This way they could wield their swords against a common religious enemy, the Muslims, rather than against one another.

Chapter 9 introduces the 12th century, A.D. 1100-1200, the period during which so many of the romantic and colorful stereotypes of medievalism were born. During this century the population grew, and with that growth new towns and cities developed. Inspired and complex new architectural projects—cathedrals, guildhalls, hospitals, fortresses, and castles—were begun.

The 12th century saw the military and political efforts of the Second and Third Crusades, as well as the flowering of art and philosophy, now called the 12th-century Renaissance, with the development of the concept of courtly love and the resurgence of philosophy that depended on faith in natural law.

Among the unintended results of the Crusades was the importation of new luxuries, manners, and ideas from Asia and the Middle East into Europe, which contributed to cultural and social sophistication. Towns grew up as centers of trade, culture, and learning in western Europe, particularly in Italy and Germany. The cities of Paris and London came into their own as centers of commerce and style.

The European crusaders returned with new ideas about what to eat and how to build castles; other ideas, from both current and rediscovered ancient works, trickled into western markets, monasteries, cathedrals, and courts. The concept of courtly love sprang up in southern France. Some say love itself was invented

In February 1301 Edward I of England appointed his son Prince of Wales, as shown above in a manuscript illumination. Thus the man who eventually became Edward II was the first English heir to the throne to bear that title, despite Welsh opposition to English domination through the Middle Ages and beyond.

The Great Mosque of Córdoba, Spain, was adapted in 784 from a previous Christian Visigothic church that had been built atop the ruins of a Roman temple.

in the Middle Ages. Certainly the ideals of romantic love combined with heroic adventure came to light in, for example, the tales of King Arthur and the Knights of the Round Table, who may well have been historic individuals but who, by their 12th-century reappearance, were already legendary and magical.

The discovery—or rediscovery—of half-forgotten works of science and philosophy from antiquity, notably many of Aristotle's works, prompted new translations into Arabic and Latin. Islamic scholars pushed into new realms of science and mathematics, while Christian philosophers and theologians like Peter Abelard sought to understand the relationship between faith and reason and to fathom the answers to hosts of prac-

tical and speculative questions. Muslim thinkers crafted their own syntheses of faith and science. Christian thinkers began to borrow freely from both the pagans of antiquity and from recent and contemporary Muslims.

Some medieval histories call the 13th century, A.D. 1200-1300, featured in Chapter 10, the greatest of the Middle Ages. In England, Magna Carta effectively made the English king a constitutional monarch—a leader who would always be answerable to Parliament and no longer be above the law. Henceforth the king of England would be regarded as "first

among equals," unlike the kings of France, who still tended to view themselves as ordained by God to a station well above that of ordinary mortals. France had one of her great kings in Louis IX, who strove to be the kind of ruler of whom the scholastic theologian Thomas Aquinas could approve: He sought to be loved more than to be feared by his people.

Few kings, however, could manage Louis IX's combination of political wisdom and religious devotion. At the other extreme was Frederick II, the Holy Roman Emperor who spent most of his reign striving, and failing, to subjugate all of his nominal subjects into real ones. Among Frederick's most difficult subjects were the citizens of northern Italian towns, who were growing increasingly wealthy and were far more interested in establishing sturdy republican governments for themselves than in supporting Frederick's schemes to subdue them.

Chapter 11 presents an overview of the 14th century, A.D. 1300-1400, which was in many respects the beginning of the end of the medieval era. The Black Death, in mid-century, wiped out one-third of Europe's population, forever changing the economic and social con-

> WE HAVE GRANTED TO GOD, AND BY THIS PRESENT CHARTER HAVE CONFIRMED FOR US AND OUR HEIRS IN PERPETUITY, THAT THE ENGLISH CHURCH SHALL BE FREE, AND SHALL HAVE ITS RIGHTS UNDIMINISHED, AND ITS LIBERTIES UNIMPAIRED.

> MAGNA CARTA
> *London, 1215*

ditions of the Continent. The Hundred Years War, a war between France and England over disputed territories on the Continent, began in 1337 and continued intermittently, actually lasting for 116 years. Meanwhile, eastern Europe was beginning to feel the threat of Islamic warriors who, in the next century, would bring the Byzantine Empire to its end. And the Great or Papal Schism—a fierce contest over who was the rightful holder of the power of the papacy—served, in the final decades of the century, to undermine confidence in the institution that, more than any other, symbolized the earlier unity of Christendom.

Chapter 12 moves through the 15th century, A.D. 1400-1500, calling it the dawn of a new age—and indeed many historians would consider this the beginning of the Renaissance. This century set the stage for the end of the medieval world and the beginning of a new world spirit, which was acted out in the 16th century and beyond.

Internal divisions shook the foundations of the western Church, in, for example, the controversy over the teachings of Jan Hus, an avowed disciple of John Wycliffe, key figure during the Papal Schism of the previous century. Both of these theologians had preached for more lay involvement in the church.

At the same time, a reform movement sought, and failed, to make the authority of the papacy subject to that of councils, just as England's king had been made subject to Parliament.

The Hundred Years War continued on its futile way, but neither dazzling victories—such as that of the English king Henry IV at Agincourt—nor inspirational prophecies—such as those of French martyr Joan of Arc—could bring the struggle to a real conclusion. The war officially ended in 1453, and while it did result in the English abandoning claims to land on the Continent, its chief consequence was an enduring hatred between the rival powers—France and England.

POWER AND RELIGION IN THE MIDDLE AGES

Worldly and Heavenly Rewards

Religion was central to the medieval world, in the daily lives of individuals, in the social rules within which communities operated, and in shared, often unconscious, assumptions underlying worldviews. As such, great power derived from the prominent religions, Christianity and Islam, which led to both good and disastrous ends.

In the Christian world of the Middle Ages, abbots, bishops, and popes became powerful leaders, mingling religious influence and worldly power in ways that challenged civic leaders and spurred endless battles both intellectual and military. In response, new austere monastic orders formed during the Middle Ages, and popular piety movements proliferated. Some of these movements formed semireligious knightly orders, such as the Knights Templar, that led Crusades to retake Jerusalem and Palestine from Muslim control and extend Christianity elsewhere.

During the later Middle Ages, inquisitions were formed by combined papal and royal decree, and religion became a feature by which leaders could separate the loyal from the politically dangerous. The momentous split between Western and Eastern Christianity—between the Roman world and the Byzantine—carried significant political and theological consequences.

In the Islamic world of the Middle Ages, religious and political leadership were often one and the same. In Islam's early years, the community was small, and the unified vision between heavenly and worldly goals probably galvanized Muslims in their missionary zeal.

As the religion's influence spread, the Islamic world fractured into geographic subdivisions whose leaders claimed religious power yet battled with one another over worldly wealth and territory. Muslims just as righteously battled to maintain control of the holy lands of Jerusalem and Palestine as did the Christian crusaders who traveled hundreds of miles to retake them. ■

This animosity lasted even longer than the war itself, and it helped to fuel the growth of a kind of patriotism based on shared national identity that would in centuries to come inform the spirit that has powered more recent (if similarly inconclusive) wars.

The year 1453 also saw the end of the Byzantine Empire, overtaken by the Ottoman Empire, an Islamic state that would threaten the Christian states of Europe for the next several centuries. Finally, near the end of the century, explorers would venture forth over the western sea seeking shortcuts to the riches of the East, only to discover a strange new world that even the wisest of the ancients seemed not to have known about.

It is a telling irony of history that the year 1492 marks two significant events: Christopher Columbus's arrival in the New World and the definitive Christian recapture of Spain, effected by a military victory against Muslim forces and by a ruthless expulsion of Jews from the land. At the end of the 15th century, the world looked back—to the religious and territorial conflicts that had driven spirit and identity for the last thousand years— and looked forward, to a new land, and to the possibility of new civilizations.

CONTINUING INFLUENCES

In certain ways, our modern world takes its shape from the ideas, conflicts, challenges, and solutions of the Middle Ages. Some of our institutions began to form during these centuries—for example, the modern university.

The structure of a cluster of colleges, all encompassed by a larger educational entity, began in medieval universities. The very subjects in which those colleges specialize, the liberal arts, were distinguished and defined in the medieval era. And the very idea of preparing for life with the broad,

This stone figurine of elephant and driver, unearthed in modern-day Iran, was carved by craftsmen in the eighth or ninth century for use as a chess piece.

culturally focused initiation of a liberal arts background, in preparation for further studies in professions such as law, medicine, and theology, took root in medieval times. These debts to a medieval past show through not only in the organization of college catalogs but also in the architecture that we instinctively associate with university campuses

today: tall, heavy stone buildings with Gothic arches, courtyards, and colonnaded walkways—the design of an abbey, applied to the academy.

By the same token, our sense of church architecture—vaulted ceilings, stained-glass windows, the cross-shaped transept, chapels to the side—derives from the floor plans of great Gothic cathedrals. Likewise today's mosques include elements established during these early centuries of Islam: minarets from which voices call out to the faithful, intricate decorative work neither representational nor perfectly symmetrical in its design, and broad open spaces where the faithful gather daily to pray.

More abstractly, the modern democratic notion of the separation of church and state traces back to bitter arguments over power in the Middle Ages. The very idea that there are matters of the world distinct and separate from matters of the spirit, and that different sets of principles apply to each of these realms, emanates from some of the important events and arguments that weave through much of medieval history, as chronicled in this book.

In important ways, the modern sense of community stems from developments of the Middle Ages as well. From the close-knit ties between lord and vassals to the network of trade and specialization at the heart of any city, and even extending to the larger sense of a national or cultural identity shared among people who may have never met one another but who can connect through history, beliefs, and fidelities—the seeds of every one of

In this 15th-century illumination from an English history, a monarch looks down upon representatives of the five estates, or social classes, from his vantage point at the apex on the wheel of fortune, with Fortune herself controlling the wheel as it turns.

these communal feelings can be found in the history of the Middle Ages.

On the other hand, the people of the medieval world seem to have experienced a deep and foreboding sense of the Other. The more one feels a part of the community of "us," the more those outside the community become an alien "them." Some of the most ruthless events that blot this thousand-year span of history—the Crusades, the Inquisition, the expulsion of the Jews from Spain—emanate from a sense of estrangement, even fear and hostility, toward those deemed different.

One thing that the modern Western world clearly does not share with the world of our medieval forebears is a fundamental and unswerving belief that religious certainties hold everything together. There were many fears and unknowns in the lives of medieval women and men, to be sure, but the existence of God and the

> I SEE THAT YOU HAVE A GREAT AND NOBLE DESIRE TO GO INTO THAT COUNTRY [TO THE EAST] WHERE THE SPICES COME FROM… IF I HAD A GLOBE IN MY HAND, I COULD SHOW YOU WHAT IS NEEDED.

ASTRONOMER PAOLO DAL POZZO TOSCANELLI TO CHRISTOPHER COLUMBUS
Italy, 1474

truth of God's laws remained steady, a glue that held community together and a strand of connection through times past and future. For those who lived in the Middle Ages, the church was the center of life that all shared, the source of truth and wisdom, and the end for which one

labored. Most modern humans are not quite so firmly centered.

And perhaps that is one reason why we remain so enchanted by things medieval: the kings and queens, the trolls and fairies, the damsels in distress, the knights and sorcerers. The stories populated by these characters are first and foremost entertaining. But, more deeply, they tell us of a time long ago in our own heritage, when things were very different and yet human nature was very much the same.

These are stories of suspense and adventure, of romance and chivalry, of the common fears of humankind and the perennial battle between good and evil. In retelling these stories, we figure out our own—and in browsing through this colorful and engaging history of the medieval world, we learn more about our own past, present, and future.

CHANGING WORLDVIEW

Trade, Travel & Treaties Reshape the Map

As Roman society disintegrated during the fourth and fifth centuries, it meant a decline in the Silk Road trade, the loss of accumulated science and technology, and a generally more insular outlook as people concerned themselves more with subsistence than philosophy. Germanic customs and laws, introduced by groups such as the Goths, Lombards, and Saxons, gained predominance as territorial principalities reemerged in northern and western Europe.

Powerful individuals built up self-sustaining strongholds against invasion by Vikings, Magyars, Muslims, and their own neighbors, and an agrarian barter economy was the model of the day. Long-distance trade was impossible until landed nobility could be convinced to give up their forest hunting grounds to be turned into fields for agriculture. After that,

agricultural innovations spurred a food surplus that allowed population growth and the reemergence of towns and cities. A transformation in outlook and learning occurred in these cities as a new merchant class created a commodity-based economy dependent on trade. Trade fairs were held in many European cities, and demand for exotic goods pushed adventurous Italian mariners back into the larger economy of the revived silk roads, while German traders established the Hanseatic League of the Baltic and North Seas.

Constantinople was an especially vibrant crossroads of trade, where Venetian and Genoese businessmen established lasting commercial enterprises. Manufactured goods were not the only products coming into the cities of Europe: Intellectual property circulated, too, as the writings of Aristotle were translated into

Latin from Arabic and Greek sources, along with commentaries by the renowned Muslim philosopher Averroes. Aristotle's rational analysis of the world clashed with the ecclesiastical worldview that had dominated early medieval Europe. Europe's first universities reintroduced the dialectical method of Aristotle, while scholastic churchmen, such as Thomas Aquinas, sought to synthesize classical and medieval thought. Other borrowings from abroad included new crops such as coffee and spices, new technologies such as paper production, new sciences such as algebra, and new diseases, notably the plague. Even in the wake of the Black Death and the financial crisis that followed, Italy's universities continued to cultivate a renewed interest in the knowledge of the classical world, a movement we refer to today as the Renaissance. ■

This 13th-century map represents Jerusalem at the center of the world and the Mediterranean Sea extending downward toward
an ocean that encircles the known landmasses.

ARCHITECTURE IN THE MEDIEVAL WORLD

Popular throughout Europe from the 12th century onward, Gothic architecture distinguished itself from the Romanesque style by elaborate stonework and pointed archways, as shown in this detail from Venice's Palazzo Ducale.

erhaps no other architectural style in history has captivated the modern imagination quite like the Romanesque and Gothic styles of the medieval era. Millions of tourists flock to the cathedrals and castles of Europe each year; significant modern churches, such as the National Cathedral in Washington, D.C., echo the centuries-old style. Both secular and religious buildings were constructed in Romanesque and Gothic styles, but we tend to look to the cathedrals as the era's landmarks.

Romanesque structures were characterized by round arches, stone piers, large towers, and decorative arcading. The simple, often symmetrical style can still be seen across Europe, most importantly in the great abbey churches—Cluny Abbey in France, for example. Like the Gothic churches that would follow them, Romanesque abbeys followed the Latin cross, or cruciform, floor plan, which consisted of a long nave bisected by a transept. The balanced, orderly, and symbolic layout reflected faith in a universe designed and governed by God.

Gothic architecture, more extreme and technically daring than the Romanesque, first appeared in the middle of the 12th century. It included pointed arches and intricately sculpted facades. Ribbed vaults and flying buttresses allowed these cathedrals to be built to even greater heights and added a new element of exterior decoration. Other ornamentation added bursts of color and embellishment: Large stained-glass windows depicted biblical scenes; figures carved into columns or archways were often painted vividly.

The overall effect, meant to inspire religious awe, could also be excessive and ornate. Renaissance architects looked back to the style preceding theirs and named it Gothic—a term that carried a bit of disdain.

Bursts of color in painted stonework and decorative embellishments characterized as well as secular architecture. Here, medi strels adorn the columns of St. Mary's C Yorkshire, England.

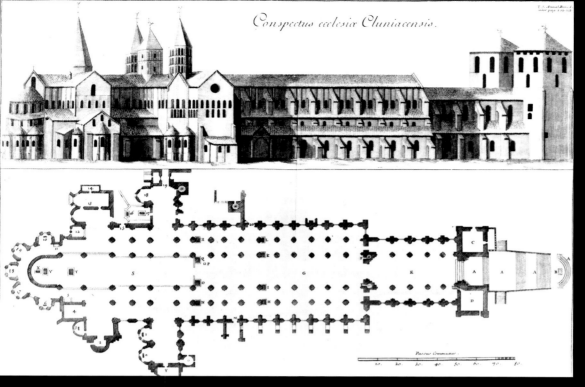

Romanesque cathedral architecture typically followed a cruciform plan, visible in the floor plan for Cluny Abbey in Burgundy, France. Designed as a cross, the abbeys were believed to reflect God's desire for a balanced universe.

Medieval architectural traditions still persist today, visible in the halls and libraries of modern universities, as well as in churches and cathedrals. The vaulted ceilings and stonework of Grace Church in New York City are prime examples.

400 – 500

E START OUR STORY OF THE MIDDLE AGES WITH THE ENDING OF ANOTHER AGE—the great Roman Empire, which had lasted for centuries but finally came to an end in the fifth century. The story of the rise of medieval Europe may overshadow the story of Rome's demise in fascination and intrigue. The empire of the Caesars and their legions fizzled ignominiously over several decades, as the vast territory gave way, piecemeal, to outsiders, until finally imperial Rome succumbed in 476. Rome's decline set the stage for the rise of new powers in Europe during the Middle Ages; thus we begin with a detailed look at the empire in its last days. In the early fourth century, the empire was guided by the emperor Constantine, whose conversion to Christianity had an enormous impact on European history and Western civilization. Constantine became the first Roman Emperor to embrace Christianity, as this strange religion, with its

message of spiritual equality, spread beyond its Near Eastern origins. Giving credit to Jesus Christ for military and political victories, Constantine not only made Christianity fashionable but also paved the way for it to become the official state religion by century's end. Paganism was waning, and Christianity was becoming a powerful force in shaping European culture over the next few centuries.

In the meantime, though, Rome had a serious problem. The many tribes who lived north of the empire's borders—known collectively as barbarians—wanted in. They were looking for better land and opportunities to the south; they wanted protection from the nomadic Huns; and they wanted some of the good life that Romans had enjoyed for centuries. From the late fourth century through the fifth century, barbarians came streaming across the natural borders of the Rhine and Danube Rivers. From the east came Ostrogoths and Visigoths, from the west came Burgundians, Franks, Saxons, and Vandals, among others. Some of these outsiders were allowed in as refugees, while others forced their way in behind armies. But however they came, these groups of newcomers rapidly spread out into Gaul, Spain, and North Africa, and within three decades the Roman Empire had to abandon these western provinces. The economic and military resources of Rome were simply overwhelmed.

In the long run, the lands of the empire became home to hundreds of thousands of new settlers, many of whom were encouraged to keep land in return for military service. Their displacement of old Roman families caused friction far and wide, as people with strange habits and languages

The art of Byzantine mosaics reached its most expert expression during the reign of Justinian I, who commissioned works such as this one of the baptism of Jesus. *PRECEDING PAGES:* Totila, Ostrogoth king, kneels before the renowned monk, Benedict of Nursia, around 542, when the church was taking on a larger political role.

insinuated themselves among the populace. Resentment flared on both sides, although after intermingling over a few generations, the provinces settled in with newly mixed-race identities. As the population grew, governance by Rome became more difficult. Small, local kingdoms arose, presenting the challenge, during much of the early Middle Ages, of inter-tribal warfare, one small kingdom battling another for territory.

The powerful Germanic king Odoacer toppled the last of the Roman emperors in 476, establishing a Gothic kingdom in Italy. At the same time, to the east, Byzantium was still very much alive.

The Byzantine emperor formed an alliance with King Theodoric of the Ostrogoths, who then was able by warfare and treachery to kill Odoacer and take over Italy. Theodoric's long reign, taking him well into the sixth century, was marked by a policy of *civilitas*, whereby the Goths proclaimed themselves not the enemies but the restorers of Rome. But his territorial ambitions would ultimately bring down the wrath of the Byzantines, those living in the surviving eastern portion of the old empire.

BECOMING CHRISTIAN

The 1,000-year Roman Empire was about 800 years old when Diocletian became emperor, in A.D. 284. Rome was still enjoying a golden age of power, wealth, and peace, its territory wrapping around the Mediterranean and extending as far north as Britain. Its provinces included lands south of the Danube River and in what is now Turkey, as well as the rim

In the fifth century the Vandals stormed through the Roman Empire, some on horseback, ultimately establishing a short-lived kingdom in North Africa.

THE FIFTH CENTURY

406
The Vandals launch a massive invasion of Gaul.

407
The Romans withdraw from Britain.

410
Rome is sacked by the Visigoths.

434
Attila becomes king of the Huns.

449
The Anglo-Saxons arrive in southeast Britain.

455
Rome is sacked by the Vandals.

476
Having shrunk to only Italy and some of Gaul, the western Roman Empire dissolves.

481-482
Clovis I succeeds his father, Childeric, as king of the Franks.

493
Theodoric, an Ostrogoth, becomes king of Italy.

of North Africa. It was a vast empire for one city to control. Too vast—political and military power was spreading out more and more to the provinces.

The people of Germania to the north, considered barbarians by the Romans, began making numerous attacks along the borders of the empire in the third century, siphoning off money and manpower for defense. Instability was furthered by a crisis in leadership, for this was a particularly dangerous time to be an emperor. More than 20 men took their turns on the throne in the 49 years before Diocletian took over—most of them meeting death in coups or battle.

A veteran of many military campaigns, Diocletian became emperor after personally killing another contender for the throne. For the next 21 years he brought efficiency and strength to Rome and its satellites. To manage the sprawling, extensive empire more effectively, he took the groundbreaking step of splitting the empire into two parts, a western half and an eastern half. He himself ruled the eastern empire, while he appointed a man named Maximian to rule the west. This jointly governed entity created a dual empire that would eventually rupture into a Latinate West and a Greek East.

Diocletian's final years as emperor were marked by the last—and probably the bloodiest—persecution of the Christians. Since the death of Jesus in about A.D. 30, Christianity had slowly been gaining popularity among non-elite Romans, offering the hope of an egalitarian community of the spirit. Out in the provinces, Christianity not only gained strong religious influence, thus displacing the pagan gods; it also became a political force to be reckoned with.

By the year 303, when Diocletian ordered the persecution, about 10 percent of the Roman population was Christian. Until the order was rescinded by Diocletian's son-in-law 8 years later, Christians were brutally put down; in Rome alone some 40 houses of worship were destroyed.

THE TIME OF CONSTANTINE

Diocletian stepped down from power in 306. Devoting the last decade of his life to gardening, he died in his late 60s at his Dalmatian villa. In the meantime, another even more powerful ruler was coming into his own.

Of Balkan peasant descent, Constantine was born around 280 and ruled as emperor from 306 to 337. His mother was a barmaid, and likely a prostitute; his father rose from humble origins to be a general and then assistant emperor, in charge of Britain and Gaul (mostly modern France). As a young military officer, Constantine moved throughout the eastern empire, coming into frequent contact with Christians.

At some point—some say as a result of a transcendent vision of a cross, glowing in the heavens above him—he discarded his father's monotheistic Unconquerable Sun religion and embraced the Christian God. His conversion was to have a profound impact on the future of Roman, European, and world history.

A civil war broke out after Diocletian's retirement, and three contenders vied for the throne. Constantine was based in Britain and Gaul, the poorest region of the empire. In 312 he decided to gamble on marching his army over the Alps for an attack on Rome. His decisive victory

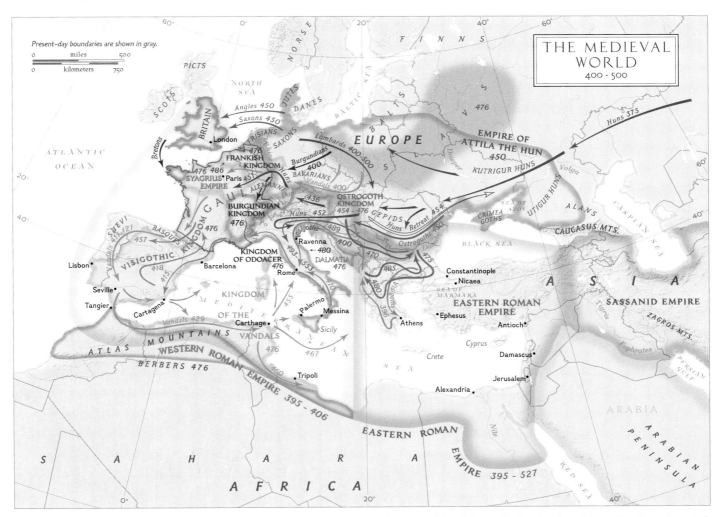

As the century began, Europe was dominated by the Western and the Eastern Roman Empires. Hun raids and Germanic migrations brought sweeping change to central Europe and the Mediterranean. By century's end, nothing remained of the Western Empire, while the Eastern Empire was on the rise, Constantinople its imperial capital.

at the Battle of Milvian Bridge outside Rome gave him supremacy in the West; he would later claim that he owed his success to his devotion to the Christian God. For the next 12 years he ruled with a co-emperor in the East, whom he then deposed, becoming sole ruler.

In 313, Constantine declared toleration for all religions in his Edict of Milan, and he went about trying to reverse the preceding years of persecution by endowing churches and elevating the status of priests. He relocated his capital to the ancient Greek city of Byzantium, on the west side of the Bosporus—the strait dividing Europe from Asia—and renamed the city Constantinople.

In 325 he called the Council of Nicaea, named for a town in Asia Minor. At this first major convening of leaders of the Christian church, he and the bishops resolved certain fundamental doctrines of Christianity. Their conclusions are codified in the Nicene Creed, still repeated as a tenet of faith today.

The Nicene Council marks a turning point in the history of Rome and of the new religion. By the late 300s, Christianity had become the official religion of the Roman Empire. Paganism was outlawed, and pagan temples were destroyed. A complete reversal had taken place, with Christianity emerging as the religion sanctioned and protected by the state.

BARBARIANS AT THE GATES

Through the fourth century and much of the fifth, Rome faced wave after wave of barbarian invasions. Not only did the Romans have to fend off outsiders, but the attacks were complicated by shifting alliances. Romans allied with Germanic tribes to fight off the Huns, and then those same Germanic tribes turned against the Romans, their protectors. Interactions were not always hostile. Trade developed along the Rhine-Danube border as well, as one culture influenced another: Germans acquired some of the civilized manners of the Romans, and Romans took up some of the German customs, games, and dress. The borderlands in particular saw a constant mixing of genes and mores.

When Germanic tribes began moving into Gaul and then northern Italy by the second century, they were not attempting a takeover but simply pushing out in search of better living conditions. The Germans were primitive herdsmen and farmers who wore cloaks and sewn skins; their artistry consisted chiefly of ornamented swords, spears, and jewelry.

BELIEF

SAINT AUGUSTINE OF HIPPO

An Intellectual Approach to Christianity

Born in North Africa to a Christian mother, Augustine of Hippo received a classical education steeped in Latin literature, rhetoric, and Hellenistic philosophy. In 383, he left for the Italian peninsula, where he met Ambrose, the Catholic bishop of Milan. Increasingly disillusioned with other theologies, Augustine was baptized by Ambrose in 387. Both his mother and his son died, leading him to ruminate on the human condition.

Over the next 40 years, Augustine wrote over one hundred titles. His best-known works are *The City of God*, an appraisal of the role of Christianity in fifth-century Roman affairs, and *Confessions*, an autobiographical reflection on his own youth, his conversion, and the development of his views on sin and morality.

A pessimist in pessimistic times, Augustine believed that human nature was essentially evil and that only through the intervention of God could men and women escape from what he considered their carnal will. Augustine is credited with the concept of original sin and the just war theory. Some of his writings on forced conversion helped propel the missionary movement and were later used to justify the Inquisition. He was also influential in subordinating women within the Roman Catholic Church.

Nevertheless, Augustine is recognized as explaining Christian theology rationally alongside Hellenistic philosophy at a time when many Romans blamed Christianity for the deteriorating political situation. By making Christianity appealing to the intellectual elite, and by insisting on universal inclusion even for the Germanic invaders, Augustine enabled the Catholic church to endure, and to outlast the Roman Empire itself. ▪

Augustine, a North African bishop, set the tone for centuries of Roman Catholicism.

The Germans held to a more pantheistic, nature-based religion, peopled by demons and witches who inhabited an imaginative geography of vast tracts of wild land and sacred groves.

Each Germanic tribe had a relatively small population compared with the Romans, who by the fourth century numbered between 50 and 70 million, while the largest Germanic tribes had only around a hundred thousand people. Chieftains or kings were local strongmen, and instead of the state, kinship was the main political unifier, tribal boundaries often shifting with the needs of a nomadic lifestyle. Settled communities ranged from small hamlets to towns of 50 or 60 families.

GOTHS, FRANKS, AND OTHERS

A multiethnic tribe known as the Goths coalesced from various forest and steppe peoples living north of the Black Sea in today's Ukraine. During the third century they began moving in on adjacent Roman territory to the south. The Roman army did its best to fight off these merciless raiders, though it had a hard time defending the empire's long borders. Resources and manpower were often stretched thin by the need to engage in more than one war at a time. In some cases, Gothic and other Germanic mercenaries fought alongside the Romans.

By the early 300s the Goths had split into two major tribes: eastern and western. The eastern Goths, who became known as the Ostrogoths, lived north of the Black Sea; and the western Goths, or Visigoths, settled in what is now known as Romania.

The Frankish Queen Radegund, portrayed in scenes from her hagiography, was such a devout Christian that her husband complained of having a nun rather than a wife.

The Visigoths allied themselves with the Romans by the early 300s. Special army units that fought on behalf of Rome were composed entirely of these "foreign" troops—all Visigoths, for example, or all Franks. Called *foederati* (federates), the auxiliary troops fought under the command of their own leaders.

The Franks occupied what is now Belgium, in northwestern Europe. Although a much smaller tribe than, for example, the Visigoths, they ironically lasted the

FOEDERATUS From the Latin for "ally," a foederatus was one of the tribes bound to Rome by treaty. Foederati were not Roman colonies; those who lived in them did not enjoy Roman citizenship, but they were required to serve in the imperial military force if needed.

longest, giving rise to the people who live in present-day Germany and France and to the first Holy Roman emperor, Charlemagne, who lived from 742 to 814.

Another tribe, the Burgundians, migrated from the region that is now Poland into present-day eastern Germany; they would later become an influential political force in eastern France, establishing a written code of law by the end of the fifth century. Yet another tribe, the Vandals of central Europe, would eventually pour down into Gaul, Spain, and North Africa.

These and other tribes began moving in on the Roman Empire in the fourth and fifth centuries, one of the many influences leading inexorably to Rome's demise.

CHANGES IN GAUL, BRITAIN, AND ELSEWHERE

If, from the Roman point of view, the German barbarians were uncouth, then the Huns of central Asia were downright brutish. These warlike, nomadic people were described by a Roman historian of the fourth century as "a race savage beyond all parallel." They "have no respect for any religion or superstition whatever," reported this eyewitness, and they "are immoderately covetous of gold, and are so fickle and irascible, that they very often on the same day that they quarrel with their companions without any provocation, again become reconciled to them without any mediator." Infants were branded so that scar tissue would prevent hair growth, he continued, and the men ate half-raw animal flesh warmed between their thighs.

Who knows whether these outlandish accounts have any truth to them. Archaeological evidence suggests that the Huns

> ON THE LORD'S DAY, WHICH IS THE FIRST DAY OF THE WEEK, ON CHRISTMAS, AND ON THE DAYS OF EPIPHANY, EASTER, AND PENTECOST, . . . THE PLEASURES OF THE THEATERS AND GAMES ARE TO BE KEPT FROM THE PEOPLE IN ALL CITIES.
>
> CODEX THEODOSIANUS
> *Rome, circa 438*

THE LIBERAL ARTS

The Proper Course of Study for a Freeman

Intellectuals in the Middle Ages sought to preserve the knowledge and writings of the classical era. In the fifth century, Martianus Capella, of the Roman province of Africa, took it upon himself to divide this knowledge into seven easily referenced categories: grammar, rhetoric, logic, music, arithmetic, geometry, and astronomy. Medicine and law were deemed earthly, not divine, and remain separate from the liberal arts to this day.

The name derived from the Latin *liber*—free, the liberal arts comprised a course of studies originally intended to be taught to Roman freemen in a university setting. In the face of political and social upheaval, this curriculum was introduced into monastic life by the Italian scholar, Cassiodorus, in the sixth century. Cassiodorus believed that to study classical writings, one needed copies of those writings, and this call initiated the emergence of monasteries as centers for the preservation and dissemination of classical texts. In this way, early medieval scholars provided not only the content of the university system to come, but also its textbooks. ■

were formidable warriors, always in the saddle, using bone-tipped javelins and twisted cords that would fetter an enemy's hands. Superior horsemen, they traveled light and were expert archers and swordswmen.

The Huns ranged across the dry, grassy plains, or steppes, of west-central Asia—modern-day Mongolia. In 376 they thundered north around the Black Sea and into Ostrogoth territory, completely overrunning it. To the south, the terrified Visigoths pleaded with Valens, Roman emperor from 364 to 378, for admission to the empire. An Arian Christian who ruled the eastern part of the empire, Valens had battled Visigoths along the border nine years earlier. It was not unprecedented to grant citizenship to barbarians, and Valens did so.

But the numbers in this case were staggering: Up to 200,000 refugees now crossed the Danube, flooding into the Balkan provinces and overwhelming the empire's ability to accommodate them. Resentful Roman residents began taking advantage of the new immigrants, charging exorbitant rates for food and necessities. One observer wrote of a slave being traded for a loaf of bread; some parents were willing to give up their children in return for basic items.

Resentment soon turned the other way. In 378 the Visigoths revolted and went to war against the Roman army, which was led by Valens himself. At the 378 Battle of Adrianople (present-day Edirne, in western Turkey), the Visigoths triumphed, and Valens was killed.

The Visigoths settled in Greece, but by 395, not content with the lands they had been given, they were on the move again. That was the year that two young, inept brothers became rulers of the empire,

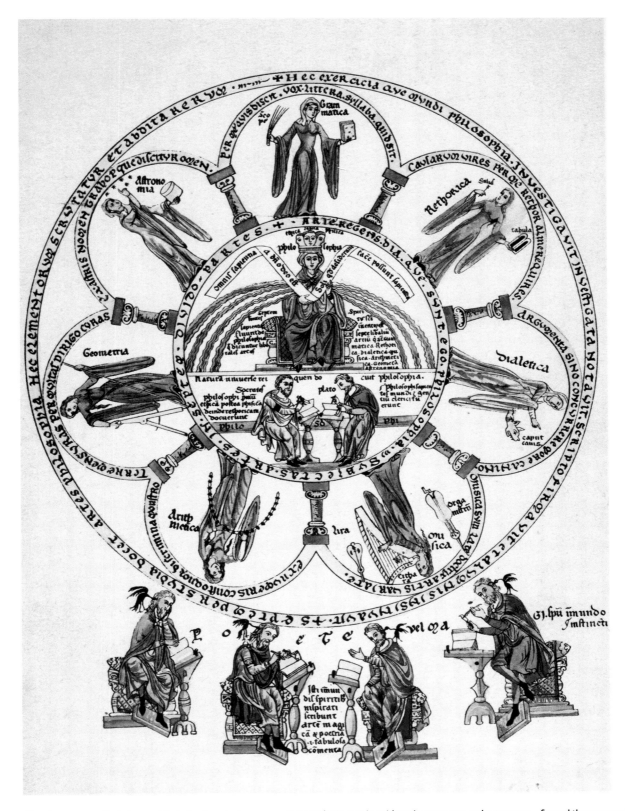

The seven liberal arts, personified above—(clockwise from top) grammar, rhetoric, logic, music, arithmetic, geometry, and astronomy—formed the core curriculum of a freeman's education in the Middle Ages. Once versed in these, a man could move on to professional studies. The concept remains in academia today.

Architects and builders of medieval Rome regularly quarried marble and other building materials from the city's many ancient ruins.

ROME
FADING IMPERIAL CITY

Power | Grandeur | Administration | Papacy

In the beginning of the fifth century A.D., Rome, the center of the known world and the magnificent capital of the great Roman Empire, was in a steady state of decline. Plagues during the second century had killed thousands; economic and political unrest during the third century had caused great upheaval; and, by 305, Rome was no longer the empire's primary city. Constantine's decision to make Constantinople the civic center of the empire hastened Rome's decline.

The city's population shrank to a quarter of its size, and few lived up to its legacy. "The magnificence of Rome," wrote Ammianus Marcellinus, the last great Roman historian, "is defaced by the inconsiderate levity of a few, who never recollect where they were born."

With the decline of the empire came the fall of the pagan state religion, countered by the tremendous growth of Christianity. Over time, Rome took on new life as the center for the growing religion. Peter, allegedly chosen by Jesus himself to lead his church, and Paul, an early convert, traveled throughout the Mediterranean, spreading Christ's message, and, according to Christian tradition, both died martyrs' deaths in Rome. Peter is considered the church's first pope, establishing Rome as the Holy See, or home of the papacy.

Christian pilgrims flocked to the city every year. In fact, as civic power moved out of Rome, Constantine abandoned

ROME THROUGH THE MIDDLE AGES

ca 337
Constantine I, Roman emperor, converts to Christianity.

410
Visigoth invaders sack Rome.

452
Pope Leo I convinces Attila the Hun to spare Rome.

455
Vandals capture Rome.

476
Emperor Romulus Augustus is deposed, marking the fall of Rome.

537
Ostrogoths siege Rome, capturing it in 546.

609
Christians turn the Pantheon into the Church of Santa Maria Rotunda.

the role of *Pontifex Maximus*—Greatest Pontiff, head of the state religion. That position came to be held by the pope in Rome, whose influence was no longer so tightly pinched by imperial powers.

By the fifth century, the Roman Empire had split in half, ruled by one group from Constantinople in the east and by another from the new, more fortified Italian city of Ravenna in the west. Disputes strained the relationship between the eastern and western halves, and attacks by the Gauls and Visigoths weakened the western half of the empire.

In 410, deprived of the subsidies promised to him, Alaric I, king of the Visigoths, laid siege to Rome and plundered the city for three days. The attack horrified the rest of the empire— and symbolized the demise of the west. Alaric and his successors made no attempt to take over the local government of Rome or to assimilate into the local culture. They hoped Romans and Goths could live together peacefully, but they failed to secure land for their people and soon left Italy.

By the middle of the fifth century, Attila and his Huns had conquered central and northern Europe and were camped outside Rome, ready to strike. The Vandals had taken over Spain and North Africa, and their pirate ships patrolled the Mediterranean and periodically cut off food supplies to Rome. In 455, they attacked,

and for the second time in a century, the proud city was pillaged.

In August 476 Odoacer, a German warrior who had joined the Roman army, won the support of his troops and deposed the young emperor Romulus Augustus, who had been raised to power by his powerful father, Orestes. The removal of the emperor marked the official date of the fall of the western empire. Though he was uninterested in changing the administration, Odoacer's relationship with the eastern emperor, Zeno, was tense, and failed attempts to overthrow the German eventually led to

Rome's Vatican fortress became the center of the Catholic Church's political dominion.

Zeno's alliance with Theodoric, King of the Ostrogoths. In 493, Theodoric killed Odoacer and established himself as king over much of southern Europe, including all of Italy. His stable and fair practices led to relative peace well into the sixth century.

During these uncertain times, the church provided Romans with a sense of identity and security that their secular rulers failed to provide. Pope Leo I, recognizing the need for a central authority, used his position politically to help maintain order and is now considered the father of the papacy. Today, it is difficult to find architectural remnants of early medieval Rome. A few papal basilicas remain, most importantly the Basilica of Santa Maria Maggiore, but most have been renovated, their facades re-created in the more ornate styles of later eras.

The creator of this 15th-century map of Rome chose to plot only its ancient and medieval monuments, including the Pantheon, the Colosseum, the Vatican, and a number of cathedrals.

and also the year that a forceful leader, Alaric the Bold, was chosen king of the Visigoths. The co-emperors refused to grant the Visigoths a suitable homeland—an unwise move, for Alaric went on the warpath, and the foundations of the empire began to give way.

THE FATEFUL SACK OF ROME

From Greece, the Visigoths marched north and then headed down into Italy in 401. The following year they were checked by the capable Roman-Vandal general and statesman Stilicho.

As a regent under the young emperor Honorius, who lived from 384 to 423, Stilicho basically ruled the western empire from 395 to 408. But instead of pushing the Visigoths farther north, he pulled back his armies in 406 to try to tighten his defense of Italy. Forces that had been guarding the Rhine—a natural boundary between Gaul and Germania— were suddenly gone.

The restless German tribes in this region needed no further invitation. They streamed across the river and down into Gaul, Spain, and North Africa. Within three decades the Roman Empire had lost every one of these western provinces.

Meanwhile, the Visigoths had a path cleared for them. The emperor, somewhat foolish and ill-advised, listened to envious aristocrats and became so suspicious of Stilicho that in 408 he had him imprisoned and beheaded. With that, the years of negotiating with the Visigoths and forestalling their advance were over. The Goths from the West came marching down the road to Rome.

> IN THE FORMATION
> OF THE LAWS,
> NOT THE SOPHISMS OF
> ARGUMENT
> BUT THE VIRTUE OF
> JUSTICE
> SHOULD EVER PREVAIL.

FORUM JUDICUM
(THE VISIGOTHIC CODE)
Circa 650

Ancient Roman coins often pictured monarchs. This fifth-century coin shows Galla Placidia, royal by birth and marriage.

In the year 410, Alaric and his army sacked the capital of the once-mighty state and demanded they be given an acceptable homeland. This instance of the sacking of Rome—first defeat of the city by outsiders in a full eight centuries—horrified contemporaries, but in fact the attack caused little destruction to the city. Alaric's plan was simply to get the emperor's attention and then to

move down the boot of Italy and cross the Mediterranean into the promised land of North Africa.

Alaric I died in 410, on that march south. He was succeeded by his brother-in-law, Ataulf, who had kidnapped and married the Roman emperor's half sister, Galla Placidia. She became a resplendent queen and a worthy diplomat between the Romans and the Visigoths. Instead of pushing south into Italy, Ataulf moved his army north again, and thence into Gaul. From there, he marched across the Pyrenees into Spain, where in the Mediterranean seaport of Barcelona in 415 he was assassinated.

But by now the Visigoths had established themselves as a people who were not to be turned away, and in 418 the Roman emperor granted them territory in western Gaul. The Franks would conquer this land in the early sixth century, but by then the Visigoths had spread into Spain, where they remained, unchallenged, until the Arab invasion of the early eighth century.

THE VANDALS AND THE HUNS

Among the Germanic tribes that pounded over the Rhine border in the early fifth century, none was more remarkable than the Vandals. Led by Gaiseric the Lame, they poured into France and then down into Spain; by mid-century they had settled in the fertile province of North Africa and, operating as pirates on the Mediterranean, they squeezed off Italy's sea link with the rest of western Europe. Hard-pressed to resupply its armies in Gaul and Spain, the Roman Empire soon had to shed those provinces.

Gold inlay and ornate sculptural ornamentation adorn the interiors of Rome's many medieval churches, such as Santa Maria Maggiore, built on the site where Roman citizens saw a vision of the Virgin Mary. Renovated many times over, it still retains its medieval core. The golden ceiling dates from the 16th century.

THE BASILICA

Spaces of Worship and Wonder

The basilica traces its origins to Roman times, but it became the first characteristically medieval architectural form. Immense buildings with open colonnaded interiors, Roman basilicas served as public meeting halls for the transaction of business, the hearing of legal cases, and the administering of civic services. Once Christianity was sanctioned by the Roman emperor Constantine in 313, the need arose for the growing numbers of faithful to congregate in buildings with more grandiose stature than the secretive community houses where Christians had previously held their rituals. The model of the classical temple was inadequate, because pagan ceremonies were generally held outside in full view of the populace, with the temple serving only to house the cult statue and coffers. Christianity, on the other

hand, was a true mystery religion that had been persecuted by Roman authorities since its inception, producing the need for a clear distinction between sacred and profane, us and them. Hence the basilica, immense but still enclosed, was chosen by Constantine and his architects as the form of the new Christian churches.

The basilica's apse, which previously held a raised platform for political functionaries, was converted into an altar; the orientation of the

entrance was adjusted to provide entry on the short side opposite the apse; and transepts were often added to emphasize the shape of the cross.

One of the first Christian basilicas was Old St. Peter's in Rome, begun by Constantine by 333. Taking more than 30 years to erect, Old St. Peter's was massive, purportedly able to hold more than 14,000 people. Believed to be built on top of the tomb of Peter the disciple, the first bishop of Rome, Old St. Peter's was also a pilgrimage site. To throngs of worshipers, it stood as a physical manifestation of the divine authority passed from Jesus to Peter and on to all succeeding bishops of Rome—the popes. As Roman imperial authority waned, the popes began to wield that divine authority more and more, not only in religious matters but in civic and military situations as well. ■

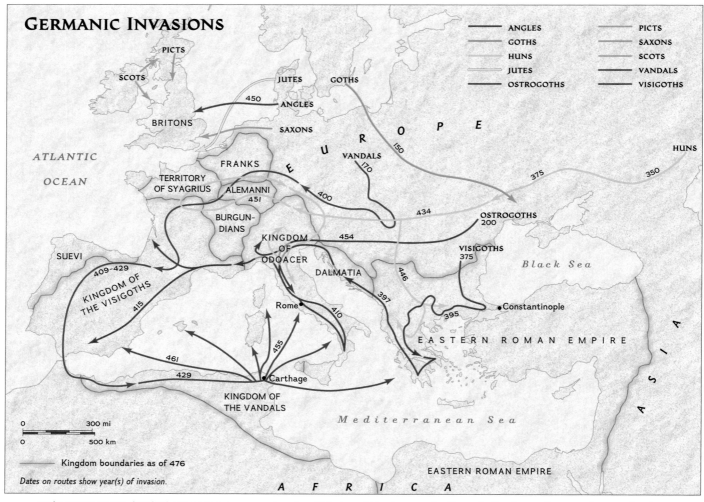

GERMANIC INVASIONS

ANGLES
GOTHS
HUNS
JUTES
OSTROGOTHS

PICTS
SAXONS
SCOTS
VANDALS
VISIGOTHS

PICTS

SCOTS

JUTES

GOTHS

450

ANGLES

BRITONS

SAXONS

HUNS

ATLANTIC

OCEAN

FRANKS

VANDALS
170

150

375

350

TERRITORY
OF SYAGRIUS

ALEMANNI
451

400

434

OSTROGOTHS
200

BURGUN-
DIANS

KINGDOM
OF
ODOACER

454

VISIGOTHS
375

Black Sea

SUEVI

409-429

KINGDOM OF
THE VISIGOTHS

415

DALMATIA

446

397

Rome

410

395

Constantinople

461

455

EASTERN ROMAN EMPIRE

A
S
I
A

429

Carthage

KINGDOM OF
THE VANDALS

Mediterranean Sea

0   300 mi
0   500 km

——— Kingdom boundaries as of 476

Dates on routes show year(s) of invasion.

EASTERN ROMAN EMPIRE

A F R I C A

As the Roman Empire dissolved, Germanic groups moved westward into imperial lands, as much refugees looking for new homes as they were invaders.
They were in turn displaced by invading Huns, and they flooded across the Rhine and Danube Rivers seeking new homelands.

At the same time, on the island of Britannia, Roman legions began withdrawing in the face of waves of an invasion from across the North Sea by a German tribe known as the Saxons. It was a good time to be a German frontiersman and not such a good time to be a Roman provincial.

As for the native Christian Celts of Britain, they were defenseless against the pagan German invaders. One sixth-century writer claimed that a British king—there being many kingdoms on the island at the time—invited the invaders to enter his lands in order to help defend against marauding Scots and Picts from the north. But however they arrived, the Saxons easily took over, their bloodletting mostly confined to the eastern part of the island. The same writer waxes poetic describing the barbarian onslaught in one town: "Swords flashed and flames crackled," he wrote.

"Horrible it was to see the foundation towers and high walls thrown down bottom upward in the squares, mixing with holy altars and fragments of human bodies, as covered with a purple crust of clotted blood in some fantastic winepress." The onslaught was so sudden and so overwhelming, according to this chronicler, that "there was no burial save in the ruins of the houses or in the bellies of the beasts and birds."

THE LEGENDARY ATTILA

Meanwhile, the Huns continued their westward drive, turning Europe into a

FREEMAN In a society based on slavery, such as ancient Rome, a freeman was a man who was not a slave—not owned by another—and who had full rights of citizenship but did not have the wealth or family title to make him a landowner or aristocrat.

pressure-cooker. Their greatest and best known leader, Attila, ruled less than 20 years, from 434 to 453, and yet he left an indelible mark in world history. His unrelenting fierceness gave him the sobriquet among western Europeans of "the scourge of God."

Attila doubled the tribute demanded from the eastern Roman Empire, to 700 pounds of gold a year. Receiving nothing, Attila annihilated cities along the Danube, including Singidunum (Belgrade) in Serbia. After a failed truce, he pushed farther south, burning Serdica (Sofia, Bulgaria) and other cities on his way to Constantinople.

Finding this walled bastion impregnable, he pursued the remaining imperial troops down the narrow Gallipoli Peninsula (in today's northwestern Turkey) and crushed them. After this he was able to exact even more payment—6,000 pounds of gold in back payment, plus an annual tribute of 2,100 pounds.

After a short-lived truce in 443, the Huns came back again, invading the Balkans and Greece. Then, in 451, Attila began a major assault on Gaul. The Visigoths and Romans combined forces to resist the Huns; following a terrific battle on the plains south of Châlons, in northeastern France—a bloody encounter that cost the life of the Visigoth king—Attila retreated from Gaul. It was his only defeat, and it was the final victory of all time for the Roman Empire. The next year Attila ravaged northern Italy, but famine and disease across the land made it impossible for his army to proceed south.

Two years later, Attila the Hun died in his sleep. He was buried with his treasures, and the attendants who buried him were killed so that no one alive knew the location of his grave.

PERSONAE

NOMADIC MIGRATIONS

Did the Barbarians Invade— or Just Migrate?

The Germanic invasions of the western Roman Empire in the fourth and fifth centuries could be called nomadic migrations. The very group that would sack the city of Rome in 410, the Visigoths, had already been living on the Roman Empire's frontier for 300 years. They settled there not to inflict any harm on Rome but to engage with Roman society and share in its wealth. They moved onto Roman land only after the appearance in eastern Europe of the Huns, an aggressive group of nomadic horsemen from the central Asian steppes. The Huns displaced the Visigoths, among others, who then sought refuge and new lands. Only after failed conciliation with Rome did the Visigoths revolt and ultimately seek a homeland in modern-day France and Spain. In the process, Rome withdrew its forces from one frontier to combat the Visigoths on the other. This opened the door to groups such as the Vandals, who went on to lay siege to Roman North Africa. The immediate effect of these migrations was widespread political upheaval; the long-term effect was a transformation of European government and society. ∎

This stylized earthenware jug, shaped like a human head with another atop it, was produced in the Roman Empire around 400.

Attila's kingdom was divided among his sons, who could not hang on to the territory he had conquered along the Danube. More and more Germanic tribes broke across to the south, including the Ostrogoths and others less well known, such as the Rugi, Sciri, Gepids, Alans, and Sueves. Each had an agreement with the Roman government, trading their labor for benefits they gained from the state.

But bit by bit the empire was collapsing on itself, unable to support the steady influx of immigrants. The last strong emperor, Theodosius I the Great, ruled from 379 to 395. His most important decision was to declare Christianity the official religion of the empire. His last reigning descendant died in 455, and for the next two decades, leadership passed from one puppet to another, as the German arrivals steadily gained control of what once was the Roman Empire.

LIFE IN THE LATE EMPIRE

What was life like during the turbulent years of the empire's fall? There was some fighting, but the transformation often called the barbarian invasion was more like a massive immigration, with significant negative impacts on towns and rural areas. Roman society could not readily adjust to the sudden injection of large numbers of people and their attendant variety of cultures and languages. Some cities swelled with refugees from the countryside, many of them vagabonds with no means of support. Other cities declined in population, then fell victim to plunder and decay. To support a crumbling civic infrastructure—roads, aqueducts, buildings, and the like—government officials raised taxes to outrageous levels, furthering the exodus from cities.

The population of the city of Rome plummeted from a peak of about a million in the early second century to less than a quarter of a million by the mid-fifth century. By the end of the sixth century, the city was home to fewer than 50,000. Though the imperial government was still officially in power until the late fifth century, these decades were a transitional period, the empire fading like an ember rather than being snuffed out like a candle, as the church became the more effective civil authority.

A 14-day sacking of Rome by Vandals in 455 probably did less harm than the spree of 410—most monuments and churches were untouched—yet it underscored the capital's vulnerability. The desperate last emperors issued decrees against stealing marble from civic buildings—a move that indicated not only the amount of lawlessness in the city but also the government's inability to prevent it.

The manners and customs of the barbarians insinuated themselves into Roman life, as many of the rising leaders, including Stilicho, were of Germanic descent. In vain did Emperor Honorius try to outlaw the wearing of "gaily coloured sleeveless coats, wide trousers, and long hair in the barbarian manner."

The truth is, many of the Germanic people were not all that much different from the Romans, after generations of living near one another on their shared

Artists in the Sassanid Empire, centered in today's Iran, produced highly refined works, such as this mosaic made of gold, rock crystal, garnet, and green glass, picturing King Solomon in the center.

borderlands and absorbing each other's customs. In fact, many of the new citizens, except the Franks and Anglo-Saxons, were already Christians, albeit of the eastern Arian variety considered heretical by the Romans. Their arts and agriculture were much the same, and those who moved into Roman territory had no interest in destroying Roman achievements or culture.

Most of the newcomers settled legally as foederati, agreeing to military service in return for land. These troops and their families were given board, lodging, clothes, horses, and fodder. And since the soldiers, like the Romans, were allowed to live with their families and slaves, they displaced many landowners, a situation that could not help but rankle. A typical arrangement was that a landowner would give up one-third of his house and produce to a resident soldier.

Writing in the middle of the fifth century, Apollinaris Sidonius, a bishop and diplomat from Gaul, protested this so-called hospitality that he had to give to the Burgundians, whom he considered interlopers. He detested their language, their songs, and even their smell, complaining that they put butter on their hair and reeked of garlic and onions. He wrote of being surrounded "as if he were an old grandfather or foster-father, by a crowd of giants, so many and so big that not even the kitchen of Alcinous could support them."

It was not long before the newcomers were taking not just the produce but the land itself—a good deal more than they were promised—and they were collecting a proportional amount of rent paid by any of the land's tenants. Instead of obliterating the Roman legal and civic structures, the new rulers wanted to keep what worked alive.

Romans and Germans alike paid taxes not to Rome but to regional Visigoth or Burgundian rulers. According to the report of a contemporary, Visigoth king Ataulf in his youthful ardor "had chosen, for his part at any rate, that he would seek the glory of renewing and

> VENERATIONI MIHI SEMPER
>
> FUIT NON VERBOSA
>
> RUSTICITAS SED
>
> SANCTA SIMPLICITAS—
>
> I HAVE ALWAYS
>
> REVERED NOT
>
> CRUDE VERBOSITY
>
> BUT HOLY SIMPLICITY.

ST. JEROME TO PAMMACHIUS
Circa 400

increasing the Roman name by the arms of his Gothic followers, and would be remembered by posterity as the restorer of Rome, since he would be its changer." Ataulf, in other words, wanted to turn Roman lands into an "Empire of the Goths," but over time he came to realize that his own people were ungovernable outside the law.

Managing the Barbarians

Religion was vastly important in the lives of the people living in the fifth century. Some newcomers only partially adopted Christianity, the newly official religion, and they were considered blasphemers. Thus the Germans' Arianism, which treated Christ as a lesser god, was to the Romans a heretical stance, representing a real obstacle in the path of cultural marriage. Ironically, in the long run the true heathens, the Franks and the Anglo-Saxons, would become more completely Christianized because they never adopted the Arian religion.

Another area separating the Romans from the barbarians was the law. While Germans often rose to high rank within the Roman army, they never became part of Rome's civilian government.

The Germans lived under their own kings and laws, the main feature of which was the *wergild* system. A wergild was literally the price on one's head—the amount of money owed a man's kindred if he was murdered. The system developed in early German society as a way to circumvent the sacred duty of the blood feud. Instead of an endless back-and-forth series of murders, an aggrieved family could obtain satisfaction by demanding a set wergild, or payment in money.

The higher a man's social status, the higher his wergild. Kings commanded the highest amount, then nobles, freemen, slaves, and oxen. Beyond this, there were prices affixed to teeth lost in skirmishes—for example, in sixth-century England, front teeth were valued at six shillings, eyeteeth were valued at four shillings, and so on.

The wergild system often came into conflict with the Roman system. Other tribes moving into the empire had their own legal systems as well. If a Burgundian brought suit against a Frank over a piece of land acquired from a Roman, the likely result was that neither party would be satisfied, because each would be looking to a different system of justice.

Intellectuals such as Apollinaris knew that the immigrant problem was the leading issue of the day, and they looked for a means to solve it. An appeal by Bishop Synesius of Cyrene, Libya, to Arcadius, emperor of the eastern Roman Empire in the early fifth century, suggests the degree of xenophobia felt by the indigenous population.

"The Emperor should purify the troops just as we purify a measure of

INNOVATION

THE HORSESHOE

Reining in the Potential of the Workhorse

The proliferation of two simple innovations in the early Middle Ages—the horseshoe and the horse collar—was a watershed development with an impact lasting for hundreds of years. Although it had been invented, the horseshoe was not widely used in Roman times. Draught animals were more often shod with a slip-on sandal of sorts, perfectly suitable on the well-paved road surfaces in the Roman Empire.

In the deep moist mud of northern European agricultural fields, however, such a sandal would have been useless. Work in this kind of soil could soften and split a horse's hooves, and a nailed-on horseshoe worked better. The horse collar, an idea imported from Asia, was fastened to a horse's chest and shoulders rather than its neck, enabling a harnessed horse to pull a greater load and a heavier plow.

These two innovations allowed wealthy European landowners to rely more heavily on horses, instead of slower oxen, to till their fields and pull their wagons. Horses were considerably more expensive to buy and keep than oxen, though, and so these technologies were slow to take hold throughout Europe. By the end of the tenth century, the cycle picked up: As more land could be cultivated through horsepower, more food could be produced, for man and horse alike. This led to an increase in population and wealth, and the helpful horseshoe and horse collar gradually came into general usage. ■

The Visigoths at first sought to engage in the wealth of Roman trade peacefully, but when they found themselves marginalized, they grew hostile and more desperate, eventually sacking Rome in 410, an event that foreshadowed the downfall of the imperial city later in the century.

wheat by separating the chaff," he wrote to the ruling Roman. "Your father, because of his excessive compassion, received [the barbarians] kindly and condescendingly, gave them the rank of allies, conferred upon them political rights and honors, and endowed them with generous grants of land." Synesius interpreted all problems as arising from the behavior of the non-Romans. "Not as an act of kindness did these barbarians understand these noble deeds," he argued; "they interpreted them as a sign of our weakness, which caused them to feel more haughty and conceited."

Bishop Synesius advised Arcadius to expect much of the tribespeople who had moved in on Roman territory, as a way to gain control and improve the situation. "Persistence must be shown in dealing with these people," he advised.

"Either let these barbarians till the soil following the example of the ancient Messenians, who put down their arms and toiled as slaves for the Spartans, or let them go by the road they came, announcing to those who live on the other side of the [Danube] river that the Romans have no more kindness in them and that they are ruled by a noble youth!" It was a matter of Roman honor, in other words, to maintain control over the barbarians—yet fate led down a different path.

THE LAST EMPEROR

The crisis in leadership that followed the defeat of the Huns by a mostly Visigothic imperial army in 451 went on for several years until a strong leader emerged in the 470s. He was a German general named Odoacer, born around 433. Around the year 470, Odoacer came to Italy with the Heruli tribe,

> HOW WONDERFUL IS
> THE SURPASSING BLESSING
> OF MORTAL WEALTH.
> AS SOON AS YOU HAVE
> ACQUIRED IT,
> YOUR CARES BEGIN!
>
> BOETHIUS
> *CONSOLATION OF PHILOSOPHY*
> **Circa 500**

native to Jutland in today's Denmark. He joined the Roman army and helped Roman general Orestes oust Emperor Julius Nepos in 475.

After that victory, however, Orestes refused to honor his promise of granting land to the Germans. Furious, Odoacer led a rebellion. On August 23, 476, his soldiers proclaimed him king of Italy, and soon thereafter they captured Orestes in northern Italy and killed him. Orestes had placed his young son Romulus Augustus on the throne; Odoacer deposed him later, in 476, and decided not to bother with a replacement. Thus the last Roman emperor of the West went away without a struggle.

For those keeping score, Romulus Augustus is considered the last emperor. But he was also a usurper, so in some sense, Julius Nepos was the last official Roman emperor. He continued to be acknowledged as emperor in Gaul and the East until he was killed four years later in Salona (modern Split, Croatia) by friends of the emperor he himself had deposed. The eastern Roman Empire would continue on as the Byzantine Empire, shrinking gradually after the sixth century until its fall to the Ottoman Turks in 1453.

With no more pretense of propping up the old regime of Rome, Odoacer now had a free hand in Italy. His main goal of obtaining land for his people was granted by the Roman senate without serious opposition. The eastern emperor, Zeno, granted Odoacer the rank of patrician, but Zeno wanted him to recognize Julius as the western emperor, which Odoacer refused to do. Instead he began attacking the westernmost fringes of the eastern empire and soon found himself at war with the Rugi, Visigoths, and Vandals. But it was the Ostrogoths who were to give him the most trouble.

OSTROGOTH INCURSIONS

In an effort to form an alliance, the king of the Ostrogoths had presented his illegitimate son to Emperor Zeno. The young boy, named Theodoric (454-526), won the emperor's favor. His eager mind sponged up culture, law, and government during the years he lived in Constantinople. After he returned to his Ostrogothic homeland, becoming king in his 30s, Zeno made a shrewd deal with him. He crowned Theodoric king of Italy in 488, hoping he would take on Odoacer, who had become such a nuisance.

Theodoric was happy to oblige, for the Ostrogoth lands had lately been ravaged by the Huns, and the Ostrogoths had been taken as slaves. Furthermore, he had a proven talent for leadership. His very name meant "leader of the people." By the time he was on his way to Italy, with a contingent reported to number 100,000, he was confident of his abilities.

Between 489 and 493 the Ostrogoths nearly demolished much of northern Italy, Theodoric engaging in three major battles with Odoacer and winning each

THE WORLD IN THE FIFTH CENTURY

The medieval era began as the classical age ended, but the influence of the cultural advances and vast empires of the ancient world would not end.

In India, a power vacuum left after Alexander's wane led to the rise of Chandragupta Maurya, who consolidated regional kingdoms on the subcontinent. Then another ruler, Chandragupta I, united India in the fourth century.

Similarly, China emerged from a time of violent unrest, as a powerful country under the Qin dynasty in the third century. Short-lived Qin rule laid the groundwork for the Han dynasty that followed and stayed in power until the third century, when China again split into smaller kingdoms, with strife continuing between kingdoms and between landowners and laborers. Buddhism, passed on along the Silk Road, also began to spread.

Civilizations rose and fell with less drama than the tumbling Roman Empire, and they entered the medieval era with relative stability. The hunter-gatherer peoples of the Americas settled into more stationary, durable societies, developing trade and agriculture. Teotihuacán, in the Valley of Mexico, was one of the most vibrant urban centers of its time. On the Yucatán Peninsula, Maya settlements grew around temple sites.

In sub-Saharan Africa and Oceania, increased trade led to more complex societies, although for the time being, individual kingdoms and tribes remained small and relatively isolated. ■

TEMPLE OF SERAPIS **The outlawing of paganism in the fourth century leads to increased tensions between Christians and pagans throughout the Roman Empire. In the city of Alexandria, Egypt, the pagan Temple of Serapis is destroyed after riots result in the deaths of several Christians there.**

TEOTIHUACÁN **In the early fourth century, Teotihuacán reaches its height of cultural sophistication and becomes one of the largest cities in the world, with more than 150,000 inhabitants. Internal warfare and external pressures, however, cause the population to decline during subsequent decades.**

CHICHÉN ITZÁ **Founded in 455 on Mexico's Yucatán Peninsula, the Maya city of Chichén Itzá features the Temple of a Thousand Columns and the Pyramid of Kukulcan, the ruins of which still stand today. At its height, the city stretches across six square miles.**

BHAGAVAD GITA Finalized in the early fourth century, the *Bhagavad Gita (Song of God)*, a sacred scripture of Hindu teaching, recounts a conversation between the divine Krishna and his pupil, Arjuna, on their way to the Kurukshetra war. Krishna shares the basic principles of Hinduism with Arjuna to guide him through his moral dilemmas.

THE SILK ROAD Increased trade along the many paths of the so-called Silk Road brings new diseases to communities throughout China, leading to significant declines in population. The Silk Road connections stretched from Scandinavia to China and the Arabian Peninsula and linked many distinct cultures and kingdoms.

BOLO NTOMO MASK The Soninké empire of West Africa emerges late in the fifth century as a major commercial center, dealing in salt and gold and developing trade throughout the Mediterranean. The Ntomo mask shown here, constructed of metal over wood, was most likely worn by boys or young men of the Soninké tribes.

one. Having failed to take Ravenna, in the northeast, he negotiated with Odoacer—they would become co-rulers of Italy. Odoacer made the fatal mistake of trusting his enemy and inviting him to his palace. Inside the palace two Goths suddenly grabbed Odoacer and held him while Theodoric slew him with his sword. Theodoric's men then mercilessly hunted down Odoacer's family and courtiers and killed them all.

Making his capital in Ravenna and wearing the royal purple of the emperors, Theodoric pretty much continued in Odoacer's footsteps, ruling over his own people as absolute king but over the Romans as the representative of the eastern emperor. The Romans had by now become inured to the idea of a barbarian kingdom existing within their own borders. There were some legal constraints on Theodoric's power—he could not grant Roman citizenship to Goths, nor appoint a Goth to a Roman civilian office, and it was not legal for Romans and Goths to intermarry.

After a decade of maintaining this status quo, Theodoric began to envision an even wider realm for his kingdom—he saw himself as ruler of Italy, Gaul, and possibly Spain. And to that end he married a sister of Clovis, king of the Salian Franks in Gaul. He created further diplomatic ties by marrying off his daughter to the Burgundian king and becoming the guardian of the young king of the Visigoths.

Like Ataulf and others, Theodoric saw himself as the restorer of the western Roman Empire. He wanted to bring back its great power and culture, but in attempting an alliance with the Franks he made a misstep. The emperor of Byz-

Wool from sheep became a valuable commodity in the rural economy of medieval Europe, making useful much of the land that was otherwise unsuitable for agriculture.

antium became suspicious of this move and made his own alliance with Clovis, giving the Frankish king official authority over Gaul.

In the meantime Theodoric continued pursuing a domestic policy that required harmonizing the Goths with the Romans, a nearly impossible task owing to the deep-seated mistrust that

each group felt toward the other. The new watchword, coined by his administrator Cassiodorus, was *civilitas*, a sort of peace slogan that proclaimed the Goths as friends, not enemies, of Roman civilization. As Theodoric's chief propagandist, Cassiodorus, himself a Roman, never referred to the Goths as barbarians.

Theodoric was sincere in this policy of civilitas, and his 33 years in office were marked by peace, prosperity, and an attempt to heal the racial divide. He promoted the arts, invited scholars to his court, and sponsored public works. Yet he also continued to seize Roman land for quartering his army, a policy which could not help but create friction.

Arian Christianity, the religion of the Goths, was too deeply engrained for them to simply convert to Roman Catholicism. Few historical sources shed light on the degree to which the Romans and Goths resented each other for practicing their own religions, but once again, Theodoric followed the policy of live-and-let-live. He allowed complete freedom of religion and further appeased the Romans by recognizing the pope as the leader not only of the Roman church but also of Rome.

Then a seismic shift occurred that made the downfall of the Ostrogoths all but certain. The papacy had for many years distanced itself from the heretical Byzantine Empire, preferring a Goth who tolerated religious diversity over an emperor with a religious ax to grind. The new Byzantine emperor, Justin I (r. 518-527), had the ambitious goal of reconquering the West, though, and thus he risked angering his own people by accepting Roman Catholic tenets. Many Roman aristocrats, fearing Theodoric's anti-Roman kinsmen and possible successors, decamped to join this strange new East-West alliance.

Theodoric rounded up suspected conspirators and condemned them to death. Civilitas was thrown out the window during the last years of his rule; barbarism was back in style. The pope was put in prison, as was the Roman world's leading philosopher, Boethius (ca 480-524).

An aristocrat, Boethius had become the head of government and court services in the imperial capital. He translated and wrote commentaries on Aristotle, and was attempting through Aristotelian logic to resolve the thorny issues of the triune God and how Christ was both human and divine. His work was of immense importance to Scholastic philosophers 700 years later, as the study of Greek had nearly disappeared from the Latin world. He wrote treatises on logic, arithmetic, and music, as well as theology, but his greatest work was *The Consolation of Philosophy*, which he wrote while awaiting execution in Pavia, in northern Italy. The triumph of Boethius was that he persevered in the midst of political turmoil. Theodoric's record bears a black mark for his execution of Boethius without a trial.

Theodoric died in 526, two years after Boethius, at the advanced age of 72. He was buried in an elaborate tomb that remains a landmark in Ravenna, along with ruins of churches from the fifth to the eighth centuries. The kingdom of the Ostrogoths collapsed shortly thereafter. In setting his sights on Gaul and thus stirring up the fear and aggression of the Byzantines, Theodoric had made a strategic blunder that abbreviated his people's tenure as overlords in the previously Roman lands.

Under their powerful new emperor, Justinian I (527-565), the Byzantines began taking back the empire. But Theodoric had been able to create a kingdom within the framework of existing western politics and culture. It would take almost 200 years—not until the Frankish

Thick double (and in some places triple) walls enclosed the city of Constantinople. One set was built by Constantine in the fourth century and another, farther west, to protect a growing city, was built by Theodoric in the fifth century. Not until the Ottoman Turks attacked in 1453 were the walls penetrated by outsiders.

According to the quasihistorical legend of King Arthur, the young prince (left) was tutored by Merlin, a magician (center). The story animated the adventure-romances of troubadours in the later Middle Ages.

Constantine, Eusebius is best known for his *Historia Ecclesiastica (Ecclesiastical History)*, a groundbreaking work of early church history.

Eusebius argued that the success of the church depended on the success of the state, and vice versa—harmony between them meant harmony throughout society. Despite this argument, the collision between assumptions within the Christian church and the state set a pattern for the future. The antiestablishment thrust that had characterized the early Christian movement never quite died out, and it would appear again in the late Middle Ages. Meanwhile the Christian tenets of love, faith, and forgiveness remained integral to church teachings, and those who held them in esteem hoped to see them become the guiding principles for statesmen as well as churchmen.

THE FIRST CHRISTIAN SAINTS

Dissent in the Eastern church was different from that in the West, generally taking the form of mysticism or asceticism—in other words, personal instead of social revolution. The first Christian monk, Saint Anthony of Egypt (c. 250-355) became an ascetic at age 20, and from about age 35 to 55 he lived in solitude on a mountain above the Nile. He then rejoined society and spent the rest of his long life teaching and organizing communities of hermits—the first Christian monasteries.

These devout men prayed, fasted, and denied themselves sleep, sex, and material possessions—all ways of stripping away sin, battling demons, and opening themselves to God. Anthony himself represented the ultimate in spiritual self-denial. A contemporary described

king, Charlemagne (742-814), rose to power—before another great European ruler would appear.

A NEW KIND OF LEADER

Emperor Constantine was tolerant of Christianity, if not a convert himself, and at the end of his life, he requested a Christian baptism. Whereas practicing Christianity had once been unwise for upwardly mobile Romans, it was now beneficial. It was as though a whole new administration had arrived in town, permanently sweeping aside the old.

It was a longheld Roman assumption that the religious and civic institutions of society would each have the back-ing of the other—the empire operated through the sanction and support of the church, and the church gained its moral authority through the confidence of the empire. Because of the circumstances of its early development, Christianity presented a different model: a separation, sometimes to the point of alienation, between church and state. In the old model, an act of treason was also an act of heresy; in the new, one could stand on solid ground with one institution and question the other.

Many continued to argue for harmony between church and state, chief among them Eusebius of Caesarea (ca 260-339). A Palestinian bishop and adviser to

him as he emerged after years of solitude "as one initiated into sacred mysteries and filled with the spirit of God." He was not only purified but had become a healer and miracle worker. "Through him the Lord cured many of those present who were afflicted with bodily ills," so it was reported.

In the fifth century, Christian asceticism was taken to new levels by Saint Simeon Stylites (ca 390-459) of Syria. He began as a shepherd, became a monk, and then was forced to leave the monastic community because of his overly austere approach. He decided to live on a six-foot-high stylite, or pillar, making him the first known stylite hermit—others took up the practice in centuries to come. Simeon built up the stylite on which he perched until it measured 50 feet tall, and he lived on it, exposed to the elements, sitting or standing on the small space at the top. Disciples brought him supplies, and until his death, pilgrims continued to visit him seeking spiritual guidance and enlightenment.

Another early Christian saint, Ambrose (339-397)—governor and bishop of Milan in northern Italy—set precedents for the relationship between church and state by wrangling with Emperor Theodosius and winning. His wily political maneuvers in 384 caused the Roman senate to overturn an appeal for tolerance of pagan members. A year or two later, Ambrose refused to allow Arians to use an established church in Milan, and then in 388 he censured the emperor for punishing a bishop who had destroyed a synagogue. These moves may hardly seem charitable, but they do illustrate the growing power of the clergy in the political affairs of the Middle Ages.

O LORD, MY HELPER AND MY REDEEMER, I SHALL NOW TELL AND CONFESS TO THE GLORY OF YOUR NAME HOW YOU RELEASED ME FROM THE FETTERS OF LUST . . . AND FROM MY SLAVERY TO THE THINGS OF THIS WORLD.

ST. AUGUSTINE
CONFESSIONS
Circa 400

PERSONAE

KING ARTHUR

The Quintessential Legend of Medieval England

The legend of King Arthur emerges from Celtic folklore, likely originating in Wales although associated with rocky Cornwall ruins called Tintagel. A hero of post-Roman Britain battling the invading Anglo-Saxons, whether Arthur actually ever lived is widely debated.

The story appears in many of the great literary works of the Middle Ages: Geoffrey of Monmouth's *History of the Kings of Britain* and Chrétien de Troyes's romances, both 12th-century, and Thomas Malory's *Le Morte d'Arthur*, an English work of the 15th century, all tell tales of Arthur.

Over the centuries, the story evolved into this: As a young boy, Arthur was aided by a magician, Merlin, and pulled a sword out of a stone, thus proving his royal nature. As king, he convened his knights at a round table, planning military missions for a greater Christian good, symbolized by the Holy Grail—a goblet, symbol of the crusaders' quest. Arthur's wife, Guinevere, succumbed to dalliances while Arthur was at war, and her love for Lancelot, a knight of the round table, made for a steamy story of passion and betrayal. ■

On the more noble side, Ambrose made the emperor do public penance for a massacre of riotous citizens in Thessalonica, in northeastern Greece. In his writings, he defined the emperor as a loyal member of the church "serving under orders from Christ"—a characterization that put church first, state second.

In his conservatism, Ambrose cautioned against the influence of heretics who "dye their impieties in the vats of philosophy." Yet his sermons could be tinged with a pagan mysticism. He is perhaps most well known for advice given to a fellow cleric who asked him whether his mother, while visiting Milan, should fast on Saturdays, as was the custom in Rome. Ambrose replied with a motto that has long outlived him in reputation: "When you are at Rome, live in the Roman style; when you are elsewhere, live as they live elsewhere."

One father of the Latin church who struggled with the demands of a devoted Christian lifestyle was Saint Jerome (ca 347-419), who was a scholar and an ordained priest. After early studies in Rome, he had a famous dream in which he was accused by a divine tribunal of being a follower of Cicero—a Roman statesman, orator, lawyer, and philosopher of the first century B.C.—rather than of Christ.

Disturbed by his dream, Jerome spent at least the next two years as a desert hermit, giving up reading the classics that he loved. It was a big sacrifice, for language and learning were of immense importance to Jerome, a sensitive and gifted writer who might have been a poet in a different time. His spiritual crisis resulted in one of the great accomplishments of the early medieval era—he translated the Bible into the vulgate, the language of the common Romans, making scripture available to the masses.

Like most writers of the time, Jerome commented on the changing political scene, his words evoking the sense of incredulity at the empire's fall: "The whole region between the Alps and Pyrenees, the ocean and the Rhine, has been devastated by the Quadi, the Vandals, the Sarmati, the Alani, the Gepidae, the hostile Heruli, the Saxons, the Burgundians, the Alemanni and the Pannonians," he wrote, naming one barbarian group after another that had moved into the old imperial lands. "O wretched Empire!" he continued. "Our tears are dried by old age. Except a few old men, all were born in captivity and siege, and do not desire the liberty they never knew. Who could believe this?"

Jerome put into words what many thoughtful people must have asked themselves during that century of change. "Who could believe that Rome, built upon the conquest of the whole world, would fall to the ground?" Who could believe, he continued, "that today holy Bethlehem should shelter men and women of noble birth, who once abounded in wealth and are now beggars?" His questions foreshadowed the crusading spirit that informed history in the centuries soon to come.

Augustine, Saint for All Ages

Although he was as pessimistic about the empire as his contemporaries, one man saw the Christian church as an institution that could and would survive into the future as a moral bedrock. Saint Augustine (354-430) of Hippo—a seaport in what is now Algeria—had more influence over the church than anyone else in the Middle Ages.

The literary efforts of St. Jerome, revising the Bible into more accessible language, broadened Christianity's reach. Medieval monks were responsible for copying and preserving many classical and religious texts.

The son of a Christian mother and a pagan father, Augustine from early on wrestled with questions of spirituality. He dabbled in Manichaeism—a mystical practice from Persia based on a view of the world as a constant struggle between dark and light, evil and good—and he explored other non-Christian religious movements. He vividly recounted these experiences in one of the world's first autobiographies, titled *Confessions*. In the early 380s Augustine taught rhetoric in Carthage (a North African city near Tunis), in Rome, and then in Milan. There he began reading the ancient Greeks and listening to Ambrose, the bishop, preach.

In 382 Theodoric had outlawed Manichaeism and declared Christianity the official religion of the empire. Augustine, convinced by the tenets of Christianity, was baptized by Ambrose in 387. He returned to Hippo and became a priest. His writings and teachings were the most intellectually advanced of his time, extending Christian theology beyond the current conceptions of Greek philosophy. The ideas still resound today.

Whereas classical philosophers believed that man could think his way toward good decisions, Augustine viewed human nature as fundamentally flawed. One can know right from wrong, yet because of essentially selfish human impulses, one can still commit evil actions in spite of that knowledge. Only with God's help can the spiritual will triumph over the natural or carnal will.

Augustine's insightful worldview took into account man's violent nature, which continued to be exhibited rampantly in the medieval world, among even the highest classes, despite all the teaching and preaching, learning and listening going on.

Though pessimistic in its outlook on human nature, Augustine's philosophy was ultimately optimistic in its view of history. The Greeks and Romans saw history as an endlessly repeating cycle of rises and falls; Augustine believed the arrival of Christ was a unique event that set in motion a linear progression toward a better future, the Second Coming. In his long treatise, *The City of God*, he depicts human history as a struggle between the Earthly City, comprising pagans and heretics, and the City of God, home to devout Christians.

"In this wicked world, in these evil days, when the Church measures her future loftiness by her present humility, and is exercised by goading fears, tormenting sorrows, disquieting labors, and dangerous temptations, when she soberly rejoices, rejoicing only in hope, there are many reprobates mingled with the good," he writes. Those who dwell in the City of God are fellow-citizens with the angels, and they can look forward to being "clothed in immortal and spiritual bodies" during a time "when the flesh shall live no longer in a fleshly but a spiritual fashion."

Augustine was the first to admit that his writing was filled with ambiguity and contradiction—for example, he both

The baptism of Clovis I, around A.D. 500, was historic—one of the first pagan kings to convert, he embraced Catholicism rather than Arian Christianity.

denied Platonic philosophy and employed it in his arguments. But this very tension was important for Christianity. Augustine realized that for the church to survive it had to become universal, embracing all the jumbled masses of German tribes filling the empire and beyond. The church thus had to be both authoritarian in structure and catholic in appeal.

By the end of the fifth century, the church and state were two separate, powerful bodies, but in the minds of church leaders the political rulers derived their power from the church, not the other way around. The tension between church and state would continue to shape the course of medieval history, with monarchs gaining power from and challenging the papacy and other church institutions.

ILLUMINATION Before printing, books were created by hand. Usually the lettering was made in black ink but often decorated with ornaments in gold and colors. Illuminated manuscripts may include marginal decorations, illustrations, and intricate capital letters.

The dragon was revered and feared as the most powerful of all creatures. It became the symbol of both London and Wales, and images of the dragon appeared in many family crests. On the other hand, the legend of St. George casts the dragon as the embodiment of worldly sin and greed, to be slain by the purest of knights in a triumph of Christianity.

ANIMALS IN THE MEDIEVAL WORLD

Beasts real and imagined were part of the tableau of the Middle Ages. They adorned coats of arms as symbols of valor, and they lent their names to the constellations. They provided daily essentials: food, clothing, and transportation. They even supplied the materials for the earliest books: animal skin parchment and feather quill pens.

Animals provided evidence of God's divine plan. Bestiaries—illuminated, book-length manuscripts that depicted animals known and imaginary—provide us today with some of the era's most remarkable illustrated manuscripts, noting characteristics of each beast. The dragon, for example, the most powerful of God's creatures, hid in shadows and strangled victims with its powerful tail. The rare but beautiful unicorn could only be captured by virginal maidens. The phoenix rose from its own ashes. The majestic griffin had the body of a lion and the head and wings of an eagle. Medieval believers also thrilled to the terrifying beasts of the apocalypse and the ancients, such as sea monsters and sirens.

Dogs made popular companions and became symbols of devotion. Oxen and horses served in the fields, pulling plows and powering mills. A newly invented horse harness redistributed weight and allowed workhorses to pull even heavier loads. As the foundation of medieval cavalries, horses became an essential part of warfare. A strong, healthy warhorse could cost up to 800 times as much as a farm horse.

Animals served important practical purposes in everyday life. Cows, sheep, and goats provided milk, meat, and clothing. Their hides could even be used for making parchment.

The frightening beasts of the apocalypse—when divine judgment will send the wicked to eternal damnation—were widely illustrated and imagined. In this 13th-century illumination, a dragon wages war on a beast of the sea.

The unicorn was the most rare and magical of imaginary beasts. Considered a symbol of purity, courage, and strength, a unicorn—so tradition had it—could only be captured when a virginal maiden was nearby.

Horses not only eased the hard labor of agriculture, they also carried knights to battle. The introduction of the horseshoe and the stirrup, brought to Europe from the East, increased the efficiency of medieval cavalries.

500 — 600

NCE THE FALL OF THE ROMAN EMPIRE WAS COMPLETE, WESTERN EUROPE SETTLED INTO A LONG and turbulent period, which subsequently came to be known as the Dark Ages. Lasting from the sixth through the tenth centuries, this period of the early Middle Ages was not as unremittingly grim for everyone in Europe as the common term might suggest. Lively markets flourished here and there, and a few leaders, notably Gregory the Great, Charlemagne, and Alfred the Great, made strides toward an enlightened, higher civilization. Life was short, hard, and often violent, as tribes warred against each other and tried to defend against the invasions of Vikings, Saracens, and Magyars. Learning and the arts gave way to simple survival, and those few who could afford a measure of learning could lament with Gregory, the bishop of Tours: "Woe to us, for the study of letters has disappeared from amongst us!"

The Franks became dominant in Gaul—which became known as Francia—under the sword of Clovis. Though his family, the Merovingians, would keep supplying Francia with kings for the next two centuries, none was as capable as Clovis himself. Their history of brutal internecine strife was made more bearable in the late sixth century by the civilizing influence of the Catholic Church under the wise guidance of Pope Gregory the Great.

In the East, the controversial emperor Justinian reigned for nearly four decades, during which the Byzantine Empire would climb to its height of power and wealth, and then begin a steady decline. Under Justinian, the Byzantines made great strides in jurisprudence and architecture, and they took back some of the territory lost to the barbarians. But in his efforts to reunite the eastern and western empires, he drained the treasury, fighting a long, expensive war against the Ostrogoths in Italy, a quagmire that turned him into an unpopular ruler.

Part of the reason for Justinian's failure in the West was that he was engaged in conflict to the East with the Persians. Since the third century, Persia had been united under the Sassanid dynasty. King Khosrow I and his grandson Khosrow II ruled for a combined 85 years in the sixth and early seventh centuries, restoring territory and grandeur to Persia that had been lost earlier. But the Persian-Byzantine wars weakened both states, making them vulnerable to Arab invasions in the 600s.

In western Europe, the monastic movement and the papacy served to keep the populace from sliding into abject misery. Though it began as a self-involved movement of men and

The dramatic life-story of Brunhilde, the manipulative queen of Austrasia at the center of generations of family rivalries over the throne, ended in three days of torture.
PRECEDING PAGES: The regal court of the early Byzantine Empire was epitomized by Justinian I and his wife Theodora, here depicted in mosaics from Ravenna, Italy.

women interested only in their own souls, the institution of monasticism became Europe's intellectual and spiritual bastion. The black-robed followers of St. Benedict became Europe's main body of teachers. And Pope Gregory I, himself a Benedictine monk, was their greatest champion. By sending missionaries to the British Isles, establishing bonds with European rulers, and strengthening the papal administration, he set the course for the medieval papacy.

THE WESTERN EMPIRE

While the fifth century belonged to the Goths, the sixth saw the rise of the Franks, the Germanic tribe with the most staying power. The branch that was to have the most impact, the Salian Franks, hailed from what is now west-central Germany. Living far from the Rhine, the old border of the Roman Empire, they were culturally and economically isolated from the empire and, unlike the Visigoths and other tribes, they had not converted to Arianism or any other form of Christianity when they began streaming into Gaul in the fifth century.

The Franks were a settled, agricultural people whose rudimentary army was made up of a small group of nobles and a large number of peasants. They were colonizers who spread out in search of arable lands. Their royal family, the Merovingians, claimed divine descent, taking their name from a mid-sixth-century patriarch, Merovech. The Franks were noted, according to their chronicler, Bishop Gregory of Tours (538-594), for their extreme antipathy toward the Romans.

As they began to spread south of the ancient Roman city of Paris, the Merovingians moved into settled Gallo-

THE SIXTH CENTURY

511
Clovis I dies; the Frankish kingdom is split among his four sons.

527
Justinian becomes Byzantine emperor after his uncle, Justin I, dies.

529
Justinian closes the School of Athens.

529
St. Benedict founds the first Western European monastic order.

537
Hagia Sophia is completed in Constantinople.

542
Carried on trade routes from Egypt, the bubonic plague reaches Constantinople.

570
Muhammad is born.

588
The Lombards, led by Authari and Theodolinda, convert to Christianity.

597
Pope Gregory I sends missionaries to Britain.

Jewelry was a luxury of the nobility in early medieval Europe. A sixth-century lady probably wore this polished rock crystal suspended from a ring.

Roman territory, and by necessity they picked up the Roman tongue. But with the decline of the Roman Empire, the Franks were poised to assert themselves in this region.

The leader who would take the Franks into three centuries of dominance in western Europe was Clovis (ca 466-511). The son of a military commander likely employed by the Roman Empire, Clovis succeeded his father in 481 and five years later scored his first major victory at Soissons, north of Paris, defeating the final Roman ruler in Gaul. He spent the next several years consolidating his power in northern Gaul, proving himself a brilliant military strategist and ruthless leader.

During a raid, according to Bishop Gregory's account, one of Clovis's soldiers took a vase from a church; Clovis asked for its return so he could restore it to the bishop. The soldier instead broke it with his ax. A year later, Clovis found occasion to criticize the soldier and threw the man's ax on the ground. When he bent to retrieve it, Clovis hefted his own ax and split the man's head open. Gregory related the story to explain not only Clovis's fearsome nature but also his devotion to his new religion.

Clovis's conversion to Christianity around A.D. 500 was compared to Constantine's, but it appears to also have had political consequences. By declaring allegiance to the god of his Burgundian wife, Clotilda (ca 470-545), he had gained victory over the Alamannis along the Rhine—or so claimed Gregory. Mainly, his public baptism, along with 3,000 of his warriors, announced that he was the sole Catholic Germanic king in western Europe, which meant that now the church and the

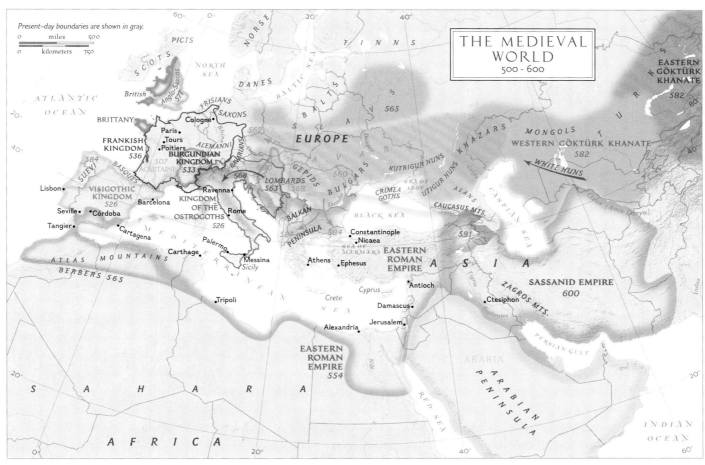

A Frankish kingdom began to form in western Europe, despite an Ostrogoth-Visigoth alliance. The Eastern Roman Empire approached old glory as Justinian drive the Vandals from the west, invaded Visigothic lands, and held off the Persians in the east. The Anglo-Saxons, now one, are well established in Britain.

Gallo-Roman populace had a champion they could support.

In 508 Clovis captured Toulouse (in southern France), the capital of the Visigoths. As we noted, Theodoric's death in 526 precipitated the ruin of the Ostrogoths, but in the early 500s the Eastern Empire was already moving against him. The Byzantines' allies in Gaul were the Franks under Clovis.

The Frankish kingdom of Francia, which held together until about 768, included Aquitaine in the southwest, Neustria to the north between the Loire and the Seine, and Austrasia between the Meuse and the Bohemian Forest to the east. As long as the Franks occupied this

territory, the Merovingian family ruled it only in name. The Franks had a limited concept of government, which mostly consisted of military leadership and personal enrichment of the royal family. A strong autocratic ruler like Clovis could provide structure and some measure of benefit to the people, but the Frankish custom of dividing property among one's male heirs made it impossible for the nascent state to cohere.

EMERGING SOCIAL STRUCTURE

Most of Clovis's descendants turned out to be weak, short-lived, and ineffective, and the Frankish territory broke apart into warring petty principalities. Bloody

feuds and corrupt, illiterate rulers were the unfortunate lot of the Merovingians, who failed to make use of the Roman system of government and, instead, let local thugs gain power. Tax collection was unpopular and so dangerous that a king who wanted to dispose of an enemy could simply send him out to gather revenue.

A few generations after Clovis, the Franks and Gallo-Romans had intermarried and intermingled enough to form common bonds, and one of their strongest points of agreement was their disgust with the avarice and incompetence of the royal family. The Merovingians tried placating the nobles by granting benefices of property, as well as offices they could hand down to their heirs. The titles "duke" and "count"—military and legal representatives—eventually became inherited aristocratic titles that were attached to large estates.

By the end of the century, the provincial aristocracy had sapped the power and wealth of the kingdom, so that in the seventh century the Frankish king was but a figurehead amid a sea of bickering dukedoms. Many of those who inherited kingship were children who died young, and so the office was controlled by the increasingly powerful *major domus*, or mayor of the palace.

The nobility—royals, lords, and bishops—comprised only about 2 percent of Frankish society by the year 600. Beneath them, about 25 percent of the population was made up of minor aristocrats and free soldiers. A small middle class, about 10 percent, consisted of free peasants, lower clergy, and merchants.

At the bottom of the heap, up to 60 percent of the people were dependent serfs. Though these serfs were not generally abused as much as Roman slaves had been, they were not free—they worked the lord's land in exchange for protection and some degree of stability. Serfs theoretically had legal rights, but their lives and prospects were just above the livestock—they could not leave the manor, and legal matters were handled by the lords' courts. Ancient superstitions and fertility rituals played a large part in their Christianity. For at least another six centuries, the lot of the lowest peasant would change little from the cycle of working, procreating, and dying.

In medieval Europe, clothes were fastened by metal brooches, some ornately wrought, like this one in the shape of an eagle.

After Clovis

The history of Francia after the death of Clovis in 511 contains some sensational stories, its brutality giving little hint that the Franks would survive into the ninth century. Clovis's four sons split up the kingdom, making their capitals in Reims (northeastern France), Orléans (north-central France), Paris, and Soissons (northern France). In 561 the last of these sons died, and the kingdom was further divided. One of the heirs, Sigebert, king of Austrasia, held the lands in the northeast, between the Meuse and the Rhine. When he married a formidable Visigothic princess named Brunhilde, trouble erupted.

Sigebert's jealous half brother Chilperic decided to marry Brunhilde's sister Galswintha. When Chilperic later took up with his former mistress, Fredegund, Galswintha complained—for which he strangled her. Now Brunhilde's sisterly wrath was stirred, and the ensuing feud allowed her to rule Neustria and Austrasia through her son and grandson. In the meantime, Chilperic's mistress had Sigebert killed in 575.

Finally, in 613 Chilperic's son imprisoned Brunhilde and charged her with the deaths of ten kings, though he himself was guilty of a few of these murders. She was tortured for three days, after which she was tied to a wild horse and dragged to her death. Some historians have seen Brunhilde as the inspiration for the Valkyrie described in the *Nibelungenlied,* the Norse epic poem depicting the court of Burgundy as the home of the gods. The German composer Richard Wagner enlarged on the tale in his 19th-century opera cycle, *The Ring of the Nibelungs.*

The disruptive civil wars were not a complete drain on the Franks' prosperity. They had a large, rich landholding in France. The Visigoths had retreated south behind the Pyrenees into Iberia, and the Lombards were safely tucked away in Italy. Furthermore, the church under Pope Gregory I the Great (ca 540-604) gave its blessing to the Franks. As

MEROVINGIAN The first Frankish dynasty, lasting more than 200 years. It was founded in the mid-fifth century by Merovech, father of Childeric, and is named for him. It ended when Pepin III became king and initiated the Carolingian dynasty, which included Charlemagne.

pope from 590 to 604, Gregory worked with Brunhilde to spread the influence of the Catholic Church. The one practice he adjured her to crack down on with military force was pagan sacrifices.

With Brunhilde's backing, Gregory sent the first Catholic mission into England, partly in fear that the Irish and Scottish monks, already under the influence of the Eastern Church, might gain control of the mission. The native Celtic Britons had never been totally controlled by the Romans; when the Romans left in the fifth century and the Saxons arrived, some Britons melted into the western mountains or escaped across the English Channel and settled in what became known as Brittany, the peninsula jutting from western France, while others simply stayed put.

Lacking the Romans' political institutions and traditions, the Germanic tribes in Gaul, Spain, and Italy could not build effective state governments quickly. The Romans had not established

> THE GREAT DOOR OF THE NEW-BUILT TEMPLE GROANED ON ITS OPENING HINGES, INVITING EMPEROR AND PEOPLE TO ENTER; AND WHEN THE INNER PART WAS SEEN, SORROW FLED FROM THE HEARTS OF ALL, AS THE SUN LIT THE GLORIES OF THE TEMPLE.

> **PAUL THE SILENTIARY REGARDING THE OPENING OF HAGIA SOPHIA**
> *Constantinople, 562*

an extensive trade network within the empire. Luxuries were still traded with the East, but for essentials, communities fended for themselves.

As for literature and learning, the last years of the Roman Empire had not produced much of originality; writers instead churned out encyclopedias, condensing within a few hundred pages vast amounts of knowledge. No one bothered to write down the Germanic legends—either they were considered inferior to the sophisticated Latin masterpieces, or people were too busy fighting or farming. But their tales and poems survived in oral form for several centuries before they were recorded. Most of the new Germanic Romans could not read or write Latin, nor had they much interest in classical Greek or Roman literature. A few books of basic grammar and law were produced, though beyond Italy and the monasteries not many people bothered with education.

THE EASTERN EMPIRE

The Western Empire had caved in, but the Eastern Empire still held its own. Citizens still considered themselves Romans, though their language, Romaic, was really Greek as the common tongue. The Byzantine Empire—as it was known by the end of the fifth century—was going

THE RULE OF ST. BENEDICT

Monasteries: Creative Centers of Medieval Society

Benedict founded Monte Cassino, his monastery near Rome, around 529. Its practice, articulated as the Rule of Benedict, would influence the Roman Catholic monastic movement, even up to today.

Informed by his Roman sense of order, Benedict expected his monks to follow a rigid daily routine of communal prayer, individual study and meditation, manual labor, and personal time for eating and sleeping. According to Benedict's Rule, monks took lifelong vows of chastity, poverty, and complete obedience to the abbot, their leader, who was elected for life by the monks themselves. Monks could keep no personal possessions and were not allowed to leave the monastery. They received food and shelter and were tended when they were sick.

There is no indication that Benedict meant his Rule to apply to any monasteries other than the few he founded, and he certainly did not foresee establishing an institution of scholasticism and leadership in the medieval world. But within a century of his death, monasteries throughout western Christendom followed his Rule as their guiding principle. With the active support of the papacy, monasteries also became centers of learning, agriculture, politics, and economy. The monasteries became so integral to medieval Europe that the period has been called the Benedictine Age. ■

Benedict of Nursia (seated) set a precedent of rigor for centuries of medieval monasticism.

Justinian I receives his general, Belisarius, who commanded short-lived reconquests of Italy, Sicily, Spain, and North Africa. His military expertise helped the Byzantine Empire expand and dominate the Mediterranean.

its own way, its walled capital city of Constantinople an impregnable fortress and its blooming culture influenced by cultures to the east, particularly Persia, its closest eastern neighbor.

By the mid-600s the Byzantine Empire was prosperous and growing, with an educated middle class and an expansive civil service. Under Justinian (r. 527-565) the empire reclaimed some of the recently lost Roman territory.

JUSTINIAN AND THEODORA

The long, controversial reign of Justinian took the Byzantine Empire to its apogee of power and prestige. Born in what is today eastern Serbia in 483, Justinian went, like many young men of the time, to Constantinople for schooling. His native tongue was Latin, but he learned to speak Greek with an imperfect accent. His uncle made him co-emperor in 527. On the death of his uncle later that year he became sole emperor. But it was his wife, Theodora (ca 500-548), who had the most influence over his reign.

Daughter of a bear keeper at the Hippodrome circus, Constantinople's chariot-racing stadium, Theodora was a mesmerizing actress and belly dancer when Justinian met and "fell violently in love" with her, to use the words of Procopius, a historian of the day. "No role was too scandalous for her to accept without a blush," Procopius wrote of Thoeodora. "At first [Justinian] kept her only as a mistress, though he raised her to patrician rank. Through him Theodora was able immediately to acquire an unholy power and exceedingly great riches." Justinian married Theodora two years before he became emperor.

Petite, dark-haired, and dark-eyed, Theodora was both beautiful and smart. Soon a rumor arose that she was more in charge of the empire than her husband. Certainly he consulted her on many legislative matters, and he let her receive and correspond with foreign ambassadors and rulers.

Some of the earliest laws protecting women's rights were sponsored by Theodora, including a ban on using young girls as prostitutes and the granting of wider benefits to divorced women. She also stemmed the persecution of Monophysites, a heretical group mostly in Egypt and Syria who went the opposite direction from the Arians—instead of viewing Christ as less than divine, they believed he was *only* divine and not partly human.

Procopius describes Justinian as a man who cared little for sleep, food, or drink—he would sometimes fast for two days at a time, living on wild herbs and water. Theodora, on the other hand, reveled in the luxurious life of an empress. Justinian's overriding goal was to take back the lost Western Empire, and though not a military leader he had the wisdom to surround himself with capable advisors and commanders. He himself possessed a potent mix of intelligence, ambition, and willingness to work.

A turning point in Justinian's career serves to illustrate both his power and also his dependence on those around him. In 532 a riot broke out in the Hippodrome between rivals known as the

Greens and the Blues, curious blends of sports fans and political factions. Rioters set fire to public buildings, including the imperial palace, and then demanded that the emperor sack two unpopular government ministers. Justinian tried to negotiate, but the next day the mob grew even more unruly and moved to the Hippodrome to proclaim a new emperor.

At this critical moment, Theodora urged Justinian not to back down. He enlisted one of the empire's most capable generals, Belisarius (ca 505-565), to marshal the troops and quell the riot. He and other generals then attacked the Hippodrome. Although numbers tended to be exaggerated by medieval chroniclers, the unfortunate result was a brutal massacre of as many as 30,000 citizens. As a result, Justinian's rule was never seriously threatened again.

THE MEETING OF MANY PEOPLES

Later in the same year Justinian concluded a peace treaty with the Persians, whom he had been fighting along the Byzantine border since he became emperor. His troops were now free to turn to the reconquest of the West.

Within two years, imperial forces under the command of Belisarius had taken back the Roman provinces in North Africa from the Vandals. They then wrested southeastern Spain from the Visigoths. Now Justinian and Belisarius turned their attention to the Ostrogoths in Italy, and by 555 the Mediterranean was once again a "Roman sea," much of the land skirting it part of the Byzantine Empire.

But the so-called Gothic war for the bulk of Italy dragged on and on, ruining once great cities and turning Italy into a cultural and economic backwater. Italy

PERSONAE

THEODORA

A Woman of Power in the Byzantine Empire

Theodora, the wife of Justinian I, served as Byzantine empress from 527 until her death in 548. The daughter of a bear trainer in the circus, she was inducted into burlesque theater and prostitution as soon as she was old enough. She escaped that fate and fortuitously met the heir to the imperial throne, Justinian. In 523, after changing the law that forbade marriage between a patrician and a commoner, the two were wed.

In her 21 years as empress, Theodora was a valuable and intelligent advisor. She helped pass legislation that empowered women, outlawed exposure of infants, and protected the rights of prostitutes. She was also a conniver: She conspired against political enemies, sanctioned the massacre of tens of thousands of people, and actively intensified the Christian schism, which her husband had worked hard to reconcile. A ruthless partner in power and a compassionate reformer for the destitute, Theodora was one of the most influential women of the Middle Ages. ■

Byzantine empress Theodora rose from obscurity as a circus performer to become one of history's most powerful women.

would not recover from this humbling devastation until the late tenth century, and by then its future as a fractured political landscape was assured.

The Lombards, another Germanic tribe, invaded northern Italy in 568, three years after Justinian's death. Constantinople held most of southern Italy until the mid-700s, though the Muslims took the strategically important island of Sicily in the 600s. Thus four powers—the Lombards, the Byzantines, the Muslims, and the pope—each had a grip on the Italian Peninsula, which was not unified again until the late 1800s.

Justinian's campaigns to regain the glory of Rome also drained the empire of resources. To pay for expensive foreign wars, he had to enact a policy of heavy taxation that caused widespread resentment. While trying to retake the West, he also let his neighbors grow strong enough to threaten the empire's borders. His successors had to contend with hordes of Persians, Mongolians, Slavs, and Bulgars. And by leaving the borders unattended, he ultimately made it easier for a new enemy to sweep in and take over the most profitable and populous sections of the empire—North Africa and the Mediterranean coast. The Muslim invasions of the seventh century forced the empire to give up the Balkans to the Slavs and Bulgars, and then to grant everything else except Constantinople and Asia Minor to the incoming Islamic power.

While his empire building may have sapped his empire, many historians have pointed out that Justinian was simply acting as any other Byzantine emperor would have done. Up to that point, after the barbarian invasions, emperors still considered themselves Roman emperors, albeit without Rome to rule.

Crusaders lay siege to Antioch with a catapult in this 12th-century manuscript illumination.

ANTIOCH
CROSSROADS OF TRADE

Antiquity | *First Christians* | *Martyrdom* | *Siege*

Antioch-on-the-Orontes, as the city was called, was often envied for its cool Mediterranean breeze, fruitful fields, and multiple water sources. Built on the western bank of the Orontes River, in modern-day Turkey on the border with Syria, Antioch was only a day's travel by boat from the Mediterranean port of Seleucia Pieria. Throughout its history, Antioch represented a stopping point for those traveling north to Turkey, south to Alexandria or Jerusalem, east to the Euphrates and the Arabian Peninsula, or west to the sea. The city's low-lying geography contributed to both its rise and its fall. Though its fields were well watered and could support many crops,

Antioch stood on a geologic fault incredibly susceptible to earthquakes, and, surrounded by mountains and hills, it was easily attacked from above. In the long run, the city could not survive these geographical shortcomings.

Antioch was founded in 300 B.C. by the Greek General Seleucus I, who served under Alexander the Great and founded the Seleucid dynasty. He named the town after his father, Antiochus. Foreign traders soon began arriving, and with them came profit. A neighborhood called Daphne, just south of the city, held its own Olympic games, and throughout the city's history, rich families built their houses there. A number of those houses have yielded stunning mosaics, mostly from the Roman period, and they are on display today in the city's archaeology museum. In the fourth century A.D., Antioch became the seat of the Roman Empire in the East, and it grew to become one of the largest cities in the realm before the rise of Constantinople.

Antioch holds a special place in the history of the early Christian church. According to the Bible's Acts of the Apostles, it was in Antioch that the followers of Jesus were first called "Christians." Peter was said to have founded the church there. The involvement of these first Christians greatly elevated the status of the church of Antioch, and disputes with Rome were often quashed with reminders that the authority of both the pope and the patriarch of Antioch could be traced back to Peter. The

ANTIOCH THROUGH THE MIDDLE AGES

A.D. 388
Emperor Theodosius orders pagan altars destroyed.

400s
Palestine and Cyprus split from the Patriarchate of Antioch.

458
A great earthquake destroys most of the city.

459
Simeon the Stylite, Christian martyr, dies; his remains are brought to Antioch.

484
Leontius, claiming to be Byzantine emperor, reigns from Antioch.

526
A major earthquake kills nearly 250,000 people.

528
Justinian I rebuilds the city and names it Theopolis, "City of God."

Antiochene School of thought flourished in the fourth and fifth centuries, and its reputation as a center of learning rivaled that of Alexandria. A number of early scholars came out of that school, most notably Diodore of Tarsus, who defended Christianity against the return of paganism in the late fourth century.

During the latter half of the fifth and into the sixth century, the city suffered from a number of natural disasters, and efforts to rebuild it were thwarted by more misfortunes. Within less than one hundred years, massive earthquakes toppled buildings and killed thousands; fires ravaged what the earthquakes had not destroyed; and plague swept through the population. Outside efforts to support the battered city failed, and Antioch's reputation for wealth, scholarship, and aesthetics quickly disappeared.

Shortly thereafter the Persian army, eager to extend their borders, took advantage of the city's weakened status and attacked. Positioning themselves on the slopes of the surrounding mountains, they trained weapons down on the city and easily seized it. In 637 the Arabs took Antioch into their domain, and it faded into obscurity, surviving for several centuries as a small town under Muslim control.

Its key combination of proximity to the Mediterranean and passes through the mountains nevertheless made Antioch an object of desire for a number of armies in the 10th and 11th centuries, in particular those traveling to the Middle East from Europe on crusades. At that time Antioch shifted from hand to hand until, after a long and difficult siege, Frankish crusaders made it a principality in 1098. Amid constant unrest, trade agreements were still negotiated between Christians and Muslims, and the city slowly began to prosper again. Spices, dyes, silk, and porcelain were carried in from the east, wood was imported from Lebanon, and locally grown olives and lemons were traded in return.

Despite an increase in commerce, the continued wars of the crusaders meant

The ancient city of Antioch was renamed Theopolis, City of God, by Byzantine Emperor Justinian I.

The sixth-century Antioch Chalice was once touted as the Holy Grail, communion cup used at the Last Supper, but it may be an altar lamp instead.

tensions remained high throughout the region. Antioch was always on guard, its surrounding geography making it particularly inviting for attackers. The city succeeded for a while by building up its military and capitalizing on divisions within the Muslim Empire. By 1130, however, the Muslims were again a threat, although they would not capture the city for another century. Antioch did not recover from this last blow, and even after it was taken over by Ottoman forces in 1517, it remained small.

Today there are few reminders of Antioch's tumultuous past. The town itself, now called Antakya, is part of present-day Turkey, near the Syrian border. Few traces of the ancient city remain, chief among them St. Peter's Grotto, a cave church outside the town reputed to have been established by Peter and enhanced with a stone facade by crusaders in the 11th or 12th century. ■

540	637	969	1085	1098	1098	1266
Sassanids under Khosrow I take Antioch.	Battle of Iron Bridge: Arabs capture Antioch from the Byzantines.	Byzantine Emperor Nicephorus II Phocas recaptures Antioch.	Seljuk Turks capture Antioch from the Byzantines.	During the First Crusade, Bohemond I takes Antioch and becomes prince.	The lance that pierced Christ's side is discovered in Antioch.	Mamluk army, led by Baybars I, Sultan of Egypt and Syria, captures Antioch.

The Sassanid Empire's capital city, Ctesiphon, in modern-day Iraq, was a hub of commerce, importing exotic crops such as rice, sugarcane, citrus, eggplant, and cotton.

Though trying to reunite the empire was a costly failure, Justinian did leave several noteworthy monuments. The greatest of these was the *Corpus Juris Civilis*, or Justinian Code, an orderly compendium of civil laws that has formed the basis of most Western legal systems ever since.

To create the code, a team of the greatest legal minds labored for years to put into a few volumes several centuries' worth of jurisprudence. The Justinian Code strove for equity and outlined procedures for judges to follow. Although the code was originally set down in Latin, most of the Novels, or new laws, were written in Greek, and the West remained unenlightened by the code for hundreds of years. Until the code was rediscovered in western Europe in the 11th century,

legal systems there were a hodgepodge of Germanic folk law, Roman law, Old Testament law, and church law.

The other great accomplishment of Justinian was the rebuilding of the Hagia Sophia church, which had burned to the ground during the riot of 532.

Justinian hired 10,000 workers to construct a massive basilica decorated with 20 tons of silver and topped by a gold-covered domed ceiling. Magnificent mosaics and icons graced the interior. The crowning achievement of Byzantine architecture, Hagia Sophia is one of the greatest masterworks of the entire

medieval period. The Turks converted it into a mosque in the 15th century, and in 1935 it became a museum.

Justinian also built other churches, as well as aqueducts, fortresses, harbors, monasteries, and public buildings, and during his time there was a flourishing of the arts and sciences.

Offsetting Constantinople's progress in the sixth century, a horrific outbreak of bubonic plague in 542 killed a large percentage of the population. The plague and the demands of war combined to turn the empire's quick rise into a steady fall, from which it would not recover for another three centuries. During this time Constantinople was besieged by a number of tribal groups, but none strong enough to break through.

The Gothic war was such a drain on the Byzantine Empire that by the end of Justinian's reign he was hated by those closest to him, including the chronicler Procopius, whose *Secret History*, published posthumously, depicted the emperor as "deceitful, devious, false, hypocritical, two-faced, cruel." Procopius blamed him as "a faithless friend" and as "a treacherous enemy, insane for murder and plunder."

MY OPINION IS THAT, ALTHOUGH WE MAY SAVE OURSELVES BY FLIGHT, IT IS NOT TO OUR INTEREST. . . . GOD FORBID THAT I SHOULD EVER BE STRIPPED OF THIS PURPLE, OR LIVE A SINGLE DAY ON WHICH I AM NOT TO BE SALUTED AS MISTRESS.

EMPRESS THEODORA DURING THE RIOT
Constantinople, 532

Theodora died in 548, and with her went much of the energy and focus of Justinian's rule. His final 17 years lacked enthusiasm and accomplishment. Western Europe would seek leadership again from its own ranks—particularly in the church and the Frankish monarchy.

THE PRE-ISLAMIC MIDDLE EAST
Justinian's peace treaty with Persia in 532 was merely a hiccup in what became a long-running conflict with peoples east of the empire. The necessity of waging this border struggle was one of the main reasons for the emperor's failure to reconquer the West. Who were these pre-Islamic people?

The Sassanid dynasty rose to power in the mid-third century, gaining control of a large area that included Khorasan (today's northeastern Iran), Kerman (southeastern Iran), Mesopotamia (central Iraq), Armenia (northwest of Iran), Azerbaijan (east of Armenia), Fars (southwestern Iran), Khuzestan (southwestern Iran), Syria (south of Asia Minor), Egypt, and part of Asia Minor.

Until their lands were overrun by the Arabs in the seventh century, the Sassanids developed an extensive network of roads and cities. Art blossomed, most notably metalwork, gem engraving, and giant rock sculptures carved into limestone cliffs at Taq-e Bostan, near today's Kermanshah in western Iran, in the Zagros Mountains. The monotheistic state religion of the Sassanids was Zoroastrianism, founded sometime in the sixth century B.C. by the prophet Zoroaster, who proposed a view of the moral universe as an unending battle between good and evil.

By the sixth century, the Sassanid Empire was on the decline, but King Khosrow I (r. 531-579) helped restore its vitality, mainly by a Roman-style method of fixed-amount taxation. Honored by the title Khosrow the Just, this leader reformed the state bureaucracy and reorganized the army. He also fought against the Byzantines, and in 540 he captured the ancient city of Antioch, southern Turkey's Antakya today. The city was vulnerable, having been partially destroyed by a fire and two earthquakes in the 520s.

Although unable to permanently hold the city, Khosrow did take a huge number of prisoners, and he forced them to resettle near his capital city of Ctesiphon, on the Tigris River south of modern Baghdad.

A legendary king, Khosrow has probably been credited with more buildings

TRADE LINKS ACROSS EURASIA

Ideas, Religion, and Disease Travel the Silk Road

Trade routes by land and sea between East Asia and the Mediterranean, collectively known as the Silk Road, suffered a decline in activity following the fall of the Roman Empire in the West and the Han Empire in the East—but they never disappeared altogether. When large-scale states such as the Byzantine Empire and the Sui dynasty in China reemerged in the sixth century, trade reenergized with them.

Constantinople, the Byzantine capital, was a crossroads along the revived Silk Road, passage point for silk and porcelain from China, spices and gems from India, rugs from Persia, and textiles from Europe. Merchants in Constantinople also maintained commerce with lands to the north, importing timber, furs, honey, and slaves from Russia and Scandinavia. Most of this merchandise was then exported throughout Eurasia with the financial support of bank loans and business partnerships.

Not just goods traveled the Silk Road. Christianity, Manichaeism, and Buddhism were all spread by missionaries traveling the Silk Road around this time. Agricultural innovations, such as the heavy-wheeled plow, traveled from Asia to Europe. Following an increase in trade through the Red Sea, the bubonic plague also made its first appearance in the Byzantine Empire in 541, decimating half the population of Constantinople. ■

and works than he actually sponsored. It is possible that he authorized the codification of the Avesta, the Zoroastrian holy book. Of great significance is the fact that many of Khosrow's policies and institutions became so ingrained in Persian life that the Muslims adopted them. The Abbasid dynasty, which ruled the Muslim world from the 8th century to the 13th century, modeled its lavish court after his and considered him an exemplary ruler.

Yet the opulence of his palace was not reflected in statewide economic prosperity. As was also the case for the Frankish monarchy, taxes and the spoils of war brought Khosrow I and his attendant nobility personal riches. Thousands of horses, camels, elephants, women, musicians, and poets graced his palace, where he sat upon a tremendous golden throne upheld by legs of ruby. Meanwhile, however, tradesmen, merchants, and the lower classes continued the daily struggle known throughout the early medieval world.

THE PERSIANS ADVANCE

Under an even more militant king—Khosrow II (r. 590-628), grandson of Khosrow I—the Sassanids began reclaiming territory that had been lost in the last few centuries. In the early 600s, Khosrow II marched his army into Byzantine lands in Armenia and

Highly refined trade goods, such as this silver bowl, were produced in Persian workshops, situated at a crossroads of trade between markets in China, India, Europe, and Africa.

Mesopotamia. Then in 613 he conquered the great city of Damascus in southern Syria, and the following year took Jerusalem, just to the south, in Palestine.

His troops then burned the Holy Sepulchre—the church reputedly built on the site of Jesus' burial and resurrection—and carried away the True Cross, believed to have been the very one on which Jesus was crucified. It was an assault on the religion. Although Khosrow II was tolerant of Christianity, and had in fact married an Armenian Christian, his top general oversaw and approved the torture of thousands of Christian prisoners by Jewish soldiers.

The Persian juggernaut continued rolling: In 617 Khosrow II captured the city of Chalcedon, opposite Constantinople, on the east side of the entrance to the Bosporus. Then in 619 he conquered Egypt.

Shortly after these victories, however, the Sassanid power began to decline. The Byzantine emperor Heraclius (r. 610-641), a brilliant military commander, began fighting back in northern Syria and Mesopotamia. By 630 he had regained everything recently lost to the Persians. Although the net result would appear to be zero, the long years of war had wreaked havoc upon the cities and people of the Near East; furthermore, the treasuries and armies of both the Byzantine Empire and the Sassanid Empire were nearly spent.

The failure of Khosrow II to stop Heraclius was considered a disgrace, and it caused a revolt within his kingdom. His top general was executed, and the royal family was captured. Khosrow was forced to watch the execution of his youngest son and heir, after which he himself was murdered.

Another pre-Islamic dynasty, the Lakhmids of southern Mesopotamia, cooperated with the Sassanids in their wars against the Byzantines. Existing as a kind of vassal state to the Sassanids, the Lakhmids were Christian Bedouins who fought against pro-Byzantine Arabs in Syria. One of the Byzantine allies was the Ghassanid dynasty, which occupied

ZOROASTRIANISM A monotheistic religion dating to the sixth century B.C., founded by the prophet Zoroaster, who described the struggle between good and chaos or nothingness in the world. Through good work, man can contribute to the ultimate triumph of good.

EDIFICES

Built by Justinian I by 537, the Hagia Sophia, or Church of Holy Wisdom, was in its day the most technologically advanced building in all of Christendom. In its 15 centuries of use, it has been an Eastern Orthodox church, an Islamic mosque, and a museum. Its interior mosaics were restored in the 1930s.

As the Byzantine Empire expanded, so did its state religion. The two were so closely linked that Byzantine emperors practically treated the church like another branch of government. They appointed officials to high church posts, called ecumenical councils, and intervened in establishing church policies.

Meanwhile, bishops wielded authority in matters political, social, and cultural, serving as judges in court, conducting business, and engaging in civic administration. Paganism was effectively snuffed out during the sixth century, with the last recorded persecution occurring in 580. As the number of adherents to the church continued to increase, so did donations. Large-scale building programs were conducted in all the empire's major cities, and in many smaller ones as well.

THE BYZANTINE CHURCH

Domed Basilicas of Grandeur

The church of Hagia Sophia—"Holy Wisdom"—a massive, domed basilica, was erected in Constantinople by Emperor Justinian I by 537. Designed to be the spiritual and awe-inspiring center of the empire's religion, it was the largest building in all of Christendom, rivaling in scale any construction from the classical period. Its dome, in reality a dome resting atop another larger dome, was a first in architectural engineering. Other Byzantine basilicas were built at remote pilgrimage sites,

such as the four in northern Syria that together form a cross centering on the pillar on which the ascetic monk, Simeon Stylites, perched for many years.

Hagia Sophia established some architectural traditions that were followed, and codified, in subsequent Byzantine churches. A large, open, square-shaped space was topped with a massive dome. In later centuries, the floor plan evolved into a Greek cross, with each of the four arms equal in length, or a quincunx, with interior columns emphasizing four corners and a fifth in the center.

Often the exteriors of Byzantine churches were relatively plain and unadorned, but the inside more than made up for it, with fine sheets of marble and porphyry lining the walls and exquisite mosaic work on the ceilings of central and subordinate domes. ▪

parts of present-day Syria, Jordan, and Israel. The Ghassanid king throughout most of the sixth century was a Monophysite Christian, much to the displeasure of the Byzantines, who considered this heresy.

But the Ghassanids served as protectors of the spice trade route up the Arabian Peninsula. This role gave them favored status, and they prospered through the century. Though sometimes warring against each other, the Lakhmids, the Ghassanids, and other dynasties served the Byzantine Empire as a buffer against the Bedouins and other Arabs to the south. The Lakhmids were unsupported by the centralized Sassanid regime, however, and by 602 they had disappeared.

In 611, Arabs won a victory over the Sassanids, prefiguring the coming Muslim raids a few decades ahead. The Ghassanids fell to the Muslims later in the century.

Sassanid Culture
Before their swift demise in the seventh century, the Sassanids had regained territory and made lasting contributions to government, literature, and the arts, many of which would be enfolded later into Muslim culture. The massive barrel-vaulted palace at Ctesiphon in Mesopotamia, now preserved as ruins, was a masterpiece of architecture. Greek and Indian literature was translated into the Sassanian language of Pahlavi, or Middle Persian, and Sassanid works of religion and history represented the vanguard in the transition from oral to written literature.

Under Khosrow I, the Sassanids welcomed neoplatonist philosophers into their culture. In 529 Byzantium's

Justinian, in a fit of Christian zeal, had closed the revered school of philosophy originally founded by Plato. His rationale was that the neoplatonic philosophy was anti-Christian. Seeking a more intellectually stimulating environment, many scholars escaped to Persia, but most of them became disenchanted with the Sassanid court and returned home.

> FREEDOM . . . IS THE NATURAL POWER OF DOING WHAT WE EACH PLEASE, UNLESS PREVENTED BY FORCE OR BY LAW. SLAVERY IS AN INSTITUTION OF THE LAW OF NATIONS, BY WHICH ONE MAN IS MADE THE PROPERTY OF ANOTHER, CONTRARY TO NATURAL RIGHT.
>
> CORPUS IURUS CIVILIS
> (BODY OF CIVIL LAW)
> FROM THE JUSTINIAN CODE
> *Constantinople, 535*

The Sassanids were generally intolerant not only of other religions but also of variations within their own. Christians, Jews, Buddhists, Brahmins, Nazoreans, and others were suppressed, sometimes by force. In some places, such as the Aramaic-speaking regions of Mesopotamia, Christians were left alone by the Sassanids until the Roman Empire officially adopted Christianity—and then, because the religion had became associated with an enemy state, Christians found themselves targeted. Despite repeated persecutions, pockets

of Christianity survived in Persia until well after the Sassanid dynasty.

An offshoot of Christianity called Manichaeism had developed in Persia in the third century. Inspired by the prophet Mani, a self-proclaimed disciple of Jesus, the religion stressed the two conflicting kingdoms of light, or good, and darkness, or evil. Abstinence was a key virtue of Manichaeism. Although Mani ran afoul of the Persian royals and was executed in the 270s, the religion he inspired resurfaced in both western Europe and central Asia.

Within Zoroastrianism itself, the dominant faith of the Sassanids, fewer variations were accepted as time went on. As in Christianity, religious leaders made narrow distinctions between dogma and heresy, and with their decrees they wielded power. Fire played an essential role in the Zoroastrian religion, symbolizing the one deity, known as Ahura Mazda. Rituals were practiced at numerous fire temples, some of which still exist. By the late Sassanid period, rigid rules defined elaborate purification rites, and anything outside these rules was considered an insult to Ahura Mazda.

The Monastic Movement
Christianity spread slowly across Europe throughout the sixth century. Though a long way from the dominant religious and political force it would be by the year 1000, the church was already drawing, educating, and protecting the most learned men of the time. The lower clergy were often illiterate and ignorant, but the bishops and other high prelates, whose ranks were filled by the nobility, were among the most influential people in society. Soon a new form of Christian devotion, monasticism, would emerge

Under Emperor Justinian I, shown here in a mosaic from Ravenna, Italy, the Byzantine Empire expanded during the sixth century, encircling the Mediterranean. The boundaries did not hold, however: The power and territories of the empire dissipated after Justinian's death.

of religious devotion and its deliberate separation from society—did not have ways of influencing society beyond its walls. To elevate the spirit by practicing abnegation of the flesh, the early ascetics had to remove themselves from the temptations of urban life—particularly sex, food, and material comforts. The fleshpots of the great Eastern cities provided a stark contrast with the harsh desert favored by anchorites—devotees committed to solitude—such as Syria's Simeon Stylites.

In the wilderness of the west, however, cities were few and not large, and an ascetic who wanted to set an example by living in solitude risked dying unnoticed. Surviving as a farmer in this colder climate was hard enough. Thus by necessity, the monastic movement in the west became a communal effort. The cenobitic, or communal, monks lived a prescribed life with their own kind, but over time monks, their institutions, and the products of their labors influenced the outside world tremendously.

One of the earliest monastic communities in western Europe was started by St. Martin of Tours (316-397), who was born to pagan parents but who at the age of ten decided to become a Christian. Refusing to fight in the Roman army, he was branded a coward—until he offered to stand on the front lines armed only with a cross. Martin later preached against the heresy of Arianism in the Balkans, and then he started a hermit community in Ligugé, in west-central France: the first monastery in Gaul.

In 415, Greek-trained St. John Cassian (360-435) founded a convent and abbey

Fifth-century monastery ruins near Rasafa, Syria, seem to rise up out of the desert on which they stand. Byzantine monasteries were often situated in remote locations to facilitate meditation and transcendence.

to shape the intellectual landscape of Europe and, ultimately, the world.

Neither the bishops nor the lower clergy could eradicate the heathen superstition—with its devils, magic, and nature worship—that the Germanic tribes had developed over the centuries, let alone replace it overnight with a monotheistic system imported from the Near East. The Christianization of western Europe was going to take several more centuries. In the meantime, primitive beliefs were simply incorporated into Christian doctrine and practice, in much the same way that

Native American converts of a later age wove their ancient religious beliefs and practices in with those of Catholicism.

The central leadership of the church, itself led by the papacy, would emerge time and again during the Middle Ages as a moral balance to the worldly power of European monarchs. But on the street level, the rank-and-file clergy, whose offices came to be filled by monks, provided the church and hence the people with a much-needed social stability.

The early monastic movement—with its inward-looking interpretation

MONASTICISM Dedication to the monastery lifestyle, which includes frugality, celibacy, relinquishing of material possessions, and a meditative routine, often including silence, ritual, and prayer. Some monastic orders encourage work in the community; others, isolation.

in Marseilles, on the French coast of the Mediterranean. A champion of cenobitic monasticism, he also wrote about both the benefits and failings of the practice of a desert hermit lifestyle.

The monastic movement of the fifth and sixth centuries was most vigorous in Ireland. Perhaps because the island was such a remote outpost, the Irish monks turned out to be a hardy and inspirational breed of missionary enthusiasts.

Sometime around the 430s, St. Patrick brought Christianity to Ireland. A real person who left a credible account of his life called *Confessio*, Patrick was born into a wealthy Celtic-Roman family in Britain. At age 16 he was kidnapped by pirates and sold into slavery in Ireland.

After working for six years as a herdsman, he escaped back to Britain. Not long after his return, though, he had a dream that changed his life. "There, in a vision of the night, I saw a man whose name was Victoricus coming as if from Ireland with innumerable letters," Patrick wrote.

"And he gave me one of them, and I read the beginning of the letter: 'The Voice of the Irish.'" Patrick recalled in his *Confessio* that in the dream, as he was reading the letter, "I seemed at that moment to hear the voice of those who were beside the forest of Foclut which is near the western sea, and they were crying as if with one voice: 'We beg you, holy youth, that you shall come and shall walk again among us.'" He believed that the dream was a sign from God that he should return to Ireland.

After a period of study in Britain, Patrick followed his dream and traveled back to Ireland. He began preaching all over the countryside, bringing Christianity to the island. Though sometimes hounded by Druid priests, Patrick managed to secure the protection of local kings. He remained in Ireland for the duration of his life, and he is said to have baptized more than 120,000 people and founded some 300 churches. He also introduced Latin as the language of the church.

BENEDICT AND HIS RULE

While the Irish monks could leave and return to the monastery as they pleased, the more common model for western monasticism was the somewhat stricter order established by St. Benedict of Nursia (ca 480-547). The Italian monk started out as a hermit, living alone for three years in the Simbruinian hills in central Italy, then in a lakeside cave near the ruins of Nero's first-century palace in the Abruzzi foothills above Subiaco, 40 miles east of Rome. His biographer, Pope Gregory I (ca 540-604), described how Benedict once overcame a temptation of the flesh: "A certain woman there was which some time he had seen, the memory of which . . . did so mightily inflame [him] with concupiscence . . . he was of mind to have forsaken the wilderness. But suddenly assisted with God's grace, he came to himself," wrote Gregory.

Benedict's response was not simply self-control but self-punishment. "Seeing many thick briers and nettle-bushes to

TALIESIN

❖

The First of the Welsh Bards

Taliesin Ben Beirdd—Taliesin, Chief Bard—was one of the earliest poets of Wales. He was known for his works even in his lifetime, late in the sixth century. What remains of his poetry are songs to royalty in praise of military prowess or laments over lost loved ones. "I will praise the sovereign, supreme king of the land, / Who hath extended his dominion over the shore of the world," reads one. Full of symbolism and powerful language, they were likely first sung at the courts of the kings addressed.

The alliteration and rhyme schemes found in the works of Taliesin set standards for centuries of Welsh sagas to come—sagas in which

Taliesin himself would appear, an exalted figure of poetry past.

Because poetry was passed on orally in Taliesin's own day, the oldest extant copy of his writings, the *Book of Taliesin*, dates to 700 years after his death. By that time, a variety of works and a magical upbringing were attributed to him. The mythological Taliesin appeared in later Welsh poetic tales alongside figures such as King Arthur and Merlin. He also appears in Alfred, Lord Tennyson's 19th-century *Idylls of the King*, a retelling of the Arthurian legends.

Few details are known about the historical Taliesin, yet he is counted one of the fathers of the rich tradition of Welsh storytelling. ■

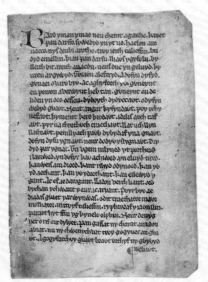

From the 6th century, transcribed in the 13th, the *Book of Taliesin* is Wales's first great poem.

THE WORLD IN THE SIXTH CENTURY

Although Islam would not begin its rise until the following century, the birth of the prophet Muhammad in Mecca in 570 planted the origins of this religion firmly in the sixth century, while elsewhere on the continent, Christianity continued to push into new regions and cultures. The Byzantine Empire increased in power significantly under Justinian.

In India, the Gupta Empire fell to nomad invaders in 550, and the country split into smaller states, ending a golden age of art, architecture, and science. Buddhists and Hindus continued to coexist peacefully. Indian traders spread Hinduism throughout southeast Asia, into Cambodia and Vietnam. The Rulers of Funan—in southern Cambodia and Vietnam—fell to the Khmers in the sixth century, and the kingdom ultimately transitioned from Hinduism to Buddhism. In China, the Sui dynasty backed Confucianism, but their efforts did little to suppress the practice of other religions and philosophies there.

Elsewhere in the world, religious beliefs were central to culture but not to the makings of empire. While northern Africa was grappling with Christianity and the Byzantines, western Africa was witnessing the rise of the kingdom of Ghana, a trading center for gold.

In the great civilizations in the Americas, sacred sites were constructed, from the pyramids and temples of the Maya to the more humble burial mounds of the Hopewell—sites that we can still visit today. ■

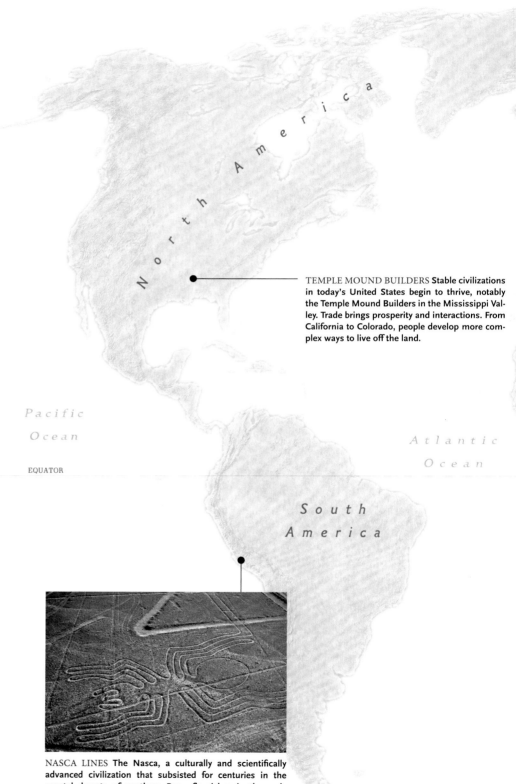

TEMPLE MOUND BUILDERS Stable civilizations in today's United States begin to thrive, notably the Temple Mound Builders in the Mississippi Valley. Trade brings prosperity and interactions. From California to Colorado, people develop more complex ways to live off the land.

NASCA LINES **The Nasca, a culturally and scientifically advanced civilization that subsisted for centuries in the coastal deserts of southern Peru, flourishes in the early medieval period. Today, however, they are known primarily for the Nasca lines—a puzzling set of gigantic geoglyphs visible only from the air.**

Ocean

RUINS AT QASR IBRIM Perched high on a cliff above the Nile, the city of Qasr Ibrim lies at the heart of Africa's Nubian kingdoms. Though the Roman Empire declares Christianity its official religion, Qasr Ibrim is slow to convert. Some Egyptian temples persist well into the sixth century.

GUPTA HEAD SCULPTURE India's Gupta Empire dates to 375, when Chandragupta I ascended the throne. Weakened by decades of nomadic attacks, it collapses in 550. Rival groups compete for power in various regions, initiating a period of instability.

A s i a

A f r i c a

Pacific Ocean

SUI DYNASTY Fractured by warring kingdoms and internal strife, China suffers through a period of instability in the early part of the sixth century. By 589, however, the Sui dynasty consolidates the empire, ushering in scientific and cultural advancements.

EQUATOR

Indian Ocean

Australia

KHOSROW II The Sassanid king Khosrow II, shown here in front of the palace of Shirin, continues the war with Byzantium that his father started. During his reign from 590 to 628 he also has to defend his lands against incursions from Azerbaijan.

After sacking Rome in 410, the Visigoths ultimately settled in Spain, where they carved out their own Christian empire ruled by the kings shown above on a manuscript page in a volume dating from around A.D. 1000.

grow hard by, off he cast his apparel, and threw himself into the midst of them and there wallowed so long that, when he rose up, all his flesh was pitifully torn; and so by the wounds of his body he cured the wounds of his soul, in that he turned pleasure into pain." The act of inflicting pain as a spiritual discipline was performed in remembrance of the suffering of Christ by some medieval monks.

Finding the hermetic life too lonely, Benedict joined a loosely organized, Greek-style monastery. The son of old-line Roman aristocrats, he had been brought up to respect order and discipline, and he tried to introduce reforms into the relatively lax monastic life. After surviving an attempted poisoning, he decided to found his own monastery, and he went on to found 12 communities, each with 12 monks living in it. Traveling south, he established the famous monastery at Monte Cassino, between Rome and Naples, around the year 529. Among his visitors at Monte Cassino was Totila, the Ostrogothic King of Italy (541-552).

The *Rule of Benedict*, which the monastic founder based partially on an anonymous work, *The Rule of the Master*, was a set of regulations for an orderly life in the monastery. Its reasonable, flexible nature made it the standard for the next 600 years.

The Rule specified that the abbot—elected for life by his fellows—was the absolute leader of the monastery: a heavy responsibility, for he was answerable to God for the salvation of each monk's soul. On entering the monastery, a monk took vows of poverty, chastity, and obedience; that is, he had to give up all his worldly possessions, abstain from sex, and obey the Rule and the abbot's orders. Since these vows exacted a sacrifice few

PERSONAE

GREGORY I

The Pope with Worldly Understanding

Gregory I was unwillingly anointed bishop of Rome, or pope, in 590. It was a particularly challenging time in Rome. Centralized civic order was becoming impossible with the economy increasingly agrarian, literacy on the decline, the encroaching Lombard kingdom, and the bubonic plague coursing through Italy.

In Gregory's hands, the work of the papacy expanded beyond just spiritual leadership. He conducted war and diplomacy, defended Rome from attack, ransomed hostages, enacted land reforms, and repaired aqueducts. His jurisdiction, though, did not extend far beyond Rome's city walls. Provincial Christian policies were taking hold in the Byzantine Empire, North Africa, Spain, Gaul, Ireland, and northern Italy. In response, Gregory sent letters and missionary envoys throughout western Europe, which ultimately allied the Roman church with the Frankish monarchy and brought cultural and spiritual cohesion. Immediately after he died, Gregory was canonized. He is a saint in both the Roman Catholic and the Eastern Orthodox Churches. ■

Through diplomacy, warfare, and ransom, Pope Gregory I preserved the office of the papacy during a difficult era.

people could stick to, the Rule imposed a mandatory one-year training period to determine if the novice was cut out for the monastic life.

The day was divided among four activities. Four hours were devoted to Opus Dei—God's Work, communal liturgical prayers; four hours to individual prayer and reading religious literature; and six hours to farm work or other activities that contributed to the community. The remaining ten hours were reserved for sleeping and eating. Talking was kept to a minimum. The idea was not to indulge in physical privation but to live a harmonious, self-sustaining, self-governing, communal life devoted to God.

The Rule of Benedict required prayer and work, the fundamentals of monastic life. His monasteries thrived amid the spread of Christianity and provided centers of devotion and learning that preserved Rome's legacy in books. Over the next few centuries, as western society grappled with wars and other calamities, monasteries remained stable local institutions that provided both leaders, educators, scholars, and artists. Benedict's black monks—named for the color of their robes—became Europe's earliest teaching organization.

It was the Roman statesman and writer Cassiodorus (ca 490-585) who founded monasteries in which monks were engaged in scholarship beyond Christianity—they copied and translated Roman, Greek, and pagan writings to preserve the ancient knowledge. Most of these were books and manuscripts on history, theology, politics, and grammar, but there were also writings on mathematics and music theory, among other topics. Cassiodorus's creation of the monastic scriptorium, a workshop where scribes made copies of classical and religious works, set a pattern for future monasteries. The medieval monastery became school and library, a place where learned and devout men taught the next generation and carefully preserved works of art and knowledge for future appreciation. During the next 500 years, about 90 percent of all literate men were educated in monastic schools.

GREGORY THE GREAT

The first monk to become pope was Gregory I (r. 590-604). A Benedictine, his work as a reformer earned him the title "architect of the medieval papacy."

Born to aristocratic parents, Gregory became in his early 30s Rome's urban prefect, or administrative president. Later he turned part of the palace that he inherited

Of pagan birth, Martin of Tours founded the first monastery in modern-day France and helped spread Christianity and monastic values throughout western Europe.

with the post into a monastery. He apparently had no ambition to be pope, yet when he was elected to the office at around age 50, Gregory accepted and vowed to use his power to help those most in need. To that end he embarked on a campaign to rid the church of corruption, centralize its administration, and extend its social services. "We do not want the treasury of the church defiled by disreputable gain," he wrote.

Gregory was pope during a period of explosive politics in Italy's history, with the primitive Lombards controlling the north, the Byzantine Empire holding the south as well as Ravenna, and Rome lying somewhere in the middle. Navigating delicately between powers, Gregory wanted to win over the Lombards, who were Arians and thus considered heretics, yet he had to be careful not to offend their enemies, the Byzantines. He opposed Byzantine taxes, which had grown so high that parents were often forced to either sell their children or move into Lombard territory, whereupon the Lombards extorted money from the papacy to accommodate these Christian refugees. Byzantine Ravenna, surrounded by Lombards, wanted to fight the latter, but was even more hostile toward a pope they considered a meddlesome nuisance.

Some 850 of Gregory's letters survive, more written material than from any other early clergyman, and from them emerges a complex personality. He was both a capable administrator and a theorist of education, a shrewd diplomat and a theologian who put faith in superstition and miracles—for instance, he attributed all sorts of minor miracles to Benedict.

Gregory's devotion to the destitute was genuine. On seeing English slaves in a Roman slave market, he is said to

This gold-plated copper plaque depicts the story of Agilulf, King of the Lombards, who encouraged the peaceful conversion of his people to Christianity.

have remarked, *"Non Angli sed angeli—* They are not Angles but angels"—or, as St. Bede (ca 672-735) reported the comment, "They have the faces of angels, and such should be the co-heirs of the angels in heaven." Gregory himself bought and sold slaves, but he also sometimes freed them, and he advocated punishment for those who mistreated them.

Gregory's organizing ability, coupled with his intelligence and devotion, helped the papacy to become what he called *servus servorum Dei*—the servant of the servants of God. The pope as the vicar of Christ on Earth had the most responsibility, because all other clergy were under his care and direction.

But implied in this principle is another: The pope wields absolute authority over the entire Latin church. The reason for strengthening the papacy was to enable it to preside over a church that was spread across a western Europe of so many different cultures and languages that Europe's only meaningful bond was Christianity. Gregory had the wisdom to realize this

and to understand that missionary work at this stage was crucial for the church's ascendancy, if not for its very survival.

STRATEGIES FOR CONVERSION

Gregory certainly understood the importance of politics. Some 200 years before Charlemagne became the first Holy Roman Emperor, Gregory saw that an alliance with the often inept Frankish kings was the key to the long-term success of the church, and, in his way of thinking, it would therefore be a benefit to the people. To that end, he began corresponding with the Merovingian king Childebert II (r. 575-595). Not until the eighth century were the fruits of Gregory's diplomatic efforts realized, however, when Frankish rulers finally woke up to the idea that the papacy could actually help them consolidate their own power. In the meantime, Gregory's missionary work had more immediate results.

He sent emissaries to England, partly to gain an edge over the rising Celtic church. He chose as leader a Benedictine monk in Rome who came to be known as St. Augustine (not to be confused with St. Augustine of Hippo). In 597 Augustine journeyed to England with 40 monks, landing on the southeast coast. They were taken in by King Aethelbert I of Kent (r. 560-616), who let them preach in an old church in Canterbury—literally, "Kent Town." Aethelbert's gracious reception of the missionaries was probably due to his recent marriage to a Christian princess, Bertha, daughter of the king of Paris.

The missionaries quickly made converts, including the king himself. On Christmas Day 597 they baptized thousands of converts in a public ceremony that recalled noteworthy precedents, including the conversion of Clovis and his 3,000 soldiers early in the century.

In the seven years preceding his death, in 604, Augustine became the head bishop of Britain and established a cathedral and monastery at Canterbury. Though

SCRIPTORIUM A room in a monastery where monks copied manuscripts, usually holy books. The work performed by medieval monks in scriptoria is handed down to us in rare illuminated manuscripts covering history and theology and rich with art and calligraphy.

his missionary efforts were fruitful in southern England, he was unsuccessful in gaining the allegiance of the Celtic churches in Wales, in the west, which had no interest in following the dictates of Rome.

Augustine's queries to Gregory about how to bring religion to the heathen Anglo-Saxons, and Gregory's responses, reveal Gregory's tact in dealing with potential converts. They also tell us much about the concerns of the church and the life and beliefs of the Anglo-Saxons.

For example, Augustine asked, "May an expectant mother be baptized? How soon after childbirth may she enter church? And how soon after birth may a child be baptized if in danger of death?" Such rules were only then in the making. "How soon after childbirth may a husband have relations with his wife?" he continued discreetly. "And may a woman enter church at certain periods? And may she receive communion at these times? And may a man enter church after relations with his wife before he has washed? Or receive the sacred mystery of communion?" As if to explain why his mind dwells on such matters, Augustine added, "These uncouth English people require guidance on all these matters."

Pope Gregory's replies always tempered dogma with political strategy.

I AM READY TO GIVE
EVEN MY LIFE
WITHOUT HESITATION;
AND MOST WILLINGLY
FOR HIS NAME.
I AM GREATLY GOD'S DEBTOR,
BECAUSE HE GRANTED ME
SO MUCH GRACE,
THAT THROUGH ME
MANY PEOPLE WOULD BE
REBORN IN GOD

ST. PATRICK
CONFESSIO
Circa 450

TO BETTER TILL THE FIELDS

Agricultural Advancements of the Early Middle Ages

The wooden plow functioned well for thousands of years, breaking up the weeds of light Mediterranean topsoil, but it was no match for the heavy mud of northern Europe, where new technologies were needed to work the land. Two inventions of the Middle Ages, the moldboard plow and the iron-tipped plowshare, advanced agricultural practices and productivity tremendously.

The moldboard plow does not just break up the soil but also turns it over, aerating furrows and pulling up weeds by their roots.

Another improvement was to equip the plow with wheels instead of runners (an idea from eastern Europe), which allowed draught animals to pull heavier plowshares tipped or faced in iron.

An expensive commodity, the heavy-wheeled, iron-tipped moldboard plow was slow to spread throughout Europe, where landowners often spent their money on war instead of food. When it finally did come into common usage, between the 10th and 12th centuries, a sudden food surplus resulted. ■

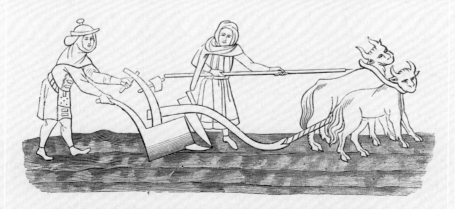

The iron-tipped moldboard plow opened up new lands for agriculture by breaking up and aerating even the heavy mud of northern Europe.

"We have come to the conclusion that the temples of idols ... should on no account be destroyed," he advised Augustine, who was to "destroy the idols, but the temples themselves are to be aspersed with holy water, altars set up, and relics enclosed in them.

"In this way, we hope that the people may abandon idolatry . . . and resort to these places as before," he continued. "And since they have a custom of sacrificing many oxen to devils, let some other solemnity be substituted in its place. . . . They are no longer to sacrifice beasts to the devil, but they may kill them for food to the praise of God." Gregory's tactic of incorporating non-Christian rites into the practice of Christianity was one of the methods by which the religion won

Moscow*

Rome
Constantinople*

THREE ROMES

THE BYZANTINE WORLD
AT HEIGHT OF EMPIRE, UNDER JUSTINIANI I (527–565)
● SIGNIFICANT CENTER ✤ MONASTERY ✕ BATTLE SITE

Map labels: VENICE, RAVENNA, ADRIATIC, ROME, Barcelona, Cordoba, Cartagena, MEDITERRANEAN, PALERMO, CARTHAGE, Naples, Tripoli, Kosovo ✕1389, Kleidion Pass 1014 ✕, CONSTANTINOPLE, THESSALONICA, MISTRA, EPHESUS, BLACK SEA, Heraclia, Chalcedon, NICAEA, Caesarea, Manzikert 1071, Edessa, Tarsus, ANTIOCH, St. Symeon Stylites, Laodicea, Tripoli, Beirut, Damascus, ✕Yarmuk River 636, JERUSALEM, Gaza, Bethlehem, ALEXANDRIA

souls. "If the people are allowed some worldly pleasures," he suggested, "they will come more readily to desire the joys of the spirit. For it is impossible to eradicate all errors from obstinate minds at a stroke; and whoever wishes to climb to a mountaintop climbs step by step."

BRITAIN IN THE VANGUARD

Over in Ireland, churchmen of the sixth and early seventh centuries followed in the wake of St. Patrick and other fifth-century missionaries. Many of these Christian newcomers came north from Gaul, fleeing the barbarian invasions. There were also Mediterranean Greeks, traveling to the British Isles by following trade routes. Their makeup, combined with the character and history of the island itself, made for a different sort of Christianity.

The Irish had never been under Roman rule, and so classical culture had not permeated their territory in the days

At the height of its expansion under Justinian I, the Byzantine Empire stretched from the eastern shores of the Black Sea to the straits of Gibraltar, the full latitude of the Mediterranean Sea.

of the empire. They made up for it in their monasteries by copying and collecting volumes of classical texts for their libraries and by continuing the study of Greek, which had been practically lost in early medieval western Europe in the spirit of rejecting paganism. So rare was the knowledge of Greek elsewhere in the west that through the ninth century, clergy who knew Greek were assumed to have come from Ireland. By the early seventh century, the Irish monasteries were the most advanced intellectual centers in the West.

A century later the influence of the Celtic Church began to wane, as missionaries of the Roman Church converted everyone else in Europe, and Ireland was handicapped by distance. The island's

own social hierarchy nurtured a growing national culture, with wealthy patrons sponsoring the production of manuscripts in Gaelic and Latin. Ireland's literary culture was well established by this time, more so than anywhere else in Europe.

Yet over the next few centuries, the papacy and the Anglo-Saxon monks would work together to effect a surprising transformation on European life and education. Historians suggest that intellectual and cultural change often starts with outlying colonies, because those colonies are the most apt to work hardest to prove their worth to the dominant culture; thus whereas the Continent and its Frankish rulers were content to stumble along as they always had, the British Isles fostered new kinds of creative thinkers and workers. The Anglo-Saxon monks then began coming across the English Channel, spreading their own intellectual brand of Christian civilization.

Some of the medieval era's most popular amusements evolved into the games we know today. This 11th- or 12th-century carved-wood gaming piece might have been used in a primitive type of board game.

MEDIEVAL AMUSEMENTS

rom cards and chess sets to dolls and spinning tops, some of today's most popular games and amusements trace back to the Middle Ages. Agricultural advancements provided the upper classes with a fair amount of leisure, which they filled with sport and play. Even peasants found time for recreation, celebrating the religious holidays with games and festivals, and all children played with toys, such as dolls and miniature horses, and invented games, such as jousting and hide-and-seek.

Chess originated in India in the sixth century and did not reach Europe until the tenth, but then it rapidly became popular among the nobility. Some of the oldest known chess sets, such as the ivory set belonging to the Frankish king Charlemagne, contain elephants instead of horses—a holdover from India.

Playing cards, too, were a common amusement. The earliest cards had suits of staves, cups, coins, and swords. What we know today as tarot cards were in the Middle Ages part of a regular playing deck. And today's cards showing king, queen, and jack (or servant) were established as such by the 14th century.

Outside, nobility entertained themselves with hunting games. Farming now provided most of the necessary food, and hunting became a sport for amusement. Hunters used bows, swords, and spears. They rode on horseback with dogs at their side. The poor hunted, too, but often sold their game or turned it over to their lords.

Public spaces hosted a variety of entertainments. Miracle plays moved from the church to the marketplace, rendering Bible stories and the lives of the saints in song. Jesters, sporting brightly colored clothing and eccentric hats, poked fun at society. Troubadours, or minstrel singers of love, parodied the romance of knighthood and performed in vernacular languages. Just outside of town, traveling carnivals provided a venue for trading goods and witnessing friendly rounds of jousting.

An early 15th-century illustration shows a king and queen playing chess—a pastime by that time aptly dubbed the game of kings. Chess originated in sixth-century India, and enthusiasm for it spread west to the Middle East and then Europe within a few hundred years.

No longer a necessity of survival, hunting became an amusement of the nobility, especially in the late medieval era. Armed with bows, swords, and spears, men hunted on horseback with specially trained dogs at their side.

An 11th-century Italian chess piece made of ivory exhibits the elaborate carvings typical of its time: The king sits on a throne in a curtained alcove with an attendant at each side.

Playing cards provided a variety of entertainments for people in the medieval era. These four examples from a 52-card playing deck show the similarities between our modern-day cards and

600 – 700

THE EASTERN MEDITERRANEAN REGION SEEMED SET ON A WAR BETWEEN PERSIA AND BYZANTIUM, but in the seventh century the region's history was knocked off that course by the sudden arrival of a new religion. From the deserts of Arabia, Islam would come whirling north, east, and west, conquering Persia and much of Byzantium, and ranging from North Africa to Armenia. The establishment of a large and powerful Islamic empire would begin affecting western Europe by the early eighth century, setting up a shifting East-West fault line that endures to the present day. Born into a Meccan merchant clan, the Prophet Muhammad grew up during a time of political instability and religious flux. Nomadic Bedouins ruled the Arabian Peninsula, their tribal raids on each other and on north-south trade caravans a long-standing tradition. They made pilgrimages to Mecca, and bowed to a number of idols and nature gods. Pagans, Jews, and Christians of various denominations lived in many of the oasis towns and desert outposts, separated perhaps by neighborhood, but more or less tolerant of each other's beliefs.

At around the age of 40, Muhammad became a religious mystic and began receiving messages from Allah, the Arabic word for God. He started preaching and soon had a loyal following for a new religion called Islam, which means "submission to Allah." Morally and politically, Islam emphasized the practice of charity and demanded social justice, or equity.

Unnerved by this new movement and its eloquent prophet, the aristocracy of Mecca opposed him. Muhammad and his disciples moved north to Medina. They supported themselves by caravan raiding, and they continued to meet and meditate on the lessons that their leader, Muhammad, had to offer. Soon they had sufficient followers and the strength to go back and take on the army of Mecca. Returning to the city, they defeated those in power there. The victory affirmed their sense of divine right and their belief that the new religion was a revelation.

In 630, two years before Muhammad's death, he led some 30,000 armed men on a march to Syria, conquering and making alliances as he went. By now Islam had become a religion at war and on the move. Those who submitted were granted mercy; those who resisted were killed. Christians and Jews were not forced into conversion, and, in fact, the tax they were required to pay instead made them valuable contributors to the exploding Islamic state. Many of the conquered peoples, bitter from years of repression by the Byzantines and Sassanids, welcomed the invaders.

Medina, home to Muhammad during the years when he built the first community of Islam, is one of the religion's most holy cities, together with Mecca, his birthplace.
PRECEDING PAGES: The open courtyard of Muhammad's house in Medina served as a prototype for Islam's first mosques. Mosques still have an open area for prayer today.

While the Frankish kingdoms muddled along from one inept Merovingian king to the next, and the rest of western Europe quietly smoldered in its own inter-kingdom struggles, the Byzantine Empire held together against depredations from all sides. Emperor Heraclius regained much of the territory lost to the Persians and Balkan peoples in the previous century. His reorganization of the military would keep Byzantium strong for several centuries, and his recapture and delivery of the True Cross to Jerusalem gave him hero status. But in his final years, he was broken and dispirited, standing by helplessly as the Muslims took Syria, then began picking off citadels farther and farther afield. They did so mainly under the caliphs Umar and Mu'awiyah. Before the century was out, Islam, while its adherents were still mostly Arabs, had endured internal war and broken into two sects, yet it emerged as a strong and expanding religion.

The Birth of Islam

By the late 500s, the Arabian Peninsula, which extends like an ax head between the Persian Gulf and the Red Sea, was occupied by warring tribes in its desert interior and the waning Yemeni civilization at its fertile southern tip. The Abyssinians, who lived in Ethiopia, had been trying to take southern Arabia to cut in on the profitable caravan trade of Indian spices and Arabian incense flowing to the Mediterranean. The two dominant states of the region, the Persians and the Byzantines, were

THE SEVENTH CENTURY

603
A truce is formed between the Lombards and the Byzantines.

CA 610
Muhammad undergoes his spiritual transformation.

613
Chlothar II reunites the Frankish kingdom by executing Brunhilde.

615
The Persians sack Jerusalem.

630
Muhammad leads his followers on a *hajj*, or pilgrimage, to Mecca.

637
Arabs take over the Persian capital, Ctesiphon.

644
Earliest evidence for the use of windmills, in Persia.

661
The Umayyad caliphate forms, based in Damascus.

698
Arabs capture Carthage, the last Byzantine base in Africa.

too exhausted from fighting each other to become involved in a struggle to the south. Thus a period of lawlessness ensued on the Arabian Peninsula.

The people who came to dominate the area were the desert nomads and semi-nomads known as the Bedouins. Descended from Mesopotamians, they considered their wandering lifestyle superior to that of the peninsula's agricultural groups to the south. Some tribes lived in tents and herded sheep, goats, or cattle; others lived at oases and raised date palms. The people of these disparate tribes wore loose robes woven from animal hair, and the men usually had multiple wives. Manliness—comprising bravery, honor, and generosity—was the virtue most prized by the Bedouin. An illiterate people, they took pride in their poetry and their storytelling tradition, a highly evolved oral literature with its own vernacular. Their stories, like northern sagas or Greek epics, were of legendary heroes and their deeds.

The most elite of the tribes, or clans, were camel herders from whose name comes the word "Arab." Fiercely loyal to their clans, the Arabs chose a male elder as the tribal leader, or sheikh. Internecine raids were common and followed prescribed, though unwritten, rules. These rules included one that banned raids during four holy months. Raiders would suddenly move in on an enemy camp and steal camels, cattle, women, and other property. Often some of the victims would join the victors, thus increasing the stronger clan's wealth and

This gold purse lid, inlaid with garnets and glass, was unearthed at Sutton Hoo, a seventh-century Anglo-Saxon cemetery in Suffolk, England.

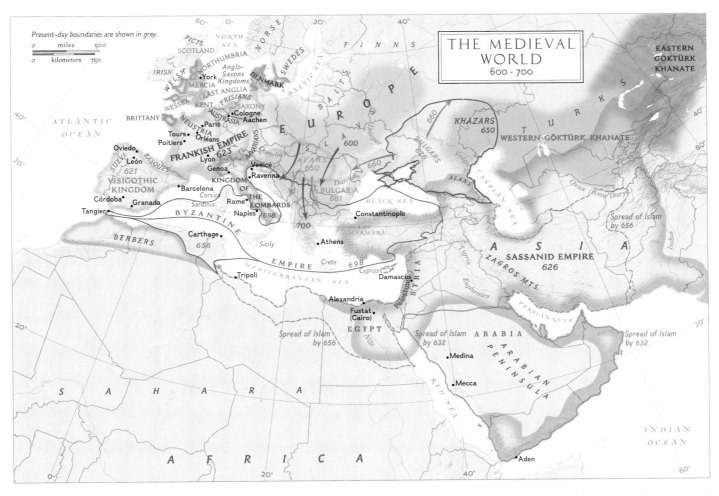

Present-day boundaries are shown in gray.

THE MEDIEVAL
WORLD
600 - 700

The Eastern Roman Empire, now called Byzantine, is losing territory to the Lombards and incursions of the Avars and Slavs in the north, while the spread of Islam changed the map of the Middle East and the southern Mediterranean. The Frankish Empire was divided into the kingdoms Austrasia, Neustria, Aquitaine, and Burgundy.

numbers. Though the raids were generally without violence, those who resisted were often subjected to bloody assault.

The Bedouin worshiped the moon and the stars, and different tribes venerated particular objects in nature—often important landmarks such as a spring, a well, a tree, or a stone. During the holy month of Dhul-Hijjah, they would make a pilgrimage, or *hajj*, to these sacred sites. The most revered site was a small granite shrine, the cube-shaped Kaaba, situated in the middle of the city of Mecca, which lay in a valley about 50 miles from the Red Sea, halfway down the peninsula. Here the Bedouin bowed to hundreds

of idols, including Christian icons, and prayed to a high god called Allah. The mixture of gods at this time and place was unsurprising given the proximity of Palestine to the north and the confluence of trade routes from East and West. Jewish and Christian communities lay scattered all around, and Arabs and Jews were by tradition all descended from the sons of Abraham—the Jews from Isaac, the Arabs from Ishmael.

It was into this environment of religious fluidity that Muhammad was born in Mecca around 570. An orphan at age six, he was raised by a grandfather and uncle to become a merchant. Little is

known of his early life, except that he was quiet and worked hard as a shepherd and camel driver. At age 25 he received a proposal of marriage from his cousin Khadijah, a rich widow whose trading caravans he managed. Though she was some 15 years his senior, he accepted the offer; she gave him four daughters and the leisure to contemplate the relationship of man to God.

One of Muhammad's favorite retreats was a cave on Mount Hira, three miles outside Mecca. Here in the month of Ramadan around the year 610 he saw his first prophetic vision. An accompanying voice told him to worship Allah:

Recite, in the name of your Lord
who created,
He created man from a clot,
Recite, by your Most Generous
Lord,
Who taught by the pen/ He
taught man what he did
not know.

Muhammad later recalled, "It was as if the scripture were written on my heart." For the rest of his life he continued receiving messages from Allah through the angel Gabriel, as tradition has it. He memorized them so that a scribe could write them down.

These revelations form the 78,000 words of the Koran, the holy book of Islam. Its name comes from the Arabic for "to read" or "to recite," and Muslims ever since have believed that the holy book contains the words of Allah as conveyed to Muhammad, which he then transcribed.

The Koran, written in Arabic, embraces human history, prophecy, the afterlife, and the legal and moral standards men and women should follow. There are specific rules governing property, personal behavior, and the family. The Koran teaches that there is only one God, creator of the universe, who demands *Islam*, or submission to Himself. Muhammad is referred to as the last of a long line of prophets that includes, among others, Abraham, Moses, and Jesus.

Daily prayers are specified in the rules, and there were to be no intermediaries between God and the individual. The

Viking warriors summoned the power of pagan deities such as Tyr, the Heaven and War God (left), by embossing his image on their helmets.

Koran further promoted humility, temperance, courage, charity, and justice. Early Islam raised the status of women by prohibiting infanticide, which applied particularly to baby girls—implying against custom that their lives are just as sacred as baby boys'; by limiting polygyny to four wives; and by providing for female inheritance.

For the first century of Islam, women and men prayed together. Muhammad himself took ten wives after the death of Khadijah, but before the Koran's limiting edict. Some were widows of followers who died in battle; others he married for political purposes.

Muhammad had begun preaching with eloquence by 613, and he had drawn

a body of loyal followers. Early passages in the Koran teach of the need for generosity and the coming of a judgment day when men's deeds on Earth will result in their going to heaven or hell after death. Muhammad found it easy to draw followers with this message, since wealth was concentrated among the few richest merchant families. It was not long, though, before the wealthy tribal leaders began feeling threatened by what they took to be a political as well as a religious message.

Believers read in the Koran, for example, that "The unbelievers, among the people of the Book and the idolaters, shall be in the Fire of Hell, dwelling therein forever. Those are the worst of creatures. . . . Those who have believed and did the righteous deeds—those are the best of creatures. Their reward with their Lord will be Gardens of Eden, beneath which rivers flow."

Attempts to bribe Muhammad to tone down his critique of the elite failed, and persecution of his followers began. Violence may have been threatened but not carried out—psychological torment included leaving waste outside the enemy's door. There were also boycotts of merchants who followed Muhammad, and there were probably some beatings.

In 619 both Muhammad's wife, Khadijah, and an uncle died, and another uncle became head of the Hashemite clan to

PAGANISM A spiritual practice that envisions multiple deities, especially spirits of nature. In monotheistic religions such as Judaism, Christianity, and Islam, paganism has sometimes been characterized as primitive, dangerous, threatening to social order, and evil.

which Muhammad belonged. This uncle aligned himself with the elites, leaving Muhammad vulnerable to attack. The Prophet decided he had best leave town, and in 622 he and his followers left on their historic *hegira*, or flight, from Mecca to Medina, an oasis 200 miles to the north, where supporters awaited them. This migration marks the traditional beginning of the Islamic era.

Medina was an oasis, green with date palms and cereal plants. A mix of Arab and Jewish clans farmed the region, though the Arabs had gained the upper hand in recent times. A war had broken out among the Arab clans a few years before Muhammad's arrival, and many Arabs likely hoped that the new prophet would help calm the strife. The new arrivals began settling in, Muhammad living in a house with apartments that came to surround a central courtyard. Here, on the spot where he preached, a mosque was later built.

The Growth of Islam

The followers of Muhammad came to be called Muslims, a word derived from the Arabic for "those who submitted." By 623 they had decided to try their hand at the Arab practice of caravan raiding. Muhammad personally led three raids, but none of them was successful. The next year, Muhammad and his followers grew bolder and attacked a caravan outside Mecca.

Muhammad's success both enriched the Muslims and also punished Mecca for its treatment of the new religion. Mecca was a sacred site, and thus traditionally a safe zone, and those in power there viewed the attack as indicative of the growing audacity and power of the Muslims. The city retaliated by sending

an armed force numbering some 800 men to punish the raiders.

Muhammad and 300 of his followers marched out to meet the Meccans at Badr, a town known for its wells. They spent the night in prayer, then fought a battle the following day that involved about 150 casualties. The Muslim victory raised Muhammad's profile and reputation. At the same time, though the early battles

were defensive, Muhammad began to realize that conquest was the best way to spread Islam.

After minor setbacks, the Muslims withstood a tremendous siege of Medina by 10,000 Meccans in 627. Political opponents in Medina were now reconciled to Muhammad, with the exception of most Jews. Muhammad had attempted to make concessions to the Jews, but the rabbis had

PLAGUE YEARS

An Excruciating Epidemic

In October 541, the plague first appeared in the Mediterranean basin, arriving by way of trade routes through the Red Sea. Over the next 225 years, 15 epidemics ravaged the populations of Byzantium, western Europe, North Africa, and Asia. The plague traveled along trade routes, and its effects were most devastating where people and rodents congregated: in cities and military camps.

Neither cause nor treatment for plague was understood in the Middle Ages, but the effects were known all too well. In the neck, armpits, and groin, inflamed lymph nodes, or buboes, would swell and turn black or purple due to internal hemorrhaging. Most victims died within days of showing symptoms.

A bacterial infection, the plague spread from flea to rodent to human. It struck all classes, young and old, clergy and lay, rulers and ruled. It decimated a quarter to two-thirds of a population with every outbreak. It was called Justinian's Plague, perhaps because the Byzantine ruler fell ill with it.

Two plague epidemics swept the Middle Ages, this one in the 6th century and the Black Death in the 14th. The huge loss in lives—perhaps as many as 100 million people all told—caused economic strain and social unrest. Massive labor shortages put more power into the hands of individual workers and may even have helped end the practice of slavery in the Byzantine Empire. ■

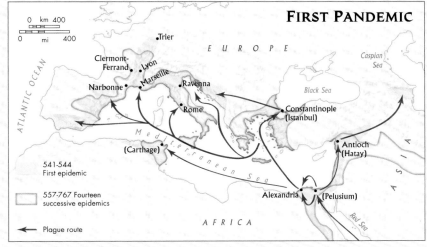

The first outbreak of plague began in 541, traveling via trade routes to Egypt, Constantinople, and beyond.

Mecca was a holy city even before Islam. At the center of the city stood the Kaaba, a shrine enclosing a sacred black stone. Muhammad's triumphant return to his birthplace in 632, after years of exile in Medina, is repeated by Muslims every year as they perform the *hajj,* or pilgrimage to Mecca—one of the Five Pillars of Islam.

only mocked him as a false prophet ignorant of the Bible. He had already banished two Jewish clans from Medina, but when a third refused to help with his crusade against Mecca he cracked down. The entire clan was wiped out—some 800 men were killed, and the women and children were sold as slaves. Medina's few remaining Jews reluctantly declared Muhammad a prophet and were left alone.

In March of the following year Muhammad led some 1,500 followers on a hajj to Mecca. They were not permitted to enter the city, but he was able to secure a ten-year truce. An attack by Meccan allies in 629 gave Muhammad a reason for breaking the truce, and by 630 he could marshal 10,000 men. Mecca could do nothing to stop them: Muhammad returned to his native city in triumph.

Meccan resistance was minor. Having occupied the city, Muhammad ordered the execution of several enemies, including three poets. He then extracted loans from rich Meccans. Astride a camel, he made seven ritual circuits of the Kaaba, ordered all its idols destroyed, and rededicated the shrine to "Allah, the Beneficent, the Merciful."

The call to prayer resounded throughout Mecca. The vanquished city was left intact, and Jews and Christians were allowed to worship as before. A precedent-setting tax was required of those who wanted to keep their former faiths. This mild discrimination proved so lucrative that there was little incentive to convert these people.

Later in 630, Muhammad commanded 30,000 troops on his biggest raid, a month-long trek to the border of Syria to the north. The conquests and treaties he made along the way became models for later Islamic expansion. Creating alliances with various nomadic clans added to the all-important *ummah*, or community of the faithful, and laid the groundwork for the coming Muslim state.

> O PEOPLE, NO PROPHET
> OR APOSTLE WILL COME
> AFTER ME AND NO NEW
> FAITH WILL BE BORN. . . .
> I LEAVE BEHIND ME
> TWO THINGS, THE KORAN
> AND MY EXAMPLE . . .
> IF YOU FOLLOW THESE
> YOU WILL NEVER GO ASTRAY.
>
> MUHAMMAD
> THE FAREWELL SERMON
> *Mount Arafat, 632*

During what is considered his farewell sermon, Muhammad addressed a multitude on a hill near Mecca. "O People, lend me an attentive ear," he began, "for I know not whether after this year I shall ever be amongst you again." He went on to exhort them to give up the tribal practices of raiding and vendettas. "Hurt no one so that no one may hurt you," he continued. "Remember that you will indeed meet your Lord, and that he will indeed reckon your deeds."

To the men, he said, "it is true that you have certain rights with regard to your women, but they also have rights over you." And on race relations, he remarked that "an Arab has no superiority over a non-Arab nor a non-Arab has any superiority over an Arab . . . except by piety and good action."

He declared that there would be no new prophet or faith after him. "This day [God has] perfected your religion for you . . . and [has] chosen for you . . . Islam."

Tradition has it that during this sermon, Muhammad also laid out the Five Pillars of Islam, although details of these central tenets of the religion were not finalized until the eighth and ninth centuries. Confession of faith requires the acceptance of Allah as the only god, and Muhammad as his Prophet. Prayers must be said at dawn, noon, late afternoon, sunset, and after nightfall, the faithful first washing with water or sand, then prostrating themselves and facing toward Mecca. Almsgiving is practiced as a means of purification. Fasting is required for spirituality during Ramadan, the ninth lunar month of the year. Finally, one pilgrimage, or hajj, to Mecca is expected of all Muslims.

Muhammad became ill on returning to Medina. One morning in 632 he rose from the chambers of his favorite wife, Aisha, and went to an assembly where his followers had gathered for prayers. Smiling, he reminded them that the faithful would follow him to paradise. Returning to his wife's side, he laid his head in her arms and died.

Christian medieval scholars, disturbed by the notion of infidels in the Holy Lands, would portray Muhammad as a fraud, lecher, and murderer. Not until the early 18th century did the western world take a more balanced view of the founder of Islam, seeing him as a social reformer and a man of vision and exceptional leadership ability.

At his death, Muhammad was the most powerful man in Arabia. Within 20 years, the united Muslim states had scored victories over both Byzantium and Persia, and Muslims occupied a vast territory from Libya in the west to Persia

Syria's capital today, Damascus was also the capital of the Umayyad Empire, founded in the seventh century.

DAMASCUS
GOLDEN CITY OF ISLAM

Stronghold | *Mosque* | *Caliphates* | *City Gates*

The city of Damascus, in today's Syria, has been inhabited for well over 5,000 years, and in fact it may well be the oldest city in the world. It nestles geographically in a prime location: at the base of the protective Anti-Lebanon Mountains, where the Barada River, a constant source of water, feeds into the Al Ghutah Oasis. Extensive irrigation systems engineered early on have helped make Damascus a lush, self-sufficient landscape that has supported thousands over many centuries.

From the Bronze Age to the present day, the city has been important because of its strategic position. It is the easternmost stopping point before entering the Arabian Desert; it has excellent access to the Mediterranean; and it stands as the midway point between the important cities of Antioch (now Antakya), Beirut, and Jerusalem—for many centuries, a crossroads for Greeks and Romans, Jews, Christians, and Arabs.

Almost nothing from the Greek period can be seen in Damascus today, as the Romans were quick to modify the cityscape. Some outer walls of the massive Temple of Jupiter Optimus Maximus Damascenus remain, hinting at the temple that brought the city tourism and fame in ancient days. Saul, persecutor of Christians, was en route to this pagan city in the first century when he had a vision, became a missionary for Christ, and took up the name Paul. The Emperor Julian called Damascus "Jupiter's only worthy city" in the fourth century; shortly thereafter, the temple was destroyed and replaced with a church dedicated to St. John the Baptist.

With the division of the Roman Empire in 395, Damascus became an important military outpost for the Byzantines, who were concerned by threats from Persia to the east. But by the sixth century, tension had mounted between the residents of Damascus and the powers in Constantinople over the capital's attempt to mandate orthodox Christianity across the empire. Content in their religious ways, practicing their own versions of Judaism and Christianity, Damascenes refused to conform. The relationship between Constantinople and the outpost would not recover.

In 612, the Persians briefly occupied the city but did not sack it. Within a few

DAMASCUS THROUGH THE MIDDLE AGES

395	612	635	661	705	750	878
Damascus becomes an important outpost for the Byzantine emperor.	Persians seize Damascus and rule for more than a decade.	Khalid ibn al Walid takes Damascus; Muslims are welcomed.	Mu'awiyah, the first Umayyad caliph, establishes his court in Damascus.	The Umayyad caliph Al Walid I begins building the Great Mosque.	The Abbasids seize Damascus, ending the Umayyad reign.	Ahmad ibn Tulun, ruler of Egypt, takes Damascus, threatening the Abbasids.

decades the city was back under Byzantine rule. Preoccupied with issues elsewhere, the Byzantines ignored the minor incursions on Damascus by a new force from the south, but their lack of interest backfired when in 635 they were overwhelmed by the Arab general Khalid Ibn al Walid. The city suffered neither destruction nor mass exodus as a result of the Muslim capture. In fact, the citizens, members of different Christian and Jewish sects who had never reconciled with the Byzantines, welcomed the Muslims, known for their tolerance toward other religions.

Damascus served as Islam's cultural and political center for centuries. In 661 Mu'awiya assumed the caliphate and made Damascus his capital city. His rule began the Umayyad Dynasty, which lasted well into the eighth century and represents the golden age of Damascus. In 705, the Christians finally ceded the Church of St. John the Baptist, and the Muslims began the construction of a new mosque on the very site that had previously housed a Roman temple and that Christian church.

The Great Mosque of Damascus, also called the Umayyad Mosque, is still considered one of the most outstanding examples of Islamic architecture, known for its incredible size, bold design, massive cupola, and intricate glass mosaics depicting houses and buildings surrounded by trees and flowing water.

As the Umayyad Dynasty declined and the Muslim capital was relocated, Damascus fell to the status of provincial city. By the 12th century, it was divided into segregated communities. In 1145 Nur al Din conquered the city and reinstated it as the Muslim capital. Building projects expanded the city, and Damascus became a center for Muslim education and religion as well as a key military stronghold during the Crusades. The four greatest leaders from that great period are buried in the Great Mosque:

Present-day boundaries are shown.

SYRIA

Damascus

| 0 | 100 mi |
| 0 | 150 km |

Damascus was settled as early as 3000 B.C. in a fertile desert oasis on the Barada River.

Nur al Din, Saladin, al'Adil, and Baybars I, a Mamluk sultan.

In the later Middle Ages, two major blows in quick succession all but destroyed the city of Damascus. The first was the plague, which arrived in 1348 and swept through the city, killing nearly half the population. The second was the sack of Damascus in 1401, when Timur forced all the city's artisans to move to his capital of Samarkand, in today's Uzbekistan, leaving no one in Damascus able to rebuild it.

At the close of the 15th century, the city once known for its magnificence and success lay in ruins, primed for the Ottoman conquest that would take place in 1516, initiating another round of restorations.

The old walled city of Damascus sits at the base of the Anti-Lebanon Mountains. Mount Kaissoun, elevation 4,000 feet, towers above the city, while the Grand Mosque's minaret towers within.

969
The Fatimids establish themselves in Damascus and begin a long rule.

1069
Fire destroys parts of the Great Mosque.

1076
Seljuk Turks overthrow the Fatimids; Prince Duqaq rules Damascus.

1145
Nur al Din saves the city from crusaders and is welcomed as its ruler.

1174
Nur al Din dies, and control of Damascus goes to Saladin, his vizier in Egypt.

1260
Hulagu, an Iranian Tatar, sacks Damascus; the Mamluks defeat him.

1401
Timur (Tamerlane) conquers Damascus.

in the east, from Yemen in the south to Armenia in the north: It reprsented the beginnings of an Islamic empire.

Muhammad's father-in-law Abu Bakr (ca 573-634) was chosen as successor, or caliph. His first act was to gather the faithful and tell them, "O men, if anyone worships Muhammad, let him know now that Muhammad is dead. But if anyone worships God, let him know that God is alive and immortal forever." He then recited a verse from the Koran: "Muhammad is but a messenger. Messengers . . . have passed away before him. Will it be that, when he dieth or is slain, ye will turn back on your heels?"

By the time of Muhammad's death there were already some 30,000 Muslims. The Arabs now had a homegrown monotheistic religion that would in short order challenge the other major religions of the Near East—Judaism, Christianity, and Zoroastrianism. Like these three, Islam relied on belief in one supreme power, faith in prophets, and adherence to scripture written by humans but originating from God.

Over time the caliphs would direct a theocratic state that would gain wider influence and power than the old Roman Empire. They began by capturing the Persian capital of Ctesiphon in 637, then went east and took down Persepolis (ancient Persian capital) in 648, followed by Nishapur to the north in 651.

To the west, the Byzantine strongholds of Antioch and Damascus fell

The violent death of the fourth caliph, Ali—depicted here in an Indian miniature of the 19th century—caused conflict within Islam that ultimately resulted in the split between Sunnis and Shiites.

in 635, Jerusalem in 638, Alexandria, in Egypt, in 640, and Carthage, on the Tunisian coast, in 697. The unstoppable Islamic wave rolled eastward, taking the great cities of Kabul in 664 and Samarkand in 710.

From the second millennium B.C., Arabic tribes had attempted to break through to the Mediterranean. The Roman Empire had stopped massive Arabic invasions, but with that empire gone and with Persia and Byzantium played out from their wars against each other, the Arabs had finally succeeded. They did so for a number of reasons.

The great empires were being exhausted, and they had made enemies of potential frontier allies. Egyptian Copts, Syrian Monophysites, and Palestinian Jews had been persecuted by Byzantium; many Zoroastrians felt the Persian government overly repressive as well. Thus when the new Arab regime arrived, many people hoped for lighter taxes and better treatment.

Islam promised specific eternal rewards in return for living according to strict rules of conduct: Pleasures forbidden in this world were attainable in the next. The greatest rewards were held out for those who died for their faith, an idea like that of the Norse and Germanic tribes that appealed to Arabs' notions of manliness, bravery, and justice. And unlike Jesus, Muhammad was a skilled political and military leader, as well as a prophet—just the sort of person needed to unify the diverse Arabic tribes.

Infighting among the Muslim leaders in the 650s led to civil war, but it did not stop a rapid Islamic expansion that would shape world history. By the next century the Mediterranean was almost entirely under Muslim control, and for the next three centuries the Muslim Empire would continue to grow and prosper.

Mapmakers worked hard to keep up with the expanding Islamic world. In this tenth-century map, the Mediterranean Sea divides the land from the left, the Indian Ocean from the right. The Arabian Peninsula sits in the center, with Mecca's Kaaba clearly visible. Constantinople is indicated by a red crescent.

A Turkish miniature depicts the death of Muhammad, surrounded by family and followers.
As is the custom in Islam, Muhammad's face is veiled, its brilliance unattainable by human art.

ISLAMIC EXPANSION

The Arabs had been fanning out under the leadership of Umar I (ca 586-644), who had succeeded Abu Bakr as caliph in 633. More a statesman than a military commander, Umar had the organizational skill to make the many Arab conquests part of a permanent empire. This required diplomatic tact as well as power, for his decision to let conquered peoples keep their land and religion tended to soften the impact of invasion.

> WE SHALL NOT DISPLAY
> OUR CROSSES OR OUR BOOKS
> IN THE ROADS OR MARKETS
> OF THE MUSLIMS.
> WE SHALL USE ONLY
> CLAPPERS IN OUR CHURCHES
> VERY SOFTLY.
> WE SHALL NOT RAISE
> OUR VOICES WHEN
> FOLLOWING OUR DEAD.
>
> THE PACT OF UMAR
> (RULES FOR NON-MUSLIMS
> LIVING IN MUSLIM LANDS)
> *Seventh century*

For the loss of expected loot, he paid his fighters a pension out of an increasingly large fund of land and poll taxes levied on the conquered populations. The new subjects found these taxes less onerous than the imposts collected by the Byzantine and Persian governments. Umar even kept local governments intact, if they worked. Byzantine administrations continued operating much as before. There was no time or necessity for imposing a new language and government on newly conquered cities, and there was much to be gained by simply collecting money.

Not since Alexander the Great (356-323 B.C.) had so much land been conquered so quickly. In 11 years, Alexander had created an empire that spread all the way from Greece and North Africa to India. Alexander's empire was forged in a lightning-fast blitz, but it did not hold together long after his death. The Muslim empire lasted much longer, and though it eventually fragmented, it brought permanent cultural and religious change to the Near and Middle East.

True, the Persian and Byzantine armies had little resistance to offer, but credit must be given to the Muslim armies. Fired by the promise of booty and spiritual glory, they had quickly put together effective command structures and battle tactics. They were a culture gearing for war; thus nearly all receipts went into weapons, horses, and supplies.

An army of a few thousand was all it took to subdue Syria, and about 12,000 to occupy Persia. Their 636 victory at Yarmuk over a much larger Byzantine force gave themselves proof of their ability to withstand fearsome battle conditions and emerge victorious. When the Arab general feigned a retreat, the Byzantines moved forward, allowing a Muslim unit, hidden on the riverbanks, to slip in between the Byzantine infantry and cavalry. Then when the cavalry tried to wheel and retreat, horses slid down the steep embankment, and the Byzantine infantry ended up atop a writhing mass of crushed and drowning horses and men. The Arabs pursued the few Byzantines who managed to regroup, overtaking most of them during the night.

With Syria under his belt, Umar looked to Persia, where his forces were running into some difficulty. The elephants, which the Persians had imported from India and deployed with the cavalry, presented a problem. When the Muslims realized their arrows would not pierce the elephants' hides, they shot at their eyes and trunks. This tactic, coupled with a providential windstorm, swept the Muslims to victory at Kadesiya (south of present-day Baghdad) in 637.

In this colossal four-day battle, the largest the Arabs had engaged in, 30,000 Persians were ranged against 6,000 to 12,000 Arab cavalry. On one day the fighting was so intense the warriors had to say their noon prayers by nodding their heads while still in the saddle. The Arabs finally prevailed by forcing the Persians into the Euphrates River, which ran red with blood.

The capital city of Ctesiphon fell later in the year, and its seven opulent palaces yielded up their dazzling riches to the conquerors—a trove of gold, silver, silks, weapons, and women. The military commander's wide-eyed report to Umar crowed, "How many gardens and springs have [the Persians] abandoned, how many sown fields and noble habitats, how many comforts in which they took delight." To keep his warriors from dissipating their energy on the temptations of the cities, Umar had to enact a strict policy of garrisoning his soldiers outside the places they conquered: "No land suits Arab tribesmen except that which suits their camels."

A final battle in 642 effectively ended Persian resistance, though the entire land was not finally subdued until 651 when Muslim assassins came after the last Sassanid ruler, Yazdegird III. He fell on his sword, ending a 1,100-year-old civilization. Yet the proud Persians would assimilate the new Muslim culture and give it a uniquely Persian flavor. And with the rebirth of Persian pride, expressed

THE KORAN

Scripture of Islam, Dictated to the Prophet

Around the year 610, an Arab merchant named Muhammad underwent a spiritual transformation in which a vision of the archangel Gabriel revealed to him the nature of the one true God, or Allah, and instructed him to preach this revelation to others. When Muhammad died, in 632, after 20 years of public sermons explaining his understanding of Allah and morality, he had established not only a new religion but also a powerful state founded on its ideals.

One of Islam's early leaders, Muhammad's son-in-law Uthman, mandated a standard written set of Muhammad's teachings, which was compiled around 650. Known as the Koran, this compilation has been the most sacred book of Islam ever since. Believed to be the very words of Allah, conveyed to Muhammad through the angel Gabriel, the Koran is the primary basis for all Islamic law, doctrine, and social organization. It sets down not only a system of belief but also a program for reforming and unifying society. Its language is bold, assertive, and respectful of the wisdom and prophets of the Judeo-Christian tradition.

In the Koran, no distinctions exist between human beings, not even Muhammad; all are equally subject to the will of Allah. Women are equal before Allah, though for the most part the Koran reinforces perceived male superiority. Held sacred today by over a billion people worldwide, the Koran is one of the most important books ever written. ■

The Dome of the Rock, built in Jerusalem in the 690s, was sited on the Temple Mount, from which Muhammad is believed to have ascended with the angel Gabriel to heaven. Later in the Middle Ages, Muslims and Christians alike believed it to be the temple of Solomon. Knights Templar occupied it during the Crusades.

in the 11th-century national epic, *Shah-nameh*, the people would remember where they came from: "Damn this world, damn this time, damn this fate,/ That uncivilized Arabs have come to make me a Muslim."

ISLAM'S FOUNDING FATHERS

A disgruntled Persian slave killed Umar in 644, putting an end to his reign. By the early 640s the great Sassanian dynasty of the Persians was no more, and the Byzantine Empire had shrunk to one-fifth its previous size. Almost afraid of his own success, Umar is said to have remarked that Allah "never gave [as much as] this to any people without that giving rise to mutual envy and hatred." Yet Umar's tight control over his armies and his policy of treating the conquered people with mercy and fairness kept his mushrooming empire from getting out of hand.

The inner circle of the faithful chose Uthman ibn Affan (r. 644-656) as the next caliph. A compromise choice over stronger rivals, Uthman never wielded the same power as Umar. Known as "the possessor of two lights," he had married one of Muhammad's daughters, then, after her death, married another, and thus had a holy pedigree to go along with his descent from the wealthy Umayyad clan of Mecca. Besides holding the empire together, Uthman's main claim to immortality was his decision to codify the diverse parts of the Muslim scripture into a single book.

Until now the Koran had existed only in fragments and in unofficial variations that had proliferated since the time of Muhammad. Uthman's sharp memory and close relationship to Muhammad made him a good choice for overseeing the compilation, and his secretary, Zayd, who was directly in charge of the scribes, had been a friend of Muhammad's. To

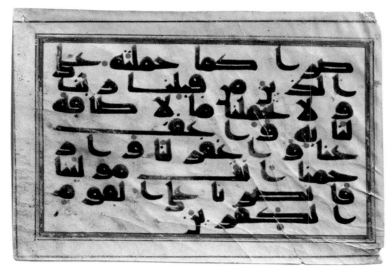

Limited in their use of figurative representations in Islamic art, Muslim calligraphers elevated their craft to works of sublime beauty—such as this ninth-century Koran, painted on parchment.

create a definitive text, Uthman ordered the destruction of all variants. Uthman and his team decided what would go into the Koran and what would not—the result was a book of 114 suras, or chapters, arranged by length.

Uthman's good intentions as a Muslim were in conflict with his greed as a caliph. Loot from victories too often went directly into the pockets of his own family. He was furthermore accused of replacing dozens of high-ranking emirs (commanders) with members of his clan. He personally owned a thousand slaves and a thousand horses, as well as several luxurious houses.

Uthman roused resentment among the faithful by using his wealth and his power for corrupt and selfish ends. These choices on his part—combined with his lack of a firm grip on authority—doomed him to an ugly death and the nascent empire to civil war. One day in 656, soldiers converged on his house in Medina. One man—possibly Abu Bakr's son—grabbed him by the beard, while others struck him with their scabbards. He was then beaten to a bloody pulp.

RIGHTLY GUIDED CALIPHS

The next caliph was Ali ibn Abi Talib (ca 600-661), who was both a cousin of Muhammad's and the husband of Muhammad's favorite daughter, Fatima. Muhammad had adopted Ali as a struggling young man, just as Ali's father had once adopted Muhammad. One of the first converts to Islam, Ali is reputed to have risked his life by sleeping in Muhammad's bed, impersonating him in the dangerous days when the prophet was fleeing Mecca.

After Muhammad's death a dispute arose as to whether he had chosen Ali to be his successor. Twice rejected by the elders, Ali finally was chosen at around the age of 55, by which time he had

DYNASTY A dynasty is created by a powerful ruling family that maintains its power and influence over a region or a nation for generations, even centuries; it can also mean rulership by leaders who spring from the same line of descent.

relinquished his ambitions to be caliph and taken up the contemplative life of a religious writer.

As caliph, Ali made clear from the outset that his rule was to be built on the principles of justice and equality, a position that was not especially palatable to the wealthy ruling class of Mecca. To challenge him, they demanded that he bring the murderers of Uthman to justice. Ali refused to be bullied—not only did many of his followers think Uthman's assassination justified, Ali also knew that sorting out the murderers would be "to bail out the floods from the Euphrates."

A rebellion broke out, led by Aisha, Muhammad's third wife, who had a long-standing hatred for Ali. Like many Arab women who fought along with the men, Aisha rode camelback into combat with the troops at the Battle of the Camel, in 656, near the city of Basra in what is now southern Iraq. Ali's forces handily won the day by disabling Aisha's camel. They captured Aisha and brought her back to house arrest in Medina. She would live another 18 years, dying at age 64.

In the spring of 657, Ali began moving his capital from Medina up to the more strategically located city of Al Kufa, on the Euphrates. His army of about 8,000 was checked by a Syrian army of 10,000 loyal to Mu'awiya, emir of Syria and Egypt.

In a few years Mu'awiya would become the fifth caliph (r. 661-680). Born around 602 into a Meccan clan that opposed Muhammad, he had not become a Muslim until Islam was gaining hegemony. Working his way up the military ladder in Syria, he scored a number of impressive naval victories—the first for Islam—against the Byzantines, including the capture of Cyprus, off the coast

BATHILDE, QUEEN OF THE FRANKS

Sold into Slavery, Married into Power

Bathilde was queen of the Frankish kingdoms of Neustria and Burgundy, modern-day France and Switzerland, for 16 years from around 648 until 664. She was born in England to an aristocratic Anglian family but was sold into slavery at an early age to the court of Neustria. There she was presented to and wed the Frankish king, Clovis II.

Having married into a dynastic family of kings largely controlled by court officials, Bathilde assumed a dominant role in her husband's administration. When Clovis died around 657, Bathilde became ruler, serving as regent to her young sons. In this capacity, she is said to have outlawed the trade in Christian slaves and worked against the practices of enslaving children and selling church appointments. Perhaps for this reason, she clashed with a number of Frankish bishops, some of whom she may even have had assassinated. She also helped to establish a number of monasteries, to one of which she retired—or perhaps was forced to retire—in 664.

Though details of Bathilde's life and career are scant and sometimes contradictory, they nevertheless reveal a strong-willed, capable politician and a powerful woman in an era of powerful men. ∎

The life story of Bathilde known today derives from hagiographies that blended history with spiritual aggrandizement.

of Syria, in 649 and a crushing victory over the Byzantine navy off the southern coast of Anatolia in 655.

Now, two years later, Mu'awiya faced off against a caliph who had come to power through the murder of one of Mu'awiya's kinsmen—he and Uthman were both from the elite Umayyad clan. The two forces clashed in the Battle of Siffin, along the Euphrates, in what proved to be a strange conflict. Two short bursts of intense fighting were followed by long periods of negotiation, with a resulting loss of prestige for Ali.

A few years later a splinter group known as the Kharijites rebelled and one of their members stabbed Ali with a dagger or a poison-tipped sword. At the time of Ali's death, Islam suffered its first and only major schism: Those who favored Ali of the lineage of the Prophet were known as the Shiites, whereas the others, the Sunnis, thought lineage from the prophet less important than ability to lead. The Sunnis favored Mu'awiya, who became caliph in 661 and moved the capital to Damascus in Syria.

Well-educated and politically astute, Mu'awiya moved first to clear out potential opposition. Though dispassionate as a fighter, he deemed it wise to offer Ali's son Hasan (Muhammad's grandson) a pension to go away, which Hasan readily did. Mu'awiya's firm hand guided Islam through what could have been a period of decay caused by further internal dissent; instead, he reorganized the Muslim army, began centralizing the government, and in the process expanded Islam's reach. His no-nonsense, non-fanatical approach to both government and religion established a model for Sunni statesmanship and orthodoxy.

After a failed seven-year campaign to take Constantinople, Muʿawiya turned his attention farther east, seizing the cities of Bukhara, Fergana, and Samarkand, all important stopping points on the Silk Road and now in modern Uzbekistan. His forces took several Aegean Islands and enlarged his holdings in North Africa, thus cementing his

> READ THE KORAN
> CONSTANTLY;
> I SWEAR BY HIM
> IN THE HANDS OF WHOSE
> MIGHT IS MY LIFE,
> VERILY THE KORAN
> RUNNETH AWAY FASTER
> THAN A CAMEL
> WHICH IS NOT
> TIED BY THE LEG.
>
> ———————
>
> THE SUNNAH
> (TRADITIONS OF MUHAMMAD)

grip in the southern and eastern Mediterranean regions. Besides keeping the peace, garrisons at the new outposts were set up mainly to collect taxes. In these towns, the governing hierarchy of Arab Muslims remained aloof from both the *kafir* (unbelievers) and the *mawali* (non-Arab) converts.

In the capital city of Damascus—one of the oldest continuously occupied cities in the world—Muslims and Christians both worshiped at the Temple of Jupiter until the early 700s, when an enormous mosque was built on the site. The irrigated city, lush with vegetation, had a grand central avenue with

a colonnade along its wide center lane. The caliph occupied a regal stone palace topped by a green dome. Before his death, Muʿawiya manipulated the tribal leaders to agree to the succession of his son Yazid (r. 680-683).

Though his three years were marked by progressive financial and agricultural reforms, Yazid is probably best known for his struggle against Ali's younger son, Hussein. The Shiites continued to support the lineage of the prophet, and they now placed their hopes in this grandson. Yet their hopes were slim against the huge armies of Yazid and a Syrian population that was afraid to speak up against the Sunni majority.

Unlike Muʿawiya, Yazid moved immediately to get rid of whatever competition remained from the prophet's family. At Karbala (south of present-day Baghdad)

While Islam was taking hold in southern Europe and North Africa, Christianity thrived in Britain. In the 600s Yorkshire's Whitby Abbey was a locus of activity, home to Benedictine monks and nuns.

Hussein and a mere 70 followers were caught by several thousand Syrian cavalry. Archers annihilated the tiny force of true believers. Hussein's infant son bled to death in his lap, and Hussein died fighting; his head was cut off and given to the commanding officer. Yazid then ordered that his enemy's head be displayed at the mosque in Al Kufa, Ali's former headquarters.

Instead of quashing resistance, Yazid's violent reprisal only stiffened the resolve of the Shiites. The martyrdom of the prophet's grandson gave them a stronger sense of unity and purpose. Shiite Muslims to this day commemorate the massacre of Hussein, performing

THE WORLD IN THE SEVENTH CENTURY

The seventh century was shaped by the rapid rise of Islam. In 610, Muhammad of Mecca received a spiritual message to obey the one God, Allah. For his beliefs, he was driven out of Mecca, but he returned in 630, and soon the disenfranchised tribes of the surrounding Arabian Desert, empowered by his message of Islam, united as one nation. Upon Muhammad's death in 632, his father-in-law, Abu Bakr, carried the message of Islam to Arabia, Syria, and Palestine. The new Muslim state annexed much of the Middle East, including Persia, and the region experienced an economic revival, particularly in farming and trade.

For China, the seventh century was also a period of rapid expansion. Under the Sui dynasty, laborers and engineers built hundreds of miles of the Grand Canal; a building spree from 605 to 611 linked the Yangtze and the Yellow Rivers. In 618, the great Tang dynasty took power, ushering in a golden age of poetry and culture at home and expanding the Chinese empire abroad. By mid-century, China reached as far north as Mongolia and as far west as Korea.

Empires in Central and South America grew as well, from the Huari in Peru to the Tiahuanaco in southern Peru and Bolivia. The Maya of Mexico expanded the city of Palenque, building a pyramid and temple there and fostering the city's cultural significance. In North America, civilizations remained relatively small and isolated, although the Hohokam of modern-day Arizona began to spread throughout the southwest. ■

Arctic

HOHOKAM PEOPLE Irrigation and advanced farming techniques allow the Hohokam to thrive in the arid climate of today's Arizona. Along with a complex network of canals, the Hohokam create colorful pictographs, or rock paintings.

Pacific Ocean

EQUATOR

Atlantic Ocean

South America

PALENQUE Situated on the western edge of the Maya empire, the city of Palenque grows in cultural significance as Pakal the Great orders a grand temple and pyramid built there. Exquisite glyphs—picture-laden writings carved in rock—decorate the buildings' walls.

Ocean

Europe

Asia

Africa

NOMADS OF NORTH AFRICA **In the Sahara, in one of the harshest climates of the world, nomadic tribes rely on camels for transportation and survival. These camel herds become essential to the region's salt trade, increasing contact among peoples of Africa and beyond.**

POTALA PALACE **King Songstan Gampo unifies a fractured Tibet in the first decade of the seventh century, introducing Buddhism and building Potala Palace and Jokhang Temple.**

Pacific Ocean

EQUATOR

Indian Ocean

HORYUJI TEMPLE **The Buddhist Horyuji Temple in Japan is completed in 607 under the direction of the emperor's son, Prince Shotoku. Buddhism has only recently arrived in Japan via the Korean Peninsula but will ascend rapidly to a place of importance within Japanese culture.**

Australia

BILAL IBN RABAH **An Ethiopian slave in Mecca is emancipated and becomes an early follower of Muhammad. Known for his graceful yet powerful voice, Bilal ibn Rabah becomes Islam's first muezzin and remains close to Muhammad through his life.**

passion plays to honor his martyrdom every year on the day that he died.

CHALLENGES IN THE WEST

While the Byzantine Empire was reorganizing in the face of the advancing Muslim tide, western Europe was meanwhile groping toward cultural unity under the twin, and often conflicting, banners of monarchy and Christianity. An unimpressive assortment of semi-civilized kingdoms, the western Europeans were living amid Roman ruins. Old roads, bridges, and buildings had been left to crumble and decay, and old Roman institutions of government and commerce were undergoing important transitions, but very slowly. Meanwhile, western Europe's new Germanic occupiers were seeking cohesion, but they also brought in the complication of different strands of tradition and belief.

Travelers would have noticed a great variety in medieval life as they moved from north to south across the European landscape. Up in the British Isles, some three quarters of the many kingdoms were of native Celts; the rest, Anglo-Saxons. Farmers worked their fenced-in plots and lived with their kin in long, low wooden buildings, four or five such farms to a community. In southern England, villages with markets and various forms of commerce had begun to flourish.

Across the English Channel lay Francia, the former Gaul, which stretched from the Pyrenees in the south to the Rhine in the east. In northern France travelers would have encountered such commercial centers as Dorestad and Quentovic. Located at the confluence of the Rhine and Lek Rivers in what is now the Netherlands, Dorestad was one of the key trading towns in early medieval Europe. From the seventh to mid-ninth centuries, when it was attacked by Vikings, it thrived as a North Sea emporium, particularly for the trading of wines from the south.

This little whalebone box, produced in Northumbria, England, in the seventh century, is intricately carved with mythic tableaux and runes, or writing, that may have served as magic omens for the owner.

The old Roman city of Paris, Lutetia, dating from the first century B.C., was now a religious center, with up to 35 churches—including the villages Montmartre, Saint-Laurent, and Saint-Martin-des-Champs. Outside the greater city, villagers lived a rural, agricultural life similar to that of England, with the occasional stone building cropping up from place to place. Heading east into the Moselle River Valley, travelers would have passed vineyards on the slopes, planted by the Romans, and woods interspersed with fields and meadows, as well as villages with perhaps a mill and a church. Tenant farmers in this region ranged from slaves to independent men who owned some or all of the land that they worked.

In southern France and in Italy, fields were planted with olive trees and grapevines. Major Roman cities dotted this region, though much diminished in population. Our travelers would have found old Roman walls, baths, amphitheaters, and other structures. Countryside farms held fewer animals than in the north—peasants cultivated fields of cereal crops with hoes and the occasional light plow. Most people barely managed to scratch a living from the soil, but money was still minted—more silver than gold. Royalty and nobility hoarded coins, jewelry, and other treasure, which they distributed to their allies, followers, and churchmen, as reminders of both their power and their generosity. Small transactions were becoming more common in a new Baltic Sea trading link, with items such as glass and ceramics traded by northern merchants for wines and grains from the south.

Although they were an inconsistent lot, the Merovingians maintained their status as Francia's leading family into the seventh century. By forming alliances with the preeminent nobles and clergy, showering them with wealth and benefits, and using military force when necessary, the Merovingians kept themselves at the pinnacle of Francia's large kingdoms: Austrasia included most of what is now Belgium, Luxembourg, and the Netherlands, plus part of northern France and western Germany; Neustria spanned western France; and Burgundy spread over southeastern France. To the southwest lay a large semi-autonomous duchy called Aquitaine.

Until the line weakened, the kings themselves wielded the most power. Clothar II ruled Neustria from 584 to 629, part of that time ruling Austrasia and Burgundy as well. He is mainly remembered for getting rid of the power-hungry Brunhilde, granting land to magnates, and extending the power of the ecclesiastical courts. It was also Clothar who established the office of mayor of the palace. The man in this position soon became the most important power broker among the kings' courts.

Clothar's son Dagobert I (605-639) was the last of the Merovingians to rule a united Frankish kingdom as more than a figurehead. To do this took quite a bit of work. He had to make a treaty with

> WHATEVER WE HAVE
> DEVOUTLY GRANTED
> FOR THE RELIEF
> OF THE POOR,
> WE BELIEVE WE SHALL HAVE
> RETURNED TO US
> WITH PROFIT
> IN THE NEXT LIFE.

—————————

DAGOBERT I
GRANT OF AN ESTATE TO THE MONKS
OF ST. DENIS
France, 635

Byzantine emperor Heraclius in 629, fight the Spanish Visigoths two years later, defeat an uprising from Brittany on the west coast in 636, then put down the Gascons in the far southwest.

Moving his capital from Austrasia to the more centrally located Paris, Dagobert still had to keep tabs on potential Slavic invaders from the east—this

involved large monetary support to the buffering nobility in Austrasia. He also made significant reforms in law and government, and he patronized the arts.

In short, Dagobert had stayed constantly on the go; few successors were up to this kind of effort. Or they were simply too young, as was the case with his son, Sigebert III, whom Dagobert placed on the throne of Austrasia at the age of three. He did this to appease the Austrasians, who wanted their own official monarch. But on Dagobert's death in 639, when Sigebert was eight or nine years old, a mayor of the palace named Pepin the Old gained power.

After the mayors had established their own parasitical dynasty, it became increasingly hard for the nominal kings to assert themselves, assuming they had the gumption. The last one to try, Dagobert's grandson Childeric II (653-675), became king of Austrasia in 662—with his mother Balthilde as regent—and king of Neustria

ARTS & LETTERS

THE LINDISFARNE GOSPELS

Fantastical Illuminations

The *Book of Lindisfarne*, an Anglo-Saxon illuminated manuscript of the four gospels of the Christian Bible, was created around the turn of the eighth century. It is the product of a monastery school that was located on an island off the northeast coast of England, founded by an Irish Celtic monk at the invitation of an Anglo-Saxon king.

When itinerant Irish Celtic missionaries settled the islands of northern England, they brought with them their own distinctive brand of Christianity, which blended elements of pagan, Anglo-Saxon, and Roman Catholic influences. The *Book of Lindisfarne* is the product of this unique blend of aesthetics.

The curving motifs of Celtic art, together with animal-like figures of Germanic tradition, decorate its pages, alongside ornaments suggesting Roman and Byzantine influences as well. Full of intricate spirals and knots, this amalgam style—known as Hiberno-Saxon—combines dynamic bird and animal forms often set with crosses or human figures. The result is a maze of complex patterns that ranks among the greatest abstract art ever made.

An Old English translation of the Latin text is written in between the lines of Latin in the book itself, and this text is considered the earliest English-language version of the Christian gospels. ∎

The Lindisfarne Gospels were written in half-uncial, a script invented by Irish monks.

and Burgundy in 673. He managed to depose his brother, Theuderic III, but politics was a dangerous game for those lacking the skill to play it extremely well. An anti-Austrasian movement developed in Neustria, and Childeric was assassinated at age 26.

Childeric's mother, Balthilde (ca 626-680), had become one of the most powerful women of her time, rising from obscurity as an English slave. Her beauty attracted King Clovis II, and as it was not unusual for kings to marry slaves, he took her as his wife. Her biographers noted her kindness: "To the princes she showed herself a mother, to the priests as a daughter, and to the young and the adolescents as the best possible nurse." She also made substantial donations of land and money to the church and retired to the Abbey of Chelles. She was canonized two hundred years after her death.

Frankish women were for the most part limited to their roles as keepers of the family. Marriages in early medieval times took place at home or in the village, but not in the church. The bridegroom gave his bride a substantial dowry of clothes, bedding, livestock, and land.

The rich could also take women as concubines, bestowing upon them small "morning gifts" such as furniture, after consummating the relationship. Wives and concubines had a good deal of control over their dowries, and they could inherit property as well—in this way

This cross was found when the tomb of St. Cuthbert, seventh-century bishop of Lindisfarne, was opened in 1827. Its workmanship and materials, gold and garnet, match the Anglo-Saxon times.

women were often involved in sales of land and stock.

Thanks to monasticism and the support of the monarchy, the church flourished in seventh-century France and Italy. Some 320 new monasteries were established in France in the 600s, many of them peopled with young children given by local parents, in the spirit of sacrifice, for the spiritual benefit of their families. In Spain, the church underwent a huge shift in the late 500s and early 600s when first the monarchy, and then the bishops, converted from Arian to Catholic Christianity, creating important ties between Spain and Rome. The move also

cemented a lasting relationship between Spain's monarchy and clergy.

But the Spanish church was soon to go into hiding, when Spain became the staging area for an Islamic invasion of Europe in 711. Though the Muslims would not get far beyond the Pyrenees Mountains, they would hold most of Spain for the next 500 years.

A NEW TENSION

After the death of Justinian in 565, the Byzantine Empire went through several decades of instability and, in addition to continuing an exhausting struggle with Persia, endured losses of territory in Spain, Italy, and the Balkans. Emperor Maurice (r. 582-602) organized what was left of Byzantine North Africa and Italy into two new administrative units, called exarchates, at Carthage and Ravenna. He also drew the Persian war to a tidy end in 591, and still had strength to take on the nomadic Slavs and Avars in the Balkans to the north.

In 602 the Avars gave in and joined the Byzantine side, but the imperial army was still deeply involved in the Balkans. After years of war and high taxes, a revolt broke out in the ranks and, led by an officer named Phocas, troops marched on Constantinople. They killed Maurice and his son, and declared the brutish Phocas (r. 602-610) the new emperor.

Phocas's reign was marked by persecutions of the Jews and Monophysites in the eastern provinces, and tyranny of the patricians in the capital. Soon the Avars and Slavs began moving in on one

CANONIZATION In the Roman Catholic tradition, a person is canonized—or declared a saint by the church—if he or she lived a life of heroic virtue and effected or experienced more than one miracle attributable to divine intervention.

side, the Persians on the other. With the spirit of rebellion again in the air, the son of the exarch of Carthage came and seized power. Heraclius (r. 610-641) would have the most distinguished reign of the century.

With foreign powers gathering ominously near, Heraclius considered moving the capital to Carthage. He decided, however, to stay and reorganize the remaining Byzantine holdings in Asia Minor into military districts called themes. The theme system, which was probably based on the exarchates, continued to serve Byzantium well into the tenth century. Instead of a roving army of frontier guards, the Byzantine forces were now concentrated in regional units within the empire. Generals known as *strategoi* led the units, which were filled by conscription.

The themes could more readily protect a region because they were easily resupplied with men and materiel. Soldiers within a theme—often peasants moved from elsewhere—were granted land and thus a means of buying weapons and uniforms. Now, instead of out-of-control mercenaries, a well-trained body of stakeholders was being groomed for national defense. The theme system replaced the civil rule of the Roman praetorian prefects, but the honed-down Roman-style army was better able to equip itself and thus to defend the homeland.

Having begun to restore a depleted treasury and a demoralized army, Heraclius had no time to lose in attempting to thwart invaders. He first turned his attention to the Avars in Thrace, in the eastern Balkans. During a parley in about 617, they broke the rules of war and tried to capture him, but he escaped on horseback to Constantinople.

In 622, the blond-haired, gray-eyed emperor, in penitent's garb, rode out with an image of the Virgin Mary to recover Jerusalem and the Holy Cross from the Persians. This early crusade was a success, at least in removing the Persians from Asia Minor, if not in making peace—King Chosroes II defiantly rejected truce

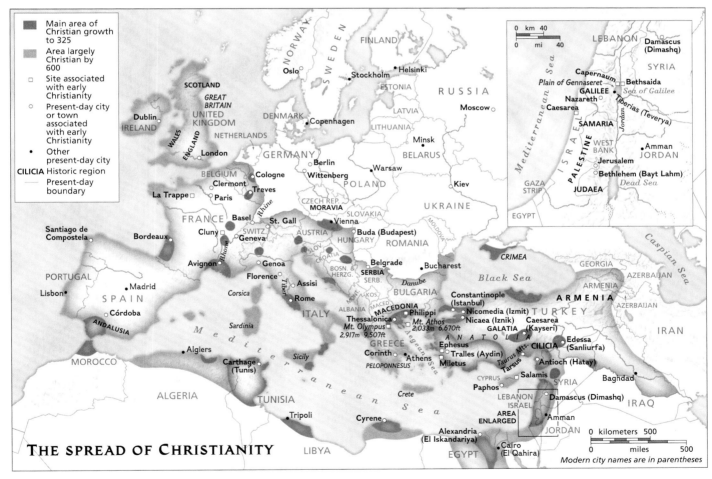

THE SPREAD OF CHRISTIANITY

Main area of Christian growth to 325

Area largely Christian by 600

□ Site associated with early Christianity

○ Present-day city or town associated with early Christianity

• Other present-day city

CILICIA Historic region

Present-day boundary

Modern city names are in parentheses

By 600 Christianity had gained influence beyond isolated pockets and had spread throughout the countryside of the Mediterranean world and western Europe, forming a powerful counterpoint to the equally dynamic growth of Islam over the course of the seventh century.

EDIFICES

The fourth-century Coptic monastery Deir el Abyad, or White Monastery, near Sohag City in Upper Egypt, was joined to a church named for St. Shenute, its abbot from 385 to 465. (He was said to have lived to the age of 118.) More than 2,000 monks and 1,800 nuns once lived and meditated here.

Monasticism began as religious individuals took to caves in the desert, rejecting the pleasures and conveniences of the everyday world. Some lived alone as hermits; others formed communes: the first monasteries. Medieval monasteries became a common feature in city and country—havens of religious, social, and intellectual life.

Hermitic monasticism often arose in response to the urban luxuries of a parent culture. Simeon Stylites, for example, lived atop a pillar in northern Syria for many years, until his death in 459. Elsewhere, Byzantine monasteries took on a communal aspect, characterized by devotion and meditation within a loose, nonhierarchical structure. For the sake of meditation and silence, they were often sited in remote locations, such as Mount Athos, on a cold, rocky peninsula in northern Greece.

THE MONASTERY

A Place for Peace and Piety

Byzantine monasticism may have influenced Irish monasticism as clergy followed trade routes in the sixth century. Irish monks were extremely well educated, zealous missionaries, whose communities also tended to be loose and nonhierarchical.

In western and most of northern Europe, on the other hand, monasteries were perhaps the most rigidly structured organizations in society. Hence resident monks came to wield political and military clout at the same time

that they provided social services: refuge, almsgiving, agriculture, and education.

The architecture of a medieval monastery was designed to promote seclusion and quiet. Typically at the heart of the monastery was a garden encircled by a cloister, a colonnaded walkway, from which passageways led to attached or nearby buildings including a dormitory, a refectory (dining hall), common rooms, and a chapel.

A cornerstone of medieval European society, monasteries were everywhere. All the major cities had one, and many were located on islands in the north Atlantic or the Mediterranean and in Christian communities of North Africa. So pervasive was the monastery's reach that legend has it when Norse settlers landed for the first time ever on the shores of Iceland, they found Irish monks already living there. ■

offers. A taunting letter from Chosroes to Heraclius begins: "I, Chosroes the son of the great Hormisdas, the Most Noble of all the Gods, the King and Sovereign-Master over all the Earth, to Heraclius, my vile and brainless slave."

After a successful two-year campaign in Armenia, Heraclius returned to Asia Minor and managed a spectacular victory over the Persians in 625. Personally engaged in hand-to-hand combat, he kept the enemy from crossing the Sarus River. In a decisive battle in 628 at the ancient Assyrian city of Nineveh on the upper Tigris, he killed the Persian commander and, raising the loser's head on his spear, rallied his troops and won the day. A month later he forced the Persians into a peace treaty. The Persians gave up the Byzantine lands they had conquered, returned prisoners, and handed over the stolen cross, which Heraclius himself took back to Jerusalem in 630.

Hailed as a conquering hero, Heraclius had kept Byzantium out of the grasp of the Muslims, yet they continued to erode his army and the edges of the empire. He died unsure of his succession and the future of his wife, Martina. She was his niece, and the clergy viewed the match as incestuous. A son by his first marriage died soon after becoming emperor, and Martina's political opponents accused her of poisoning him. They cut out her tongue and lopped off her son's nose to prevent him from taking the throne.

In 636, in a momentous battle in southwestern Syria, on the Yarmuk River, the Muslims defeated the Byzantines—the first in a series of punishing losses for the empire. During the long reign of Heraclius's grandson Constans II (r. 641-668), the Arabs spread out across North Africa, Asia Minor, and Armenia, expanding the

According to tradition, St. Cuthbert of Lindisfarne walked into the cold waters of northern England, praying. When he came back to the rocky shore, friendly sea otters came and warmed his feet, a sign of God's love.

Muslim Empire. In 655 they succeeded in destroying the mighty Byzantine fleet. Constans moved to what he felt was a safer location—Syracuse, in Sicily—but controversy followed him there, and he was assassinated. His son, Constantine IV (r. 668-681) fought off the Arab fleet with the use of Greek fire, a medieval incendiary. He died peacefully, but the battles were not over.

The world's new religion had changed the map of the medieval world.

Carved into the stonework of the Cathedral of St. Etienne in Bourges, France, this depiction of the devil pushing a damned man into the fires of Hades was a firm reminder of the importance of righteousness leading to salvation.

EVIL & INTOLERANCE IN THE MIDDLE AGES

he spread of Christianity meant new rules of law and morality for many communities. Christian rites of birth and death, along with their accompanying concepts of heaven, hell, and purgatory, began to influence the lives of the converted. By the late 12th and 13th centuries, the pope's power was unmatched, and his rule extended to the farthest reaches of Christendom through a sophisticated bureaucratic system.

This meant, of course, that non-Christians found it increasingly difficult to practice alternative religions or hold to variant systems of belief. The church used gruesome and often frightening visions of evil to prove the value of salvation on its terms. Art and architecture often reflected these beliefs, and cathedrals— intimidating in size and scope to begin with—were animated with sculptures and tableaux picturing the devil leading the damned, or the last judgment, or the fires of hell: vivid reminders to the faithful to stay to the straight and narrow.

Even Christian movements outside of the institutional church, especially those that viewed the church bureaucracy as antithetical to Christian values, could be labeled as heretical. Popes and bishops did all they could to eradicate those they considered heretics, such as the Waldensians and the Cathars, Christian sects whose members were often vilified and imprisoned. Heretics were less frequently burned at the stake though this image of the Inquisition has stayed in the popular imagination.

As fear and intolerance took further hold of the lay population the later Middle Ages saw an increased persecution of deviants, from Jews to homosexuals, witches to magicians. Such trials reinforced anti-Semitism and laid the groundwork for the witch-hunting crazes of the centuries to come.

Frightening images of hell, such as this 13th-century French illustration, helped deter Christians from committing evil and also helped to promote conversion for the sake of salvation to non-Christians.

The aggressive spread of Christianity in the medieval era led to the increased persecution of deviants, including witches. A bureaucratic system helped identify alleged heretics; tests of the person's mettle were subjective, illogical—and irrefutable.

Popular among medieval Christian stories was the legend of Theophilus, who was said to have bargained with the devil for a position in the diocese. Theophilus later repented, and the Virgin Mary interceded with God on his behalf.

700 – 800

THE EIGHTH CENTURY WAS A PERIOD OF SWEEPING CHANGE ACROSS EUROPE AND THE MIDDLE East. New dynasties overthrew the old, religions fought for land and converts, and parts of Europe that had fragmented in the wake of the Roman Empire began uniting as tribal states clashed and coalesced. Europeans still looked to Rome as their spiritual center, yet political and social innovations had to come from elsewhere. Three cultures sought to build their worlds out of the ruins of Rome—Frankish, Byzantine, and Anglo-Saxon—while a fourth culture, springing out of the new religion of Islam, swept the Mediterranean world. Muslims brought the art of war to new levels with their blazing cavalry attacks, moving ever forward in their pursuit of more land, more wealth, more tribute, and more converts. The Muslim quest for land and subjects was likely foremost, more important even than their quest for converts to the new religion. Once they took over a territory, Muslims treated the Jews and Christians there with more tolerance than Christians had generally shown to Jews.

By the early 700s most of the countries edging the Mediterranean had become Muslim territories; only north and central Italy and France remained unconquered. Notable battles occurred as the invading Berbers, or North Africans, clashed with the local Visigoths in Spain, scattering the Christian princes to mountain holdouts in the north. The Muslim tide advanced as far north as Poitiers, France, where in 732 it finally met its match in the Frankish army led by the redoubtable Charles Martel.

Europe was just beginning to awaken from a long daze after the Roman pullout. Since the time of the mighty ruler Clovis, the Frankish kingdom—composed of today's France and western Germany—had been ruled by the Merovingian dynasty, but by the mid-600s that family was a shadow of its former self. Charles Martel's son Pepin the Short started the new dynasty of the Carolingians. Though short-lived, this family line would produce one of Europe's greatest leaders, Charlemagne. Under his strong and able leadership, the Frankish kingdom grew, the arts flourished, and the Christian influence spread across formerly pagan regions, bringing a common culture to disparate tribes.

At the same time, the burgeoning Muslim empire was experiencing growth pains of its own. The Umayyads, who had been in power almost since the death of Muhammad, were overpowered by the Abbasids in a series of violent uprisings. These

---

Charlemagne's Carolingian Empire began to dissolve almost immediately upon his death in 814. Mourners grieve in this 14th-century French evocation of those times. PRECEDING PAGES: The Christian victory over Muslim forces at the Battle of Tours in 732 was considered by 19th-century historians to be a turning point in history, the halt to Islam's advances into Europe, as memorialized in this 1837 oil painting by the French artist Charles Auguste Steuben.

internecine power struggles momentarily checked the Muslim advance. The new rulers moved their capital from Damascus to Baghdad, and the empire became decentralized. Emphasizing religion over race, the Abbasid culture easily incorporated people, converts and others, into its fold.

While Rome forged an allegiance with the emerging Frankish empire under the regal Charlemagne, Byzantium held on as the heart of eastern Christianity, breathing easier after decades of Muslim attacks. A succession of emperors in the seventh and eighth centuries took the throne, many of them acquiring it through bloody dramas at the same time that Anglo-Saxons in England were settling into a relatively peaceful period marked by the widespread acceptance of Christianity.

The Moors Reach Spain

The Muslims, enticed by the prospect of riches and religious converts, pushed their way northward. Here lay a Europe fractured into many kingdoms and loose confederations that, without the central authority of a Rome, was vulnerable to the incursion of Muslims, seeking converts to their religion or, at the least, more land and richer tribute from a population of subjects that had grown exponentially in the seven decades since the death of their prophet, Muhammad, in 632. No longer could Rome look out on the Mediterranean and call it "our sea." Now Syria, Egypt, and other North African and Middle Eastern countries joined together through their religion.

Backed by the powerful caliph of Damascus, Berber Muslims—native peoples of North Africa, recently converted to Islam—invaded Spain in 711.

The Hunterston brooch, produced in Ireland and made of gold, silver, and amber, was a luxury good symbolizing the power and wealth of its owner.

THE EIGHTH CENTURY

732
Bubonic plague recurs in Constantinople; up to 200,000 die.

732
In the Battle of Tours, Charles Martel defeats the Moors.

750
The Abbasid dynasty overthrows the Umayyad caliphate.

751
A paper mill is built in Samarkand, first in the Islamic world.

751
Childeric III is deposed by Pepin the Short, first Carolingian king of the Franks.

762
Baghdad is established as the Abbasid capital.

793
The monastery of Lindisfarne is sacked— first recorded Viking raid.

800
Pope Leo III crowns Charlemagne Emperor of Rome.

ca 800
Castles are first built in western Europe.

Spain was at that time under the rule of the Visigoths, the western division of the Goths, who had sacked Rome. Their current (and final) king was a usurper named Roderick. The Berbers were led by a daring general, Tariq ibn Ziyad, who had established a beachhead at Gibraltar with about 7,000 men.

In early July 711, Tariq's mounted troops headed northwest up through the mountains and ushered in the historic beginning of Islam in Europe. "Oh, my warriors," invoked Tariq, "whither would you flee? Behind you is the sea, before you, the enemy. You have only the hope of your courage and your constancy. . . . The spoils will belong to yourselves." Roderick's much larger force met them on the plains near the village of Sidonia, in southern Spain.

For several days, the armies clashed, the Visigoths clad in Romanesque breastplates and plumed helmets, the helmetless Berber infantry wearing sandals and white tunics. The Berber cavalry, somewhat better outfitted, wore leather jerkins under light mail and metal caps under turbans. Swords and spears were the weapons of the day. Whereas the Visigoths battled by massing in tight formations, the Berbers swooped in for repeated lightning attacks and withdrawals. At a cost of some 3,000 warriors, Tariq managed both to defeat the Visigoths and to kill Roderick. He sent severed heads and gold rings back to Damascus as proof of his great victory.

Its king toppled, Spain tottered and collapsed under the impact of such bloodbaths. Despite a depleted force, Tariq raced onward to the mountain stronghold of Toledo, in central Spain, which had been the Visigoth capital for nearly 200 years. Expecting a fierce struggle from the well-fortified city, to his surprise Tariq found Toledo nearly empty, its defenders fleeing northeast with the city's precious bejeweled altar. Toledo's Jews had not fled their home city, however. After years of anti-Semitic treatment by the Visigoths, the Spanish Jews were happy to make deals with the Muslim conquerors. That done, Tariq's army charged after Toledo's escaping Visigoths and slaughtered them.

And so the Moors—as these Berber Muslims moving into Europe would come to be called—first occupied Spain, and there they would remain for more than 700 years. Muslims now had nearly complete economic and political control of the Mediterranean, while across Spain the muezzin's calls to prayer echoed from sinuous minarets whose elaborate architecture borrowed from Persia, India, and Byzantium.

Martel Meets the Saracens
Not long after taking the Iberian Peninsula, the Muslims crossed the Pyrenees Mountains and marched into what is now France, part of the Frankish kingdom, named after the Franks, the west Germanic people originating farther east along the banks of the Rhine River. In 721 a Frankish leader, Duke Odo of Aquitaine, routed a Muslim force at Toulouse. It was the first victory of the Europeans over the invaders. And yet the Muslims were not seriously checked. That would happen 11 years later at the watershed Battle of Poitiers.

As their numbers advanced into Europe, the Muslim invaders gained another name: Saracens. They swept across France like "a brush fire fanned by the winds," according to one chronicler, and not even Odo could stop them. Their emir, or leader, Abd al Rahman al Ghafiqi, was a charismatic new governor-general in Spain; accompanying him over the mountains were 15,000 soldiers.

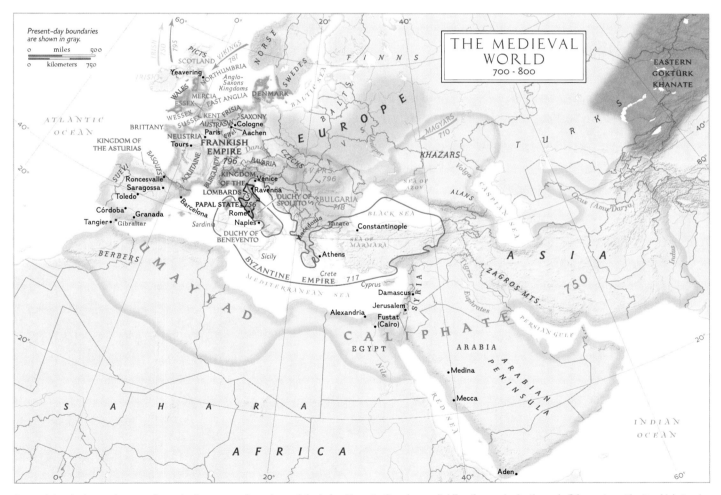

By 715, Islam had spread west as far as the Pyrenees and east beyond the Indus River. Factions began dividing the empire by the end of the century. The Frankish Empire also expanded in all directions, its growth culminating in the reign of Charlemagne. The Vikings make their first voyages to the British Isles.

After pushing the duke aside near Bordeaux, Al Ghafiqi's forces came rolling on, banners waving, up the old Roman highway to Poitiers. Here they paused to plunder the richly decorated basilica, and then it was on to the venerated holy city of Tours, which lay 60 miles north. Odo had fallen back to Tours, and now with only a few thousand men, he sent out for the assistance of Charles Martel.

Though he would become known as Martel—the Hammer—he started as Charles the Bastard. He was an illegitimate son of Pepin of Heristal, who was mayor of the palace of Austrasia, the eastern part of the Frankish kingdom. Charles survived his legitimate half brothers and became a serious contender for the power wielded by Pepin's widow, Plectrude. He was strong, confident, and bent on proving himself a worthy successor to his father. The mayor of Neustria, the western part of

the Frankish kingdom, regarded Charles as a threat. The headstrong young man went about gathering allies to defeat the western mayor, but Plectrude had her husband's son imprisoned. Charles managed to escape, however. He raised an army, defeated the Neustrians, and, by 719, five years after his father's death, Charles Martel had ascended to rule the entire Frankish kingdom.

In 732, Charles engaged in one of numerous expeditions against the Saxons and people along the Rhine and Danube Rivers. At the same time, he had to address the threatening presence of the Saracens to the west. Marshaling an army of about 10,000 infantry and cavalry, Charles led a forced march across Frankland to Tours, where he joined with Duke Odo. There, in October, the soldiers under Charles and Odo gathered in the Basilica of St. Martin, and in the candle glow and swirling incense they

prayed to their Christian God, dedicated themselves to victory or death, and began marching south.

On a tilted plain between the two towns of Tours and Poitiers, Al Ghafiqi's juggernaut came pouring onward. For a few days the armies tested each other, feinting, skirmishing, and reconnoitering. On around the fourth day, Charles crossed the Vienne River downstream of Al Ghafiqi and made a surprise attack on his rear. Rattled but hardly deterred, Al Ghafiqi regrouped for the showdown two days later.

Charles positioned his men on a slight plateau where the road made a gentle rise. Knowing that his army's speed was no match for that of the Muslim forces, he formed them in tight shield-to-shield lines and ordered them to stand there and take the assault waves he knew would come. After their noon prayers, the Saracens attacked. They began with a furious volley of arrows, directly behind which came the cavalry, battle-hardened horses snorting beneath yelling riders in their conical helmets. But soon they found themselves pushed back by the Franks, who came slowly forward in one great phalanx of glittering steel. Then all the terrors of war thrummed the air, as long swords clashed and found their targets in flesh. Two decades later an unknown scribe (or scribes) known as Isidore Pacensis wrote this description of the scene: "The men of the north stood as motionless as a wall. They were like a belt of ice frozen together, and not to be dissolved as they slew the Arabs with the sword."

Finally, when he saw the opportune time, Charles wheeled out his cavalry and smashed into the teetering Muslim center. In the melee, Al Ghafiqi was struck by an arrow and killed. The Saracens folded their tents, and by cover of

INNOVATION

CROP ROTATION

Improving Productivity & the Soil

The three-field system of crop rotation was an agricultural development of the Middle Ages that almost doubled the amount of food that could be produced on a tract of land. At the time, the staple food of Europe was wheat, which sucks nutrients out of the soil such that half a field has to lie fallow, replenishing itself, while the other half produces a harvest—a two-field system. The new idea, a three-field system, involved sowing wheat, barley, or rye in the autumn; beans, peas, or oats in the spring; and leaving one-third of a field fallow at any given time. The nitrogen-fixing legumes, such as beans and peas, actually enriched the soil while producing a crop. Incorporating legumes into the system not only resulted in higher crop yield

but also a greater variety of food and more dietary protein.

As with other agricultural innovations of medieval Europe, wide adoption of the three-field system happened slowly. The common open-field system divided arable land into strips, not plots, that were apportioned to individual farmers. Plowing, sowing, and harvesting were communal affairs, which could discourage personal ingenuity. As its advantages became better known, though, the three-field system of crop rotation produced a food surplus that served as the commodity base for a reemerging economy and in turn increased social mobility, the division of labor, and mercantilism, enriching and enlarging the entire medieval world. ■

First mentioned by Romans in 192 B.C. and occupied by Visigoths into the eighth century, the city of Toledo, situated at the center of the Iberian Peninsula, thrived as the location for government headquarters and as a crossroads of trade and commerce after the Moorish invasion of Spain.

night collected their dead and began retreating south.

There would be other Muslim incursions into what they called the Great Land—Frankish Europe—over the next several years, but the Franks, united under Charles, had proved that the invaders could be stopped. Historians have characterized this battle as the high-water mark of the Muslim expansion. Edward Gibbon, writing in the 1700s, speculated that without Charles's victory at Poitiers, "perhaps the interpre-

tation of the Koran would now be taught in the schools of Oxford." Instead, Muslim invasions unified Europe, and thus created the concept of Christendom, the term used by thinking Europeans for their culture from this point forward through the entire Middle Ages. Isidore Pacensis named the victors the "Europenses." For the first time since the Roman Empire, the idea of a people, unified by culture and religion, took root on the continent. The battle also proved that, bastard or not, Charles was father

to a new line of rulers, and Frankland, which contained most of modern France and western Germany, was the dominant power among the new Europeans.

While Charles Martel's efforts kept the Muslims' European reach limited to Spain, the rest of Europe still had to worry about internal divisions and invaders from other lands, who would come in hordes before the eighth century was over. Of course, the Franks at the time were not aware of the meaning and magnitude of the victory. Nor were the

CAROLINGIAN The Carolingian dynasty included Charlemagne at its peak and ruled western Europe from the middle of the eighth century through most of the ninth century. The term also refers to that period of history or to styles and artifacts from that time.

Saracens, for they continued for at least a decade to try pushing on beyond the Pyrenees. In the ninth century the Muslims would conquer Sicily and southern Italy, thus turning the entire Mediterranean into an Islamic shoreline. By then an entire paradigm of competition was emerging between the rising civilization of Christendom, based in Europe with its primary spiritual center in Rome, and the relatively advanced civilization of Islam, based primarily in North Africa and the Middle East, its spiritual center in Mecca.

THE TRANSFORMATION FROM MEROVINGIAN TO CAROLINGIAN

The Merovingian dynasty, which had ruled the Frankish people since the beginning of the sixth century, had by the middle of the seventh degenerated

> IN THIS YEAR PEPIN
> WAS NAMED KING OF
> THE FRANKS . . . BUT
> CHILDERICH, WHO HAD
> THE NAME OF KING,
> WAS SHORN OF HIS
> LOCKS AND SENT
> INTO A MONASTERY.
>
> ANNALS OF LORSCH ABBEY
> *Germany, 751*

into a weak line of incompetent rulers, most of them women, children, or (in the words of historian Norman Cantor) "mental defectives." Merovingian noblemen were marked by their hair, which they wore long and flowing to signify their royal lineage back to a primeval, hirsute sea-god. As Christianity gained influence, this sea god heritage held less sway, and the last of the Merovingian leaders were largely ignored by the local aristocracy.

Something had to be done to prevent the provincial aristocracy from simply taking royal lands and property. Enter the so-called mayors of the palace, household officials working directly for the royal family. Charles Martel, for example, first seized the title of mayor of Austrasia and then the title of mayor of Neustria as well, and a new line of power and authority emerged: the Carolingians, as they came to be called, from the Latin *Carolus,* Charles.

Charles Martel turned out to be not only a skilled warrior but also a success-

Pepin III, the son of Charles Martel and the father of Charlemagne, was the first in the line of Carolingian kings. He was also the first Frankish ruler to be sanctioned by the Catholic Church.

ful diplomat. He courted St. Boniface and other Anglo-Saxon Christian missionaries, because he knew that gaining the support of the Church would legitimize his claim to the French monarchy. He also reasoned that Christianizing the Germanic tribes on the northern and eastern frontiers of Frankland would make them more pliant.

Charles wielded considerable power, yet his son, Pepin the Short, was not the recognized heir to the throne of Frankland. That title was held by a Merovingian longhair. According to Frankish law, only the pope in Rome could authorize a switch in ruling families, so Pepin the Short sought papal support for his claim. He saw his chance when the Lombards, a Teutonic tribe, were attempting to overtake Ravenna, the final Byzantine city in Italy. Pepin knew that he could capture Ravenna for the papacy, and so he sent word to Rome, asking if his assumption of the throne would be sanctioned. The pope replied that the man exerting power was more deserving of the crown than a figurehead. To Pepin, that was a challenge, and he did what he needed to exert power. He brought together an assemblage of soldiers, noblemen, and clergy to witness an elaborate coronation ceremony. St. Boniface anointed him with holy oil, symbolizing Pepin as a descendant not of a pagan sea-god but of the kings of the Bible. And so in 751 Pepin became king, and the last Merovingian was sent off to a monastery, where his hair was cut monk-style, and the door closed on the once great dynasty.

Pepin did make good on his vow to recapture Ravenna for Christendom. More important than that, though, he is known for fathering the man who would put his stamp on Europe like no one

Ci comence listoire du Roy pepi
filz de charlee martel. ou quelfail
li la lignee des Roys de france. q̃
auoient este par auant. xlix.
pres ce que li Roye chil

Archbishop Boniface crowns Pepin III, also known as Pepin the Short, King of the Franks. Challenged by his half brother, Grifo, who led an army against him in Bavaria, Pepin maintained his rule. Ultimately his son, Charlemagne, became one of the greatest leaders in the medieval world.

The cathedral at Aachen, built around 792, was the site of the coronation of 30 German kings and 12 queens.

AACHEN
CROWNED OF GOD

Springs | Chapel | Coronations | Pilgrimage

The city of Aachen, located close to the modern border between Germany and Belgium, is small in comparison to many of the historically important cities across Europe. Its time in the spotlight was comparatively short—only about 50 years—but from it originated great change for Europe, and for the world.

Aachen is the German name for the town, but it also goes by the French name Aix-la-Chapelle. The site was inhabited from an early date: Archaeological evidence suggests that Neolithic peoples quarried rock outcrops in the area. Little is known about habitation here until the first century A.D., however, when natural hot springs drew the Romans to the area, which they

called Aquisgranum. They established spring-fed spas, but the Roman tenure was short; they left the site almost completely abandoned.

Aachen remained virtually uninhabited for centuries until the Merovingians, Frankish kings, built a small residence and chapel beside the springs. The Carolingian takeover accomplished by Pepin the Short, father of Charlemagne, included many Merovingian residences, but Charlemagne did not visit Aachen until he was already established as King of the Franks. Charlemagne admired the great leaders in history such as King David and Constantine. Like them he wanted to create a city to serve his own purposes: a place where he could establish himself as a new leader interested in culture, the arts, and religious reform. Aachen was to be a new center of civilization to embody his ideals of a Europe conquering the barbarism and lawlessness that had become commonplace since the fall of the Roman Empire.

Within several years of his first visit to Aachen, Charlemagne ordered a palace and cathedral built there. No expense was spared in the design and construction; materials and skilled laborers came in from all over Europe, with Charlemagne paying out of his own treasury.

Of all the buildings Charlemagne had constructed at Aachen, most have disappeared over time. One building still stands, however: the Palatine Chapel, part of the Aachen Cathedral, which is

AACHEN THROUGH THE MIDDLE AGES

1st century A.D. Romans settle Aquisgranum, named for the nearby hot springs.

790 Charlemagne begins building the Palatine Chapel.

794 Aachen becomes Charlemagne's favorite royal residence.

814 Charlemagne dies in Aachen and is buried in the Palatine Chapel.

843 Charlemagne's grandson Lothair I keeps Aachen as imperial capital.

936 Starting a tradition, Otto I is crowned King of Germany in Aachen.

1002 Otto III, Holy Roman Emperor, dies in Italy but is buried in Aachen.

widely regarded as the preeminent surviving example of Carolingian architecture. The Carolingian style incorporated architectural motifs from around the empire: Germanic, Celtic, and Mediterranean elements combined to produce a distinctive look. Chapel architects departed from typical German or Frankish architecture and looked to Italy for inspiration, basing their design on the sixth-century Basilica of San Vitale in Ravenna. The chapel in Aachen is defined by its double-shelled octagonal dome, which rests on thick piers, reminiscent of late Roman architecture. An ambulatory and its overhead gallery occupy a second story, looking down into the center of the building, and the cupola that crowns the dome reaches a height of more than one hundred feet. Charlemagne had works of art—mosaics, frescoes, and marbles—removed from churches elsewhere in the empire and reinstalled in his chapel, symbolizing the unity formed from diversity of Charlemagne's rule.

Charlemagne's even hand and multifaceted personality allowed him to gain respect and loyalty, and many people visited his court. Aachen blossomed overnight into a major cultural center, and from it emerged a new and cosmopolitan sense of society, upon which many European countries base their values and governments today.

Louis the Pious, Charlemagne's eldest surviving son, inherited the throne in 814, and he maintained the court at Aachen. But with his death, in 840, arguments over succession broke out. The empire was soon divided into three parts, and Aachen seemed too far out of the way to be a capital city for any of them.

Thus, after about half a century of being one of the world's most important cities, Aachen sank back into obscurity. A few factors kept the city from completely disappearing from the map, however. Starting in 936, with the reign of Otto I, and lasting for the next 500 years, until the reign of Ferdinand I, the Aachen Cathedral served as the coronation site for German kings, a sign of its legacy as the seat of power. During these centuries Aachen remained a free imperial city, subject only to the rule of the emperor, which brought it certain privileges. At the end of the 12th century, Charlemagne was unofficially canonized (though never officially recognized by the Holy See), and his burial place in Aachen Cathedral, already a repository for relics, became a pilgrimage center.

Aachen was founded in the Rhine Valley near the western border of modern-day Germany.

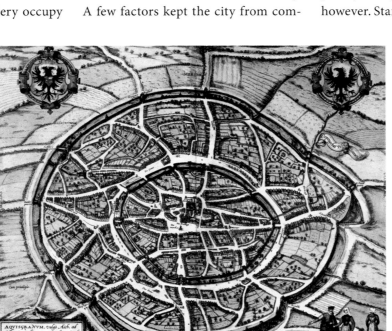

Charlemagne chose Aachen as the capital city of his Carolingian Empire; there he built a grand imperial palace and other municipal buildings. Today's Rathaus, or town hall, stands on his palace site.

1165
Charlemagne is canonized, and Aachen becomes a pilgrims' destination.

1168
Emperor Frederick Barbarossa installs the cathedral's bronze chandelier.

1171
The citizens of Aachen pay for city walls to be constructed.

1215
Charlemagne's remains are placed in a golden shrine.

1250
Aachen becomes a free imperial city.

1330
Rathaus (town hall) construction begins atop Charlemagne's palace ruins.

1531
Ferdinand I is the last German king to be crowned in Aachen.

before and very few since: Charles the Great, Carolus Magnus, Charlemagne.

The Great Charlemagne

It's an irony of history that Pepin the Short sired a giant in the history of the world, not to mention a man who stood at a height seven times the length of his own foot. Tall, strong, eloquent, and dignified, Charlemagne (742-814) was an expert swimmer and horseback rider. He valued learning and culture, though he was himself illiterate. He married many times and had several concubines and at least 13 children. When his father died, in 768, Charlemagne and his brother Carloman became joint rulers of the Frankish kingdom, which included what is now France, Belgium, Luxembourg, the Netherlands, and part of western Germany. Three years later Carloman died, and Charlemagne became sole ruler.

He immediately set out to enlarge his domain. First he went to war against the neighboring states of Bavaria and Lombardy, handily taking them within the fold. He enriched the kingdom's coffers by raiding the Avars of eastern Europe. The toughest military challenge lay with the pagan Saxons to the north: Though early gains were made, it ultimately took some three decades to, in effect, tame them with Christianity. During a break in that action, Charlemagne marched his army over the Pyrenees to see what he could do about Spain, lately taken by the Moors.

In 778 he laid siege to Saragossa, an inland city in northeastern Spain, but, failing to capture it, he began to retreat. It was in the village of Roncesvalles, farther north toward the Pyrenees, that his rear guard was fiercely attacked by a contingent of Basque fighters. Though not an especially important event, the

PERSONAE

THE VENERABLE BEDE

Venerated English Historian

Northumbria, in the north of England, was such a center for scholarship in the eighth century that the era's most respected historian, a monk known only as Bede, never departed from his sparsely populated homeland, yet left a legacy for the centuries.

Bede wrote more than 60 books on topics of history, religion, science, and grammar. Around 731, he completed his most influential work, *An Ecclesiastical History of the English People*, which charts the course of English Christianity from the invasion of Julius Caesar to the time of writing. Glorifying the Roman Catholic Church as the prime mover in English civilization, Bede's history omits some unsavory details and includes miracles that are clearly not historical. It also introduces the convention of dividing history into times before and after the birth of Jesus.

Bede collected his sources from the libraries of England and firsthand popular accounts, compiling a massive amount of information that has informed historians ever since. He was so highly honored in his lifetime that not long after his death, he came to be called "The Venerable Bede," a name that has been used ever since. ■

Bede lived in provincial northern England and became a key chronicler of his time.

battle resulted in the death of Charlemagne's trusted paladin, Roland, and the episode became the subject of a number of medieval romances and epic poems, the most famous of which was *La Chanson de Roland* (*The Song of Roland*), originating in mid-11th-century Brittany. The poem tells of a treacherous knight who betrays Roland and his troops— exaggerated to 20,000 strong—as they are ambushed not by Basques but by an army of 400,000 Muslims. As in many medieval retellings of history, the truth was embellished for the sake of the story. In the end, Charlemagne destroys the Muslims and rules supreme, to the greater glory of Christ.

After battling in Spain, Charlemagne traveled to the northeast to put down a rebellion in Saxony, part of today's Germany. In fact, between 772 and 804 he frequently waged war with the unruly Saxons, wreaking violence on those who had broken earlier vows of allegiance and bringing more lands and people under his rule, all with the blessing of the Christian Church. Though some of Charlemagne's methods were criticized, his results were approved. Among those taking note was Pope Leo III. Seeing Charlemagne as both a powerful ally and potentially dangerous enemy, the pope decided to recognize Charlemagne's unique position as both a mighty ruler and a friend of the Church by granting him an ancient title of honor.

In 800, at a Christmas Mass held in Rome, the pope crowned Charlemagne Emperor of the Romans. Though the leader gained nothing substantial in territory or power, the coronation signified that Leo and Charlemagne had just created what would become known as the Holy Roman Empire. A confederation that would last for a thousand years, it reached from Rome to the North Sea, from French Burgundy in the west to Austria in the east, a solid band of territory in the middle of the European continent.

Charlemagne had spent so many early years on the battlefield, solidifying his kingdom, that not until 794 did he build a permanent home. He returned to the city very likely to have been his birthplace: Aachen (Aix-la-Chapelle in French), about 45 miles west of Cologne at the meeting point of today's borders between Belgium, the Netherlands, and Germany. Sitting amid rivers tributary to the Rhine River, at the foot of the Eifel Mountains, Aachen had long been visited by the Romans for its spa, hot sulfur springs creating natural mineral baths believed to have healing powers. In Aachen, Charlemagne erected a chapel and palace, parts of which still stand.

With Aachen as a base, Charlemagne began introducing political reforms and improving the cultural literacy of his people, extending and promoting the learning that had for so long emanated out of Rome. During this Carolingian Renaissance, he granted estates to the nobility in return for their promises of military service and continued maintenance of local roads, bridges, and fortifications. In this way, Charlemagne exerted a lasting influence on the material culture of his times. With equal or perhaps even more importance, he exerted a lasting influence on his intellectual world.

Charlemagne established a palace school and a vast library at Aachen. Here the top teachers and clergy were trained and then sent to various parts of the empire. In an age when hand-copying ancient and modern texts was the only

Charlemagne ruled the Carolingian Empire from 768 to 814, temporarily establishing a centralized imperial state that encompassed much of western Europe.

way to preserve them, Charlemagne's scholars devised a new script called Carolingian minuscule. While Roman script had used all capital letters, Carolingian, which looks much like modern handwriting, used upper- and lowercase letters, made each letter distinct, and left breaks between words—all linguistic innovations. Henceforth all laws, all liturgical documents, all government records, and all Bibles were written in this uniform script.

Once in Aachen, Charlemagne himself pursued intellectual interests that he had not had time for as a younger man. He spoke Old High German and prob-

ably understood the Old French dialect; to these he now added a knowledge of Latin and some Greek. He learned the basics of mathematics and astronomy, and he hired learned men to read aloud to him.

Whereas the Roman emperors had been able to maintain an extensive empire for centuries, Charlemagne's kingdom was tenuous and relied on the strength and ingenuity of one man. He did not have the road network, standing army, navy, paid civil service, or money economy enjoyed by the Romans. Plots and rebellions against him surfaced both near and far, but he was able by dint of

his forceful personality to hold his empire together and hand it off to one more generation. His two oldest sons having died, Charlemagne crowned his third son, 35-year-old Louis the Pious, co-emperor in 813. Now 71 years old and walking with a limp, Charlemagne was still in good enough health to take to his horse for the fall hunting season. But in January he became seriously ill. After his death, a contemporary biographer wrote of omens that foretold his end: eclipses, and a ball of fire in the sky that had startled the emperor's horse and caused him to throw his rider.

Louis reigned from 814 until his death in 840. Devoted to religion but lacking in skills as a statesman and soldier, he watched the empire fall to pieces. His three sons divided the kingdom, and civil war broke out. But Charlemagne's contributions remained—he gave Europe a profound new sense of a common religious, cultural, and political identity.

FROM UMAYYAD TO ABBASID

While Europe's leading dynasty was shifting from Merovingian to Carolingian, the Arab world just to the south was undergoing a similar sea change. The Umayyads, in power from 661 to 750, gave way to the Abbasids, who would rule until the Mongol invasion of 1258.

The first four successors to the Prophet Muhammad, called the rightly guided caliphs, led the Muslim faithful into the middle of the seventh century, but then a power struggle broke out, ultimately leading to a schism that continues to this day. After the death of Ali, the fourth rightly guided caliph, a family named Umayyad held the ruling power of Islam until the middle of the eighth century. They made their capital

Louis I, called Louis the Pious, was the son and heir of Charlemagne, yet he was unable to defend himself against sons and nephews who conspired against him, banishing him to a monastery.

Immense open-air mosques were built in every town and region as Islamic forces advanced and as many new converts sought places to worship Allah. The Great Mosque of Córdoba, Spain, built in the eighth century and expanded later, is one of the largest of all mosques in the Islamic world.

THE MOSQUE

Buildings of Prayer & Praise

The Islamic empire exploded out of the Arabian peninsula in the seventh and eighth centuries, when the Persian and Byzantine empires were both in decline. Wherever Islamic armies conquered, from Spain to the Indus River, Arab leaders, or caliphs, would inaugurate massive building programs of mosques and palaces. Though strictures against sumptuousness were outlined in the Koran, mosques were built on a grand scale, perhaps out of the necessity to accommodate large numbers of new converts or perhaps out of the drive to surpass in splendor the ruins of non-Islamic predecessors. In either case, mosques were a tangible symbol of the wealth, power, and devotion of the new rulers.

The first mosque was of humbler origins, no more than the courtyard of Muhammad's house in Medina, but it nevertheless served as a model for much larger mosques to follow. The open space of Muhammad's courtyard is reflected in the open interiors of later mosques. Muhammad's house was not just a place of worship, either, but also served social, political, educational, and military functions. This is also the case with medieval mosques, which often housed schools, libraries, and law courts.

Regional variations in the architecture of mosques display the great diversity of cultures in the Islamic empire. The arches, pillars, and minarets characteristic of modern mosques were inspired by Persian and Roman examples, while the Great Mosque at Córdoba, begun around 784 in Islamic Spain, drew inspiration from Visigothic and Byzantine precedents.

Built on the site of both a Roman temple and a Visigothic church, the Great Mosque is vast, supported by some 850 pillars of variably colored jasper, marble, and granite, many recycled from the previous Roman building. Each pillar supports horseshoe-shaped arches, a design that was likely of Visigothic origin but is now closely associated with Islamic architecture. The walls and roof are ornately decorated with Byzantine-style mosaics, gold inlay, and arabesques, which are distinctly Islamic motifs of repeating geometric patterns intertwining into an abstract representation of the infinite nature of Allah. ■

in Damascus, from which they directed an empire that included Arabia, Persia, Iraq, Syria, and Egypt—and from which they ventured out to conquer even more lands. By 750 the Islamic world spread across three continents, from Tashkent on the border of China in the east, to Spain in the northwest, to Morocco in the distant south.

As they spread the influence of their religion, Muslims mixed a rich melange of cultures from the various lands they had taken. Artists from Constantinople were hired to build the Great Mosque at Damascus, new coins were issued, and a new postal service was founded. Arabic was designated the official language and was used by both Arab and Byzantine officials. As Muslims moved into new territories, many people welcomed the new regime. The rulers taxed those in the garrison cities but otherwise generally left people alone and did not try to convert them. An Islamic cultural renaissance occurred in formerly war-torn regions. Scholars put together a definitive version of the Koran and a book called the *hadith,* a narrative of Muhammad's teachings and sayings. New forms of prose and poetry also arose, fostered by a literary class of former Persians and Syrians.

There was still one prize that the Muslims sought: Constantinople, the great capital of the Byzantine Empire, was a rich fortress on the Bosporus, the narrow water link connecting Mediterranean Europe with Asia and the Black Sea. In 672 Muslim invaders had conducted a

> GLORIFY THE NAME
> OF THY GUARDIAN-LORD
> MOST HIGH,
> WHO HATH CREATED,
> AND FURTHER,
> GIVEN ORDER
> AND PROPORTION;
> WHO HATH
> ORDAINED LAWS.
>
> ———————
>
> THE KORAN

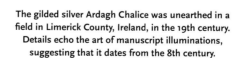

The gilded silver Ardagh Chalice was unearthed in a field in Limerick County, Ireland, in the 19th century. Details echo the art of manuscript illuminations, suggesting that it dates from the 8th century.

seven-year siege and taken the walled city. With apparently endless reserves of men and materiel, the Saracens attempted to strangle the great bastion of Christianity. Yet the Greek navy's fast-sailing ships, notorious for propelling bombs termed "Greek fire," repelled their efforts. In

717 the Arabs made one final attempt to humble Constantinople. Incendiary bombs, a committed Greek fighting force, and an outbreak of bubonic plague among the invaders saved the citadel on the Sea of Marmara once again.

One hundred years after Muhammad's death, his followers had created a formidable, expansive empire. Until the mid-700s, an autocratic Umayyad caliph in Damascus ruled the Islamic world, making him one of the most powerful men on earth. But more and more, his subjects clamored for a better life and a voice in governmental affairs. To appease the non-Arab Muslims, the caliph enacted fiscal reforms, but an economic crisis resulted. Old feuds flared up again among tribes in Syria, Iraq, and Khorasan (today's northeast Iraq), straining the central military. Discontent grew into outright revolt, and taking advantage of the atmosphere of dissension, a clan called the Abbasids wrested control of the empire.

Aided by Shiite Arabs and Persians, the Abbasid family led a rebellion against the caliph in the late 740s. The final coup came in 750 at the Battle of the Great Zab River, named for a tributary of the Tigris that flows from Turkey into Iraq. There the caliph's army faced a much smaller but more motivated force led by the Abbasids. A veteran cavalry of Umayyads charged into an Abbasid line of lances, and the Abbasids cut the attackers down like so many stalks of winter wheat. Other Umayyads drowned in the river, and the caliph himself fled the scene and hid in a village on the Egyptian Nile for several

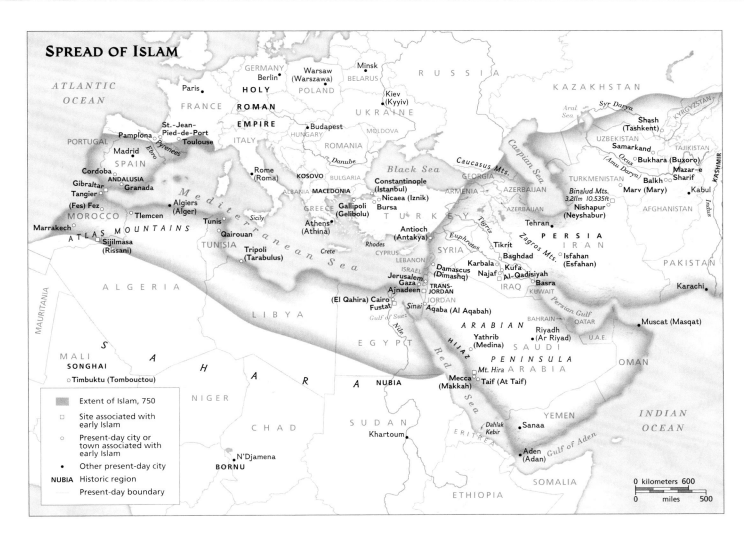

SPREAD OF ISLAM

Extent of Islam, 750

□ Site associated with early Islam

○ Present-day city or town associated with early Islam

• Other present-day city

NUBIA Historic region

— Present-day boundary

0 kilometers 600

0 miles 500

months. Ultimately the caliph was killed in a brief battle, and an Abbasid replaced him as caliph, declaring that whereas the Umayyads could not trace their line directly to Muhammad, their people were direct descendants from his uncle. A new Islamic dynasty had begun.

Most of the Umayyad leaders were tracked down and murdered. One hold-out escaped to Spain. Abd ar Rahman became the progenitor of the Umayyad dynasty of Córdoba and managed to drive Charlemagne out of Iberia.

Establishing a new capital in Baghdad, the Abbasids had their work cut out for them—rebellion was widespread

Islam took root in the Arabian Peninsula, and within a century, the new religion had spread west through North Africa into Europe and through Central Asia to the borders of modern-day China.

throughout Islam, despite the religion's unifying power. By the middle of the ninth century the caliph had lost his influence. Still the Abbasids, promoters of trade, industry, science, and the arts, kept Islam's profile and power high.

BYZANTINE POWER STRUGGLES

Just as the eighth century saw the overthrow of dynasties in the Frankish and Muslim worlds, so it witnessed political and cultural upheavals in Byzantium

as well. During the late 600s and early 700s, the Byzantine Empire spent much energy fending off Muslim attacks. With the breakup of the Muslim empire in the mid-700s, Byzantium could finally return to the artistry and trade that had made it an enviably prosperous dominion.

The culturally rich Byzantine Empire gained in power and influence, becoming the primary hub of Christianity, the pulse point of trade and ideas, and developing a distinctive identity of its own, with new art and architecture arising from the fusing of its numerous attendant cultures. The city of Constantinople dominated the empire. Rich and crowded, it offered entertainments for all classes. Its large stadium, the Hippodrome, rivaled Rome's Coliseum. Chariot races were particularly popular, and two clubs of racing fans, the Blues and the Greens, became so powerful that they turned into political parties. The empire, strategically located along major east-west trade routes, soon became the wealthiest and best-governed realm in Christendom.

In rural provinces around Constantinople a loyal peasantry and work force, which doubled as an army when needed, produced crops and goods valuable for trade—olives, wine, and skillfully worked gold. These were exchanged for ivory, spices, and other luxuries from India and Arabia; grain from Egypt; silks from China; and slaves, furs, and other goods from Russia. The trade network was extensive: Silk found in a Viking grave in Sweden probably originated

in Byzantium. The Byzantine currency, the *bezant*, was accepted throughout the Mediterranean for some 700 years.

But as Constantinople gained prestige, competitive forces arose in Europe. Independent ideas in both politics and religion eventually led to significant theological differences between the Christians of Byzantium and the Christians of western Europe, who still followed the lead of Rome. In 800, when a grateful pope crowned Charlemagne emperor, Byzantine Christians respected the coronation, yet the empire was by then technically two sectors, east and west, governed by two different heads. Cooperation had existed for 500 years, but its hold was giving out. Byzantium had become its own empire; the Franks had carved out a new power. Latin had virtually disappeared as a common language, giving way to Greek in the east, German and the Latin-based Romance

languages (Italian, French, Portuguese, and Spanish) in the west.

We still use the term "byzantine" to describe a web of archaically intricate design. And the power struggles of the Byzantine emperors were surely tangled and labyrinthine affairs. The twists and turns of the Heraclian dynasty, which ruled from Constantinople through the seventh century, continued into the eighth. Like their Roman predecessors, Byzantine emperors considered themselves God's representatives on earth. The emperor's word was law. His palace was a wonderland of riches and opulence, designed to emphasize his power and glorify his divine nature. Hundreds of courtiers, officials, guards, and servants busied themselves in and about the emperor's sumptuous household, the hierarchy among them designated with impressive titles and symbolic robes. Anyone who came calling was humbled beyond words by the stately grandeur and rigid pomp of the place; no one without official business dared presume upon the emperor's presence. To be born into the royal family was to know intrigue from birth.

Becoming emperor at 16, Justinian II immediately formed treaties with the Arabs, receiving tribute and land. He marched his army west into the Slavic regions of Thrace and Macedonia, part of today's Greece, where he won territory and new soldiers. He could be as ruthless with his ministers as with his enemies, and in 695, ten years after taking the throne, he was deposed and his nose was cut off—for which he earned the nickname Rhinotmetus, "cut-nosed." He was exiled to the Crimean Peninsula, on the outskirts of known civilization at the time. Within three years, the new emperor was also noseless and out of

ICONOCLASM

The Clash Between Image & Spirit

In 730, Byzantine emperor Leo III issued a decree outlawing the pictorial representation of religious figures such as Jesus, Mary, and the saints. While the early Christian Church did not venerate portraits of Jesus or the saints, by the end of the sixth century, icons played a major part in the Catholic faith, believed to be a way to increase knowledge of and reverence for holy figures. Pope Gregory I even claimed that icons were the Bible of the illiterate.

Obeying Leo's decree, the iconoclasts—literally, image breakers—went about destroying the images in churches and monasteries. They believed they were following the commandment that forbids worship of graven images. Leo may truly have viewed

icons as sinful, or he may have been trying to strengthen the power of the state. In either case, the result was conflict and division.

Protests and riots erupted from clergy and laity alike, setting off more than a century of debate over iconography in the Christian religion. Theologians and artists who valued icons migrated west to Italy, where Pope Gregory II had openly rebuked Leo's policy and established the doctrinal independence of Rome. Monks throughout the Byzantine Empire opposed iconoclastic measures and faced persecution and execution under Leo's successor, Constantine V. Iconoclasm was finally abandoned as an imperial policy in 843, but the split between eastern and western Christianity remained. ∎

work, and his replacement was plotting against Justinian II, who had escaped his exile and found refuge with the khan of the Khazars in Russia.

After marrying the sister of the khan, Justinian II discovered that the new Byzantine emperor had bribed the khan to kill him. He raised an army and made his way back to Constantinople. When his allies let him down, he crawled through an aqueduct, regained control of the throne, and had the current emperor executed. During his second reign, from 705 to 711, Justinian II rekindled Byzantine relations with the pope, but he overstepped in seeking revenge on former opponents. After one too many mass executions, he and his family were killed, and the dynasty that had begun a century before with Heraclius finally came to an end.

The next emperor who made a lasting mark in Byzantine history was Leo III, who ruled from 717 to 741 (and who should not be confused with Pope Leo III, who crowned Charlemagne some decades later). Emperor Leo III managed to beat back another Arab assault on the empire, and he brought out a new legal manual. His was considered more practical and liberal than Justinian's earlier one, although the new one did codify corporal punishments, such as cutting off the nose, feet, and hands.

THE FIRST ICONOCLASTS

Leo III is perhaps best known for supporting the new religious principle known as iconoclasm. Byzantium had a long and rich history of decorating its churches with images of Jesus and the saints, before which the faithful would

Cyril and Methodius, Byzantine missionaries and educators, converted Slavic peoples to Orthodox Christianity and devised a new alphabet so they could translate the Bible into local languages. Russian uses Cyrillic today.

pray. In contrast, the newly developing religion of Islam had at its core a deep distrust of the physical portrayal of any prophet or holy figure. Muslims had been so successful conquering former Byzantine lands, some began to argue

that their dominance should be interpreted as a sign from God: Perhaps God himself disapproved of the Christian use of icons that portray the faces and bodies of holy saints and prophets. In 730, Emperor Leo III decreed that icon

ICON An icon is a painting or a sculpture that depicts a holy figure and is used in religious practice. Those who believe in icon worship use the icons as an aid to prayer, believing that the physical representations serve as intermediaries between them and God.

These illustrations depict scenes from *The Song of Roland,* one of the oldest works of French literature, a 12th-century epic that tells the 8th-century story of Charlemagne and the Battle of Roncesvalles. Above, Roland calls his men to battle by blowing a horn; below, the horn becomes a weapon in battle.

worship should end in Byzantium. His military gains, together with the consent of key church leaders, seemed proof that his policy of iconoclasm (from the Greek for "image breaking") was divinely inspired. All over Constantinople and beyond, thousands of icons were taken

> THERE SHALL BE
> REJECTED AND REMOVED
> AND CURSED . . .
> EVERY LIKENESS
> WHICH IS MADE OUT
> OF ANY MATERIAL
> AND COLOR WHATEVER
> BY THE EVIL ART
> OF PAINTERS.

> ICONOCLASTIC COUNCIL
> *Constantinople, 754*

down, painted out, or smashed. To many, this policy amounted to sacrilege—outraged crowds killed officials who tried to remove a statue of Christ from a public place. A split arose between iconoclasts and iconophiles—"image lovers." Tens of thousands of iconophilic monks fled for their lives to Italy, where they found the Roman Church more accepting of physical representations of Christ and the saints to which they prayed.

From 741 to 775 Constantine V, Leo III's son, enjoyed a long and energetic reign marked by stunning victories over the Bulgars and the Arabs. His son Leo IV reigned a mere five years, but his ambitious wife, Irene, claimed her own notorious place in history.

Regent for her son Constantine VI, Irene set about repealing the iconoclasm

decrees. The action met with approval from the majority of her subjects, as well as the clergy, who argued that praying to icons was not the same as idolatry. Once Constantine VI grew up, he and his mother began plotting against each other. To silence dissenting uncles, he had four of them detongued and one of them blinded. Just as reprehensibly, he banished his wife so that he could marry his mistress.

For a while his mother, Empress Irene, was able to maintain sole rule. But when a rebellion broke out in Asia Minor in 790, Constantine VI took the throne and banished his mother from court. But she was far from finished. Conspiring with bishops and courtiers, she maneuvered her way back into favor, then had her son arrested, blinded, and likely killed.

For five years, from 797 to 802, Irene claimed the title of emperor—not empress. During that time she contemplated a marriage with Charlemagne. Such a marriage would have represented a remarkable alliance between the two arms of the empire, Byzantine and Roman—but it did not occur. Instead a cabal of generals deposed Irene and exiled her to the island of Lesbos, just off the coast of Turkey. And there she died, in 803, at the age of 51. For restoring icons to religious practice, many historians and commentators through the ages have overlooked Irene's violent past and considered her a saint, although she has never been officially canonized.

The legal status of religious icons remained the issue during military conflicts through the next few years. Iconoclasm was finally outlawed in 843, during the reign of Emperor Michael III. (In fact, his regent mother enacted the decree, since Michael was only five at the time.) By this point the bitterness over iconoclasm had created the rift between what

THE SILVER PENNY

England's First Standardized Coin

King Offa rose to power in the English region of Mercia in 757. One of the most powerful Anglo-Saxon kings, he unified most of southern England and established the country's first uniformly minted coin: the silver penny.

A previous coin, the *sceat*, had been minted in Kent, but Offa's silver penny was the first with a uniform size and weight. It invariably bore Offa's name and usually that of the issuing mint as well. These coins often bore portraits of Offa and displayed a high quality of workmanship derived from Roman and Germanic influences. Some coins, in typical Roman fashion, bore the name and portrait of Offa's wife, Cynethryth.

Offa's coins have been found throughout continental Europe as well, an indication of their widely accepted value and of the esteemed position of Offa himself. The standards governing coinage established by Offa continued to be used in England for over 700 years, making his little penny a remarkably influential coin. ■

Silver pennies stamped with the name Offa Rex—King Offa—were England's first true currency of guaranteed value.

THE WORLD IN THE EIGHTH CENTURY

Trade and exploration spurred in part by the advance of Islam led to further contact between various regions of the world. Muslim seafarers traveled from the Persian Gulf to the South China Sea. They carried ivory, pearls, incense, and spices to India, Vietnam, and China, and they returned with silk, paper, ink, tea, and porcelain. They also traded with the east coast of Africa and the Mediterranean. Silk Road trade remained vibrant.

Religions spread along the routes of commerce. Buddhism traveled through Korea and southern Asia into Japan and Oceania, while Islam pushed into western China. Indeed, China's western border was a place of contention as the powerful Tang dynasty led campaigns against Arabs in present-day Kazakhstan. Yet China remained economically and culturally strong, and art—especially poetry—flourished.

Japan grew economically as well, and the city of Nara became a prominent urban center. Meanwhile, in the Pacific Islands, the Srivijaya kingdom extended its domain throughout Sumatra, Java, and the Malay Peninsula, Buddhism becoming the dominant religion.

Central and South America saw the decline of formerly stable civilizations, including the Moche and Nasca of Peru and the Zapotecs of Oaxaca in Mexico; even the great city of Teotihuacan was attacked and burned by invading Toltec, but the Maya continued to prosper. In North America, the Caddo of the south-central states built alliances and engaged in long-distance trading. ■

CADDO CULTURE On the plains of present-day Texas and Oklahoma, the mound-building Caddo culture prospers. Known as able farmers and craftsmen, the Caddo trade surplus crops and goods across long distances and develop a loose federation of local tribes.

MSHATTA PALACE This desert castle near Amman, Jordan, is a classic example of early Islamic architecture, blending Roman and Byzantine traditions with those of the Middle East. Islam continues to spread throughout the region, introducing new art forms and mores.

TIKAL TEMPLE The observatory at Tikal, in present-day Guatemala, demonstrates the advanced astronomical knowledge of the Maya. It is situated so that in certain years the planets Venus and Jupiter align perfectly over its highest point.

Arctic

North America

Pacific Ocean

EQUATOR

South America

Atlantic Ocean

EMPEROR XUANZONG A silk print shows Xuanzong, the seventh emperor of the Tang dynasty, who rules from 712 to 756, as China reaches the height of its power. He enacts bureaucratic reforms, revives the canal system, and leads military campaigns into surrounding regions.

BAGHDAD Founded in 762 as the Abassid capital by Caliph Al Mansur, Baghdad quickly becomes one of the world's great cities, a center of Islam and Arab culture. Shortly after its founding, Baghdad matches Constantinople in size and population; it will reign unrivaled for nearly 500 years.

SRIVIJAYA KINGDOM The thriving Srivijaya empire extends its domain from Sumatra through Java, the Malay Peninsula, and southern Thailand, gaining economic power by controlling the Strait of Malacca.

would become two separate churches: the Catholic Church in Rome and the Orthodox Church in Byzantium.

As Michael reached adulthood, he conspired with his uncle Bardas to seize control of the throne from his mother and her circle of ministers. During his reign, Michael lent support to the brothers Cyril and Methodius, missionaries who became known as the apostles of the Slavs. Besides bringing the gospel to the Khazars and Moravians, these two men invented the Cyrillic alphabet as a tool for translating the scriptures into Old Church Slavonic and sharing them with those whom they hoped to convert. Based on Greek characters, the Cyrillic alphabet forms the basis for Russian writing today.

During campaigns against the Arabs, Michael III became influenced by a crafty Macedonian horse groom named Basil, who poisoned his mind against Bardas. In 865 Michael let Basil murder Bardas; the following year Basil murdered Michael. Basil then became emperor, initiating a new era of Macedonian rule. During this vigorous dynasty, Byzantium took back from the Arabs several great Roman cities: Antioch, Alexandria, Beirut, and Caesarea.

Anglo-Saxon England Emerges

Since the fifth century, the people called Saxons had been spreading out, and by the eighth century their territory stretched from the Baltic coast to northern Germany, west through Gaul, and across the channel to the coast of Britain. Moving westward, they clashed repeatedly with the Franks, especially in the late 700s.

The Bell of Clogher was wrought in Ireland in the eighth century and belonged to the monastery of Donaghmore, said to have been founded by St. Patrick 200 years before. The bell is now in the National Museum of Ireland in Dublin.

Under Charlemagne's relentless pressure, those in Germany became part of the Frankish empire.

But the Saxons farther west mingled with other invaders on the island of England, most notably a Germanic tribe called Angles and a people of Scandinavian origin called Jutes. The Angles settled in Northumbria and Mercia (now northern and middle England), while the Jutes took to Kent and southern England. The Saxons adopted the vernacular of the Angles, a language they called English. The Anglo-Saxons, as they came to be known, dominated England until the Norman Conquest of 1066.

The Romans had vacated the British Isles in the early 400s. The Roman Christians who remained coexisted with the pagan Saxons, while ancient Celts still clung to distant kingdoms in Scotland and Ireland. Over the next 200 years Christianity gradually took hold of the entire island, starting with Wales and then spreading, thanks to such missionaries as St. Patrick.

In the late sixth century, St. Augustine, first archbishop of Canterbury, worked to convert the Anglo-Saxons. His effort was carried on by St. Benedict Biscop of Northumbria, the father of Benedictine monasticism in England. A highborn thane, Benedict forsook a life of privilege to devote himself to evangelizing. He went on five separate pilgrimages from Britain to Rome, which was no easy task in those times. He brought back books, pictures, saints' relics, liturgical vestments, and even a choir director. After so much travel, he was unable to walk during his last few years. But the famous monasteries he founded in Wearmouth and Jarrow established a tradition of scholarship and art that influenced all of northwestern Europe. The finest of all the monastic arts that flourished in eighth-century England was manuscript illumination; many exquisite examples survive.

From the pen of one of Benedict's students, St. Bede, comes much of our knowledge of Anglo-Saxon life and history. Called the Venerable Bede, this man created a five-volume *Ecclesiastical History of the English People* that starts with Roman raids on Britain in the first century B.C., moves through the missionary appearance of St. Augustine in

RELIC A relic originally meant a preserved part of the body of a saint or holy figure and came to mean anything that had been in physical contact with a holy person, like clothing or possessions. Considered sacred, relics were displayed in ornate boxes called reliquaries.

Kent, and continues up through the author's own lifetime. Though the focus is church history and legends, the texture of daily life seeps through the text. For example, Bede writes that when England "began to abound with such plenty of grain as had never been known in any age before," a sense of luxury developed, leading to "drunkenness, animosity, litigiousness, contention, envy, and other such like crimes."

Archaeology in the British Isles fills out the picture of Anglo-Saxon life. In Northumberland, on the border of Scotland, aerial photographers in 1949 noticed the outlines of a complex of buildings now identified as Yeavering Palace, a royal villa belonging to Anglo-Saxon kings including Edwin, who ruled Northumbria from 616 to 633. The Venerable Bede describes sermons and baptisms there, identifying the place as Ad Gefrin, "at the hill of the goats." Ruins suggest that the complex included a great hall, an enclosed area where animals grazed, and a Roman-inspired amphitheater. Like many Anglo-Saxon communities, it was built atop an old Roman settlement.

In the days of Yeavering, the landscape was dotted with fenced farmsteads. Fields were planted in oats, wheat, rye, and barley (used for a thick beer), and farm animals included horses, sheep, cattle, goats, pigs, and dogs. Well-to-do farmers had iron plows, though most of the land and much of the equipment was owned by a lord, to whom the farmer gave a share of the produce. Kinship was the closest of all social bonds. Social classes were stratified by a family or clan's *wergild*—"man payment." Indeed, conventional legal values were assigned to every person, animal, and thing.

PERSONAE

EMPRESS IRENE

The Woman Who Would Be Emperor

Empress of Byzantium for 27 years, Irene was born an orphan in the shrunken provincial town of Athens, Greece. She married in 769 and became empress in 775. Five years later her husband died—some suspect that Irene may have had a hand in his demise—and she became ruler of the Byzantine Empire, serving as regent to her ten-year-old son.

As empress, Irene was strong willed and ambitious, and soon she threw her influence against the forces of iconoclasm. Despite resistance, she succeeded in temporarily restoring icon veneration in 787, by which time her son, Constantine VI, was coming of age and becoming resentful of his continued subordination. Constantine seized power in 790 but made his mother co-ruler two years later. In 797, Irene conspired against her son, had him blinded, and assumed control of the empire, calling herself not empress but emperor. Irene was the first woman ever to become sole ruler of the Byzantine Empire, a post she retained for five years until deposed by palace officials in 802. ∎

Byzantine Empress Irene reigned for 27 years, despite hostility from her political enemies, her allies, and her own family.

Up through the ninth century, England encompassed several kingdoms: Northumbria stretched north and east, straddling today's boundary between England and Scotland. To the south lay smaller kingdoms—Wales, Mercia, and Wessex to the west; Sussex, Kent, Essex, and East Anglia to the east. Some of these place-names are still used today, while the rest remain a part of the culture, even though they may have been replaced officially.

Anglo-Saxon society was distinctly stratified, the levels determined by ownership of property and slaves. A freeman of the lowest rank was known as a *ceorl,* from which "churl" derives. In some places the next highest rank was noble, which was attained either by birth or service to the king. In Kent, the wergild of a noble was three times that of a ceorl; in other places it was six times. Both ceorls and nobles could possess slaves, known in other parts of Europe as serfs (from a Latin word for "servant"). In other places, lower classes were distinguished as, in ascending order, *cottar* (cottager), *villein* (from which the word "villain" derives), and *sokeman* (one under the legal jurisdiction of another). Above all was the king: He could grant land and favors, and he also had a number of rights. He could demand compensation for offenses against himself or anyone in his protection; he could charge rent on all land; and he could demand military, construction, and other services.

A man accused of a crime could bring "oath helpers" to try to establish his innocence. For tough cases, a king might convene a *witenagemot,* a council of *witan;* these wise men consisted of local nobles, prelates, and officials. Or the accused might undergo a trial by ordeal, which

The *Book of Kells* is one of the few surviving examples of the Hiberno-Saxon artistic style, a combination of Germanic, Celtic, and Christian influences. An illuminated volume of the four Gospels, it may have been created in Scotland and carried to Ireland for protection during Viking raids.

put the verdict in God's hands. In the most popular method, a priest would say prayers and incantations over a cauldron of boiling water: "We beseech thee, O Lord, to send down from heaven thy Holy Spirit upon this water, which is now hot and steaming from the fire, that through it we may have a just judgment upon this man." A judge would drop a stone into the water, and the accused would reach in and pull it out. His hand was then bound in linen. If there was no infection after three days, he was presumed innocent. In a variant of this trial, the accused was bound by rope and thrown into a pond; if he sank, he was considered guilty.

By the eighth century, Christianity had spread across all of England, yet the Anglo-Saxons held on to their legends and language. The Middle English of Chaucer and the modern English of Shakespeare developed directly from the Anglo-Saxon language, or Old English. Middle English, in use from the middle of the 11th century to the middle of the

> AND NEXT BY THE HAIR
> INTO HALL WAS BORNE
> GRENDEL'S HEAD...
> AN AWE TO CLAN
> AND QUEEN ALIKE,
> A MONSTER OF
> MARVEL: THE MEN
> LOOKED ON.
>
> *BEOWULF*
> **Circa 700**

15th century, incorporated many Latin and French words, but at its core still were the strongly inflected growls of Anglo-Saxon. For that reason, the English language includes words with both Germanic and Latin origins.

The greatest extant piece of Anglo-Saxon writing, the epic poem *Beowulf*, probably dates to the early 700s. Written by an unknown author, it comes out of the German heroic tradition and fuses

Norse legends with historic events. Like Bede's work, but written in the guttural, consonant-loaded vernacular, it gives us a wonderful window onto medieval English life. We see a king and his followers gathered in a great hall like Ad Gefrin, boasting of their prowess and courage, cheering and toasting those who prove their mettle by bringing back spoils from the battle—like the hero Beowulf, who displays the severed arm of the monster Grendel and, for his bravery, is rewarded with riches from the king and songs and all-night feasting in his honor.

The Anglo-Saxon culture was distinctly different from the Frankish, Islamic, and Byzantine cultures that were emanating from other geographic centers in the medieval world of the eighth century. Yet all shared a common impulse: the desire to build new and viable social, political, and religious identities from out of the ruins of the Roman Empire—and, in some cases, literally on top of those ruins.

BEOWULF

A Hero Meets a Monster—and the Monster's Mother

Beowulf, one of the earliest and most elaborate examples of Old English literature, is the first known European epic to be written in a vernacular tongue. It was set down in its modern form by an unknown poet sometime between A.D. 700 and 750, but its origins may extend over one hundred years earlier to the heroic traditions of continental Germanic balladeers, whose art was sung, not read, and passed down by word of mouth. From the original recitations, the eighth-century poet borrowed aspects of the story, themes, meter, and style, but he also undoubtedly added his own commentary and reflections, including an explicit Christian veneer.

The legend is set in sixth-century Scandinavia. Some characters and events may be historical, but the plot is pure folklore. Beowulf and his men come from Sweden to Denmark to challenge the monster Grendel, who has been terrorizing an ally's kingdom. Victory is swift but impermanent, as Beowulf incurs the wrath of Grendel's mother and a fire-breathing dragon. A somber, elegiac tone pervades most of the poem, which closes with Beowulf's death.

Written at a crossroads of history between the Anglo-Saxon and the Viking invasions of England, *Beowulf* depicts the traditions, ideals, and mores of the very people who were soon to raid the poet's own homeland of England. ■

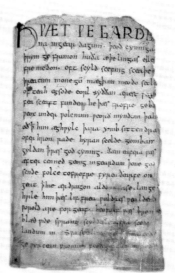

A single fragile, charred manuscript is the only existing copy of the famous *Beowulf*.

The tunic formed the foundation of the medieval wardrobe, worn by peasants and nobility alike. This tenth-century Egyptian example, made of linen, shows simple embroidery work, a humble effort in the spirit of adornment.

CLOTHING OF THE MEDIEVAL WORLD

Clothing in the medieval era ranged from the simple functional garments of laborers and peasants to the elaborately draped costumes of the nobility. Ordinary fabrics were linen spun from flax grown in northern Europe and the Middle East, and wool from various coarse- to silky-haired breeds of sheep. Luxury fabrics, such as silk and velvet and thread wrapped in gold and silver came from the Far East especially China, where silk had been woven since 3000 B.C.

Buttons grew in importance through the Middle Ages. Typically made of coral, copper, or glass, they were first considered an extravagant decoration sold by jewelers rather than a functional item. But beginning in 13th-century Italy, buttons were used to fasten sleeves and bodices, leading to figure-accentuating dresses and tight, elegant sleeves.

Sleeves themselves were often one of the more lavish elements of medieval dress. A person might don an ornately decorated, fuller sleeve to go out, while a basic sleeve would be worn to work around the house. Sleeves often detached from the tunic, so that a work sleeve could be replaced with a clean dress sleeve. Beneath the main garment, nobility often wore thin tunics and shorts or tights. Tights were not elastic, and so had to be laced from waist to foot; soles on the feet of the tights allowed them to function as shoes.

Hats took on many shapes and ornaments. Popular among women—yet perhaps more in our modern imagination than in actuality—were tall, cone-shaped hats adorned with veils. Simple bonnets were worn for chores and labor. In the fields, peasants often wore large-brimmed straw hats to shield their faces from the sun, while noblemen typically sported rounder, flatter hats with upturned brims. Shoes, made of leather and pointy in shape, were owned almost exclusively by nobility.

Form-fitting bodices and tight sleeves characterized women's dresses of the late medieval era in Europe. Tall, cone-shaped hats adorned with veils may have completed the ensemble, though not as often as our fairy-tale images might suggest.

Shoes were almost exclusively the province of nobility, and even among the wealthy they were something of a luxury, not a part of everyday attire at all. Most shoes were made of leather and offered little in the way of protection or support.

People of means liked to display their good fortune, in part, with elaborately draped clothing made of costly imported materials.

Noblemen wore hats with upturned brims and a rounded or flat shape. Such hats would not be useful for workers, who needed hats that shielded them from all kinds of weather.

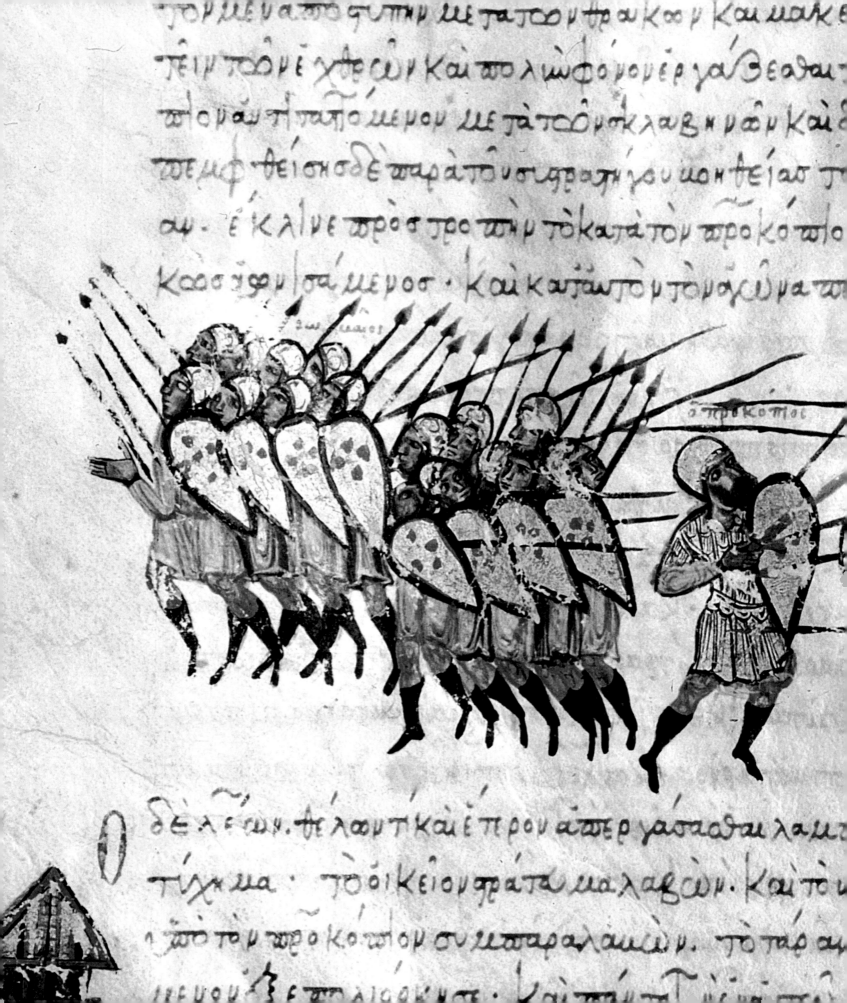

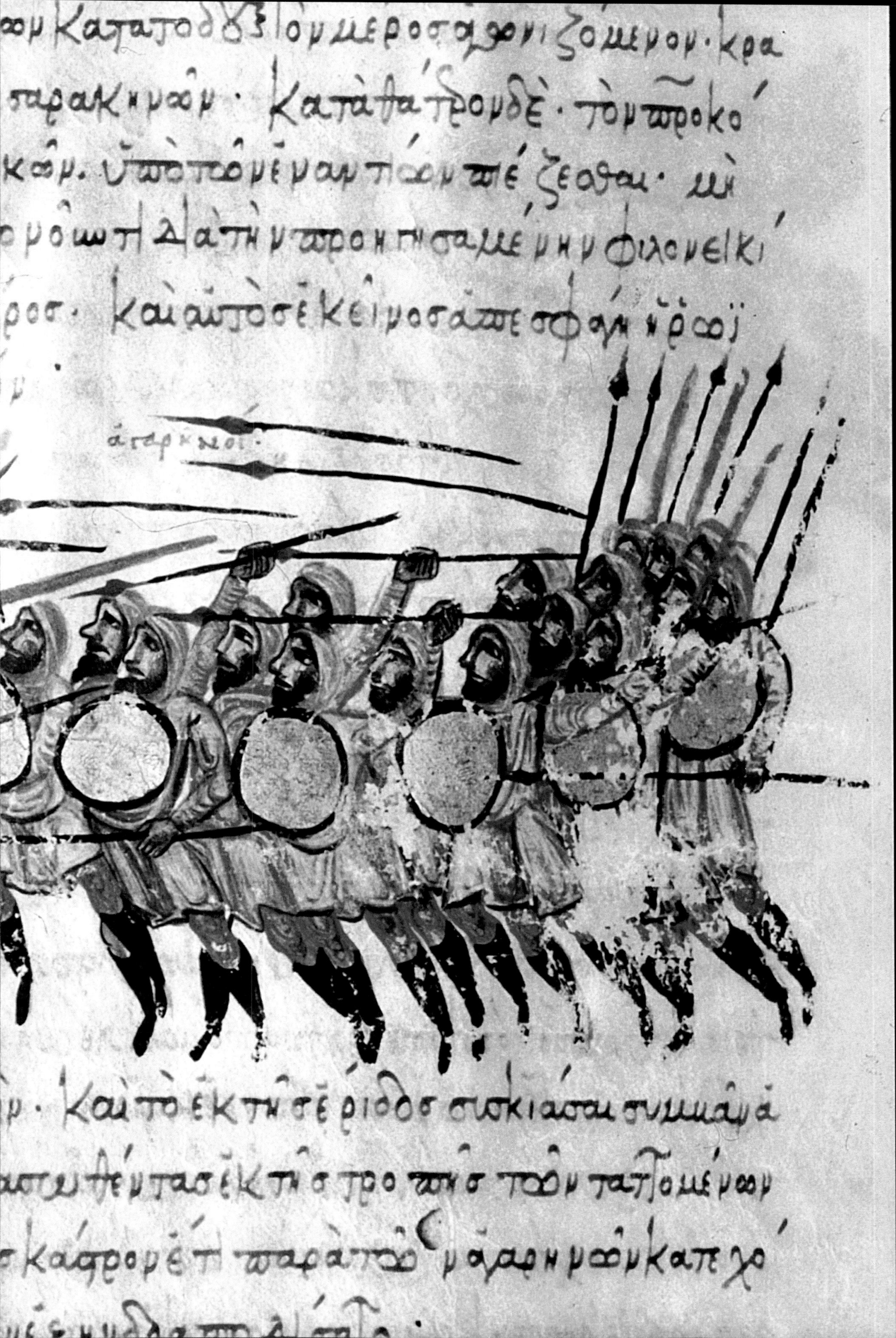

6 A WORLD DIVIDED

800 – 900

THE STORY OF THE MEDIEVAL WORLD OF THE 800S IS POPULATED BY REMARKABLE MEN AND women, leaders of their time, who followed no established regimen or routines. Through their actions and inclinations, for good or ill, they carved out their roles in society. Emperors and caliphs, queens and kings promoted scholarship and the arts, making their cities—Baghdad, Córdoba, Paris, Constantinople—more beautiful. Blind to their own mortality and lacking established patterns of succession, however, one ruler after another built a power structure that collapsed soon after he died. Religious affiliations remained the one lasting link through all such permutations. Three powerhouses arose: the Kingdom of the Franks, united by Charlemagne; the empire of Islam, arising out of Baghdad but stretching as far west as Spain; and the Byzantine Empire, defining itself more and more as the legitimate heir of Rome. Religion was a tremendous force, both at the political level and in the daily life of rich and poor. While imperial forces rallied behind one religion or another—Roman Christianity, Byzantine Christianity, or Islam—in day-to-day life, traditions blended. Jews and Christians living under Muslim rule followed their own practices; pagans converted to Christianity, which happened more easily since its practices borrowed elements from their own festivals and pantheons. Institutionalized religion assimilated popular religion as much as possible, and that which it could not assimilate, it demonized, setting up the grounds for bigger schisms yet to come.

During this century England evolved on its own, a distinctive branch of the European culture of the Franks and the Roman Church. Tribal realms that had been separate since the departure of the Roman rulers began combining into a single kingdom. Anglo-Saxon kings had battled for territory and made deals throughout the previous century, but now, in the ninth century, a new enemy made cohesion a matter of survival. Starting with easy monasteries, Danish Vikings made hits along the coastline, robbing, pillaging, and murdering. A strong line of kings—Egbert, Aethulwulf, and Alfred the Great—gathered armies from various regions and won key battles against the invaders, keeping them from taking over. This father-son-grandson dynasty, ruling most of the century, was the first to bring all of England together under one ruler.

For the Vikings, England was but the first target. Scandinavian raiders penetrated deep into Russia, Germany, and the Mediterranean. Wherever there were rivers to navigate,

The Ada group of illuminated manuscripts—named for a woman who may have been Charlemagne's half sister—is the earliest known Carolingian art.
PRECEDING PAGES: Byzantine forces (left, with long shields) retreat from advancing Arab soldiers (right, with round shields) in this chronicle by a medieval historian.

the Vikings penetrated, seeking booty. The ruddy, blue-eyed, merciless pirates swooped through like the Vandals and barbarians of an earlier age, spreading terror through a Europe that was in many places too disorganized to put up a strong resistance. Communities cowered and prayed—or ran off in terror. Those who did not resist the marauders were often spared, and Vikings settled permanently here and there, blending their culture and genes with the local population. The Frankish kingdom, churned up by its own internal wars, did all it could to fend off the Viking assaults. Recently unified under Charlemagne, the kingdom was split among his three grandsons, who then kept up a steady, bloody wrestling match, further dividing the kingdom.

The culture of Islam, led by the Abbasid caliphate, grew in achievements, wealth, and influence. The Abbasid dynasty gained power over all the Muslim world save Moorish Spain. Like the Umayyads before them, they struggled with wars external and internal, but they counterbalanced those struggles with tremendous cultural and commercial gains. With the caliphate now in Baghdad and other Islamic states allowed more autonomy, an elite ruling class could enjoy the riches brought by a widespread trade network. Sumptuous palaces and mosques went up, and scholars, poets, and artists brightened the torch of civilization.

Likewise, the Byzantine Empire thrived, this period representing new building, scholarship, and cultural achievement, particularly in the second half of the century. With fewer attacks to fend off and a final repeal of iconoclasm, Constantinople and her satellites could

THE NINTH CENTURY

801
Charlemagne takes Barcelona from Islamic forces.

812
Byzantine rulers recognize Charlemagne's title.

814
Charlemagne dies; Louis the Pious succeeds him as emperor.

842 & 851
Vikings attack London.

ca 841
Dublin is founded as a Viking base and slave market.

860
Two hundred Viking ships raid Constantinople.

867
Macedonian dynasty begins in Byzantium.

872
First hospital established in Cairo.

881
Pope John VIII crowns Charles III emperor.

This coin from the reign of Charlemagne, with a cross where a royal portrait would normally be, was testament to the growing political sway of Christianity.

focus less on destruction and more on creation. Byzantium stood apart from Rome and its allegiance to the pope—more and more often, the Orthodox and Catholic Churches charted their own independent futures. As the two branches of Christianity competed for souls, they used and were used by rulers in a symbiosis of politics and religion.

THE CHANGING MAP OF ENGLAND
From the eighth to the tenth centuries, England struggled toward unification in a haphazard fashion, as friction between kingdoms flared and died. Vigorous government, a Christian culture, and increasing wealth animated the land. The so-called Heptarchy of Anglo-Saxon kingdoms divided the land into seven distinct realms: Mercia (central), Kent (southeast), Northumbria (north), Wessex (southwest), Sussex (south), Essex (southeast), and East Anglia (east)—familiar place names, part of the vernacular if not the official geographic nomenclature in Britain today.

In the early seventh century, when Augustine and other missionaries were beginning to Christianize southern England, the rest of the island was controlled by a number of Anglo-Saxon kings. Edwin, who died in 633, was the first such king to become overlord, ruling all the English kingdoms but Kent. The Northumbrian ruler did make one significant conquest in Kent—he married a Kentish princess, under whose influence he himself converted. He took north Wales, but in so doing apparently wrote his death warrant. A Welsh king named Cadwallon of Gwynedd teamed up with a Mercian king, invaded Northumbria, and killed Edwin.

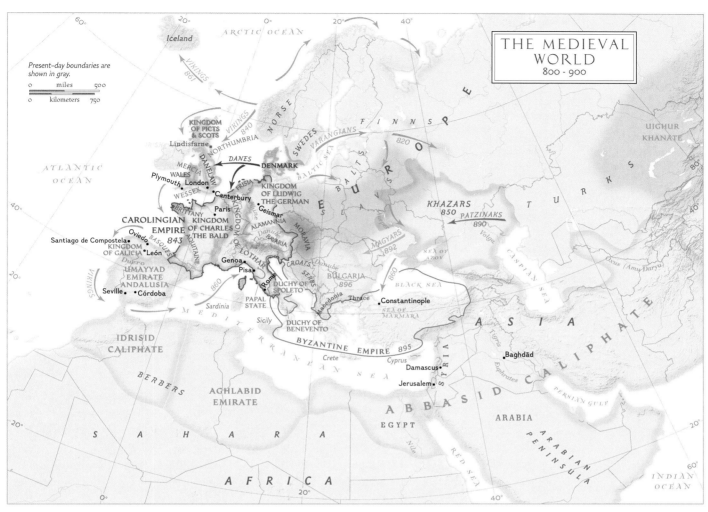

THE MEDIEVAL WORLD 800 - 900

The Carolingian Empire reached its largest extent the year Charlemagne died, 814, and was divided among his three grandsons in 843. The Muslim Empire fractured as well during this century, the Abbasid caliphate taking the largest share. Vikings fled crowded homelands, raiding mainland Europe and the British Isles and inhabiting Iceland.

The Mercian king, Penda, outlasted Cadwallon and became a powerful military leader who drove into Middle and East Anglia, killing three kings. Promoting paganism over Christianity, Penda reinvaded Northumbria. He was killed in 654 by a king named Oswiu, who let his former enemy's son take control of southern Mercia. Within a year the young man was murdered. Oswiu soon fell from power, but he had reconciled the region's Celtic and Roman churches.

Kings with colorful names—Wulfhere, Aethelwalh, Ecgfrith, Aethelred—duked it out as Mercia tried to extend its domain. By 716 a king named Aethelbald had gained control of all England's midlands, including London. In the 720s he captured Kent and Wessex. By staying in power until 757, he became the longest-lasting ruler of the Anglo-Saxons to date, calling himself the "king of Britain." Riotous living earned him a rebuke from St. Boniface and other German missionaries; he responded by loosening the tax burden on churches. Over his 51-year reign, he made too many enemies to die peacefully—his retainers killed him.

The next ruler, Offa, reigned from 757 to 796 and gained even more power and control, further solidifying England below Northumberland (in other words, south of the Humber River). Descendant of an ancient royal Mercian family, Offa was ruthless in putting down rebellions on the edges of the kingdom, thereby maintaining a tight-knit sovereignty. He practiced the age-old rule of creating family for diplomacy's sake: He married his daughters to Northumbrian and Wessex rulers and thus helped cement relations with his neighbors. Moreover, he reached out to continental leaders, giving the pope a larger hand in the English church and forging a commercial treaty with the Frankish king, Charlemagne. The latter referred to him as "dearest brother," and urged a marriage between his son and Offa's daughter.

As part of the deal, Offa wanted his own son to marry Charlemagne's daughter. The ensuing dispute led to a three-year moratorium on trade between the two regions. With the treaty, the English Channel was open again to trade, and economic stability returned. One of Offa's most noteworthy achievements augmented that stability—the creation of a mint in East Anglia, which produced coins bearing his likeness. Offa's economic resources made it possible for him to erect a great earthen dike marking the border with Wales; lasting to modern times, it forms the path of one of Britain's National Trails.

What of Northumbria—the lands north of the Humber River? This large northern kingdom was not simply a wilderness. The school of York, founded by a disciple of St. Bede, was an intellectual center that drew pupils from Ireland and the continent. A key figure in the school, the Anglo-Saxon scholar Alcuin (also called Ealhwine), lived from around 732 to 804.

Alcuin served as headmaster at York until invited by Charlemagne to head up his soon-to-be-famous school and scriptorium in Aachen. In a letter to Charlemagne, written about 800, he reminded the king, "The voice of the people is the voice of God."

Alcuin ultimately wrote a biography of Charlemagne, a primary source for our information about him. He was a seminal figure during the Carolingian Renaissance and helped develop Carolingian minuscule script, a new, uniform way of forming the letters of the Roman alphabet. Carolingian script eventually became the norm among those few who could write. A revolutionary advancement, it influenced reading and writing for centuries. It is the basis of the type that we today call Roman.

LONGSHIPS ON THE HORIZON

With the death of Offa and, just a few weeks later, his son and heir, a ruler named Cenwulf took over in 796, and he enlisted the aid of Charlemagne to help quell the Northumbrians. But he lacked the power of Offa, and when a stronger king came along, Mercia's days as England's foremost kingdom ended.

That king's name was Egbert. Son of a Kentish underking, Egbert had been exiled by Offa and spent his youth in Charlemagne's court in Aachen. Returning to England after Offa's death, he took the throne of Wessex in 802, conquered what is now Cornwall, and by 829 had become ruler of Mercia and everything to the south. Even Northumbria considered him its king. He was thus the first overlord of all England. Yet that glory was short-lived; within a year Mercia broke away.

Egbert nevertheless remained in power for almost another decade, during which he fought an adversary the

IVAR THE BONELESS

Fearless Invader Despite the Name

During the ninth century, Scandinavian mariners known as Vikings struck out from their homelands to trade, settle, conquer, raid, and plunder. One of the most colorful of those, at least in name, was Ivar the Boneless. Details of Ivar's biography blend history with legend, and theories abound as to the origin of his name. Some say he had a debilitating brittle-bone disease and had to be carried into battle on a shield. Others see the nickname as ironic, contrary to his strength, an interpretation confirmed by history.

In 865 a "great heathen army" flooded the eastern coast of England. Led by Ivar and his brothers, this army went on to subdue the kingdoms of East Anglia, Northumbria, and a large part of Mercia, carving out a new Viking territory known as Danelaw. Then they attacked Wessex, in the south of England, but were repulsed by the Anglo-Saxon king Alfred, who fended off Viking attacks for the 28 years of his reign.

Scattered Viking settlers remained on the agricultural lands of Danelaw after Ivar's invasion, but never did a Viking army subdue the whole of England. On the contrary, the common threat of Viking incursions encouraged the unification of regional Anglo-Saxon kingdoms into a single large state. At the time of Ivar's death around 873, however, Danelaw was still powerful and seemingly invincible. ∎

Norse craftsmen in Iceland produced this silver cross, crafting a dragon's head on one end.

Charles II, also known as Charles the Bald, a Frankish king, receives a lavishly illuminated Bible in this ninth-century illustration.

likes of which had not been seen in English history.

Up on the isolated northeast coast of England, the monastery of Lindisfarne had since 635 perched on a skinny peninsula jutting out into the North Sea. One day in June 793, longships emerged from that frigid gray expanse of water. Pairs of rock-muscled oarsmen rowed the ships, which had prows of serpents' and horses' heads. Perhaps the monks believed the Vikings had come on some friendly mission, and, in fact, the boatmen themselves were not sure of their own intentions. Yet coming ashore, when they found the monastery much richer in treasure than any place they had seen before, and so poorly defended, they could not resist, and they plundered it for its silver and gold. They killed anyone who resisted, drowning some, taking others off in chains, and leaving a few stripped naked in humiliation. Lindisfarne was lucky to have survivors to record the event, the first known Viking raid on Europe. "Never before," moaned Alcuin, "has such a terror appeared in Britain."

So began a period of attacks that went on through more than two centuries, waged by the dreaded seafaring warriors of the north. Within two years they had raided the monasteries at Jarrow (south of Lindisfarne) and Iona (all the way around the north end of the British Isles, on an island in the west of Scotland). By the early 800s, coastal monasteries had nearly disappeared from Britain under repeated Viking assaults, their church-

Lothair I attempted to seize full control of his grandfather Charlemagne's empire but fomented civil wars against his brothers and half brother.

men murdered, their treasuries pilfered. These Norse raiders were impressed by the wealth that the Christians of England and Ireland had accumulated; in the long run, they came to be impressed by the apparent power of the Christians' God, too.

Recruiting an army of Britons in Cornwall, Danish Vikings went up against Egbert in 838, near the end of

the king's life. At Hingston Down, just north of today's Plymouth, Egbert decisively crushed the invaders. Yet this one victory could hardly hold back the unceasing waves of Viking intrusion. Egbert's son Aethulwulf shrewdly realized that only by combining his Wessex forces with those of Mercia could the English stand a chance of long-term victory. In 851 Aethulwulf beat a Viking army that had marched on Canterbury and London, but with such a long coastline to protect, he could not ultimately keep the Norsemen out.

By this time the Vikings were picking off other easy European targets, although England continued to bear the brunt. Over time, their invasions had an unexpected effect. As local citizens banded together, organizing themselves to defend against the next Viking invasion, a sense of community developed, helping to unify England as well as other northern European states. At the same time, arriving Vikings settled in and colonized the places where they had been raiding or trading. The Danish Vikings upped the ante, deciding not simply to rob and pillage but to conquer the English lands. One of Aethelwulf's sons finally succeeded in subduing them: the man we now call Alfred the Great.

Alfred lived from 849 to 899 and became king in 871. He scored a major victory over the Danes in 877, driving them from Wessex to northeastern Mercia. When they attempted another fight the next year, Alfred's tenacious forces

LONGSHIPS Sleek wooden Viking boats up to 100 feet long, powered by square sails and multiple oarsmen. Their tall prows were sometimes adorned with mythological figureheads. Shallow drafts allowed coastal navigation. Some may have reached a speed of ten knots.

pushed them back to East Anglia. There they settled, and their king was baptized. One way Alfred beat the Vikings was to build his own fleet—longer and swifter than those of the Danish, his boats held 60 or more oarsmen. He also erected a series of 33 forts some 40 miles apart, each manned by a peasant militia; captured Danes were hanged as an example.

For the rest of the century, England was relatively peaceful. Though monasticism had been practically wiped out, Alfred was able to renew interest in learning and the arts. Viewing the Viking invasions as God's punishment for neglecting loftier pursuits, he enacted enduring educational and judicial reforms. He was literate—one of the first medieval royals to be so—and championed St. Augustine's *City of God* and Boethius's *Consolation of Philosophy,* turning their Latin into Anglo-Saxon and correcting their ideas when he found it necessary. He set up the British system of shires, or counties, which continues to this day. And he established a sort of taxation system, regulating the amount of tribute due to him from thanes.

THE VIKING GRIP

The English were only the first to feel the icy grip of the Vikings. The Norse pirates were formidable in their daring booty raids, hacking their way into the farthest reaches of the civilized world. Centuries of trade and peaceful travel before this era had given the Norse an extensive knowledge of the coasts and trade routes of Europe. Swedish Vikings rowed down uncharted Russian rivers into the Black and Caspian Seas. They set up a dynasty in faraway Kiev, and even tried to take Constantinople. Impressed by the Vikings' gumption, the Byzan-

> LO, IT IS NEARLY 350 YEARS
> THAT WE AND OUR FATHERS
> HAVE INHABITED
> THIS MOST LOVELY LAND,
> AND NEVER BEFORE
> HAS SUCH TERROR
> APPEARED IN BRITAIN
> AS WE HAVE NOW SUFFERED
> FROM A PAGAN RACE.

FROM ALCUIN TO KING ETHELRED
Northumbria, 793

PERSONAE

THEUTBERGA

Medieval Marriage Woes

Theutberga's arranged marriage to the Frankish Prince Lothair II sparked such a controversy that it needed a pope as final arbiter. At the time, marriages served many functions among the nobility, including the acquisition of power and the production of heirs. Theutberga's family was to gain prominence in the royal court and Lothair's dynastic line was to continue; but after two years without children, Lothair initiated efforts, on the grounds of incest, to divorce Theutberga and marry his mistress, with whom he already had a son.

Theutberga's brother Hucbert, with whom her husband accused her of relations, was the abbot of a wealthy monastery. He came to her defense. Lothair appealed to two loyal archbishops, who sanctioned the divorce. At that, Theutberga appealed to Pope Nicholas I. In unprecedented fashion, Nicholas restored the marriage and deposed the two archbishops in an attempt to assert supreme papal primacy over church and state.

Theutberga and Lothair never had children. When he died in 869, the kingdom was divided between his uncles. ■

tine rulers recruited them into an elite military unit that for centuries served as imperial shock troops.

To the west, Danes and Norwegians probed into every inlet and stream from the North Sea to the Pyrenees Mountains in search of treasure and trade goods. They besieged Paris, ransacked Pisa, burned mosques in Andalusia, and even took slaves in North Africa. In western France, Viking bands occupied the lands they had ravaged. Their progeny, called the Normans, would prove significant in the history of Europe. One of them, William the Bastard, conquered England in 1066, disrupting Anglo-Saxon life and leaving an imprint on language, culture, and government that endures to this day.

Their homeland surrounded by cold seas and dotted with deep fjords, the Vikings became master mariners, their skill and bravery in the open waters unmatched in their day. Expert shipbuilders chose timber from dense Scandinavian forests; a shallow draft and light weight meant the boats could travel up streams. Large woolen sails powered the boats at sea. By adding a keel to the design of their vessels, they gained stability, improved steering control, and increased the speed and distance an expedition could travel. The Oseberg and Gokstad ships, excavated in the late 19th and early 20th centuries from Viking burial mounds in Norway, show what technological marvels Viking ships must have been. These two each measured more than 70 feet long and must have held about 30 oarsmen.

Especially vulnerable to Viking raids were churches—filled with silver and gold objects, and manned, if at all, by peace-loving monks. Churchgoers learned

Commerce and wealth flowed freely through the Golden Horn, as Constantinople's natural harbor was named.

CONSTANTINOPLE
GATEWAY TO THE EAST

Gold | Opulence | Iconography | Empire

Built on the crossroads between Asia and Europe and on the main waterway from the Black Sea to the Mediterranean, the city of Constantinople blossomed out of the ancient Greek maritime site of Byzantion and the later Roman settlement of Byzantium. The city began on a peninsula surrounded by the Golden Horn, a flooded valley that provided a natural harbor, and the Bosporus, with its challenging currents. The site proved to be incredibly strategic. In A.D. 330 the Roman emperor Constantine claimed the city as his new capital, calling it New Rome, and named it after himself: Constantinople. Constantine wanted to build a Christian city; although Christianity was swiftly taking hold throughout the empire, older pagan cities were not so easily converted, and a new city allowed the unthreatened development of the new religion. Constantinople's growth and success signaled the end of the old pagan empire and the beginning of a new Christian one.

The city grew quickly. Early in the fifth century, Theodosius II ordered new walls built to protect the population that had grown to nearly half a million. A powerful earthquake in 447 destroyed some of the Theodosian walls. They were restored and still surround the modern city.

In 532, dissatisfaction with government corruption led to the Nika revolt: disastrous riots that left the city destroyed and thousands of people dead. In response, the emperor Justinian I undertook a number of major projects, rebuilding many of the structures lost during the riots.

Of the new constructions, Hagia Sophia—the Church of Holy Wisdom—far surpassed anything else in size, grandeur, and beauty, and it remained unrivaled for centuries. Constructed of traditional Greco-Roman mortar and brick, the building's scale had never before been attempted and its dome, a common feature in churches from the period, spanned the largest space in the world at the time.

Earthquakes were a known threat in the area and, accordingly, the builders took special precautions; nonetheless, a massive earthquake destroyed the original dome two centuries after its

CONSTANTINOPLE THROUGH THE MIDDLE AGES

A.D. 413
A new city wall more than four miles long replaces one built by Constantine.

483-565
Justinian I seeks a *renovatio imperii,* "restoration of the empire."

532
The Nika Riots cause vast portions of the city to be burned.

537
The Byzantine Church of Hagia Sophia is completed.

542
The plague sweeps Constantinople, killing three out of five citizens.

610
Heraclius's North African fleet takes Constantinople; he becomes emperor.

726 & 730
Emperor Leo III bans icons in religious practice.

completion. Undeterred, workers shored up the walls and rebuilt the dome. Converted into a mosque in the 15th century, Hagia Sophia is now a museum, its sixth-century magnificence still visible to all who step through its doors today.

Despite the new monuments, the glorious New Rome was threatened when a plague swept the city in 542. More than half the people in the city died, leaving it paralyzed. Invading armies took advantage of its weakened state, but attacks by the Persians, the Arabs, and others between the 7th and 11th centuries did not shake the fortifications, and the city did not fall.

At the same time and in the centuries that followed, Constantinople regained prestige as trade developed, driven not by Byzantine merchants but by foreign merchants stationed in the city. When Venice provided military support against invading Normans, Emperor Alexios promised the Venetians that "all their desires would be satisfied." They received special trading privileges and were granted their own commercial district, which soon grew to be the largest and most prosperous neighborhood in the city. Soon other Italian states, including Pisa, Amalfi, and Genoa, gained similar status within Constantinople, an eminent

city that continued to be a major trading nexus throughout the Middle Ages.

The wealth brought in by trade did little to stop the city's decline during the 13th century, when the knights of the Fourth Crusade marched on Constantinople. Disgusted by false promises made by the newly instated emperor, the crusaders attacked Constantinople. The city fell on April 12, 1204, and was pillaged ruthlessly for several days. The crusaders looted obvious targets such as palaces and the homes of nobles, but they also plundered churches and mausoleums, carting off anything of value. In the following days, Baldwin of Flanders installed himself as emperor, while the Venetians took control of the church, but the next several decades proved to be the worst in Constantinople's history, as the city lay in ruins with no means or motivation to rebuild.

Situated on the Bosporus Strait, Constantinople had access to the trade routes of both the Mediterranean and Black Seas.

The Byzantine Empire came to an end in 1453 when Mehmed the Conqueror's Ottoman troops blocked the Bosporus and captured Constantinople. Mehmed was determined to rebuild the city. Considered broadminded and freethinking, he welcomed foreigners in the hope that trade would resume; he brought scholars from the West to his court and collected vast libraries in Greek and Latin; and he began construction on the Topkapi Palace, a magnificent edifice that sits on the tip of the Sultanahmet Peninsula, overlooking the Golden Horn and the Bosporus. It is still possible to stroll the grounds and hear the call to prayer from minarets built by Mehmed and by the sultans who came after him.

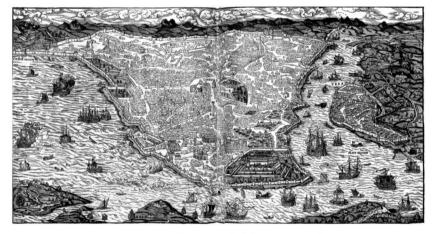

Sited strategically on an easily defensible peninsula that juts into the Bosporus Strait, passageway between Europe and Asia, Constantinople has served as the capital city of three empires.

740
An earthquake devastates the city and the surrounding countryside.

843
Icons are officially reinstated in worship.

1054
The pope excommunicates Constantinople's patriarch: the East-West schism.

1082
Venetians are given special trading privileges and living space in the city.

1204
Crusaders conquer Constantinople.

1261
Nicaean Greeks capture Constantinople, ending Latin occupation.

1453
Sultan Mehmed II names the city Istanbul; Hagia Sophia becomes a mosque.

a special prayer, "God, deliver us from the fury of the Northmen."

A typical warring party of two to ten Viking ships would land at a small, unprotected port, and several hundred warriors would storm in, often leaving towns behind in smoking ruins. Surprise attacks were lightning fast, over before the defenders could organize a resistance. Sometimes the Vikings massed a fleet of several hundred warships, overwhelming a region with sheer numbers. The warriors were wild in battle, shooting arrows, throwing spears, and swinging broadaxes to chop off limbs. They believed that if killed, they would be borne by warrior-maiden Valkyries to Valhalla, the Viking heaven, where they would battle all day, feast and drink all night. Tales of their cruelty abounded, like the legendary "blood eagle" method of killing a victim: A Viking attacker would split open a man's back and then yank out his lungs, so that with his final gasps, his lungs flapped like wings.

ACCORDING TO THEIR CUSTOM THE NORTHMEN PLUNDERED EASTERN AND WESTERN FRISIA AND BURNED DOWN THE TOWN OF DORDRECHT . . . WITH THEIR BOATS FILLED WITH IMMENSE BOOTY, INCLUDING BOTH MEN AND GOODS, [THE NORTHMEN] RETURNED TO THEIR OWN COUNTRY.

ANNALS OF XANTEN ABBEY
Germany, 846

These images of Viking brutality have overshadowed many positive aspects of their culture. They were skillful in decorative arts, as shown by the handsome cups, bracelets, and brooches that they made of intricately worked metal. Their tightly

metered poetry told the stories of their gods and espoused high ideals such as freedom and honor. In truth they traded as often as they raided, bringing furs and ivory southward. Trading networks included those connecting the Baltic to the Caspian and the Black Seas along the rivers of European Russia. Some Viking raids may have been prompted by overcrowding and hard times at home, where rocky lands offered limited opportunities for farming. Land in the Norse world was typically inherited by the eldest son; younger siblings may have needed to leave home to make their fortunes.

An Arab chronicler encountering Norse traders on the Volga River described them as "tall as date palms, blond and ruddy." Viking wives knew rights that other medieval women could scarcely imagine. They owned land, ran farms, kept their maiden names, and could divorce by simply stating their desire to do so to witnesses. Compared with feudal Europe, with its strict class

THE GROWTH OF DUBLIN

The Viking-Irish Connection

Driven from their Norwegian home by population pressure, superior maritime and military technology, and a keen spirit of adventure, the Vikings first invaded Ireland in 795. After decades of raiding and plundering, an attempted conquest began around 837, when a fleet of 120 ships landed near a small port village. From there the Vikings undertook a large-scale campaign into the island's interior.

Local resistance to Viking expansion was fierce, but the Vikings' new settlement on the Liffey River, ringed by hills and with easy access to the sea, was fortified and established

as a Scandinavian kingdom. The Vikings built a fort on the ridge above the river's south bank, where Dublin Castle now stands. Similar fortifications soon appeared farther south along Ireland's coast at Wexford, Waterford, and Cork, and on the Shannon River at Limerick.

Gradually the Vikings took up commerce and assimilated with the Irish. Dublin became a hub of trade and the site of one of Europe's largest slave markets. Excavations have revealed a large influx of wealth as indicated by the first known Irish coins, minted by Viking kings who held court in Dublin. The Vikings essentially dictated the flow of commerce,

exporting iron goods and slaves and importing wheat, wine, silk, and leather.

From the Irish, the Vikings learned more about agriculture, raising cattle, Christianity, and classical education. From the Vikings, the Irish learned about stone architecture, iron armor, fighting on horseback, shipbuilding, and sailing. In fact, nearly all the Gaelic words for large ships and their parts come from the Old Norse. Viking literature as well drew inspiration from the Irish bards who came to Scandinavia and there sang and recited stories in the court in a ceremony called Dublin of the Festal Drinking Horns. ■

The three grandsons of Charlemagne—Louis II, Charles II, and Lothair I—divided up his Carolingian Empire at the Treaty of Verdun in 843, less than a century after the empire's founding.

delineations, Viking society was highly egalitarian. "Who is your master?" a Frankish messenger called out to a Viking ship in France. "None," came the reply, "we are all equals." Some adopted Christianity and became absorbed into local populations—as did their language, which enriched English with such words as "anger," "knife," and "slaughter."

VIKING ASSAULTS CONTINUE

In 837 Egbert was defending England against the Danish, while Norwegians were invading Ireland. They struck up the Boyne and Liffey Rivers on the eastern side of the emerald isle, each fleet with some 60 warships. A historian would recount the invasion: "They made spoil-land and sword-land and conquered land of her, throughout her breadth and generally; and they ravaged her chieftainries and her privileged churches and her sanctuaries; and they rent her shrines and her reliquaries and her books." And yet, despite such destruction, it was the Vikings who established the settlement that would become Dublin, on the banks of the Liffey.

Sailing farther south, Danish marauders explored the coast of Moorish Spain in 844. A local observer wrote that "al-Magus [fire worshipers] arrived with about eighty vessels which covered the sea like so many red and black birds, and filled all hearts with anguish and anxiety." After brushing aside the coastal defenders, the Danes sculled up the Guadalquivir River and took Seville. Killing was rampant. Finding a group of old men who had taken refuge in a mosque, they murdered them.

Farther inland, in the Moorish city of Córdoba, Spain, Emir Abd ar Rahman II organized a response. A corps of light cavalry and a column of infantry advanced on Seville, skirmished with the invaders, and inflicted severe losses.

Then on a plain south of the city, the two armies clashed in a key battle. The Moors prevailed, killing more than 1,000 Danes and capturing 400.

The survivors fled in panic to their ships, and then they rowed off, watching as the Moors killed their captors in plain sight. A contingent of Vikings was left behind in the city, and to save their skins, they knelt and embraced Islam. A sturdy wall was then built around the city of Seville, and a shipbuilding program

This wood carving of an animal's head evokes the wild spirit of adventure that drove the Norsemen to distant lands. It decorated part of the Oseberg ship, a ninth-century vessel unearthed in Norway in 1904.

was initiated, with workshops in Lisbon, Seville, and Valencia.

In about 859 a Viking chieftain named Hasteinn led 62 ships from France on an epic voyage, according to accounts detailed by both Christian and Muslim writers. Looting along the way, the Norsemen crossed the Mediterranean for perhaps the first time and began scouting the North African shoreline. They took captives, and they were especially fascinated to see native Africans, the first black-skinned people they had ever seen, whom they called "blue men." They then crossed the Mediterranean again and put in at various cities in Italy. And here, according to an account by the French monk William of Jumièges, possibly apocryphal, a strange series of events unfolded.

Hasteinn found himself dazzled by the towering buildings and marble walls of Luna, an Etruscan town on the Ligurian coast between Pisa and Genoa. In fact, he thought he was in Rome. When the citizens of Luna barricaded the city gates, Hasteinn tried a slyer approach. He declared that he had come in peace and that, mortally ill, he wanted to be baptized before he died. The locals took him to a church for the ritual, and then his own men helped him back to the ship. They later returned somberly, carrying their leader in

his coffin. As the bishop of Luna bowed his head and uttered a special prayer for this newly converted soul, Hasteinn leapt from the coffin and slew the cleric with his sword. "The house of God becomes the theater of crimes committed by His deadly enemy," mourned William; "the young are massacred, the throats of the old are cut, the city devastated." Not until after the bloodbath did the pillagers discover that they were not in Rome.

By the end of the century, large parts of Europe were so devastated by Vikings that the countryside was a desolate place where wolves and loose bands of marauders preyed on anyone daring to travel. The nascent economy and social structure of Europe was shaken; surviving communities walled themselves off and hunkered down, waiting for what might be out there.

A Treaty Divides a Kingdom

During his 46-year reign, Charlemagne unified Europe to a degree unprecedented since the Romans. His death in 814 precipitated the breakup of his empire, the pieces of which would reconstitute a new Europe.

It started with the ascension of Charlemagne's son Louis I, or the Pious. He misstepped from the beginning by banishing from the court anyone whose morals were questionable. Ministers and loose women alike were tossed out, and Louis publicly repented of his own sins, proving himself a devout Christian. The nobles were unimpressed; accustomed to his father's iron-fisted rule, they had little respect for a king they did not also fear.

Louis aspired to a holy life. Finding kingship incompatible with his spiritual aspirations, he passed governmental responsibility on to his sons well before they were ready for it. The political history of the next several decades was dominated by the sibling rivalry between his sons and heirs. No laws yet codified the rule of primogeniture—the right of inheritance by the firstborn son—yet Louis gave ruling power to his firstborn, Lothair, thus demoting his other two sons, Pepin and Louis (Louis the German). Pepin got

> TOWARD MIDNIGHT
> HE HEARD A LOUD NOISE
> OUTSIDE, AND VERY SOON
> THERE WALKED A HUGE
> TROLL-WIFE INTO THE ROOM.
> SHE CARRIED A TROUGH
> IN ONE HAND AND
> A RATHER LARGE CUTLASS
> IN THE OTHER.
>
> *GRETTIR THE STRONG*
> *An Icelandic Saga*

Aquitaine—the western half of today's France, minus Brittany—and Louis got Bavaria—the part of today's Germany just north of the Alps. And that was just the beginning of family squabbles. Louis tried installing a nephew as king of Italy. The ungrateful nephew revolted, and Louis had him blinded, from which treatment the young man died. In 823 Louis had another son, Charles (later called Charles the Bald), and to him, at the age of six, he gave Alamannia, along the upper Rhine.

The older brothers tried to depose their father. Then Louis decided to take Aquitaine from Pepin and give it to Charles. The three brothers revolted again, this time

with the pope's help, and yet again Louis was able to retake his crown and make peace. Lothair and Louis the German tried, independently, to stage rebellions in the 830s, but their armies were defeated.

For years Louis found himself at war with his sons, and the empire united by Charlemagne became a house divided against itself. Pepin died in 839, and the empire had to be carved up anew. Plagued by dissension to the end, Louis died in 840 at age 62. The peaceful empire that his father had hammered together by brute force and subtle diplomacy was torn to pieces by civil war. It was harder to maintain an empire than to build one.

Three years after their father's death, the brothers decided to try to reach an agreement. Their 843 family reunion became known as the Treaty of Verdun, a peace worked out in the same northeastern French town that would see a terrible battle in World War I.

The treaty divided the kingdom of the Franks into three parts: The western third (which became France) went to Charles the Bald; the eastern third (later Germany) went to Louis the German; and the so-called Middle Kingdom, between the two, went to Lothair—a slice of geography that would eventually become parts of France and Germany, Belgium, the Netherlands, Luxembourg, Switzerland, and northern Italy.

This tripartite arrangement held for a decade, after which the brothers took to fighting again. Civil war raged among them at the same time that they were fighting off attacks by Vikings from the north and Muslims from the south. The fact is, the lands they controlled were home to people of such different cultures and languages that even had the brothers succeeded in uniting, they would have had trouble keeping the empire together and safe from invasion.

THE SAGAS

Iceland's Legendary Literary Heritage

The great Icelandic sagas date back to around 870, when the island's first permanent settlers arrived from their homeland, today's Norway. They began to record their memories, history, and folklore in oral recitations, influenced by earlier Germanic and Irish ballads. Those poems and stories were passed down by word of mouth from one bard to the next. They included many details of Scandinavian culture: accounts of their kings, exploits and adventures of the Vikings, family histories and genealogies, and fictional tales of heroes, gods, dwarfs, elves, and dragons. How true to historic fact any one saga might be is a matter of debate. Many were certainly written imaginatively, without any intent to be historically accurate, and yet they often corroborate verifiable names, places, and events.

One such heroic Viking account, *The Saga of the Greenlanders*, describes the voyages of Bjarni Herjolfsson and Leif Eriksson to Vinland—yet not until 1963 did archaeologists confirm Vinland's location in modern-day Canada, confirming Leif Eriksson as the first European known to set foot in North America, around the year 1000.

Passed on orally for centuries, these compositions were ultimately written down beginning in the 11th century. Most of these writers are unknown; an exception is Snorri Sturluson, a 13th-century Icelandic poet, historian, and politician, considered one of the greatest of the saga writers. ■

As it was, they did work out another treaty, in 870. Lothair had died by this time, and his son and heir received a significantly smaller portion. Another partition in 880 divvied up the Frankish kingdom into several pieces among such heirs as Louis the Younger and Charles the Fat. Other heirs dropped out of the picture, one dying on a hunt and another losing his head chasing a girl on horseback through a low passageway—he forgot to duck.

Danish Vikings took to pillaging Aachen, the city that Charlemagne had built as his capital. They actually stabled their horses in the city's cathedral. Charles the Fat became the nominal emperor of the crumbling Frankish empire. A monk who witnessed the Danish siege of Paris in 885-886 wrote that the locals bravely withstood the attack. When the Viking leader, Siegfred, requested entrance into the city, a bishop replied, "Paris has been entrusted to us by the Emperor Charles, who, after God . . . rules over almost all the world. . . . If, like us, you had been given the duty of defending these walls, and if you should have done that which you ask us to do, what treatment do you think you would deserve?"

"I should deserve that my head be cut off and thrown to the dogs," Siegfred replied. "Nevertheless, if you do not listen to my demand, on the morrow our war machines will destroy you with poisoned arrows." And the next day catapults were drawn and arrows began flying; the defenders poured hot oil and pitch on the Danes who tried to scale the ramparts, burning off their scalps. In the end Paris was stricken but not defeated.

Yet the next year Charles conceded so much to the Danes that his subjects ran him out, and with his abdication, the Carolingian dynasty came to a stuttering, unspectacular end. Tribal chieftains took the reins of power in Germany, while in France the landowning dukes and counts seized control and did not let go until the mid-1100s. Invading Danes kept hold of one portion of northwestern France, which came to be called the Duchy of the Norsemen—later, Normandy.

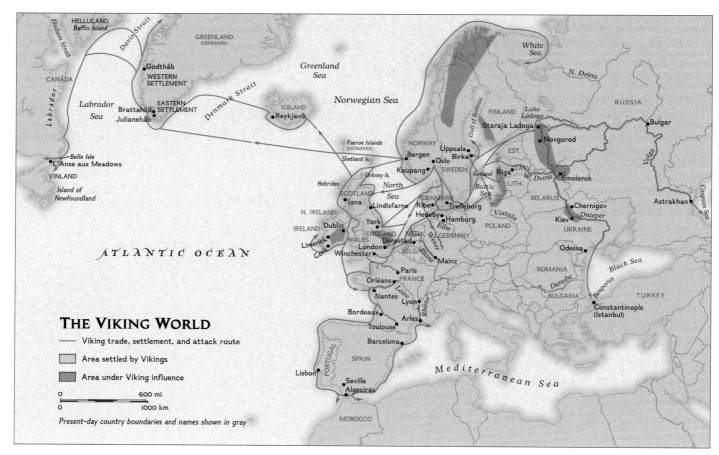

THE VIKING WORLD

— Viking trade, settlement, and attack route

▢ Area settled by Vikings

▢ Area under Viking influence

Present-day country boundaries and names shown in gray

Pushed on by population pressures and advanced maritime skills, the Vikings erupted out of Scandinavia, sailing in many directions and establishing new settlements throughout Europe and the North Atlantic. Some even reached North American shores some 500 years before Christopher Columbus.

In many ways the Carolingian world had just been hanging on until something better came along. Much of Western Europe was a wilderness of deep forest and murky swamps. Life for most was short and hard—poverty, grinding labor, poor nutrition, war, and other violence limited a lifespan to about 30 years. Most people traveled no farther than ten miles from their birthplaces.

Superstition and magic flourished alongside intellectual endeavors; many looked to local saints and other legendary figures for miracles and signs. The church found ways to assimilate pagan traditions—the celebration of the winter solstice or the spring equinox—into religious holidays, Christmas and Easter.

With the old Roman cities depleted or in ruins, three institutions remained as social anchors in ninth-century Europe: the church, the monastery, and the castle. The first two were often little more than low-slung stone edifices, some castles simply wooden forts, but each provided a locus of activity and security for people who regularly endured deprivations of one kind or another.

Barter was the generally accepted means of exchange in the Carolingian world. Some silver coins were minted, the smallest of which could purchase a cow. More often the coins in circulation were old, from other times and cultures: Byzantine and Muslim gold coins circulated, for example. To a large extent, trade was limited by a poor transportation network. Some long-distance trade did occur, thanks to those who traveled—Jews, Greeks, Muslims, and Vikings—but for the most part, Carolingian villages provided for themselves.

Though on the surface Europe in the ninth century was a poor, dirt-grubbing

Archaeologists discovered the Oseberg ship, a 72-foot-long sailing ship, in a Norwegian burial mound that also contained artifacts and human remains. Tests dated the mound to 834, but the ship may be older.

cousin to the grand and sophisticated Byzantine and Islamic Empires, it contained the seeds of intellectual and political systems that would slowly flower into one of the most powerful and wealthy societies in the world.

Charlemagne's head scholar, Alcuin, started a trend in organized education that would spread literacy and culture, via church and school, throughout the social classes. He revived the classical educational system consisting of the *trivium* (grammar, rhetoric, and logic) and *quadrivium* (arithmetic, music, geometry, and astronomy)—the standard academic areas of study.

Most monastic schools that took root in the Frankish kingdom continued to thrive into the ninth century and beyond, despite disruptions to daily life caused by Viking invaders. These important advances in education stand at the heart of what has been called the Carolingian Renaissance, a rebirth of intellect inspired by rediscovering ancient traditions of learning.

The Carolingian line flickered out in the ninth century, but it did not officially end until the tenth. Louis the Child, a great-grandson of Louis the German, was king of the East Franks (in today's Germany) until 911, and Louis V (also called Louis the Sluggard), a great-great-great-grandson of Charles the Bald, nominally ruled as king of the West Franks (in today's France) until 987. Louis V's advisers cautioned him to ally with German king Otto III, but he chose the French duke Hugh Capet instead. When Louis died in a hunting accident, Hugh Capet took over, initiating the Capetian line of French monarchs.

ARAB ADVANCES IN KNOWLEDGE

With the rise of the Abbasid dynasty in the Muslim world in the mid-700s, the Islamic center of power shifted from Damascus to Baghdad. Under Caliph al Mansur, who ruled from 754 to 775, Baghdad grew as a capital city. The caliph granted property to military leaders, who, because of such favors, eventually formed an elite ruling class.

The Abbasid caliphs understood that with so much territory under Islamic influence, each region having its own history, culture, and language, it would be to their advantage to give each region some autonomy. More successful in collecting taxes than the Umayyads had been, the Abbasids nevertheless kept only loose control over the larger Islamic world. Syria, Egypt, Khorasan (today's eastern Iran), and the lands that now make up Iraq—each region enjoyed a degree of independence. Spain and the Berber territory of North Africa took that independence to extremes, becoming unruly.

Like the Byzantine emperors, the caliphs played a dangerous game of political intrigue, which only the smartest and strongest survived. Al Mansur had a hand in the murders of numerous rivals, as well as supporters whom he viewed as potential rivals. Partly owing to this policy, Al Mansur spent much of his reign putting down insurrections. Yet in spite of this, he began building what would become the dazzling city of Baghdad. Tall and lean, he promoted a simple lifestyle, and he encouraged the translation of Greek and Latin classics into Arabic, a vast intellectual enter-

This ornately wrought water jug was presented to Charlemagne by Abbasid caliph Harun al Rashid, who oversaw a flourishing of art and science in his lands.

prise with important implications for medieval philosophy, Muslim, Christian, and Jewish alike. Considered the true founder of the Abbasid caliphate, Al Mansur ushered in a new period of cultural and economic prosperity.

In the ninth century Baghdad became a major crossroads in a vast and exotic trade network. From India came rubies, sandalwood, ebony, coconuts, tigers, and elephants; from China, silk, porcelain, cinnamon, paper, ink, and peacocks; Greece contributed racing horses, female

slaves, hydraulic engineers, and eunuchs; Arabia exported ostriches and camels; Egypt sent balsam, topaz, and donkeys. Amid this colorful bazaar, the locals assembled their own style, the decorative arts flourishing in the homes of the elite. Talent and therefore entitlement were drawn not just from the Muslim and Arabic populations but from Persians, Christians, Jews, and others.

With the Abbasids' power and prosperity came a golden age in science, law, and literature that added not just to the Islamic heritage but to world civilization forever after. Scholars translated philosophical, mathematical, medical, and astrological works from Greek and Indian into Arabic; poets and prose writers invented new forms of literature; and books of all kinds became available to a huge number of people. The caliph under whom this cultural flowering was most intense, Harun al Rashid had one of the longest reigns of all the caliphs, remaining in power from 786 to 809.

Now known as the caliph whose court inspired *The Thousand and One Nights*, or *The Arabian Nights' Entertainments*, a collection of tales assembled in the 1400s, Harun al Rashid was the son of a caliph and a Yemeni slave. As a young man he served as a leader on military expeditions and then, helped by the machinations of his mother, outmaneuvered other aspirants to the caliphate. Though he had his share of revolts to deal with, he fostered the growing intellectual atmosphere of Baghdad. His own palace was as lavish as that depicted in the romantic tales—a buzzing hive of eunuchs, concubines,

CALIPH A caliph was both the civil and the religious ruler of the ancient Muslim world, a position of honor and authority. The word comes from the Arabic for successor; the caliphate was considered a line of succession going back to the Prophet Muhammad himself.

The Mosque of Uqba in Kairouan, Tunisia, was one of the largest mosques of its day, its architecture influential throughout Muslim North Africa.
It was first built in A.D. 670 but destroyed, reconstructed, and expanded several times during the next two centuries.

THE WORLD IN THE NINTH CENTURY

Baghdad and Samarra thrived in this century, representing a dynamic Muslim culture. Enterprises flourished, from observatories and schools to papermaking facilities. Caliphs commissioned scholars to translate Greek classics into Arabic, and Arab mathematicians made remarkable advances in algebra and astronomy. In North Africa, the Berber Kharijites established an independent Muslim state. Jewish immigrants known as Radhanites developed trade between Timbuktu and the East, as far as India.

In India, Adi Shankara, a philosopher, revived Hinduism, especially in the south, where the Chola kingdom began to consolidate. The Chola dynasty also added to India's rich artistic history with lavish temples and bronze works.

The Japanese began to manufacture refined rice paper and developed their own phonetic writing system distinct from Chinese. Fractured Khmer states, in today's Cambodia, united into one under Jayavarman II. Later in this century, Indravarman I built the civilization's first temple-mountain, and established a capital at Angkor.

In Central America, the Maya, once powerful throughout the Yucatán Peninsula and Honduras, fell into decline as the Mixtec in Mexico advanced. In North America, the Caddo continued to thrive, trading with the Woodlands people of the east and indigenous plains people of the west. The Caddo traded agricultural products and sophisticated osage-wood bows to warrior communities in exchange for meat and hides. ■

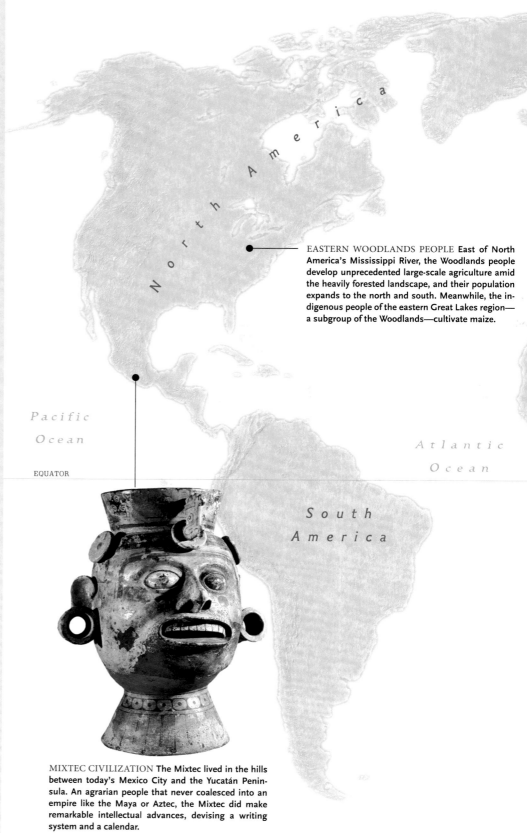

Arctic

North America

Pacific Ocean

EQUATOR

Atlantic Ocean

South America

EASTERN WOODLANDS PEOPLE **East of North America's Mississippi River, the Woodlands people develop unprecedented large-scale agriculture amid the heavily forested landscape, and their population expands to the north and south. Meanwhile, the indigenous people of the eastern Great Lakes region—a subgroup of the Woodlands—cultivate maize.**

MIXTEC CIVILIZATION **The Mixtec lived in the hills between today's Mexico City and the Yucatán Peninsula. An agrarian people that never coalesced into an empire like the Maya or Aztec, the Mixtec did make remarkable intellectual advances, devising a writing system and a calendar.**

THE GREAT PAGODA, THANJAVUR **Around A.D. 850, with the defeat of the Pallavas, the Chola dynasty becomes one of the most important kingdoms in southern India, remaining in power for nearly four centuries. Thanjavur becomes the kingdom's capital, and the city's Great Pagoda, with its impressive sculptural towers, expresses prosperity and a devotion to Hinduism.**

JENNE-JENO **At the inland delta of the Niger River, the city of Jenne-Jeno becomes one of Africa's most prosperous urban centers, with an estimated population of more than 10,000 people and trade with the surrounding region.**

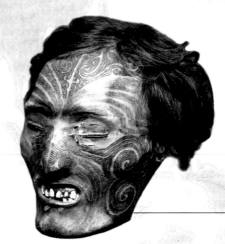

MAORI CIVILIZATION **Sailing from Hawaii or Samoa, the Maori people discover New Zealand in the middle of the ninth century, and their civilization thrives in the new landscape. Elsewhere in the Pacific, island people maintain close-knit trade networks and establish stable agricultural societies.**

THE GREAT MOSQUE, SAMARRA **Commissioned by Al Mutawakkil, the last great Abbasid caliph, the Great Mosque at Samarra, Iraq, is the largest of its time. Its spiraling minaret, built in 861, rises a remarkable 180 feet.**

singers, and servants. His wife, a member of the ruling family and Abbasid herself, required that her table be set only with gem-encrusted gold and silver vessels.

In one of the darker chapters of Harun's reign, he had his close friend and adviser, Ja'far, executed and his family imprisoned. Homosexual jealousy was rumored, though greed and political expediency may have been the motives. Considered a greater patron of the arts than ruler, Harun made the same mistake as Louis the Pious. In an age and culture in which there were no clear rules about succession or inheritance, the death of powerful leaders seemed always to precipitate chaos. Like the Franks' Louis, Harun divided his empire between his sons—who then went to war against each other.

The victor of this eight-year civil war, Abu Jafar Abdullah al Ma'mun ibn Harun, born of a Persian concubine, ruled the Muslim empire from 813 to 833. The defeat of his half brother marked the triumph of rationalism over traditionalism, as

QUOTH NUR AL DIN, "WHITHER BOUND, O CAPTAIN?" AND QUOTH HE, "TO THE HOUSE OF PEACE, BAGHDAD."

"NUR AL DIN ALI AND THE DAMSEL"
THE THOUSAND AND ONE NIGHTS
Persian folktale

Al Ma'mun was open to new ideas from Persia (today's Iran) and other lands. Known for his attempts to reconcile Sunni and Shiite factions, he also helped integrate Greek philosophy into Islamic thinking. An intellectual himself, Al Ma'mun established astronomical observatories and promoted the concepts of free will, personal responsibility, and the human rather than divine origin of the Koran. Yet Shiites and others opposed the idea of a human-created Koran. To them, the Islamic scripture was Muhammad's transcription of the words of Allah, God. Within a few decades after Al

Ma'mun's death, the theory of the human origin of the Koran had lost favor.

One ninth-century Muslim whose work survives to the present day is the brilliant mathematician Muhammad ibn Musa al Khwarizmi, who lived from about 780 to about 850 in Baghdad. Al Khwarizmi gave us the basics of algebra. His *al jabr*, as it was called in Arabic, set forth rules for solving linear and quadratic equations, for doing elementary geometry, and for calculating proportions. Although he didn't invent algebra, Al Khwarizmi extended its reach into practical applications and ensured its transmission to future generations by publishing his ideas.

Among his other great contributions are the concept of zero, the use of Arabic numerals, the word "algorithm" and the mathematical concept it expresses, and numerous astronomical calculations based on a seventh-century Sanskrit text. Surveyors, bridge builders, irrigation engineers, and inheritance lawyers

BELIEF

THE ZANJ REBELLION

Early Slavery in the Middle East

Beginning in the eighth century, Muslim merchants visited the East African coast to trade metal weapons and tools for gold, ivory, horn, and slaves. The institution of slavery in Africa already had a long history, but demand for slaves in new foreign markets meant that domestic slave-raiding increased.

By the ninth century, several thousand men from a region called Zanj—the root word for today's Zanzibar—had been transported as slaves to southern Mesopotamia to work the sugarcane plantations and prepare the marshlands for cultivation. Facing grueling conditions with little to eat, these Zanj slaves constituted over half the total population of the area.

In 869 a slave among them named Ali bin Muhammad organized a rebel uprising. It grew rapidly in size, and soon a force of some 15,000 Zanj men had joined the rebel army, which went on to raze fields, burn mosques and houses, massacre local Arabs, and even sack Basra, an important city, in 871.

The rebels formed a Zanj state, centered in the city of Mukhtarah, a stronghold that Islamic armies did not recapture until 883. Ali and other rebel leaders were executed, and many Zanj were returned to slavery, though with better working conditions and greater social mobility. This early incident left an influential legacy of slaving networks in Africa. ■

Slaves sold on the Swahili coast of Africa staged a revolt from 869 to 883.

were among those who benefited from Al Khwarizmi's work.

THE RISE OF MOORISH SPAIN

One Muslim region lay well beyond the control of the Abbasids. Moorish Spain, first established as its own cultural center by the eighth-century Umayyad governor-general Abd al Rahman al Ghafiqui, was now ruled by his grandson Abd ar Rahman II. An Umayyad enclave in what was called Al Andalus (most of present-day Spain) would last for nearly three centuries, with Córdoba its political and intellectual capital. Distinctive works of art and architecture emerged from this cultural center, influencing western Europe and the New World.

While their rulers were Muslim, the Andalusian population was diverse. Through the ninth century, only about one quarter of the population of Al Andalus was Muslim; the rest, Christians and Jews, practiced their religions freely but bore a heavy tax burden. Abd ar Rahman and other emirs used that money to create their own golden age of literature and science. Though there was doubtless some hostility between Muslims and Christians in Moorish Spain, recent scholarship indicates that for the most part the two groups mixed reasonably well, with some intermarriage.

Abd ar Rahman was emir for more than three decades, from 755 to 788; Abd ar Rahman II continued the family tradition, holding power from 822 to 852.

In Al Andalus they built regimes of other Umayyad refugees, as well as locals they could trust. Leaders in Baghdad were none too pleased at the rival Islamic culture and stronghold of power in Córdoba. The caliph Al Mansur sent an agent

Knowledge of cobalt glazes, like those used on this earthenware dish from ninth-century Mesopotamia, traveled the Silk Road to Asia, where Chinese artisans used the same blue on thin white porcelain.

to Al Andalus, and a recruited army was soon challenging the Moorish emir. Abd ar Rahman put together his own army—mostly of Visigoth slaves—and in 763 he defeated the caliph's puppets at Seville. He ordered all the prisoners executed; the leader had his hands and feet cut off before being decapitated.

Having fended off rival Muslims, Abd ar Rahman succeeded in uniting

the disparate elements of his domain. While Frankish Christians to the north commanded the Muslims or Jews in their territory to convert to Christianity, Muslims did not require conversion. In the Christian ideal of an ordered society, all adhered to the same set of beliefs; in the Muslim view, a hierarchy of social status held things together. Non-Muslims were seen as unenlightened, lesser citizens required to pay higher taxes. Over time many of the restrictions imposed on them, such as building limitations, special clothes, and so on, were dropped.

Of more concern were the Berbers, the Visigoth Muslims, and other Arab clans that continued to test the power of the Umayyad dynasty headquartered in Córdoba. And the memory of Charlemagne's stunted invasion of Spain in 778 reminded the emirs that a threatening presence loomed beyond the Pyrenees.

Despite uprisings, Abd ar Rahman and his descendants built up Córdoba, strengthened the trade and economy of Al Andalus, and unified the greater part of Spain into one Islamic territory. A lover and practitioner of poetry, the elder Abd ar Rahman wrote, "I came fleeing hunger, the sword, and death, attained security and prosperity, and gathered together a people." His son completed the Great Mosque in Córdoba, and his grandson bolstered the administrative policies of his predecessors, added more public works, and patronized poets, musicians, and religious leaders.

By the mid-ninth century, Baghdad had a population of some two million, and stood second only to Constantinople as a center of Islamic trade and culture. Though Córdoba would never quite surpass Baghdad as a commercial and intellectual capital, it would with the freedom of an outlying territory make quick strides in the sciences and humanities. The Umayyad dynasty of Al Andalus would reach its zenith of power and influence under Abd ar Rahman

III, who, ruling longer than any of his forebears—from 912 to 961, nearly a half century—made Córdoba an intellectual pulse point of Europe.

While the Umayyad dynasty was flourishing, the northern region of the Iberian Peninsula—from Spain's Duero River north to the Atlantic Ocean—was going its own way. Here amid wooded mountains and fertile valleys, the kingdom of Asturias became a haven for Spanish Christians. Centered at first in Oviedo, then in León, the kingdom would hang on, biding its time, throughout the

Moorish period. The region was associated with St. James, one of Jesus' apostles, believed to have traveled and preached in Spain. Asturians, believing that James had died there, built a cathedral upon his tomb: Santiago de Compostela, which became one of the three most important Christian pilgrimage destinations later in the Middle Ages.

ROME VERSUS BYZANTIUM

In the ninth century, the three post-Roman powers emerged as distinct personalities with clearly defined religions. The Muslim caliphate was the guardian of Islam; Byzantium was the center of Orthodox Christianity; and Frankland was an affiliation of Christianized tribes. All three were centrally controlled monarchies with a strong military and a growing amount of wealth—more in the East than in the West—and all three found expression in arts and scholarship. With Arab incursions against Europe and Byzantium ebbing in the eighth and ninth centuries, the Western world struggled to define itself as a bipolar Christian domain whose two centers—Rome and Byzantium—would not formally split until 1054.

The newest player in the tripartite hegemony, Frankland was glued together by the might of the short-lived Carolingian dynasty; when that gave way, what was left as a common factor was Christianity. More than anyone else, the Anglo-Saxon missionary St. Boniface, who lived from around 675 to 754, was responsible for the spread of Christianity through the Frankish kingdom.

Known as the Apostle of Germany, St. Boniface moved tirelessly about, establishing monasteries that added

This tenth-century Byzantine painting mixes classical and biblical references: The prophet Isaiah prays to divine light while shadowed by Nyx, a Greek and Roman divinity representing night and death.

EDIFICES

Stone ramparts still encircle the old city of Carcassonne, in southern France. Timber walls surrounded this city as long ago as the first century A.D. The medieval stone walls, built and rebuilt through centuries, fell into disrepair but are now maintained in the modern spirit of pride in history.

CITY WALLS

Protecting Against Intruders

Ravaged by lightning-quick raids from Viking, Magyar, and Muslim forces, the Holy Roman Empire was unable to defend the full extent of its territory. Local and regional authorities had to mount their own defense. Ninth-century western Europe was therefore full of small, autonomous states whose leaders sought to expand or consolidate their land and consequent wealth. Conflict often occurred between rival kingdoms governed by brothers, uncles, and cousins, and violence was commonplace. Hence poor farmers had to pledge their services to powerful lords in exchange for protection.

To provide this protection, many lords surrounded their estates with fortifications and walls. The first walls were little more than earthen ramparts, known as the motte-and-bailey type, consisting of a high mound, or motte, topped with a wooden tower and encircled by a palisade, a kind of fence constructed of cut logs fixed tightly together. The earth for the mound was taken from a ditch that was dug around the stronghold. At the foot of the mound was located an enclosed courtyard, or bailey, that was surrounded by another palisade and often another ditch.

From the motte, landowning seigneurs oversaw the protection, taxation, administration, and jurisdiction of the bailey, where the lords' peasants and animals lived. These earthen ramparts were effective in defending against small-scale sieges, but stone walls did better, especially as weaponry technology advanced. The immense stone walls of later centuries included innovations such as the portcullis—an iron and oak grate that could be quickly lowered over a gateway—and the machicolation—an opening at the top of a wall through which stones or boiling liquid could be dropped on an advancing enemy.

Walls such as these served as practical defense systems, as symbols of power, and as methods of control over nascent urban populations. By the 14th century, most towns and cities were enclosed within stone walls, many of which still stand today, encircling the oldest city center and remaining prominent landmarks in the European cityscape. ■

considerably to European cultural life. If he was sometimes too stern, Boniface certainly had courage: In front of angry German pagans in Geismar, he threatened the sacred oak dedicated to Thor, the thunder god.

According to legend, he gave the oak a single blow with his ax. At the same time, a mighty wind came rushing through and toppled the ancient tree, convincing the pagan observers of Christianity's extraordinary powers. Instantly they converted, and Boniface used the wood to build a chapel.

The felling of Thor's oak is seen by many as a symbolic moment, as the Germanic world abandoned paganism and embraced Christianity. Boniface continued traveling, preaching, and reading the Bible aloud to all who would listen. Over time he was granted authority by the pope, and Boniface crowned Pepin king of the Franks in 751. When he and a small group of followers were attacked by angry pagans in Frisia (today's Netherlands), he died a martyr's death.

Byzantium, still linked to the West by Christianity, went its own way politically. With Emperor Irene exiled to Lesbos in 802, Nicephorus I took the helm of an empire that included what is now Turkey, Greece, and southern Italy, ruling until 811. At first he refused to pay tribute to Caliph Harun al Rashid; later he was forced into it by Islamic victories.

More successful in his campaign into the Balkans, he beat an army of Slavs near what is now Sofia, Bulgaria, but overstepped in driving too far west. Bulgarians trapped his plundering forces in a narrow valley. They massacred the Byzantines and killed Nicephorus. As a trophy, the triumphant Bulgarian khan had workmen line Nicephorus's skull

THE ONE THING
TO BE AIMED AT
IS NOT TO ADORE
A CREATED THING MORE
THAN THE CREATOR.

———————————

St. John of Damascus
Apologia Against Those Who
Decry Holy Images
Circa 730

with silver so that he could use it as a ceremonial drinking vessel.

An often more effective, and less bloody, method of bringing the Slavs within the Byzantine fold was to convert their souls. Missionaries such as Cyril and Methodius went through the Slavic countryside, preaching the Orthodox brand of Christianity. As their missionary efforts continued, the Byzantine Empire grew, and Bulgaria, Serbia, and later Russia all came into the fold of Eastern Orthodox Christianity. At the same time, Byzantine forces did what they could to push the boundaries of the empire east and south, hitting up against the powers of the caliphate in Baghdad.

By the middle of the ninth century, Byzantium was enjoying a cultural renaissance. The Byzantine emperor Theophilus, called "the Iconoclast," died in 842, leaving his wife, Holy Empress Theodora, in power. Long an icon worshiper in secret, Theodora used her power over church and state to revive the religious and artistic tradition, and suddenly Byzantine art blossomed in exquisitely rendered, hauntingly mystical religious icons, many gilt-ornamented paintings but also carvings, statuary, mosaics, and coins.

At the same time, scholarship flourished. Classical Greek texts of science

and philosophy were translated; the art of illuminating manuscripts thrived. Monumental architecture influenced grand palaces, churches, and monasteries.

A new dynasty began with Basil I, called Macedonian after his homeland. Coming into power by rising up in court ranks and then murdering the emperor, Basil ruled the Byzantine Empire from 867 to 886. An 11th-century historian wrote that Basil's dynasty was "more blessed by God than any other family ... though rooted in murder and bloodshed."

Despite his ruthless rise to power, Basil promoted the arts and brought in legal reforms long overdue. He and his son Leo VI (Leo the Wise, emperor from 886 to 912) worked to build the empire's power, partly by maintaining friendly relations with Rome. Naval power was increasingly important as the Muslim influence spread around the Mediterranean. Islands such as Cyprus and Sicily became important military prizes that Rome and Byzantium, as allies, struggled to maintain.

Just before Basil's reign, rumblings of discontent between Rome and Constantinople had flared into an open rift, called the Photian Schism, which presaged schisms to come. Photius, a highly educated and well-traveled man who lived from about 820 to 891, became patriarch—head bishop—of Constantinople in 858. The pope at the time, Nicholas I, questioned his eligibility and refused to recognize him as patriarch. Photius showed his own muscle by excommunicating the pope. Numerous intrigues and changes in power characterized the rest of his life, and the irritating conflict laid bare the possibility that the two Christian empires might divide irreconcilably.

Charlemagne and his heirs were patrons of the arts, inspiring a new era of artistry often called the Carolingian Renaissance, as exemplified in this illumination.

SCIENCE IN THE MIDDLE AGES

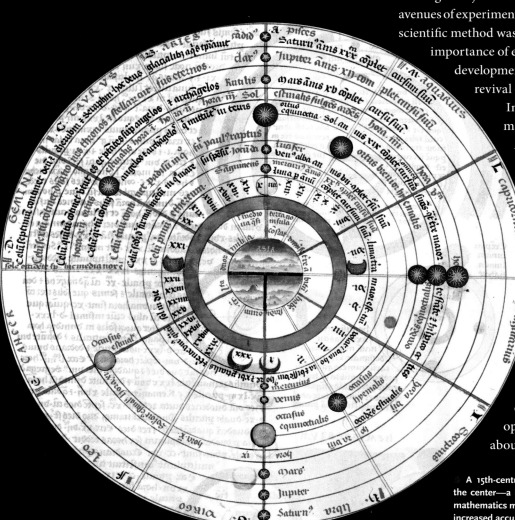

An illustration from a 14th-century surgical manual may seem primitive by today's standards, but a renewed interest in empirical evidence led to important surgical innovations in the late medieval era.

cross Europe and especially in the Middle East, medieval astronomers, mathematicians, scientists, alchemists, and philosophers reinvigorated and further refined knowledge in all fields of science. They studied and built upon the lessons of classical antiquity, which they read in meticulously translated volumes. The establishment of the self-governing university—a uniquely medieval development—aided this expansion of knowledge and investigation. Though learning centers, such as the library at Alexandria, had been in existence for centuries, the founding of other independent institutions run by scholars forever changed the culture of learning.

Medieval thinkers came to separate science from philosophy. No longer subject to abstract theory, science could now pursue new avenues of experimentation and practice—and out of this shift, the scientific method was born. Late-medieval scientists stressed the importance of empirical evidence, giving rise to important developments in medicine and ultimately inspiring a revival of rational thought.

In mathematics, most major advances were made by Arab, Persian, and Indian scholars. Arabic numerals replaced Roman numerals, and in 873, Muhammad ibn Musa al Khwarizmi announced the concept of zero. He also introduced algebra, which made possible new developments in astronomy and mechanics, which allowed medieval engineers to design remarkably complex irrigation and water supply projects.

Muslim scientists also began experiments in alchemy, the forerunner of chemistry. Though turning common metals into gold was often the endgame, alchemists made significant advances in creating dyes, glazes, and glass; in developing distillation processes; and in learning about the physical properties of the elements.

A 15th-century astrological planetary chart places Earth at the center—a belief shared by most at that time. Advances in mathematics meant that stars and planets could be mapped with increased accuracy.

Advances in algebra by mathematicians of the Muslim world led, in turn, to important developments in the field of engineering and irrigation, as demonstrated by this 13th-century Turkish diagram for pumping water into a basin.

A lavishly ornamented bronze mortar, its handle in the shape of a lizard, may have been used in the laboratory of an alchemist. The practice of alchemy refined the art of metalworking, improving the utility of iron and bronze.

Giotto's 15th-century fresco of an alchemist shows a lone man in a primitive laboratory. In their pursuit of creating gold, alchemists made important advances in glass, dyes, and especially distillation.

L e dengleters out le delivs
E hymecligne sei fist e Roy
S i devenent mille gent nobles
K ft Walms e oyelsa oierent
K e Byetruis Roy de Gelaeu sivent
A ssemble ont ses Golenders
E t les zhorvell e les Vaneis
E t ceus Deslote e ceus Viislande
S i pustrent Zophthumbre lande
Y nnibre od lur gens passerent
O kastell e viles decurrierent

Q i Bretun virent la wistomt
O t le deseit faire de sont
A t senatour ont derechief
A nde par lybe e par bref
A L i senatour soulement
L es ennoieit isnelement

900 – 1000

AT THE OPENING OF THE TENTH CENTURY, EUROPE SEEMED LITTLE CHANGED SINCE THE opening of the ninth. England was still battling the Danes, Germany and France were wracked by Viking attacks and internal upheavals, and Moorish Spain was continuing on its own path, separate from the rest of Europe and Islam. Under the Abbasids, the Islamic empire was still fragmenting, defining and redefining itself as a convulsing coalition of dynastic states. Though no long-lasting change was in sight, there were signs that the tenth century at least promised some stability in politics, economics, and religion. England had just lost its greatest ruler to date, Alfred the Great, and peace with the entrenched Danes lasted only long enough for his successors to gear up for battle. By mid-century the only things that had changed were the borders between Danish and English territory. Yet despite ongoing conflict,

Alfred's political system of shires and courts became firmly rooted in English society, and the infighting of Anglo-Saxon tribes was all but over. The popular King Edgar ruled for 16 peaceful years, during which monasteries made a comeback and, with them, scholarship and the arts.

Though the tenth century opened with Germany divided into duchies run by warring nobles, the situation changed dramatically under the powerful King Otto I, whose life spanned much of the century, from 912 to 973. He made Germany whole again, and in 962 the pope crowned him Holy Roman Emperor. His skill as a military leader paid off in a decisive battle against the marauding Magyars, pushing them permanently back to Hungary. Europe's politics and economy were evolving toward the feudal system. An increase in both agricultural output and urban commerce led to an economic revival, particularly in silver-rich Germany. And with the Peace and Truce of God movements, the clergy asserted its place as the ultimate authority over the life of the people—war would be tolerated only within sanctioned limits.

In the Islamic world, half a dozen major sects, controlled by powerful dynasties, continued to decentralize the Abbasid leadership. A shrinking power base left the caliphate with no real control beyond southern Iraq. Many states maintained nominal allegiance to the caliphate but broke away politically. In North Africa the Fatimids—a rival family that traced its line back to Fatima, daughter of Muhammad—presented a direct challenge to the Baghdad caliphate and its tolerant ideology. Though they did not succeed in dominating all Islamic

The Vikings invaded England in the ninth century, carving out a large settlement known as Danelaw.
PRECEDING PAGES: Citizens of Manchester, England, defend their home against Viking marauders in this 19th-century painting by Ford Madox Brown.

territory, the Fatimids made tremendous gains in a few decades, reshaping the political landscape.

On the threshold of the new millennium, the Christian world held its breath, awaiting the doomsday that they believed to be predicted in the Bible. With end-of-century wars, famines, plagues, and disasters, many people saw the hand of God writing an earthshaking drama of good versus evil. Pilgrimages to the Holy Land increased, the pious hoping for salvation in the coming apocalypse. Others saw the year 1000 as merely a number. But few people had the resources to do much except fear the worst—and hope for a better future, either on earth or in the hereafter.

THE DANELAW

By the time Alfred the Great died in 899, the Danish Vikings had control of the northeastern third of England. This area, called the Danelaw, consisted of East Anglia, Essex, much of Mercia, and most of Northumbria. Linguistic legacies of the Danelaw remain—the suffix -thorp or -thorpe, for instance, as in the town name Mablethorpe, identifies a former Viking settlement.

The next generation of English rulers attempted to take back what had been lost. Alfred's son Edward the Elder, who lived from 870 to 924, teamed up with his sister, Aethelflaed, to make serious inroads on the Danelaw. While he was building a circle of fortresses around Wessex, she was doing the same thing in Mercia. In 912 he began a steady advance, winning first Essex, then East Anglia. Aethelflaed meanwhile moved her forces successfully against Danish-occupied Mercia. By 917 they were ready to launch a huge combined attack.

THE TENTH CENTURY

911
Charles the Simple grants land to Viking leader Rollo: origin of Normandy.

911
Louis III, last German Carolingian ruler, dies.

912
Arab forces defeat Byzantine navy off Chios.

924
Aethelstan becomes King of Wessex.

929
Germany's Henry I defeats the Wends, pagan people of Eastern Europe, and converts them.

955
Otto I of Germany defeats the Magyars at the Battle of Lechfeld.

962
Pope John XII crowns Otto I as Roman Emperor, initiating the Holy Roman Empire.

973
Edgar is crowned King of England at Bath.

987
Louis V, last French Carolingian ruler, dies.

Aggressive and violent in their raiding, Viking warriors donned metal helmets and armor to besiege cities throughout Europe.

Though quick victories gave Aethelflaed momentum, she was unable to savor triumph, for she died the following year.

Edward then was able to follow up by annexing Mercia, and, because of promises his sister had exacted from the Danes, he claimed control of Wales and Northumbria as well. He was also able to subdue, if not subjugate, the king of the sparsely settled region farther north—known to the Celts as Alba, to the Romans as Caledonia, and, since the ninth century, to those living there as Scotland. The Gaelic and other Scots had united under Kenneth I MacAlpin. From 858 to 1034, 14 of his descendants ruled, one after the other. Then a feud erupted, and a probable MacAlpin descendant named Macbeth seized the throne, later to become the subject of Shakespearean tragedy.

Edward's son Aethelstan, who ruled from 924 to 939, proved as formidable a warrior as his father. Styling himself "King of all Britain," he forayed deep into Scotland and kept the borders that his father had established against the newcomers. Yet the Viking problem was not solved. In 937, Vikings who had settled in Dublin joined forces with Celts in Scotland and invaded England. Aethelstan and his brother Edmund met them at Brunanburh (probably in northwestern England) and inflicted a devastating defeat that won them immortality in a poem written at the time:

With their hammered blades, the sons of Edward
Clove the shield-wall and hacked the linden bucklers . . .
And the host from the ships fell doomed. The field
Grew dark with the blood of men.
. . . the English king and the prince,

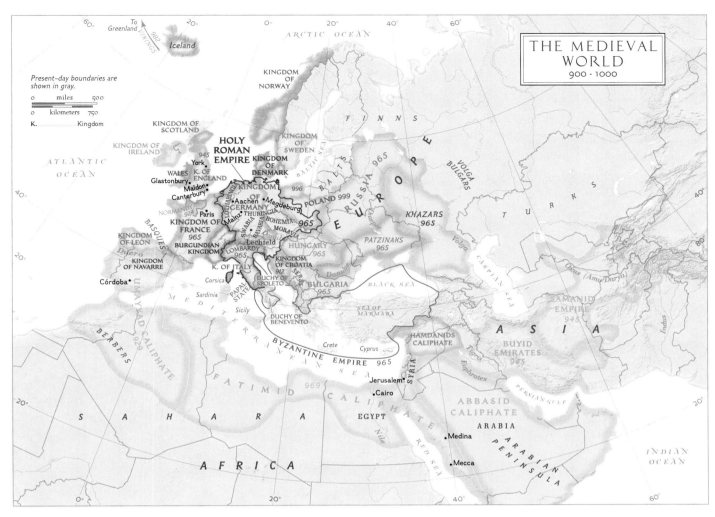

By mid-century, King Otto I of Germany annexed the Kingdom of Italy, creating the Holy Roman Empire, crowned by the pope in 962.
The Byzantine Empire battled Arabs on many fronts, while of the competing factions of Mohammed's descendants, the Fatimid caliphate rises to power.

Brothers triumphant in war,
   together
Returned to their home, the land
   of Wessex.

These words ring out from *The Anglo-Saxon Chronicle*, a collection of historical writings begun under Alfred the Great and added to through two more centuries, drawing from Bede's writing and monastic records. Vikings told a similar story of the bloody battle at Brunanburh, reporting five kings, seven Norse earls, and two of Aethelstan's cousins slain. The Icelandic *Saga of Egil Skallagrimsson*

recounts the action in detail, agreeing that "greater carnage had not been in this island ever." Yet from the point of view of the Celts, the battle was a final, failed effort to rid their land of Saxons.

Despite all the fighting in the first half of the tenth century, the Danelaw remained, although its borders changed. English kings tolerated variations in language, custom, and government from one region to another. Areas under Danish law generally saw stiffer penalties for crimes. Money was reckoned in marks and ores, not shillings, and arable land was partitioned into hides instead

of plowlands, though both these units equaled about 120 acres, enough to support a large family. Small landholders in some areas enjoyed more independence than in others, exchanging protection by nearby lords for freedom.

Viking invasions slowed down in the mid-tenth century, but then they returned with renewed intensity—and the English king in power at the time was not up to the challenge. In 978 the crown passed to Aethelred, often called Aethelred the Unready. He reigned for 38 years, trying to fend off the Vikings with might or money, but in the end his failures spelled doom for Anglo-Saxon England. It was not long before entire Viking armies were pouring ashore, the first one led by Olaf Tryggvason in 991. Aethelred could have submitted, negotiated, or fought; instead, he tried to buy the invaders off. He levied a special tax on his subjects—the *danegeld*, "ransom to the Danes"—hoping to pacify Olaf with the proceeds: 22,000 Saxon pounds of silver, the equivalent of about 16,500 pounds sterling today.

In response, Vikings came in even greater numbers. Olaf returned in 994 with a temporary ally, King Sweyn Forkbeard of Denmark, with whom he shared a danegeld of 16,000 pounds of silver. Then Aethelred made another crucial, and especially heinous, error. In 1002 he ordered a massacre of all Dan-ish settlers. It is unclear how many were actually killed, but the English Danes revolted against him in response. Further danegeld followed: 24,000 pounds in 1002; 36,000 pounds in 1007. Not all Saxons tried to buy off the Vikings, however. In 991, the men of Essex followed their leader, Brithnoth, against a Viking host at Maldon, a town at the mouth of the Chelmer River, about 50 miles northeast of London. A poem was written to record the events: "Then went forth the proud thanes," read a few lines,

> Brave men—hastened eagerly,
> And willed they all—for one of two things:
> Their lives to lose,
> or their loved lord to avenge.

Aethelred paid his last blackmail in 1012—a staggering 48,000 pounds of silver—but to no avail. The following year, Sweyn Forkbeard attacked. The English could endure no more; Aethelred fled and his people submitted. After some two centuries of warfare, the island had become a Dano-English kingdom, with the Norse in nearly complete control.

"Things have not gone well now for a long time at home or abroad," wrote Wulfstan, tenth-century archbishop of York, of this trying period. "But there has been devastation and famine, burning and bloodshed in every district again and again; and stealing and killing, sedition and pestilence, murrain and disease, malice and hate and spoliation by robbers have harmed us very grievously, and monstrous taxes have afflicted us greatly, and bad seasons have very often caused us failure of crops.... Lo, what is there in all these events except God's anger clear and visible over this people?"

Mounted duels took place, for sport as well as in earnest, in many medieval cultures. This medieval Egyptian manuscript portrays Muslim cavalry maneuvers.

VIKING EXPLORATIONS

The Vikings had by this time pushed well beyond England and the nearby European continent. Before them, explorers had cautiously limited themselves to coastlines they could see. It took the bravery and enterprise of the Norsemen to thrust westward to the Shetland and Faroe Islands and beyond. They not only visited these isolated islands but also planted there the seeds of their culture—people on the Orkney and Shetland Islands were still speaking Norse into the 1700s.

By the late 800s Norwegian Vikings were sailing ever farther out into the North Atlantic, and by the mid-900s some 25,000 Vikings had colonized Iceland. In keeping with their egalitarian principles, Viking settlers in 930 established the Althing, one of the world's first parliaments. It was but a few hundred miles from Iceland to Greenland, and in 982 explorer Erik the Red landed there with his family and soon was joined by several hundred hearty Icelanders. The final leap, beyond anything imagined by geographers of the time, was to the east coast of North America.

At first using only the sun for navigation, the Vikings developed by the late tenth century a system for estimating latitude using a table that showed the sun's midday height for each week of the year. Sometimes they released a raven, a bird known for its ability to find land, to decide their sailing direction. Viking sailors were acute observers of sun and stars, currents and winds, sea creatures and land formations—everything that could give

them clues to directions, weather, and landfall, for their lives depended on clear perception and keen memory. A 12th-century handbook gave the directions for finding Greenland: "From Hernar in Norway to sail a direct course west to Hvarf in Greenland, you pass far enough north of the Shetlands that you sight land in clear weather only, then so much south of the Faroes that only the upper half of

This pitcher, hewn out of quartz crystal, was produced during the Fatimid caliphate, which ruled North Africa from 909 to 1171.

the braes [hill] is visible above the sea, and then so much south of Iceland that you will see whales and birds." Around A.D. 1000 Bjarni Herjulfsson sailed off course from Iceland to Greenland and caught sight of a new land—presumably the first European sighting of North America.

FRAGMENTATION OF ISLAM

The fragmentation of the Islamic empire that had begun when the Abbasid dynasty took power continued at a greater pace in the tenth century. Still influential in former Umayyad-controlled lands, the Abbasid caliphs were unable to maintain political control over such a large and culturally diverse territory, and their base shrank to what is now southern Iraq. Having lost Spain in the mid-700s, they gradually lost Egypt and Ifriqiya (Tunisia and eastern Algeria) to the Fatimids and Syria to the Hamdanids. Lands to the east splintered even more, taken over by the Samanids, the Buyids, and other factions.

The most powerful of these competing dynasties, the Fatimids, rose to power in the early 900s. Before this time, the rulers in North Africa had recognized the caliph in Baghdad as the spiritual leader of Islam. But the Fatimids, tracing their descent from Muhammad's daughter, Fatima, and her husband, Ali, were the leaders of a swelling religious movement, the Shia sect of Islam. Believing that their lineage represented the rightful leadership of Islam, they sought to overthrow the Sunni political and religious leadership that dominated the Muslim world. In other words, they wanted to take down

IMAM Originally this word referred to the line of holy leaders descending from Muhammad through his daughter, Fatima, and considered the true leaders of Islam by Fatimid (or, later, Shiite) Muslims. Today the word is used more generally to mean an Islamic prayer leader.

Medieval cultures meet in this 19th-century Spanish oil showing Abd al Rahman III, the caliph of Córdoba, receiving Johannes von Gorze, an ambassador from the court of Holy Roman Emperor Otto I.

the Abbasids just as the Abbasids had taken down the Umayyads.

They never achieved such radical change, but the Fatimids did establish an imam in Tunisia in 909. He called himself Al Mahdi, "the divinely guided one." For the first half of the tenth century, the Fatimids ruled North Africa and Sicily. In 969 they conquered the Nile Valley and founded Cairo on the site of an older town. Here they made their capital, erecting a splendid new mosque and seminary. By 975 the Fatimid empire was the most powerful in the Islamic world, and its territory included North Africa, Palestine, Syria, and the holy cities of Mecca and Medina.

The last Fatimid ruler of the tenth century, Al Hakim, was named imam and caliph in 996, when he was 11 years old. Noted for his arbitrary, often cruel, decisions, he ordered the sacking of Fustat, a city near Cairo where many Jews lived. Christians and Sunnis were also persecuted, and, since he disliked barking, all dogs were to be killed. Certain vegetables and shellfish were banned. It was a time of intolerance unlike any experienced under Muslim rule before. On the other hand, Al Hakim built mosques, encouraged poets, and distributed food during famines. He must have spawned enemies, because while taking a walk one night in 1021, he mysteriously disappeared.

The Fatimids had a missionary branch whose job was to preach the faith and to denounce the Abbasid leaders as heretics and frauds. The Fatimids used a trade route that promoted the Red Sea corridor over the Persian Gulf route that the Abbasids favored. Their hegemony remained strong through the mid-1000s, then began a gradual decline. Internal disputes, the inability to win over a Sunni majority, and the arrival of the European crusaders finally closed the book on the Fatimids. Their last ruler died in 1171.

Another dynasty that bled some power away from Baghdad, the Hamdanids, controlled most of northern Iraq and Syria during the tenth century. Known as fierce fighters, they were also big patrons of Arabic poetry and scholarship.

The Samanids controlled territory northeast of Persia (today's Iran) throughout most of the tenth century. Renowned for their pottery, Samanid artisans used bright colors and worked such motifs as birds, lions, and Arabic calligraphy into the design of their bowls and plates.

The Carmathians (also spelled Qarmatians) were a dissident sect operating mostly out of Bahrain. They became infamous for uprisings in Syria and Iraq, and they sacked the holy city of Mecca in 930, stealing the precious Black Stone, which by tradition fell from heaven to show Adam and Eve where to locate a place of worship. It was kept as a sacred object of worship in the Kaaba, Mecca's most holy building, and the Carmathians held on to it for some 20 years. It is still preserved in the Kaaba today, although fractured into several pieces, very likely during the years that the Carmathians kept it. Highly principled yet in opposition to other Islamic groups—they maintained a vegetarian diet and scorned the pilgrimage to Mecca—the Carmathians controlled the Persian Gulf for much of the tenth century, exacting tribute from the Abbasid caliphs.

The Shia-inclined Buyid dynasty came to power in Iran in the early 900s, and by 946 they had seized Baghdad, leaving the Sunni caliph a mere figurehead. Under Adud ad Dawlah, who took the throne in 949, the Buyids engaged in numerous public works, building hospitals and a dam near Shiraz, Iran. Diplomatic relations were established with the Fatimids,

Hamdanids, Samanids, and Byzantines. By the mid-11th century, a weak economy and internal dissent ended Buyid rule.

Masterpieces of Medieval Islam

It was during the Buyid period that the eminent Persian poet Ferdowsi lived, born around 941 and dying in 1020. Ferdowsi labored for 35 years on the *Shahnameh (Book of Kings),* an epic of Persia's history. The 60,000-couplet poem incorporated historical sources now lost and has thus become the standard work of early Persian lore. The sultan of Khorasan (northeastern Iran), influenced by critics of the poem, gave Ferdowsi less than half the promised fee. According to one legend, the temperamental poet threw the money away on a bath attendant and a beer seller. Fearing the sultan's anger, he went into hiding, where he composed a satire on the sultan. Years later the sultan had a change of heart and sent Ferdowsi the balance of his reward, but the poet

had just died, and his proud daughter refused the payment.

Another intellectual, even more influential, who arose during the Buyid dynasty was the scientist and philosopher Ibn Sina (also spelled Avicenna), who lived from 980 to 1037. The author of some 200 works on philosophy, religion, science, and language, he was Islam's most important early thinker. In his youth in Bukhara (in today's Uzbekistan), he found patronage under the Samanids and made great use of their royal library. By the age of ten he had memorized the Koran and many works of poetry, and in his late teens he mastered medicine and Islamic law. He was becoming widely known as a physician when the Turks came to power to the south, in Khorasan. At this point he undertook a peripatetic lifestyle that would last most of his years.

Avicenna became court physician to an influential Persian. His position brought him status yet also made him a

FAMINE IN BYZANTIUM

The Dawn of Feudalism

A plague of locusts followed by four months of bitter cold struck the Byzantine territory in the winter of 927-928. Crops failed, animals died, and people starved. Emperor Romanus I Lecapenus built temporary shelters for the homeless of Constantinople and doled out money to those too poor to buy costly food. Many small farmers had to sell their land and become sharecropping tenants on the fields they once owned.

This development threatened the security of the empire, since free and independent peasants were the best pool of military recruits and also the biggest taxpayers. Wealthy estate owners, on the other hand, used their influence to gain tax exemptions

and often pressed their tenants into military service to further their own interests.

In response, the emperor issued legislation in 928 and 934 to support free peasants and curb the accumulation of land by the wealthy. Successive emperors attempted to strengthen the agrarian legislation, but continual campaigns against Muslim forces still kept taxes too high for many of the poorer peasants. Famines struck again in 961 and 967, and every crop failure produced higher food prices, more destitute peasants willing to sell their land, and increasingly prosperous lords eager to buy it. Such changes transpired throughout Europe, ushering in the system of feudalism. ∎

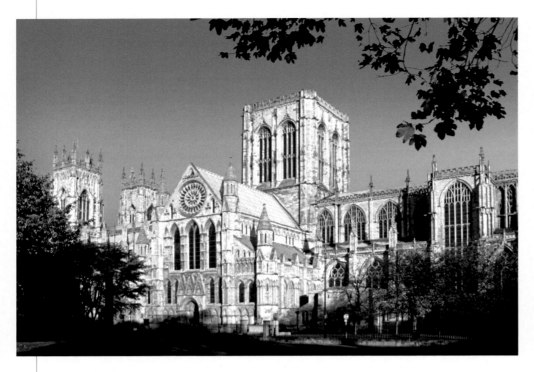

One of northern Europe's largest cathedrals, York Minster was built and rebuilt over many centuries.

YORK
CITY OF THE NORTH

Moors | Norsemen | Minster | Saints

The narrow streets and medieval architecture of today's English city of York almost give the feeling of traveling back in time. Founded in A.D. 71, the city served as Rome's military headquarters in the north. The modern plan of the city center remains largely unchanged from the initial Roman layout, and the main street, Cannongate, follows the ancient Roman road, linking the city's civic center on one side of the River Ouse with the basilica on the other. The Romans called the city Eboracum. It grew in size but then shrank when Rome's legions were called home in A.D. 400.

There is little archaeological evidence to tell us how the city fared between 400 and 600, but York would be forever changed after 601, when Pope Gregory the Great sent an envoy to England to convert the Anglo-Saxons to Christianity, designating York as the island's Christian center of the north. By the middle of the seventh century Edwin of Daria, King of Northumbria, had converted to Christianity. He was baptized on Easter Sunday 627, in a small wooden church built for the purpose and dedicated to St. Peter.

He set about rebuilding York's little church in stone, but he died in battle in 633 and did not see its completion. Although its actual position is uncertain—no archaeological remains exist of either the wood or the stone church—these buildings are considered the first built on the site of York Minster, England's grandest Gothic cathedral, which to this day towers above the city with its multiple spires and towers.

Christianity grew in importance in England during the next century. In 732, Ecgbert, brother of King Eadberht of Northumbria, became the first archbishop of York, thus gaining jurisdiction over the rest of the churches in the region. At the same time a school and library were built, expanding the church's function to include education.

Northern England and York became targets of Viking attacks during the ninth century, but eventually the city prospered under Viking leadership. By 905, the Viking leaders had themselves converted to Christianity, allying with the church. York became the region's only city to have its own coin mint, a sign of its wealth and power.

YORK THROUGH THE MIDDLE AGES

by A.D. 400	601	627	732	778	866	876
Eboracum has been settled by the Romans for nearly three centuries.	Pope Gregory selects York as center for Christianity in northern England.	King Edwin of Northumbria is baptized and accepts Christianity.	Ecgbert becomes the first archbishop of York.	Alcuin, known as a poet, becomes headmaster of York's Cathedral School.	The Danes capture York and make it their Northumbrian capital.	Called Jorvik, York is the capital of Scandinavian Britain.

Viking coins minted in York during this period are inscribed with Christian mottoes and statements of allegiance to Rome. Skillful seafarers, the Vikings soon became great traders, and before long goods from around the Mediterranean and Black Sea regions could be found in York, likely received in trade for the city's fine metal products. Cannongate, the old thoroughfare, was revitalized as the main street for craftsmen.

As successful as they were, the Vikings could not withstand the growing political and military pressure from the south, and in 1068 York fell to the Normans. Now in power in York, William the Conqueror built two castles, one on either side of the river, making it and London the only British cities with more than one castle. Today's York Castle, a massive fortification, stands where one of William's castles once stood.

In 1069 the people of York rebelled against their Norman occupiers. In what is called the harrying of the north, William and his men went on a vicious rampage, killing thousands, destroying buildings, and ruining farmland. By the following year the city lay in ruins, but the Normans began rebuilding many churches that had been destroyed. The new archbishop, Thomas of Bayeux, gained substantial political control and began the task of rebuilding the destroyed Minster, which was finished in 1100. A native of York, William Fitzherbert, served twice as archbishop of York, living through contentious times involving theological and political conflicts with Rome and with the Cistercians, at that time a relatively new and energetic Roman Catholic monastic order. He died soon after achieving the bishopric for a second time, and was canonized as St. William in 1227.

By the 13th century, York was once again thriving as a center of commerce. The primary product of the region was the wool shorn from the sheep that grazed throughout the north of England.

York was the northernmost walled city of the kingdoms of medieval England, founded near the border with Scotland.

Landmasses sit in the middle of a green ring of water in this Anglo-Saxon world map, created in England in the tenth century, clearly visualizing the ocean as encircling the known world.

England's king granted the city a charter, allowing York to maintain its own court and mayor in exchange for paying taxes to the crown. As the city prospered, it became an important military staging ground for English kings of the later Middle Ages, who were constantly at war with the Scots to the north.

Beautiful buildings were erected in the city during the late medieval period, buildings that contribute to the historic feel of the city today, including the Guild Hall and the Merchant Adventurers' Hall. Meanwhile, renovations and additions to the Norman church spanned some 250 years, so that by 1472 York Minster had assumed the stately Gothic shape that dominates its city today.

954
Killing Erik Bloodax, Eadred seizes York, returning England to English rule.

1068
York surrenders to William the Conqueror and York Castle is built.

1190
Anti-Jewish riots erupt; Jews are attacked and 150 people killed.

1212
York receives a royal charter and can govern itself.

1256
Henry III strips the sheriff of power; control of York goes to the people.

1349
The Black Death arrives in York, killing nearly one in three.

1486
Elizabeth of York marries Henry VII, a Lancaster; the Wars of the Roses end.

target of intrigues. Harassed and at one point imprisoned, he still continued his research and writing. His *Canon of Medicine*, an encyclopedia drawing on Greek writings and his own clinical work, was the world's most comprehensive medical compendium and served as Europe's standard medical text until the 17th century. Avicenna's final move was to the court of Isfahan (in Iran, south of Tehran), where he enjoyed 14 years of relative calm and finished his famous *Book of Healing*.

While Islam south and east of the Mediterranean was fragmenting into regional dynasties, Spain under the Umayyad caliphs was flourishing. Córdoba during the tenth century became the most brilliant and sophisticated city in Europe. With a population of about one million, the city spread out some 24 miles by 6 miles and is said to have contained more than a quarter of a million buildings, including shops, palaces, baths, a tremendous library, and 3,000 mosques. Córdoba was a center for architects, writers, artists, and leaders of industry. Especially noted throughout Europe and the East were Córdoba's leatherwork, jewelry, brocades, and woven silk.

The most famous building in Córdoba from this period is the Great Mosque, which was begun in the 780s under Abd ar Rahman I and enlarged during the next two centuries. Inside the edifice, a cavernous rectangle, stand 850 marble columns that support elaborately decorated double-tiered arches. Gold and marble mosaics grace the seven-sided mihrab, an interior chamber oriented to Mecca. When Córdoba was taken over by Christians, in 1236, the Great Mosque became a cathedral.

Córdoba's blossoming was largely accomplished under Abd ar Rahman's grandson Abd ar Rahman III, who ruled from 912 to 961. By suppressing rebels in the south and Christians in the north, he was able to regain power that had been lost after his grandfather's death. He kept a tight grip on state affairs, even executing a son who was plotting against him.

> THE KNOWLEDGE OF ANYTHING, SINCE ALL THINGS HAVE CAUSES, IS NOT ACQUIRED OR COMPLETE UNLESS IT IS KNOWN BY ITS CAUSES. THEREFORE IN MEDICINE WE OUGHT TO KNOW THE CAUSES OF SICKNESS AND HEALTH.
>
> ―――――――――
>
> IBN SINA (AVICENNA)
> ON MEDICINE
> *Circa 1020*

GROWING GERMAN IDENTITY

The breakup of the Frankish kingdom that started with Charlemagne's death in 814 was checked by the rise of Otto I, King of Germany from 936 to 973. The Germanic tribes—Saxons, Franks, Bavarians, Lotharingians, Swabians, and Thuringians—were each ruled by a duke. When the Carolingian line died out in 911, the dukes elected a king named Conrad. Neither he nor his successor, Henry the Fowler, were able to accomplish much, but Henry's son Otto was a new kind of king.

Born in 912, Otto the Great demonstrated his taste for power when at age 24 he had himself anointed and crowned by the archbishop of Mainz, head of the German church, in Charlemagne's former capital of Aachen. Otto wanted to gain the military and economic support of the German duchies. The German clergy was a force to be reckoned with, and Otto solidified his power by claiming royal investiture, whereby he could install his relatives and loyal underlings as bishops and heads of monasteries. Through crafty manipulation of the laws, Otto gained further property and monetary rights over the German church.

Several dukes revolted, including Otto's half brother, who was killed in battle, and Otto's brother, Henry, whom he defeated. Henry later took part in a failed conspiracy against Otto, but he was again defeated—and forgiven. Otto's instincts were right, and when his brother remained a faithful follower, he rewarded him with the dukedom of Bavaria. While dealing with these internal troubles, the king extended his sphere outward, claiming primacy over Lotharingia (also called Lorraine) and Burgundy. When Burgundian princess Adelaide, whom the Lombards had taken prisoner, asked for his help, he brawled his way into Burgundy, declared himself king of the Lombards, and in 951 took her for his bride.

Four years later Otto and his army fought a critical battle against the Magyars of Hungary. For 50 years, the horse-riding nomads had terrorized parts of Germany, France, and Italy, the warriors freely raiding farms and villages. Speaking a language related to none other in Europe except Finnish, the Magyar tribes had consolidated under one ruling house. When the Magyars invaded Germany in 955, Otto went out with several thousand men to meet them. Historical sources claim Otto had 10,000

The epic *Shahnameh*, composed around 1000 A.D., tells of Persian kings from prehistory to the seventh century. Here, the military hero Rustam kills a challenger.

heavy cavalry against 50,000 Magyars, though these are likely exaggerations.

They met at Lechfeld, the flood plains along the Lech River, south of Augsburg in southern Germany. Otto's forces found themselves at first trapped between two wings of the Magyar cavalry, but when the latter stopped to loot the German supply train, the Germans crushed the dismounted soldiers. Savage hand-to-hand combat went the Germans' way, as their disciplined ranks refused to surrender. The Germans then pursued the fleeing Magyars for two days, burning them out of hiding places and executing many captives; others went home without ears or noses.

The Battle of Lechfeld turned Otto into a hero. The victors raised him on their shields and carried him from the field, proclaiming him emperor. Their ad hoc coronation was borne out a few years later when the pope crowned Otto Holy Roman Emperor, a title not held by anyone since Charlemagne. The Reich—the empire of

the east Franks—was now firmly consolidated once again. As for the Magyars, they began settling down to an agrarian lifestyle east of the Danube and did not pose any further threat to Germany. The first king of Hungary, the Christian Stephen I, was anointed on Christmas Day in the year 1000. His coronation meant that the formerly pagan nation was now a part of Christendom. Organizing his kingdom along German lines, Stephen ruled for 38 mostly peaceful years.

Otto's son and grandson, Otto II and Otto III, extended the Ottonian hegemony into the 11th century, and both were crowned Holy Roman Emperor as well. Though not as strong as Otto I, they were able to carry on his policies through the relations he had initiated between the government and the church. Before the end of Otto III's reign in 1002, Saxon nobles were beginning to throw off the heavy hand established by Otto I. But by this point a Germanic cultural and political tradition had been created.

FRANCE AND ITALY AFTER CHARLEMAGNE

The post-Carolingian situation of France was different from that of Germany. Here the Carolingian kings did not die out until late in the 900s, and no strong leader emerged to defend the region from foreign invasions. Germany enriched itself with local silver mines and profited from its strategic relations with Italy and the pope; France, by contrast, was relatively poor in both money and connections. With the coronation of Hugh Capet in 987, a new era of leadership commenced, and it would last, in a continuous line of 15 Capetians, until the 14th century. Hugh Capet formed alliances with Otto II and Otto III, and though he himself really controlled only Paris and its environs, his descendants ruled an increasingly large domain.

The so-called Ile-de-France, a province containing Paris, was ruled by early Capetians; it may have gained its name, "Island of France," from the island at the

THE ASTROLABE

The Essential Tool of Exploration

A scribe, an astrologer, and a mathematician all benefit from observations by astrolabe.

Devout Muslims faced a difficult task in the Middle Ages. At five preordained times of the day, they were to kneel and pray in the direction of Mecca—but how could they know which direction was Mecca or, for that matter, exactly what time it was?

Arab mathematicians set to work to find a solution. The result was a refined version of the astrolabe, an astrological instrument of ancient Greece, which in the hands of Arab craftsmen became the pocket watch of the medieval world.

An astrolabe consisted of a movable map of the stars superimposed on a two-dimensional chart of known celestial coordinates. Matching latitude to the date, one could use the astrolabe in many ways—more than a thousand, according to the tenth-century Persian astronomer Al Sufi. Soon the astrolabe became an indispensable tool for maritime navigation.

Combining the compass from China, the triangular sail from India, and the astrolabe from ancient Greece, Arab mariners devised a new technology that allowed them to ply the seas between Africa, Asia, and China, trading products as diverse as silk, paper, ink, tea, ceramics, spices, jewelry, textiles, and slaves. By 1050 the astrolabe was reintroduced into Europe via Islamic Spain, and it served as a catalyst for even longer voyages soon to come. ■

heart of the city of Paris, by the confluence of four rivers that flow through the region, or because it was an island of power circled round by castles. The castellans, or lords, of these castles possessed a great deal of governing power: They had the right to collect taxes, impose fines, hear and judge court cases, and conscript men for defense.

Whereas France and most of the rest of Europe were rural, Italy retained much of the urban orientation of the Romans in the tenth century. Nobles constructed their castles within city walls, and their peasant tenants paid rent to them in cash; in turn, the peasants sold their produce to nobles, as well as middle-class shopkeepers and artisans. A rising merchant class began to appear not just in Italy but in England, northern Germany, and the Netherlands, places awash in silver coins. The Baltic port of Hedeby, Denmark, was a bustling center for European–Western Asian trade in slaves, textiles, furs, iron, weapons, honey, and wax, much of these goods pirates' booty.

All over Europe, a society of lords and vassals—people bound to lords by personal ties such as an oath of faithfulness—was based on a system of three classes. There were *bellatores*—those who fought; *oratores*—those who prayed;

This gold crown, inlaid with pearls and precious stones, was made for the coronation of Otto I of Saxony as the first Holy Roman Emperor. The face showing depicts Solomon, representing wisdom.

and *laboratores*—those who labored. The fighters included both nobles and knights; the religious group included priests, abbots, monks, nuns, and others; and at the bottom of the heap were the masses of peasants, who depended upon the higher-ups for protection. The fighters usually were both vassals and lords—they recognized a higher lord, going up the ranks to the king, and they in turn had vassals who were loyal to them. Even monasteries employed vassal warriors. Shifts in status could occur; for example, extraordinary service in battle was often rewarded with property. The

practice of primogeniture—inheritance by the oldest son—was emerging but not universal. Women could be both vassals and ladies—the female equivalent of a lord—and they could sometimes own land. They became oratores when they joined convents, and in this position, they could hire vassals.

Laboratores included serfs, who worked the land owned by lords. The lot of a serf was better than that of a slave, because serfs were generally considered human beings with certain rights, including, most important, the right to be protected by the law and by the lord whose land they worked. Slaves, on the other hand, generally had no rights; they were considered property. Serfs sometimes were allowed to farm new fields by clearing woods and draining marshes. As commodity prices rose, they could make money selling their own produce and animals. In the 11th and 12th centuries, communities of serfs developed into villages, centered on a parish church and its cemetery, around which clustered farms, mills, bake houses, breweries, and homes of craftsmen.

In these small, somewhat autonomous settlements, people depended on one another for food and defense. At feasts in the lord's castle, his vassals would share a meal and be entertained by bards and minstrels. For sport, and to keep in training, they took part in hunts

KNIGHT A knight was an armed, mounted warrior in service to a monarch or nobleman. A knight gained this elevated position after time spent in service as a page or squire. Vestiges of this post remain as the honor awarded by the crown for extraordinary service to society.

The victory of Otto I's forces at the Battle of Lechfeld ended nearly a century of Magyar raiding in western Europe and propelled Otto's political career at the same time.

clergy's effort to control the violence of war. Women, clergymen, and peasants were off limits as objects of wartime aggression, and violators of such laws were subject to excommunication. A truce was to be observed through Lent to Easter, and all year round from Thursday through Sunday. A 1065 edict held

> IN [886] ALFRED,
> KING OF THE ANGLO-SAXONS,
> AFTER THE BURNING
> OF CITIES AND THE
> SLAUGHTER OF PEOPLES,
> HONORABLY RESTORED
> THE CITY OF LONDON AND
> MADE IT HABITABLE; AND . . .
> ALL THE ANGLES AND SAXONS
> . . . PLACED THEMSELVES
> UNDER HIS RULE.
>
> ASSER, BISHOP OF SHERBORNE
> *THE LIFE OF KING ALFRED*
> *Circa 888*

that "if any one during the Truce shall violate it, let him pay a double composition." Non-Christians were not protected by these rules, however, and so the effect was to channel the violence of European warriors toward non-Christian targets instead of one another.

THE FIRST KINGS OF ENGLAND

Alfred the Great was the man for his times, preventing the Vikings from taking over the whole of England. Ruling for 28 years at the end of the ninth century, the King of Wessex was also a great promoter and practitioner of scholarship, welcoming scholars from Mercia, Wales,

and military games. War was an inescapable part of life for the bellator class, the "war season" beginning in spring when the grass was high enough to feed horses. A typical vassal might spend 40 days of

the year in military service, a lord often longer. There were rules for war, and penalties for disobeying them. The Peace of God and Truce of God movements that began in the late tenth century were the

and the Continent. The hugely important *Anglo-Saxon Chronicle* was begun under him, and a contemporary writer left a full biography, which paints a portrait of a forceful, wise, compassionate monarch deserving of his nickname. Plagued by illness for many of his 50 years, he carried stoutly on, setting a standard for future English leaders. His progeny, though a mixed lot, were able to continue his work, both in checking the Viking invasion and in advancing English culture. Although the early English kings did use force, they relied on it less than the entrenched dynasties of Byzantium. Consensus of the people was becoming more important as groups continued to rebel successfully against unpopular kings.

Alfred's successor, Edward the Elder, was king of the Anglo-Saxons from 899 to 924. He gained control of an increasingly larger portion of the island, advancing slowly northward. Edward also sealed a relationship with Germany by the marriage of his daughter Edith to Otto I. (When Edith died, he married Adelaide, daughter of the King of Burgundy.) After Edward's death, his four sons ruled in succession for the next 31 years. Replacing a brother named Aelfweard who died in 924 (and may never have been crowned), Aethelstan took the throne. During his 15 years, he continued pressing north, until he could claim title as first king with real authority over the whole island of England, Scotland, and Wales. That authority was still limited in some places, with Scotland and some areas of central England recognizing Danish law.

Nevertheless, the Anglo-Saxon kingdoms that had fought one another for some 500 years finally coalesced into one nation that shared a common history,

BELIEF

THE BULGARIAN PATRIARCHATE

The Origins of an Eastern European Identity

Institutionalized Christianity was introduced into Bulgar territory by Khan Boris I in 864. Boris foresaw that a single religion would promote greater cohesion among his people, but he did not want the Bulgars to lose their cultural identity. So in 886 he gladly approved the petition of missionary Clement of Ohrid, among others, to instruct the new Bulgarian clergy in the Slavonic vernacular, which had only recently been formalized into a written language by Clement's teachers, Cyril and Methodius. Boris also established two literary schools, where theology was taught in Slavonic, church books were translated, and Bulgarian art and literature were born.

Boris was denied an autonomous patriarchate, but Symeon, his son and successor, demanded one. During his reign, Symeon sieged Constantinople five times, declaring Bulgaria's church a patriarchate and himself emperor of all Bulgarians.

Constantinople recognized the patriarchate after Symeon's death in 927 and then rescinded it in 1018, but by then the seeds of Bulgarian Orthodoxy had already been sown. ∎

The Bulgars adopted Christianity in the ninth century and soon produced works of Christian art, such as this saintly portrait.

language, and government. The shire system created by Alfred spread throughout England, with courts on three jurisdictional levels. Kings' sheriffs acted as local administrators; manors (estates owned by lords) also employed officials called reeves. Charity for the poor and mercy for first-time offenders were laid out in the law.

Aethelstan's half brother Edmund ruled for only seven years, from 939 to 946, but during that time he had to regain parts of Northumbria and support the comeback of monasteries that had been devastated by the Vikings. Killed by an exiled robber, Edmund gave way to his brother Eadred, who ruled from 946 to 955, also facing a Northumbria problem. When the Northumbrians rebelled and proclaimed the Norwegian Erik Bloodax their king, Eadred marched north, laying waste their land. The Northumbrians ultimately recognized Eadred as their rightful king.

Eadred was succeeded by Edmund's teenage son Eadwig, who ruled for only two years before the Northumbrians, now joined by the Mercians, revolted and installed his brother Edgar as king. Deposed, Eadwig continued as ruler of southern England until his early death in 959. Meanwhile, Edgar began a reign that would last for 16 years. A champion of the monastic revival as well, he enjoyed a period of peace and prosperity. He prescribed penalties for those not tithing the church or paying their Peter's pence—the annual penny owed by every householder to the church in Rome. Edgar also sponsored three powerful prelates, who were ultimately canonized as saints: Aethelwold, builder of a cathedral at Winchester; Oswald, Benedictine monk and archbishop of York; and Dunstan, archbishop of Canterbury.

Four ninth- and tenth-century Saxon kings—clockwise from top left, Edmund the Martyr, Edward the Elder, Aethelstan, and Alfred the Great: While they ruled smaller regions, they helped unify England.

Born in 924 and educated by Irish monks who lived in a ruined abbey in Glastonbury, Dunstan became a member of Aethelstan's court at a young age, but his intellectual curiosity drew criticism. Some even accused him of reading heathen literature and performing black magic. Banished from the court, he was attacked as he departed, beaten, and thrown into a cesspool. Undeterred, he escaped to live with his uncle, the bishop of Winchester, and then returned to Glastonbury, where he lived as a hermit, waiting until the political winds shifted.

When Edmund took the throne, he made Dunstan the abbot of Glastonbury, a move with two huge consequences, for Dunstan both launched the revival of England's monasteries and also preached conciliation with the Danish. But he fell out with Edmund's son King Eadwig. Too vocal in his criticism of Eadwig's dissolute behavior, Dunstan once again had to flee, this time to Flanders. Recalled by the next king, Edgar, Dunstan could finally settle safely in England. As archbishop of Canterbury he became England's chief prelate. He established and reformed monasteries, sent missionaries to heathen Scandinavia, and fostered a vigorous intellectual movement. Energetic and resilient, Dunstan was also a musician, a draftsman, a metalworker, a scribe, and a bell and organ maker.

Dunstan proved instrumental in elevating Edgar's older son, Edward, to the throne. Unfortunately an antimonastic movement caught Edward in its crossfire, and he was assassinated in 978 while visiting his younger brother, Aethelred. It is not known whether the latter had anything to do with the murder—they were only around 10 and 15 years old—but as a result, Edward was eventually canonized as Saint Edward the Martyr and his brother was meanwhile crowned as King Aethelred II. He ruled for 38 years, until 1016; as noted earlier, Aethelred the Unready's rule was marked by weak-

With this document, composed in Latin, handwritten by scribes, and approved by King Eadwig, property near Annington, Sussex, south of London, was granted in 956.

ness and a loss of ground to the Vikings. Suspicions about his possible role in his brother's death made it hard for him to rally supporters.

Aethelred's son Edmund, born when Aethelred was about 15, became King Edmund II on his father's death in 1016. Along with the throne he inherited a huge Danish problem. He would survive in office only seven months, probably dying of natural causes, but during that short time he earned the moniker "Ironside" for valiantly—and vainly—attempting to stop a tremendous invasion led by Denmark's King Canute (also spelled Cnut). Scandinavians were by now Christian, and they had blended with the English so much over the course of two centuries that they were no longer considered outsiders. In the wake of the Danish invasion, many people sided with Edmund, but even more were fed up with Aethelred's legacy and sided instead with Canute.

Son of Sweyn Forkbeard, Canute accompanied his father as the Danish invaded England in 1013. With Sweyn's death the following year, Canute carried on the struggle against Edmund II. On Aethelred's death in 1016, the *witan,* or council of ruling lords, in Southampton decided in favor of Canute as king, yet the witan in London voted in favor of Edmund. With the kingdom split, the war continued. Resolution came only when Edmund died, later that year.

Now king of all England, Canute started out in very unpromising fashion. He stripped English landowners of their estates and gave them to his Danish compatriots. He extracted a staggering danegeld of 83,000 pounds of silver, with which he paid off his troops and consolidated his rule. Then he stamped out a potential rival by having Edmund's brother killed, and for good measure he killed or banished other English leaders. In 1017 he married Aethelred's widow, Emma, thus keeping her two sons, who were living in exile in Normandy, from

THE WORLD IN THE TENTH CENTURY

The Muslim Empire changed radically in the tenth century, as the Fatimids broke away from the Sunni Abbasids, resettled in North Africa, and took Cairo as their capital. Abbassid power began to decline in Baghdad, yet with the Fatimids, from northern Africa to Mesopotamia and Persia, the empire continued to expand and absorb many races and cultures.

Empires rose and fell throughout Asia as well. The Chola kingdom of southern India continued to prosper, producing spectacular architecture and art. By A.D. 1000 the Chola conquered Kerala and northern Sri Lanka. In China the fall of the Tang dynasty led to decades of fracturing, known as the Era of Five Dynasties. By 960 the military leader Zhao Kuangyin had reunited China under the Song dynasty, ushering in a period of remarkable cultural achievement. In Korea, too, the fall of the Silla and the rise of a unified state triggered decades of high artistic development.

In the Americas, the Toltec of central Mexico continued to grow in military might, operating out of the magnificent city of Tula and establishing commercial relationships with surrounding provinces. Farther north, the Hohokam Indians of the American Southwest developed complex irrigation systems and flourished in the harsh desert environment, while the nearby Cahokia mound builders constructed sophisticated cities in the Mississippi River Valley. All across the present-day United States, advancements in maize agriculture allowed civilizations to thrive and stratify. ∎

TOLTEC EXPANSION **A stone carving represents the birth of Toltec leader Topiltzin, son of Mixcoatl and founder, in 918, of the city of Tula. Under his reign, the Toltec invade surrounding lands and soon control most of present-day Mexico. Tula reaches an estimated population of 60,000.**

North America

Pacific Ocean

EQUATOR

Arctic

Atlantic Ocean

South America

HUARI AND TIAHUANACAN EMPIRES **Long dominant in the Peruvian highlands, the Huari and Tiahuanacan empires begin to dissipate in the late tenth century. They leave behind spectacular ruins, including signs of advanced agriculture as well as evidence of a sophisticated sociopolitical hierarchy.**

O c e a n

E u r o p e

A s i a

LI SHENTIAN, FIVE DYNASTIES **The fall of the Tang dynasty in 907 gives rise to the Era of Five Dynasties, which rule a fractured China until 960. But art and culture still advance with increased trade, improvements in printing, and the development of explosives.**

Pacific

Ocean

EAST AFRICA **They call themselves Swahili, Arabic for "people of the shore," a mix of Bantu, Arab, Persian, and Indian people in present-day Kenya, Tanzania, and Mozambique, joined by trade and Muslim culture on Africa's east coast. By 970, Islam is the dominant religion of this region.**

A f r i c a

Indian

Ocean

EQUATOR

SEOKGATAP PAGODA, BULGUKSA TEMPLE **The Silla dynasty, ruling Korea from 668 to 918, establishes a flourishing culture. Stunning architecture—such as the Bulguksa Temple's Seokgatap Pagoda, shown here—and visual arts distinguish indigenous Korean from inherited Chinese traditions. In 918 the Silla dynasty is succeeded by the Koryo dynasty.**

Australia

ARAB SCHOLARSHIP **Known in the West as Abulcasis, the physician Abu al Qasim Khalaf ibn al Abbas al Zahrawi is remembered as the medieval era's greatest Muslim surgeon. His medical treatises—which include these diagrams of the body—influenced medicine through the Renaissance.**

England was ravaged by Viking invaders throughout the reign of King Aethelred. His nickname, "The Unready," is thought to refer to the bad counsel he received from his advisers.

moving against him. (One of them eventually would return as king—but that is getting ahead of our story.) Perhaps Emma had an anglicizing effect on Canute, though, for within a couple of years his policies began to change.

He installed several Englishmen in prominent posts and took Danes out of positions when he found them unworthy. Finding a close adviser in Wulfstan, the learned and influential archbishop of York, Canute was moved to become a Christian and proved a strong church supporter. Piety and diplomacy naturally went hand in hand, and so when Canute made a pilgrimage to Rome to meet with the new Holy Roman emperor, Conrad II, he returned having gained advantages for his people: Conrad II agreed to reduce the tolls on the roads between England and Rome for English pilgrims and traders.

By 1028 Canute controlled the North Sea corridor, reigning over England, Denmark, and Norway. A formidable warrior, he became a just ruler, and thereby lived up to the medieval ideal of a king. The same could not be said of his descendants, however—Canute's death in 1035 was followed by bad rule and chaos. An illegitimate son, Harold I, ruled for five years, followed by a legitimate son, Hardecanute, who ordered his half brother's body exhumed and tossed into a fen. When two of his tax collectors were murdered in Worcester, Hardecanute torched the city. By 1042 an English king was back on the throne.

JUDGMENT DAY POSTPONED

In 1014, when the final Viking onslaught of England was at its peak and English spirits at their ebb, Wulfstan wrote an address to his people that has come down in history as the "Sermon of the Wolf to the English." "Dear Friends," he wrote in his native Old English, "This world is in haste and is drawing ever closer to its end, and it always happens that the longer it lasts, the worse it becomes. And so it must ever be, for the coming of the Anti-Christ grows ever more evil because of the sins of the people, and then truly it will be grim and terrible widely in the world." The turn of the millennium had come and gone, and until well after the turn of the century, fear and anticipation of biblical doom spread across Christendom.

As the year 1000 approached, many Europeans began looking for signs of the apocalypse. "And when the thousand years are expired," the Book of Revelation warned them, "Satan shall be loosed out of his prison." Christians believed that St. John's vision would be realized: An Anti-Christ, or false Christ, would overtake the world, ruling by the forces of evil and terror, and in a cosmic cataclysm God would meet and destroy the Anti-Christ,

A.D. 926. THIS YEAR APPEARED FIERY LIGHTS IN THE NORTHERN PART OF THE FIRMAMENT; AND SIHTRIC DEPARTED; AND KING ATHELSTAN TOOK TO THE KINGDOM OF NORTHUMBRIA, AND GOVERNED ALL THE KINGS THAT WERE IN THIS ISLAND.

The Anglo-Saxon Chronicle
Date unknown

creating "a new heaven and a new earth." All would be judged, sent eternally into the realm of the Anti-Christ, hell, or into God's new heaven.

There were plenty of signs of the coming Judgment Day for those who were looking. Halley's comet made a dazzling appearance for several weeks in

989. Comets were considered stars with tails, an oddity that to the average person presaged some important event. There were, in fact, no real breakthroughs in astronomy during the entire medieval period. Ptolemy's Earth-centered theories, originating in the 100s, held sway until the introduction of the Copernican heliocentric cosmos in the early 1500s. The changing positions of the sun, moon, and planets had been noted and used for marking calendars since ancient times, but beyond that the night skies were mostly a darkened theater for the staging of omens, good and bad.

In 998 two large, brilliant meteorites shot down from the sky, one of them crashing into the cathedral in Magdeburg, Germany. Who could deny that the destructive ball of fire was a warning from on high? Over the next couple of years, people saw lightning in the shape of dragons, blood raining from the sky, and other wonders and auguries of doomsday.

PERSONAE

SAINT MATILDA

How Saintly Was She?

Queen Matilda—wife of King Henry I, called "The Fowler"—was a pious woman, devoted mother, and model for future generations of queens to come—at least that's what her biographers would have their readers believe. Most of what scholars know about Matilda comes from two posthumous hagiographies—formulaic summations of the virtuous aspects of the lives of saints.

Matilda's hagiographies were written not only to emphasize her sainthood but also to legitimize her dynastic lineage. Born to a noble family around 895 in a region that is today part of Germany, she was raised in a convent by her grandmother until summoned to the court of

Saxony to wed Henry, the duke's son, in 909. Ten years and three-going-on-five children later, Henry became king of the East Franks.

King Henry and Queen Matilda traveled their kingdom, consolidating power and founding churches, monasteries, and convents along the way. But Matilda's two hagiographies diverge as to the nature of her life after Henry died. The first, written for her grandson Holy Roman Emperor Otto II, leaves out that Matilda favored her second-born son, Henry, over her first-born, Otto, in a squabble over succession. The second hagiography, written for Matilda's great-grandson Emperor Henry II, includes this episode, to affirm Henry's right to the throne.

A profoundly religious aspect permeates Matilda's hagiographies as well. When her charity and almsgiving to monasteries and the poor drew courtly criticism, King Otto I, her son, forced her to renounce her properties and retire to a convent. Almost immediately, her hagiographic biographers contend, misfortune struck Otto's court, instigating him to recall his mother and help her found more monasteries.

Not every word of Matilda's hagiographies can be accepted as fact, nor can they be dismissed as fiction. Either way, they paint a vivid portrait of the idealized medieval queen—and they provide insight into the motives of medieval biographers. ∎

All over western Europe, villagers did not even need to gaze up into the night sky. They could simply cast their eyes around and see war, famine, plagues, and natural disasters; they could hear the galloping of the four horsemen of the apocalypse just over the horizon. Vikings, Moors, Magyars, and other so-called barbarians had ravaged the populace for years. Though invasions had declined in the tenth century, there was still internal strife and famine left by scorched fields. "No region could be heard of which was not hungerstricken for lack of bread," wrote an 11th-century monk of food shortages that began in the 970s, "and many of the people were starved to death ... so fierce waxed this hunger that grown-up sons devoured their mothers, and mothers, forgetting their maternal love, ate their babes."

How common this cannibalism was, the writer does not say, nor whether it involved murder. He does mention a "horrible plague, namely a hidden fire which, upon whatsoever limb it fastened, consumed it and severed it from the body." That "hidden fire" is now believed to be St. Anthony's fire, an infection caused by a rye fungus that can lead to gangrene, hallucinations, madness, and death—all taken by the pious as signs of impending doom.

Natural disasters arrived right on time as well. Italy's Mount Vesuvius, which destroyed Pompeii in A.D. 79, erupted again in 993, spewing stones

for miles around. Earthquakes rumbled through Saxony in 998 and France in 1000, and major fires broke out in nearly every large city in France and Italy. Were there really more disasters than ever, or did it only seem that way? As

JANUARY. PLOUGHING.

FEBRUARY. PRUNING TREES.

MARCH. BREAKING UP SOIL—DIGGING—SOWING—HARROWING.

APRIL. FEASTING.

Despite warfare, invasions, and poverty, the work of peasants continued with the seasons. This calendar series depicts peasant life in the first four months of the year, January through March.

the year 1000 passed into history, the world seemed to remain much as it had been before.

Some continued to prophesy the end of days, rationalizing that the turn of the century was only the beginning of the

end, which would occur at the millennium of Christ's death, 1033. A massive Viking attack of England in the early 1010s seemed to prove that theory. Meanwhile, events in Spain cast a different light on the promise of the new millennium. With a weak caliphate in Córdoba, Christian princes in northern Spain allied themselves with Berbers whom the Arabs had persecuted and began moving in on Muslim territory. After a three-year siege, Berber forces sacked Córdoba in 1013, a victory heralded by Christians as a sign of things to come. Christians would not claim the entire Iberian peninsula until the 13th century, but they had begun the backlash that would come to full power during the Crusades.

WORLDS OLD AND NEW

In Scandinavia the situation was entirely different. Even though Viking warriors had brutalized and conquered parts of the Christian world, the mixing of cultures had caused Christianity to spread across formerly pagan areas. The old world was quickly dying out, doomed in the face of a new civilization. Ragnarok, the twilight of the gods, was at hand.

As in the Book of Revelation, the vision of Ragnarok predicted a new world. Norse mythology had told that giants and demons would attack the gods, that gods would die like heroes, and that the sun would go out forever, its flames licking the sky, as this poetic passage describes:

APOCALYPSE The cataclysmic end of earthly life, predicted in Judeo-Christian tradition. In this cosmic and irreversible event, God will destroy all evil and elevate all the righteous into heavenly eternity. Millenarians believed it would take place at the turn of the millennium.

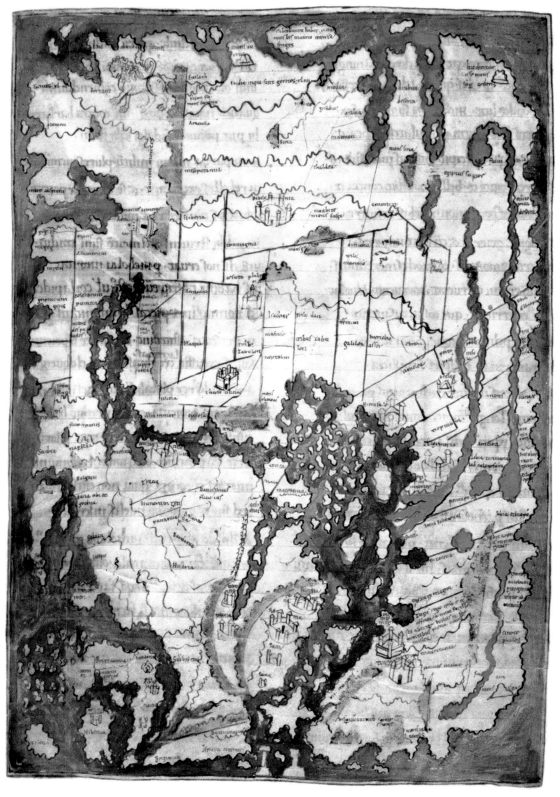

This Anglo-Saxon map of the world, probably created in Canterbury, England, between A.D. 1025 and 1050, contains the earliest known depiction of Britain and Ireland as islands, in the lower lefthand corner. Much information on this map came from earlier Roman maps.

*Brothers will fight, will kill
     each other.
Kin will break the bonds of kin. . . .
All mankind must depart
     this world. . . .
The sun blackens. The earth sinks
     into the sea.
The brilliant stars dash down from
     the skies.*

Leif Eriksson—here glorified in a bronze that stands in Rejkjavik, Iceland—established a short-lived Norse settlement in Newfoundland, Canada, around the year A.D. 1000.

Yet in the end it was not monsters but monks who came and, at least figuratively, killed off the world in which Norsemen and Norse gods dwelt together.

Among the monks who spread the gospel was Aelfric of Eynsham, considered the greatest Anglo-Saxon prose writer of his time. Known as Aelfric the Grammarian, he was educated at Winchester under the charge of Aethelwold, one of King Edgar's advisers. Among his works are a Latin-English glossary, a collection of 120 homilies, and a set of 27 life stories later titled *Lives of the Saints*. He tended to write in a rhythmic, alliterative style, using his native Old English. He challenged traditional Christian doctrine, denying the virgin birth of Jesus and transubstantiation, the conversion of wine and bread into the actual blood and body of Christ during the Eucharist. Reformation churchmen 500 years later would use his arguments. Unlike Wulfstan, Aelfric preached not the end of the world but God's mercy, assuring that "God is always near to those who sincerely call to him in their trouble."

Most people, whether or not they believed in the apocalypse, had little time for idle speculation. The daily struggle of life and work continued regardless. Even though the dawning new millennium was a time of uncertainty all over the world, not just for those numbering the years from the birth of Christ, civilization marched forward in the face of war and pestilence and catastrophe.

The unquenchable human spirit found an apotheosis in an event that occurred at the millennium. It was little noticed and then forgotten for nearly a thousand years. The Norsemen—those same people whose gods and myths were dying in the old world—reached out and discovered a new one that was real.

Sometime around the year 1000, Erik the Red's son went in search of the land that had been sighted. Sagas record the voyage and ill-fated attempts to colonize there. Sailing past Helluland, or Flatstone Land, Leif Eriksson headed south and went ashore on a sandy beach with woodlands beyond. Still farther south, he and his crew came upon a place "so choice, it seemed to them that none of the cattle would require fodder for the winter." They found "salmon there in river and lake . . . bigger than they had ever seen before" and, later, vines and grapes. Naming the place Vinland (Vineland), they built shelters and spent the winter.

For the natives, whom they called Skraelings, the visit was a harbinger of their own apocalypse. On a subsequent voyage, Leif's brother Thorvald had a run-in with the Skraelings and killed eight of them. A larger group came back and killed Thorvald with an arrow; he was buried on a headland where he had hoped to make a home. Later in the century, 160 would-be colonizers arrived from Greenland; their efforts ended after three years in a pitched battle with the Skraelings. Records from Iceland and Greenland indicate that American landfalls were made as late as 1347.

In 1960 a Norwegian scholar discovered the remains of a Viking settlement near the northern tip of Newfoundland, in an area called L'Anse aux Meadows. Evidence suggests that this was Leif Eriksson's colony; carbon-14 testing of organic material found on the site dates the settlement to about A.D. 1000.

EDIFICES

Beginning in the tenth century, the Benedictine abbey at Cluny, in eastern France's Burgundy region, became the powerful hub of a network of monasteries located as far away as England and Spain. Education, self-denial, and care for the poor were central to the Cluniac reform.

THE ABBEY

The Architecture of Righteousness

An abbey is a self-contained group of buildings that houses a community of monks or nuns living under the authority of an abbot or abbess. In many ways an abbey's design reflects medieval ideals.

Central to the abbey—and to the life of a monk or nun—is the basilica. Secular buildings were scattered just outside the basilica, their entrances oriented to the public, such as a guesthouse, a hospital, or a school. Nearby also stood a library and scriptorium for the preservation of religious and secular texts. Self-sufficient in its needs, the ideal abbey was also equipped with a kitchen, garden, bakery, brewery, workshops for artisans, and often animal pens and other agricultural buildings.

Monasteries were crucial to the development of agriculture in western Europe. They exerted an incentive and an organizing force, summoning up the labor needed to clear forests, drain swamps, and open up land for cultivation. Among the first institutions to use innovations such as the water mill, monasteries advanced agricultural technology.

While many abbeys of the Middle Ages strove to fit this model of a thriving and productive community, just as often they fell into spiritual decay. A single abbot could abuse power, especially as the reach of his control expanded. The concept of an order of several abbeys all under the direction of one central abbot was born out of the monastery at Cluny in modern-day France, founded in 910. The Cluniac reform was a response to the decadence and laxity to which monastics, including the Cluniacs themselves, were vulnerable, but it evolved into a political power system.

Subject only to the papacy, the abbots of Cluny came to wield as much power as any military conqueror, gaining influence through the acquisition of land. In medieval Europe, wealth and privilege depended on the ownership of arable land. Wealthy kings and nobles seeking to gain the church's favor granted land to the monasteries, which accumulated large tracts, along with the loyalty and labor of the peasants living on them. In exchange for land, the abbots promised blessings and salvation, at the same time waging endless arguments over whether abbot or nobleman held the supreme authority. ■

Sacred documents were often elaborately decorated and bound, as evident with this 16th-century Koran. A *thulth* style calligraphy inscription is visible on the binding of the case, which is made of embossed leather.

BOOKS & PRINTING

O f all the advancements made in the medieval era, perhaps none so dramatically affected the cultural landscape like the printing press. Though printing did not come into widespread use until the latter half of the 15th century, it quickly and irrevocably changed the way knowledge was passed on, contributing to a wider sharing of ideas, as well as the standardization of some languages. Johannes Gutenberg of Mainz, lauded as the inventor of moveable type, printed one of the most famous books of the period: the 42-line Gutenberg Bible. Borrowing from existing techniques, including the use of woodblocks to print images on cloth, Gutenberg cast his letters in metal so that they could be used repeatedly and "moved" to create new words.

However revolutionary it might have been, the printing press—as well as the concept of the book as a keeper of ideas—would not have been possible without the handwritten volumes that came before. Illuminated religious and secular texts are some of our most precious medieval documents, illustrating everything from Bibles and biblical stories to military and moral instruction. Lavishly decorated with color, fluttering script, and swashes of gold, manuscripts were also frequently bound in ornate, bejeweled covers. Each culture had its own particular style of ornamentation, from the bold colors of the Spanish Mozarabic style to the light drapery of calligraphy of the Winchester School.

The popularity of reading—or listening to others read—also led to the establishment of European vernaculars as literary languages. Referred to as the "lay emancipation," the dismantling of Latin and Greek for written works, beginning in the early 12th century, gave rise to some of the era's most well-known romances and epics, including *The Canterbury Tales*. Later, as printing and the production of paper became part of local economies in cathedral or university towns, books and the book trade laid the groundwork for the cultural movement of the Renaissance that was to come.

An illustration of the Second Coming demonstrates the ornately decorated style of calligraphy of the Winchester School. Illuminated manuscripts are today some of our most remarkable medieval documents.

The earliest illuminated manuscripts were bound with luxurious materials that promised ornate interiors. Gold, pearls, and jewels encrust the cover of this tenth-century German book.

After Johannes Gutenberg's printing innovations proved viable, presses were established all over Europe, particularly in towns with universities and churches.

Perhaps the most famous manuscript of its time, Gutenberg's 42-line Bible was printed with moveable type—an innovation that allowed wide circulation of the Bible.

ET HIC: TRANS

h

1000 – 1100

BY THE FIRST CENTURY OF THE NEW MILLENNIUM, CHRISTIANITY HAD BECOME THE SPIRITUAL foundation of European society. As the 11th century progressed, Europe's various constituent states began to organize themselves as parts of a unitary culture—"Christendom." The economic, social, and political order of feudalism was supposed to correspond to the order ordained by God, with divine authority vested in his earthly representatives—the church—and its head, the pope. The prevailing Christian view, rooted in part in Platonic philosophy, was that the world of the spirit is more real than the world of swords, men, and the flesh. The ultimate fealty of the Christian society or individual was to God. England in the 1000s found that it could not chart its own course separately from that of Europe. The takeover by Danish king Canute (d. 1035) in the early part of the century was but the prelude to

more changes significant to the course of English history. The subsequent conquest by the Normans of France under William the Conqueror (ca 1027-1087) in 1066 was a bitter pill for the English to swallow. One consequence was the destruction of much Anglo-Saxon literature and the infusion of French and Latin into the English language. But the takeover brought England more in line with continental culture; Norman feudalism became England's established social, economic, and political order.

For Europe as a whole, the biggest issue of the day was the struggle between church and state. Who really had the highest authority? When the ambitious Pope Gregory VII (ca 1015-1085) came into office at the same time as the powerful Holy Roman Emperor Henry IV (1050-1106) of Germany, the stage

was set for a dramatic showdown. The church issued sweeping reforms for its clergy. The most important reform involved investiture—the appointment of bishops. The pope claimed that secular lords had no authority to appoint high-ranking churchmen, and Henry disagreed.

By the end of this century, Christianity was spreading farther across Europe, while the Turkic Seljuks were conquering Syria and Palestine in the Middle East. To extend his power and put some of the violent propensities of Christian warriors to better use than petty civil wars, the pope called for a Crusade to take back the Holy Land.

Peasants and soldiers by the tens of thousands picked up the cross and marched eastward to Constantinople and on into Asia Minor. The Greek Orthodox and Roman Catholic

Picturing the stages in the creation of the world, this illumination opened a medieval Flemish edition of a first-century classic, *Antiquities of the Jews* by Josephus.
PRECEDING PAGES: A detail from the Bayeux Tapestry, a vast medieval depiction of the 1066 Battle of Hastings in stitchery, shows Norman forces fording a river.

Churches had split for good in 1054, and here was a chance for a reunion in a higher cause. But the Byzantine emperor did little more than point the way; the crusaders did the rest.

The First Crusade achieved its goal of setting up Latinate colonies in the Holy Land, but at a high price. Convulsions of bloodlust left a legacy of distrust in the Muslim world, while back in Europe unofficial Crusades turned into raids of rage against Jews and other minorities in the first organized pogroms.

A CHANGING ENGLAND

The 11th century brought about a fundamental shift in English history. By the new millennium, the Anglo-Saxon rulers had finally cobbled together a kingdom with the glimmerings of political stability. But under massive Viking attacks, the country yielded to an invincible outsider, King Canute of Denmark (r. 1016-1035). England would have but two more Anglo-Saxon kings.

Edward the Confessor (1003-1066) was a son of the ineffective king Aethelred. During the Danish invasion early in the century, he and his family took refuge in Normandy, France, the home of his mother. Edward succeeded to the throne of England in 1042, and he went about putting Normans and other foreigners in high government positions, thus paving the way for actual Norman conquest. A weak leader but a pious and dignified man, he married late and within six years dismissed his wife. On Edward's death in 1066, his son Harold claimed the throne, but by then forces were already at work against Harold.

Across the English Channel, Normandy, in northwestern France, had been a cultural backwater in the early

Reform movements in the church were a response to extravagances such as this gold Gospel cover, inlaid with semiprecious stones.

THE ELEVENTH CENTURY

ca 1000
Leif Eriksson reaches North America.

1012
The church begins prosecuting heretics.

1016
Denmark's Canute is crowned King of England.

1040
Macbeth becomes King of Scotland.

1042
Edward the Confessor succeeds
Harthacnut as King of England.

1046
Henry III of Saxony is crowned
Holy Roman Emperor.

1054
Rome excommunicates Byzantine patriarch,
institutionalizing Roman-Orthodox schism.

1066
At Battle of Hastings, Duke William of
Normandy defeats King Harold of England.

1097
The First Crusade arrives at Constantinople.

1099
Crusaders conquer Jerusalem and the
First Crusade ends.

tenth century. But a feudal system was developing there, which meant that the dukes grew powerful enough to elevate Hugh Capet to the French throne in the 980s. By the early 1000s they were enriching their province by building monastic schools and importing scholars. Within a few decades Normandy was the most powerful duchy in France, its duke capable of raising an army of several hundred knights. The stage was set for the rise of a dominant Norman duke with great ambition: William I.

William was born about 1027 as the illegitimate son of Norman duke Richard the Magnificent. Called William the Bastard in his early years, he owed his survival against plotters to his mother, while several of his guardians came to brutal deaths. Knighted at age 15, he soon learned how to fight and how to form alliances, and was able to outmaneuver the claims of rival kinsmen.

William was muscular, robust, smart, and harsh. He learned to lead by example—and by instilling fear. While his distant cousin Edward the Confessor was in exile in Normandy, William befriended him and apparently received the promise of succeeding him in England. Furthering William's cause, the pope disapproved of the independence and corruption of the Anglo-Saxon church, and in William he saw his best option for a strong ally.

In any event, when Harold took the throne, William decided to make his move. In September of 1066, Harold was up in the north fending off an invasion from Norway. At the same time, William was sailing the channel and landing in southern England with several thousand cavalry and infantry. Harold's men were spent, but he force-marched them south, and in less than three weeks they were facing William's deadly archers and crossbowmen. When his attendants accidentally put William's armor on backwards, legend has it that he turned it around with a laugh and said, "The power of my dukedom shall be turned into a kingdom."

THE BATTLE OF HASTINGS

The two armies met outside Hastings on October 14, and at first the English held firm. Then when William feinted a retreat, the sturdy English line broke in pursuit. William, amidst his army, ordered an about-face, and the confused English took flight.

For a while, chaos reigned—javelins flying, broadaxes heaving, men groaning and sweating in the labor of battle. The leaders themselves fought like demons, Harold on foot and William on horseback. (Horses were shot from under him three times, and he kept on fighting.)

The momentum began turning in favor of the English again, until an arrow pierced Harold's brain, at which point the English resistance collapsed. William quickly moved to put out any sparks of rebellion in the countryside. On Christmas Day he was crowned King of England in Westminster Abbey, and Anglo-Saxon rule came to an end.

The Anglo-Saxon Chronicle records William the Conqueror's personality and ruling style. He was "a very wise man, and very powerful, more dignified and strong than any of his predecessors." On the other hand, the *Chronicle* describes him as "a very rigid and cruel man, so that no one durst do anything against his will." One thing generally agreed upon is that he demanded law and order. His 21-year reign was so peaceful that "a man who had any confidence in himself might go over his realm, with his bosom full of gold, unhurt."

The *Chronicle* further notes that William was greedy and a lover of wildlife. He established a vast preserve for deer, boar, and hares, sometimes clearing out entire villages to add to the royal forests; poachers were to be blinded.

How did William's rule affect England? The introduction of French language and culture, coupled with William's heavy-handedness, was felt throughout English

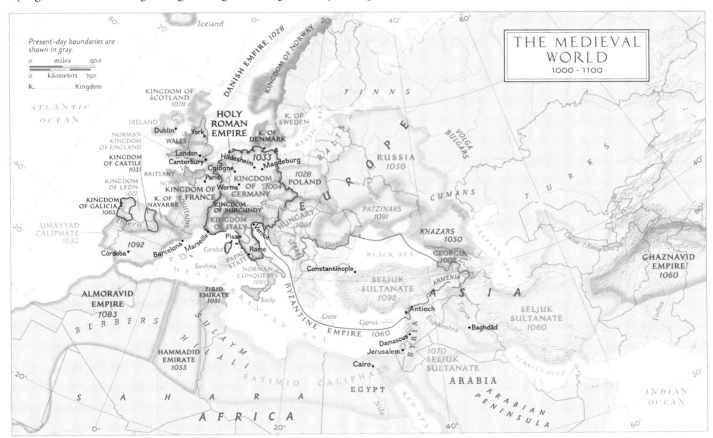

By the beginning of this century, kingdoms had begun to form throughout the continent of Europe. After the hold of the Danish empire on England failed, the Duke of Normandy—to be known as William the Conqueror—followed his claim to the crown. Successions of dynasties fought over and divided up Muslim lands.

society, most especially among the upper classes. The English nobility not killed at Hastings were for the most part disenfranchised and probably demoted to serfs. Most bishops and abbots were likewise replaced with Norman clergymen.

For decades thereafter the Normans looked down on the English: Many illuminated manuscripts and other fine Anglo-Saxon artworks were destroyed, and Anglo-Saxon became a peasant language, not to reappear for 300 years. For about a century and a half after William, England was essentially a French province.

Thus England was more closely bound to its nearer European neighbors. Crushing the English people was never William's intention, nor would it have been advisable. He tried to learn English; royal writs were sent out at first in English (though by the end of his reign he was using Latin). He preserved institutions that worked—the shire and hundred courts, sheriffs, and various government offices and agencies. He did this while maintaining tight, central control of the feudal system, so that no provincial lord could gain too much power.

One key to William's success was his unprecedented ability to squeeze taxes from every part of the kingdom. He levied taxes on estates, trade, law courts, and bishoprics, and even allowed lords to substitute money for a knight's military service. This

IF A MAN IS CALLED UNJUST WHO DOES NOT PAY HIS FELLOW MAN A DEBT, MUCH MORE IS HE UNJUST WHO DOES NOT RESTORE WHAT HE OWES GOD.

———————————

ANSELM
CUR DEUS HOMO
(WHY GOD BECAME MAN)
1099

Edward the Confessor (seated) holds court with a number of his nobles, who continually vied for more power throughout the 24 years of Edward's reign.

scutage ("shield money") enabled him to hire better-trained mercenaries to fight in continental wars. William's ability to raise and equip a crack fighting force became the envy of Europe.

William's innovations to the legal system marked another enduring contribution to English life. For land disputes in shire courts, he commissioned inquests

formed of a panel of sworn local men. Later known as juries, they had been in existence from time to time, but under William they became an institution.

MEDIEVAL CENSUS

One of William's greatest accomplishments was a detailed survey and census of all the property and landholders in England before and after the conquest. Dubbed the Domesday Book for its likeness to a record of souls at doomsday, the massive two volumes contained the most comprehensive compilation of its kind ever undertaken in Europe. Clerks and census takers went out through every village and hamlet in every shire, interviewing sworn citizens, and jotting down numbers—land amounts, numbers and kinds of workers, animals and their estimated values, mills, fishponds, and more. Citizens resented the prying, but the record gave the royal government a highly useful administrative tool—royal commissioners could more accurately assess taxes and courts had more complete information.

As the largest source of statistical information compiled in Europe up to the 19th century, the Domesday Book offers an invaluable account of medieval social and economic life. A contemporary writer observed with bemusement that William "sent his men over all England into every shire and had them find out how many hundred hides [120-acre units] there were in the shire, or what land and cattle the king himself had in the country, or what dues he ought to receive every year from the shire.... So very narrowly did he have the survey to be made that there was no single hide nor a yard of land, nor indeed ... one ox or one cow or one pig left out."

Early Anglo-Norman society had been a major breeding ground of European intellectuals. And continuing in this vein, by the end of William's reign in 1087, England was one of Europe's ablest nations and fostered one of the greatest of medieval intellects, St. Anselm of Canterbury (1033-1109). Born in Italy, he became abbot of a Norman monastery, where he began addressing philosophical questions on the nature of the divinity. Instead of simply referring to historical sources, he attempted to prove God's existence by reason, and thereby founded the ontological argument for the existence of God—the very fact that we conceive of a higher being means that one must exist. Anselm's assertion was that the idea itself is proof of the thing. Descartes in the 17th century would draw on Anselm's work for his own philosophy.

In 1093 William II Rufus (1056-1100; r. 1087-1100), William the Conqueror's son and successor, appointed Anselm archbishop of Canterbury. Showing how independent the clergy could be, Anselm refused to accept the position until William agreed to return the lands of Canterbury that he had confiscated several years earlier. He continued to knock heads with the king for years, mainly over the issue of how much authority a secular ruler had over the clergy. In one of his greatest later works, *Why God Became Man,* Anselm likened

A vassal kneels and pledges an oath of service to a lord. In exchange, he might receive a parcel of land, protection, or some other economic or military incentive.

the question of redemption to the feudal system: As in society a criminal must give satisfaction to his lord, so a sinner must make recompense to God. Since the amount of satisfaction depends on the status of the lord, a sinner must make infinite recompense to an infinite God. No human being would be able to pay this infinite debt; only Christ, both divine and human, could do that.

REFORM AND SCHISM

Anselm found himself caught up in church-state controversies that raged across Europe in the late 11th century, although William's new English kingdom was mostly peripheral to the real fireworks between the pope and Germany. The brouhaha was a reform movement that originated with the French monastery of Cluny.

Founded in 910 in Burgundy, the obscure Benedictine monastery became within a century the most important one in Europe. Free from lay interference, the Cluniac monks could chart their own destiny. They selected intelligent, forceful abbots with aristocratic pedigrees, and they observed and preached strict adherence to Benedictine rules. They were especially concerned about two abuses of recent times—nicolaitism (clerical marriage) and simony (buying of church offices). Clerical celibacy, they believed, would elevate the monks' status even higher than that of firstborn sons, and would make them more committed to God and less to acquiring property for their families. Refusing to accept bribes and gifts would help keep the clergy free of corrupting influences.

With the building of great monasteries all across Europe as symbols of prestige and power, as well as places of

AVICENNA

Persian Physician & Medical Visionary

Ibn Sina—also known by his Latinized name, Avicenna—was a prolific thinker and writer born in Persia (today's Iran) in 980. His father was well educated and gave him his first intellectual instruction. By the age of 21, Sina had surpassed his teachers in all branches of formal education and had already gained a reputation as a skilled physician.

Sina later wrote the *Kitab al-shifa'*, or *Book of Healing*, one of the most ambitious encyclopedic works ever written by one man. Expounding on philosophical and scientific subjects from logic to psychology to mathematics and metaphysics, the *Book of Healing* helped reintroduce the concepts and ideas of Plato and Aristotle to the Western world. In his lifetime, Sina penned nearly 450 books and asserted a tremendous intellectual influence on both East and West. Sina's *Canon of Medicine* served as a definitive authority in the Middle East and Europe for several centuries, and for that reason he is widely regarded as the father of modern medicine. ∎

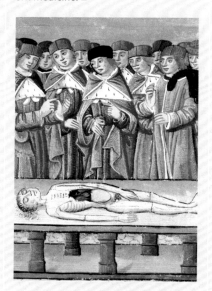

Muslim philosopher Ibn Sina (middle) mastered many sciences, including human anatomy, learned through actual dissection.

religious devotion, rulers were taking the church more seriously than ever. Hence the Cluniac movement quickly gained momentum and spread its influence far and wide. Believing that monks had the direct line to God and his mercy, nobles would often in old age hie themselves to their local monastery and spend their final days in monks' habits. It was during this century that All Souls Day, in observance of the faithful departed, was added to the church calendar.

Emperors, kings, and dukes were just as impressed by the Cluniacs as anyone, but they felt no need to subject themselves to church authority. In fact, quite the opposite. The Holy Roman Emperor Henry III (r. 1046-1056), for example, was a devotee of the Cluniac order, yet he believed his crown implied that he was Christ's earthly representative and thus had the authority to grant office to bishops and abbots and otherwise intervene in ecclesiastical affairs. In 1046 he convened the Synod of Sutri, in which he dispensed with three rivals to the papacy and elected a pope of his own choosing. He would claim this prerogative three more times, the final time choosing his kinsman Leo IX (1002-1054), who would turn the papacy around.

Leo was not content doing the emperor's bidding; reforms should be carried out under papal, not imperial, auspices. Appointed pope at age 47, this energetic man of God made the bold move of getting the Roman clergy and people to sanction his appointment. Now with a mandate, Leo set out to reform the entire Roman Catholic Church, focusing primarily on concubinage (nicolaitism), simony, and lay investiture (the appointment of clergy by secular leaders). To accomplish these he needed to strengthen the papacy's role

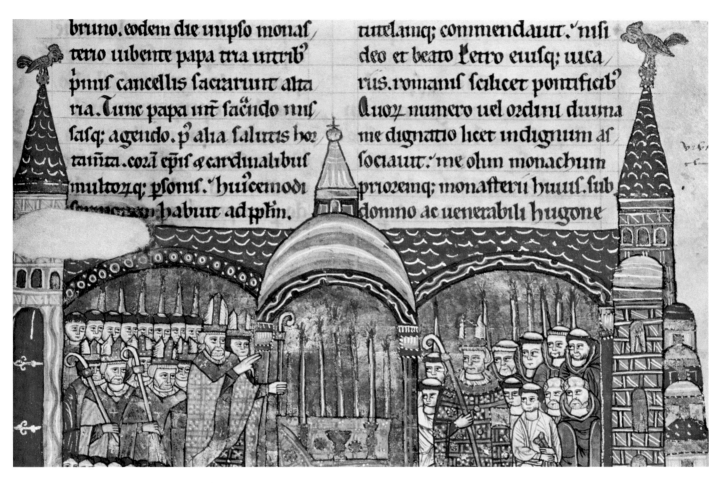

in Christian life, so he began traveling (which popes never did) and surrounding himself with major reformers. He also sponsored a book of canonical laws, the *Collection of 74 Titles*, which underscored the pope's primacy.

Among his new circle were Peter Damian (ca 1007-1072), Humbert of Silva Candida (1015-1061), and Hildebrand, who became Pope Gregory VII. Peter Damian was an adviser to several popes and an early disciple of voluntary poverty. A more zealous reformer, Humbert became embroiled in an East-West controversy when Leo sent him to Constantinople in 1054 to investigate a possible Greek Orthodox-Roman Catholic union. While there, Humbert argued with preeminent theologians.

A 12th-century illumination memorializes the opening of Cluny's third abbey, at the time the largest church in the western world. Pope Urban II performed the consecration in November 1095.

The three-century-old *Filioque* controversy came up, Humbert insisting that the Holy Spirit proceeded from both Father and Son, not just the Father. Furthermore, Humbert, frustrated with the Orthodox Greeks' refusal to accept the dictates of the Latin church, excommunicated their patriarch. The patriarch shot back by excommunicating Humbert. In what was known afterward as the Great Schism, the Roman Catholic and Greek Orthodox Churches now officially parted ways, and would not recognize each other for more than a thousand years.

GREGORIAN CHANGE

The Benedictine monk Hildebrand would go on to serve as Pope Gregory VII (ca 1015-1085), from which position he would push the reform movement to its zenith. Gregory's ultimate aim was, like Leo's, to consolidate the papacy's authority over the church and thence over the state. Many historians consider the Gregorian reform movement of the late 11th and early 12th centuries to be the pivotal point in the medieval age. Up to this time the Christian Church had been slowly penetrating western Europe, and as distinct states were emerging in the High Middle Ages, the reforms of the church, and the challenges they met from rulers, would set a new pattern. Only by holding themselves to ever

The Duomo, or domed cathedral, of Palermo was built in 1185 on the site of a previous Byzantine basilica.

PALERMO
CITY WHERE EAST MEETS WEST

Harbor | Crossroads | Tolerance | Sophistication

Sicily, the Mediterranean's largest island, has over the centuries been an important halfway point for sea travelers, both those voyaging east and west between the holy lands of the Middle East and western Europe, and those voyaging north and south between continental Europe and Africa. Control of Sicily meant significant sway over trade throughout the region, and the island remained strategically important throughout the Middle Ages.

Military and governmental control of the island changed hands a number of times, and these recurring shifts in power and influence left the island a diverse and tolerant place for much of its history. Palermo, long the island's capital city, is located on its northwest coast. There are times when it reached such levels of sophistication that its style and society became the envy of all Europe.

Palermo was founded in the eighth century B.C. by the Phoenicians, who settled many other parts of the Mediterranean as well. The beautiful bay offered a natural harbor, and a city developed around it, built on a high plateau bordered north and south by rivers so deep that they became impassable during the rainy season. The city's high elevation above the sea provided a modicum of natural protection. Palermo's geographic contours today are not what they were in the Middle Ages. Since those days, sea level has dropped, the harbor has filled in, and the city now sits farther back from the coastline than it did in medieval times.

The Romans took over the island as they expanded their empire. Palermo dwindled under Roman rule, but prosperity returned to the city with its conquest by the Byzantines in the sixth century. In 831 Muslim Arabs conquered Palermo and immediately began reconfiguring it as a city of Islam.

The emir chose a high point above the port to build his residence, completely surrounded by walls. Although little remains of his original constructions, that part of town still bears the name of his home: La Kalsa. By the time Arab rule ended in Palermo, several centuries later, over 200 mosques had been built, and the city had risen to such prominence that it was said to compete with Córdoba and Cairo in importance as a Muslim city.

PALERMO THROUGH THE MIDDLE AGES

254 B.C.
Palermo, ruled by Carthage, falls to the Romans during the first Punic Wars.

A.D. 535
The Byzantine general Belisarius wins Sicily.

831
Under Arab rule, Palermo becomes a trade hub between Europe and Africa.

1072
The Normans take over Palermo, which prospers under their rule.

1130
Roger II founds the Norman Kingdom of Sicily.

1132
The Cathedral of Palermo is constructed.

1194
German king Henry VI marries Constance, the daughter of Roger II.

The Normans took Sicily in the 11th century, ushering in Palermo's golden age. Roger II became the first Norman King of Sicily, and the city flourished under his rule. He followed the Byzantine model of monarchy, living in splendor above his subjects and acting as god's viceroy. He was an intellectual and a great leader; one scholar noted that Roger "accomplished more in his sleep than others did in their waking day." In particular, Roger was known for his high-minded tolerance of religion, and Palermo's rise is often attributed to the freedoms he granted his people.

The successful intermingling of cultures in Palermo is demonstrated in the city's architecture. The Palatine Chapel in the Palazzo dei Normanni, where Roger built his court, was commissioned in 1132 and represents an excellent example of the Arab-Norman style. The Latin plan follows that of other cathedrals in Europe, but includes Byzantine-style mosaics and a stalactite-type roof of Arab craftsmanship. This melding of distinctly different medieval architectural styles remains unique to Sicily and is eminently represented in Palermo.

Frederick II, who was Roger's grandson—the son of his daughter Constance and Henry VI of the German Hohenstaufen dynasty—perpetuated the atmosphere of religious tolerance that had defined his forebear's rule. French, Latin, Greek, and Arabic were all spoken in Frederick's court, and scholars of all ethnicities gathered there. Frederick was crowned Holy Roman Emperor in 1220, but his reign was plagued with wars and minor uprisings, signals of an empire that was beginning to break up into separate countries. He was simultaneously loved and feared. His popularity increased over time, and when Frederick II died, all the empire mourned his loss.

Shortly thereafter, in 1268, the French House of Anjou gained control of Palermo as well as the rest of the island of Sicily. The new French rulers denied the citizens of Palermo the autonomy to which they had grown accustomed, and they held on to the island with such a tight grip, it forced a major decline in the city's economy and spirit. The population of Palermo dropped

Occupied by Greeks, Romans, Muslims, and Normans, Sicily was a Mediterranean melting pot.

from 100,000 during the height of Norman rule to around 65,000.

In 1282, French oppression sparked rebellion. Angry Sicilians killed several French soldiers who had been taunting them during Easter vespers, then turned on all the French population living among them and killed over 2,000 people in just two days. The massacre led to a war between the House of Anjou and the Kingdom of Aragon, a Spanish principality that allied with the Sicilians.

The war ended in 1302 with the signing of the Peace of Caltabellotta. Aragon was granted control of Sicily, but the island, and the city of Palermo, would never again see the wealth and prestige it enjoyed during Norman rule.

The city design oriented to the harbor, and the streetscape of Palermo was home to some of medieval Europe's most advanced scientific research—and most cosmopolitan thinkers.

1220	1268	1282	1296	1301	1302	1347
Frederick II, crowned Holy Roman Emperor, moves to Sicily.	The French House of Anjou gains short-lived control of Palermo.	Sicilians riot against Charles I and Anjou: the Sicilian Vespers.	Frederick III of Aragon becomes regent of Sicily.	Pope Boniface VIII sends Charles de Valois to Sicily.	The Peace of Caltabellotta ends war between Aragon and Anjou over Sicily.	Ships arrive in Sicily carrying the bubonic plague.

Byzantine emperor Alexius I Comnenus, shown here in a stylized portrait from a manuscript on vellum, braced his empire against Normans invading from the west and Turks encroaching from the east.

yet Henry was Holy Roman Emperor only because the church said he was. The lines were drawn, the battle joined.

Henry sent a letter to the pope, calling him a "false monk," and claiming that in daring to confront Henry's own God-granted royal power, Gregory was betraying the office of the pope handed down from St. Peter. The letter further complained that Gregory had used his office to wage war (unsuccessfully against the Normans in southern Italy); for these and other infractions Gregory was eternally damned. It was not the kind of letter to appease the pope, and Gregory's reaction was to convene a synod that excommunicated Henry and challenged his very right to rule: "I deprive King Henry . . . who has rebelled against [God's] Church with unheard-of audacity . . . and I forbid anyone to serve him as king." This was a real smack in the face, for it denied not just his "Holy Roman" status but the legitimacy of his rule.

Church and state were at war with each other as never before. Gregory's denunciation touched off rebellion in Germany, as princes and bishops who had rankled under Henry's rule used the opportunity to rise up against him. Henry decided to take a diplomatic course of action. Hearing that the pope was headed north to formally depose him, Henry with a small retinue hastened south over the Alps in the winter of 1077 to intercept him. The pope learned of the king's journey and, mistaking it for a hostile move, took refuge in the Tuscan castle of a rich patroness, Matilda of Canossa. And here a great medieval drama unfolded.

For three days Henry stood a penitent, barefoot in the snow, begging the

clearer theological standards could the clergy feel a divinely granted superiority and thus hold authority over an increasingly pious public and its rulers.

The issue that turned the gears of change was that of lay investiture, and the two key players were Gregory and German emperor Henry IV (r. 1056-1106). They first came to loggerheads over Henry's appointment of the archbishop of Milan in 1075. When Henry overlooked two rival candidates and invested his own choice into the office, Gregory warned Henry either to back off or be deposed. It was a bold move for a churchman to make against the most powerful man in Europe, who was fresh off a victory over rebellious Saxons. And

INVESTITURE The act of placing an individual in a clerical, or church, office. Lay investiture occurs when a layman—someone who does not hold a position within the church—performs it rather than an official of the church. Some feudal lords assumed such a right.

forgiveness of Gregory. The pope was in a quandary—lifting the excommunication would seem a sign of weakness back in Rome. Yet the leader of the Christian church could hardly refuse to pardon an apparently remorseful soul who presented such a public display of humility. Sacrificing power for spiritual leadership, Gregory finally relented and exonerated the king. Henry was back in the good graces of the church, but the investiture conflict was far from over.

The episode at Canossa demonstrated that the pope had the strength to bring a king to his knees, yet Gregory had not won a complete victory. Henry now had a civil war on his hands, and while at first Gregory tried to mediate, he determined after three years that Henry was not to be trusted. Again excommunicated, Henry brought his forces south, defeated Matilda's army, and then lay siege to Rome itself. Several attempts at a peace settlement failed, and in 1084 Henry overran the city. Gregory fled to the Castel Sant'

Angelo, where he learned that Henry had installed a new pope, who in turn crowned Henry emperor. Gregory died a year later, his end no more ignominious than Henry's. The king's sons began rebelling in the 1090s, and one of them, Henry V, finally toppled him and put him in prison in 1105. He escaped and raised an army against Henry V, but died suddenly in August 1106.

The investiture conflict was not resolved until the 1122 Concordat of Worms. Under the agreement worked out in this German town, the symbols of church office—the ring and staff—were to be conferred by a clergyman; afterward, the emperor or his representative would touch the newly appointed bishop with a scepter to indicate the bestowal of material goods—land and possessions. It was a compromise, and rulers still had influence in church affairs. But the pope now wielded more authority than ever. The resulting civil wars meant that Germany fell far behind France

and Italy in scholarship and the arts, and would remain there through the Middle Ages.

THE ANGLO-NORMANS

The papacy had supported William the Conqueror's bid for England, but as the century wore on and William turned his back on Rome, the pontiff likely wondered if he had paid too much attention to Germany and not enough to England. Lay investiture remained a fact of English life, William continuing to confer both spiritual and temporal symbols of office on clergymen. He made it clear that he, not the pope, was the head of the English church. Only he could give consent to ecclesiastical councils, orders of excommunication, and even acceptance of letters from the pope.

The Anglo-Norman alliance, forced by William's muscle, was more than a century in the making, and the result was a model feudal state. Where had the Normans come from? They were named for

HELOISE & ABELARD

From Passion to Philosophy

Peter Abelard, renowned philosopher and theologian, arrived in Paris in 1108 and founded a school of dialectic that foreshadowed Europe's university systems. Abelard's ability to use Aristotelian logic to discredit the theories of academic rivals attracted thousands of students to his school.

One of his pupils was Héloïse, the young niece of a prominent clergyman. Héloïse was well versed in Latin, Greek, and Hebrew—rare for a woman in medieval Europe—and she attracted the affections of Abelard. An illicit relationship ensued that, in an age of strict rules concerning marriage and dowries, proved dangerous to Abelard's career.

Héloïse became pregnant and gave birth to a son, Astrolabe. She and Abelard married in secret, but her outraged family had Abelard attacked in his sleep and forcibly castrated. Abelard entered a monastery.

Around 1125, Abelard installed Héloïse as abbess of his monastery, and the two exchanged letters full at first of passion and emotion but eventually of philosophy and theology.

Héloïse and Abelard challenged social conventions of life and love at a time when such rules were considered divinely ordained. They may have been publicly condemned, but their writings provided a revolutionary framework for centuries of academic inquiry to follow. ∎

Héloïse receives a visit from Peter Abelard, castrated by order of her disapproving uncle.

To create an impermeable fortress—and to declare his domination over the English countryside—William the Conqueror built the 90-foot-tall White Tower, now part of the Tower of London, during the late 11th century. It contains London's oldest church, the Chapel of St. John the Evangelist, shown above in the 19th century.

the Northmen, the Vikings who settled in northern France. One of them, Rollo, was granted the territory of Normandy by a Frankish king in 911. Though they acquired Christianity and the French language, the Normans continued to make Viking-style raids, mostly into southern Italy. Little wonder, then, that a Viking descendant named William would have conquest in his blood. By the time William invaded England, Normandy was the most centralized state in Europe, its feudal system tightly managing all institutions from the church to serfdom.

Under William and his Italian-born archbishop of Canterbury, Lanfranc, English church-state relations prospered. Royal funds supported large monastic libraries, historical scholarship, and the building of grand stone churches in the Norman perpendicular style. One fine example is the old part of the cathedral at Durham, a town William fortified as a bulwark against the Scots.

For a while, Pope Gregory tried to bend the new conqueror to his will, demanding that Lanfranc come to Rome as a sign of submission, but the loyal archbishop made an excuse. Since there were no hostile dukedoms in England that the pope could stir up, there was little he could do. William's son William Rufus , as noted earlier, shadowboxed with his archbishop of Canterbury, Anselm, who was much more disposed to strengthen ties with the pope than his predecessor had been. But the English clergy were not interested— partly in fear of Rufus and partly because Gregorian reform was not particularly tasteful to them. Why give up marriage, land, and entitlements when your own king doesn't want you to?

William Ruthless would have been an apt name for the Conqueror's successor.

Every bit as tough as his father, but lacking William's fairness, Rufus, named for his ruddy coloring, took the throne at about age 31, favored by William over Rufus's older brother, Robert, who was given Normandy. Anglo-Norman barons who wanted Robert as their ruler fomented a rebellion in eastern England. Rufus then gained the support of the local populace by promising to

EVERY FREEMAN SHALL
AFFIRM BY OATH AND
COMPACT THAT HE WILL BE
LOYAL TO KING WILLIAM
BOTH WITHIN AND
WITHOUT ENGLAND,
THAT HE WILL PRESERVE WITH
HIM HIS LANDS AND HONOR
WITH ALL FIDELITY
AND DEFEND HIM
AGAINST HIS ENEMIES.

FROM THE LAWS OF
WILLIAM THE CONQUEROR
London, 1066

lower taxes, provide better government, and repeal his father's harsh forest laws. Handily squashing the rebellion, Rufus did nothing he had promised.

The king now concentrated on reuniting England with Normandy. Clashing with Robert's forces, he took the southern part of the duchy, and then managed to forge an alliance with Robert against a third brother, Henry. The family quarrel took time out for another rebellion of Norman nobles in 1095. This one was so brutally stamped out that no one dared test Rufus again—not with an insurgency,

that is. The following year Robert decided to go on a Crusade and mortgaged his Norman holdings to Rufus before leaving. To try to lift the mortgage, Rufus raised taxes, but before he could seize the land he died in one of those "hunting accidents" that plagued medieval royalty with odd frequency. On August 2, 1100, while riding in the forest in Hampshire, he was shot in the back by an arrow. Brother Henry, who just happened to be in the party, cantered to Winchester and took hold of the treasury. Three days later he was king.

A much better politician than his brother, Henry I helped pacify the English by marrying Scottish princess Matilda, of old Anglo-Saxon lineage. And though he did not keep all his promises to return to the Anglo-Saxon laws and customs, he did restore Anselm, lately banished by his brother, as archbishop of Canterbury, and was in general less severe and more competent as a ruler.

The first major action Henry took was to fight with his brother Robert, newly returned hero of the First Crusade. A better fighter than administrator, Robert was persuaded by a number of barons to try to take England. Not only did he fail, he ended up also losing Normandy— and more. By 1105 Robert had conceded England, but now Henry was on the move in France. The Norman clergy, disenchanted with Robert's lack of leadership, encouraged the cross-channel invasion, and Henry needed no further invitation to regain what his father had given away. Winning a key battle the following year in Tinchebrai gave Henry control of Normandy. He captured Robert and imprisoned him, and Robert moldered away the rest of his long life in castle dungeons. A son, William Clito, escaped and continued to battle for Normandy until his death in 1128.

A NOBLE SORT OF ANARCHY

The final years of Henry's life were complicated by the question of his successor. His only legitimate son perished at sea, leaving his daughter, Matilda, as his heir. On the death of her husband, Holy Roman Emperor Henry V, in 1125, she returned to England, and King Henry secured a promise from his barons to support her. No law on the books prevented a woman from claiming the throne, yet Matilda was both haughty and unwise. When Henry died in 1135, the Anglo-Norman nobility ignored the royal line and elected their own choice—Henry's nephew Stephen of Blois.

Under King Stephen, the next 19 years saw civil strife in England, a period sometimes referred to as "the anarchy." Matilda showed her colors by waging a protracted—and at times nasty—war against England's ruling house, yet the political, financial, and legal apparatus set up by William the Conqueror held firm. Lacking his uncle's political talons, Stephen was unable to control dissension among the nobility. Power in the central government was wielded by the bishop of Salisbury, his family, and the Earl of Leicester. Others were not happy about it. At one meeting of magnates and prelates a street fight broke out between factions. Demanding satisfaction, Stephen asked the bishops involved to give up their castles as a good-faith token. One of them went home and barricaded himself in,

The Battle of Hastings in 1066 was the decisive encounter of the Norman Conquest and ensured the speedy takeover of England by William I, also called William the Conqueror—a victory here romanticized by 19th-century French painter François Hippolyte.

not giving up until Stephen himself came and threatened to hang him.

From this point on the clergy began turning against Stephen. After two years of halfhearted war against Matilda, the mild-mannered king was actually captured, and for a few months she became the de facto ruler, dubbed *domina Anglorum* (lady of England). But when she tactlessly demanded allegiance, as well as higher taxes, Londoners hounded her out before she could be crowned. A prisoner exchange put Stephen back on the throne, and seven years later, in 1148, Matilda went back to Normandy. Though she did not return, in 1153 her 20-year-old son, Henry of Anjou, did; he continued the struggle for the throne, with more success than his mother had known. With the death of Stephen's heir later that year, and the erosion of baronial support, Stephen treatied with Henry. Stephen died the next year, and Henry II became the first Angevin king of England.

What was clear by now was that after William the Conqueror, the French and English were inextricably linked. England under the Normans was able to centralize power and build its cultural and economic institutions like no other European state. Henry I, like his father, managed to support the clergy without giving away power to the pope. And he went a step further by clearing monastic scholars out of government administration and replacing them with secular clerks. Though still churchmen, since there was no literate nonclerical class, these men began forming a professional bureaucracy. The crown also created a central accounting office called the exchequer, which kept careful track of royal revenue and disbursements.

THE DOMESDAY BOOK

Counting All Land Owners in England

In 1086 William the Conqueror, the first Norman King of England, completed an unprecedented survey of the wealth and property of almost all landholders across England. Compiled for purposes of taxation and litigation, this survey stirred up resentment among the Anglo-Saxons, who came to refer to the survey's two volumes as the Domesday Book. They were referring to doomsday or Judgment Day, as predicted in the Bible's Book of Revelation, and implied that the survey, like God's decisions on Judgment Day, represented final and unappealable law.

William sent out several panels of commissioners to collect information from hundreds of local juries. The results tell how the landed estates of an entire country were confiscated and redistributed to the Norman minority. It revealed that more than half of all land in England was owned by fewer than 250 people, most of them directly installed by William and only one of them female. The church controlled more than 25 percent; William himself 17 percent.

Completed in a year, the Domesday Book is one of the most ambitious administrative achievements of the Middle Ages, and still provides valuable historical, statistical, and economic information. ■

William I's survey of property holdings in England was derisively called the Domesday Book, since no one could appeal its verdicts.

Likewise, by 1135 the English and Norman court system, vertically managed under Henry I, was the most efficient in Europe.

THE FIRST CRUSADE

Around A.D. 1000 a group of Turkic people called the Seljuks rode horseback into eastern Iran. By mid-century they had united with the Sunni caliphate, pushed out the Buyids, taken over eastern Islam, and made headway in Byzantium. In 1071 the Seljuks defeated the Byzantines in a major battle that took place in what is now eastern Turkey, opening Asia Minor to militant sheepherders and threatening Constantinople.

At about the same time, Christians in northern Spain had initiated a *reconquista* of Muslim-occupied territory. By 1100 Christians occupied nearly a quarter of the Iberian Peninsula, and their reconquest was continuing steadily southward, inspired by religious zeal. Meanwhile, in Rome, the pope watched with interest. Similar pressure in the east could help assert his supreme moral authority, not only in Europe but in Byzantium. A battered Byzantium, presided over by a weak emperor, Alexius Comnenus, offered little resistance to the Seljuks.

Thus when Alexius asked for help in taking back Anatolia (Asia Minor), Pope Urban II (1088-1099) pricked up his ears. A win would add to the pope's prestige while helping to patch up relations with Byzantium. And a war directed at another religion would at least temporarily curtail the European feudal wars. Finally, it was a chance for Christianity to retake the Holy Land. Pilgrims in the past century had worn grooves on the roads to

The Norman forces of William the Conqueror stand ready for battle against the English in this detail from the Bayeux Tapestry, created to recall and honor the definitive 1066 Battle of Hastings.

Jerusalem. The growing Christian movement had spread throughout Europe, and thousands of sinners from all classes felt that the only way to guarantee the Lord's forgiveness was to make a pilgrimage. Though many Muslims apparently welcomed the added business along the route, conflicts inevitably occurred.

A mass offensive to the east seemed in order, and Urban's smooth tongue was all that was needed to rouse his followers to high-pitched fervor. "Oh, race of Franks . . . chosen by God," he importuned a crowd in Clermont, France, in 1095. "A grievous report has gone forth . . . that a race from the kingdom of the Persians, an accursed race . . . has violently invaded the lands of [Eastern] Christians and has depopulated them by pillage and fire." The Holy City, he insisted, belonged to Christianity. "Jerusalem is the navel of the world; the land is fruitful above others, like another paradise of delights." With a Koran-like promise of paradise ringing in their ears, the frenzied mob

> ENTER UPON THE ROAD TO THE HOLY SEPULCHRE; WREST THAT LAND FROM THE WICKED RACE, AND SUBJECT IT TO YOURSELVES. THAT LAND WHICH AS THE SCRIPTURE SAYS "FLOWETH WITH MILK AND HONEY," WAS GIVEN BY GOD INTO THE POSSESSION OF THE CHILDREN OF ISRAEL.

> **URBAN II AT THE COUNCIL OF CLERMONT**
> *France, 1095*

shouted, *Dieu le volt! Dieu le volt!* God wills it! God wills it!

Muslims had occupied Syria and Palestine for more than 400 years, but the illiterate masses were unaware of that, and the pope's exhortations made the matter urgent. Before an official crusading army could be organized, a charismatic French preacher named Peter the Hermit put together a ragtag horde of commoners, and off they went in the vague direction of the Holy Land. With strips of red cloth sewn in crosses on their tunics, they swaggered forward, some driven by religion, others simply for the chance to be a part of something bigger than their dirt-poor lives. Peter survived; most of his followers did not.

Detouring through the Rhineland in Germany, the motley People's (or Peasants') Crusade, armed with sickles and pitchforks, slashed through prosperous Jewish communities, many taking the opportunity to unleash pent-up racial hatred. They continued on into the Balkans with the same apocalyptic zeal, some 40,000 strong—men, women, and children. Living off the land, they clashed repeatedly with locals, then moved on, again without a plan. They slaughtered 4,000 Hungarians, then lost that many of their own in Bulgaria.

THE BAYEUX TAPESTRY

Telling History Through Needlework

The Bayeux Tapestry, a band of linen 20 inches tall and 231 feet long, skillfully embroidered as a historical tableau, was created sometime between 1077 and 1092 to commemorate the Norman conquest of England. The wool embroidery displays a continuous pictorial narrative of more than 70 historical scenes, beginning with the Anglo-Saxon heir Harold Godwinson's tumultuous visit to the court of conqueror-to-be William I in Normandy, France, in 1064. The images conclude with the defeat of Harold's forces by William's army at the Battle of Hastings in England in 1066. Additional sections have been lost or removed from the end.

Bordering the narrative are heraldic arrangements of birds and other animals, scenes from the fables of the classical writers Aesop and Phaedrus, elaborations and details of the historical scenes depicted, and other decorative motifs, including abstract symbols.

The Bayeux Tapestry conveys a vivid portrayal of arms, armor, and action. It was unique in its own day in depicting an event so soon after it took place—a kind of medieval journalism. The consistency of style and form suggests that it is the work of either a single artist or a school of similarly trained needleworkers, but the artists' identities have not been preserved. Even its place of origin is a matter of dispute.

The tapestry was likely commissioned by William II's half brother Odo of Bayeux to hang in his newly constructed cathedral in Bayeux, Normandy. Odo took part in the Norman invasion and was afterward appointed Earl of Kent, in southeastern England, and the tapestry may have been created there instead.

No matter what its origin, the Bayeux Tapestry was hung annually along the wall of Bayeux's cathedral, where it celebrated in detail the Norman Conquest for all the members of the congregation, most of them illiterate. It still serves today as a valuable source of information on medieval military equipment and strategy and as a remarkable work of medieval art. ■

THE WORLD IN THE ELEVENTH CENTURY

During the 11th century, the Islamic world fractured. The Abbasids declined as the Fatimids rose in power; Seljuk Turks took control of Baghdad and challenged the Byzantine Empire.

Asia stayed relatively isolated, yet China entered an era of prosperity: Under the efficient bureaucracy of the Song dynasty, the Chinese invented movable type, perfected gunpowder, and printed paper money. New agricultural techniques helped China grow. In Japan, Shirakawa attempted to stabilize the empire after the fall of the influential Fujiwara clan. Increased trade and agricultural innovation spurred population growth in the Pacific islands.

Northern Africa belonged largely to Islam, but sub-Saharan Africa kept fairly independent of the affairs of the Middle East and Europe. In the west, the empire of Ghana held its power as a center of commerce, while Zimbabwe prospered, trading ivory and gold. The East African coast, influenced by Swahili merchants, remained almost entirely Muslim.

In the Americas, native civilizations flourished—notably the Anasazi, whose Chaco Canyon settlement reached a population of 5,000. Smaller tribes in the Northeast and the Mississippi Valley also grew prosperous, developing new methods of agriculture and commerce and forging networks that spanned wide regions of the continent. In Mexico, too, the rise of the powerful Toltec and Mixtec empires laid the groundwork for exceptional achievements during centuries to come. ■

ANASAZI PEOPLE Settling in the plateaus of the American Southwest, the Anasazi survive for centuries and enjoy a period of prosperity in the middle of the 11th century. By 1050, more than 5,000 Anasazi populate Chaco Canyon. They construct sophisticated stone dwellings and produce finely decorated pottery.

TOLTEC IN TULA With a population of more than 30,000, the Toltec city of Tula, near present-day Mexico City, rises to the height of its power. The Toltec empire, spreading from the Yucatán Peninsula to the Gulf of Mexico, will persist into the 12th century and will then be largely absorbed by the Aztec.

North America

Pacific Ocean

EQUATOR

South America

Arctic

Atlantic Ocean

Ocean

Europe

PAPER MONEY IN CHINA The newly centralized rule of the Song dynasty, which governs China from 960 to the early 12th century, gives rise to a flourishing arts culture—including porcelains and landscape paintings—and improvements in agriculture and commerce. Among many milestones is the minting of paper money by the year 1023. *Numismondo.com*

ALMORAVID DYNASTY The city of Marrakech, in present-day Morocco, is founded by the Berber Almoravids in 1062. With a territory that stretches from northwest Africa to Spain, the Almoravid Empire reaches its largest extent in the last half of the 11th century, adopting Sunni rather than Shiite Islam.

Asia

Pacific Ocean

Africa

EQUATOR

Indian Ocean

BYODOIN TEMPLE Powerful during Japan's Heian period, the Fujiwara clan begins to decline in the latter half of the tenth century and yet still builds the Byodoin Temple south of Kyoto in 998 as a rural home of Fujiwara no Michinaga. The complex, including the Phoenix Hall (above), becomes a Buddhist temple in 1052 under Fujiwara no Yorimichi.

Australia

MUSLIM LEARNING Al Biruni (973-1048), a Muslim scientist and historian, makes lasting contributions to a wide range of disciplines, from astronomy to cartography and mathematics. From his *Chronology of Ancient Nations*, this page describes the famous surgical birth of Caesar.

In Constantinople, a nervous Alexius awaited their arrival with uncertainty. He cautioned them to wait for the main crusading army, but they ignored him and poured into Asia Minor. The Seljuk Turks killed all but a few thousand, who were rescued by the emperor's troops. The People's Crusade foreshadowed the arrival of more small bands that came pillaging their way east, and were wiped out by the wary Hungarians.

The official Crusade headed out in several armies during the summer and fall of 1096. Though no kings led the armies, the leaders were mostly capable nobles with military training. Among them were Godfrey, Duke of Lorraine, who was out for adventure; Robert, Duke of Normandy, the oldest son of William the Conqueror, who as we saw wanted a chance to prove his mettle; and Count Stephen of Blois—a future king of England, his ambitious wife urged him on. The most able leader was Bohemund, son of the fierce Norman warrior Robert Guiscard, who had conquered parts of southern Italy.

CRUSADERS EN ROUTE

The combined armies comprised as many as 100,000 knights, a prodigious fighting force for that time. Though purposeful and disciplined, they were not above massacring Jews and robbing from Balkan peoples along the way. From Constantinople, they crossed into Asia Minor and invaded Nicaea, capital of the sultanate of Rum (the Seljuk name for Anatolia). Then the Christian soldiers marched south to their next target, Antioch, the largest city in western Asia and the best fortified of the cities on the route.

Antioch was the crucial battle in the First Crusades's success. When the

The Muslim call to prayer has emanated from this ornate brick minaret since the 11th century, when architects working under the rule of Seljuk Turks built it in the north of today's Iran.

crusaders arrived in the fall of 1097, the Seljuks had occupied the city for 12 years. For months the crusaders lay siege without any success. Lack of food and water in the semiarid environment became a major problem, and the chain of command began breaking down. Stephen of Blois rounded up his knights and headed home, only to be badgered by his wife into returning. Word came of a Seljuk relief army traveling from Mosul.

Bohemund decided to try cunning instead of force. He persuaded a former Christian captain inside the city walls to turn traitor, allowing the crusaders to breach one section of wall and then take over the city. Now the crusaders had to hold the city against the besieging Mosul army.

But Bohemund organized an attack that cleared the territory of all resistance. Other cities now rapidly folded, giving the Christians even more proof of what they deemed their God-granted invincibility. But the momentum of the Crusade dwindled, as soldiers returned home and leaders set up Levantine fiefdoms.

Only about 5,000 soldiers left Antioch for the final goal, Jerusalem. The Fatimids had recently wrested Palestine away from the Seljuk Turks and were now offering the crusaders free entry to all holy places as long as they limited their occupation to Syria. But the crusaders had come too far to turn back, so in January 1099, off they went. A total of 12,000 soldiers and 1,300 knights arrived in Jerusalem in June. So did the heat, and the wells had been poisoned. The crusaders began constructing siege ladders and towers from scavenged wood. At the Mount of Olives, Peter the Hermit gave a rousing sermon. By mid-July the crusaders were ready; moving towers and siege engines into place, they stormed the city.

"Wonderful sights were to be seen," wrote a knight, eyewitness to the gory celebration. "Some of our men (and this was more merciful) cut off the heads of their enemies; others shot them with arrows . . . others tortured them longer by casting them into the flames. Piles of heads, hands, and feet were to be seen in the streets of the city. . . . But these were small matters compared to what happened

Rhuddlan Castle, built on the River Clwyd in northeastern Wales, stands near the site of an ancient pre-Norman seat of Welsh government. Its strategic design included two concentric walls, the inner one enclosing household spaces and the outer one workshops such as a stable, a granary, and a smithy.

The high nobility dominated the wealth and politics of 11th-century Europe. With no imperial centralized authority in much of the continent, kings, counts, and dukes—each with an inherited title—vied against one another in a power struggle of endless raids and wars, often at the expense of the lives of innocent peasants, forced to pledge their loyalty to a local lord in exchange for protection, a pact central to feudal society. Nobles had to build a defensive infrastructure around their land. Soon earthen ramparts were not enough, and stone castles were built at strategic locations throughout Europe.

Fulk III Nerra (970-1040), Count of Anjou, was a typical feudal lord who expanded his power through warfare and consolidated it through the construction of more than one hundred castles, keeps, and abbeys. A pioneer

THE CASTLE

Walls and Towers for Protection

in stone construction, he built one of Europe's first stone castles around 994 at Langeais, where portions still stand more than a millennium later.

Medieval castles in general followed standards of design and construction, but their designs also evolved in response to new weaponry and techniques in siege warfare. The heavily fortified central tower of the medieval castle was known as the keep, or donjon, where the lord and his retainers usually lived,

held audience, and made laws, and to which the entire garrison would retreat in time of siege. The enceinte was the outer wall of the castle precinct, usually fortified with towers, moats, drawbridges, and gatehouses.

Some medieval castle precincts developed into towns, the centers of trade and production. As that happened and populations grew, stone enclosures known as curtain walls were often built in an expanding concentric pattern. Crowded into these confining walls were crooked streets lined with wooden houses, from which emerged a new caste of merchants and craftsmen known as burghers, or bourgeois. Distrusted and often harassed by the nobility, the bourgeois merchants of medieval Europe brought with them new industry and an entirely new social order based not on land but on commerce and economy. ■

At the center of controversies pitting pope against both king and antipope, Pope Urban II roused support when he congratulated crusaders on their way to Jerusalem. As added incentive, he guaranteed salvation to those who died in the Crusades. Dying in 1099, he did not see Jerusalem captured.

at the Temple of Solomon.... men rode in blood up to their knees and bridle reins. Indeed it was a just and splendid judgment of God that this place should be filled with the blood of the unbelievers." Some 10,000 men, women, and children were killed in the temple; 40,000 Muslims were killed in Jerusalem in two days.

> THEY DESTROYED THE HOUSES
> AND PULLED DOWN THE
> STAIRWAYS, LOOKING AND
> PLUNDERING;
> AND THEY TOOK THE HOLY
> TORAH, TRAMPLED IT IN THE
> MUD OF THE STREETS
> AND TORE IT AND
> DESECRATED IT AMIDST
> RIDICULE AND LAUGHTER.
> THEY DEVOURED ISRAEL
> WITH OPEN MAW.

RABBI ELIEZER BAR NATHAN,
"THE PERSECUTIONS OF 1096"
Circa 1150

The First Crusade attained its goal because of Muslim disunity as much as Christian capability. The short-term outcome was that European enclaves were established in the Levant—the Kingdom of Jerusalem, the Principality of Antioch, and the Counties of Tripoli and Edessa. Colonists adopted the dress, food, and customs of the locals, thus broadening their cultural and religious perspective, but the crusaders who returned remained committed to wiping out the infidels. Over the next 200 years, Muslims would reclaim the European holdings, starting with Edessa in 1144, which precipitated the Second Crusade.

As for the leaders of the First Crusade, Godfrey ruled Jerusalem as "protector of the Holy Sepulchre" for one year, but he died in 1100. Peter the Hermit founded the monastery of Neufmoutier in Belgium. Bohemund was captured by the emir of Sebastea; after his release he went to war against the Greeks and, in a settlement with Alexius, became prince of Antioch.

THE WISDOM OF OUTSIDERS

The Christian militancy that developed in the late 11th century caught European ethnic groups in its backdraft. Jews and others were crushed in the wide swath cut by crusaders on their way. The First Crusade marked a turning point in Jewish history, after which anti-Semitism became a widespread stain on Europe. On the other hand, in Islam, Jews, like Christians, were generally allowed to practice their own faith, paying higher taxes and suffering discrimination but not outright persecution.

Jews in Spain during the 10th to 12th centuries enjoyed a golden age, flourishing as doctors, scientists, and business leaders. The poet Solomon ibn Gabirol (ca 1033-1070), part of an intellectual circle in Saragossa (northeastern Spain), knew the Bible, the Talmud, and the Koran. As a court poet, he wrote satires, love poems, wine songs, and dirges. His philosophical writings influenced both Jewish and Christian traditions. A Neoplatonist, he believe that a divine creative will radiates from God as sunlight from the sun.

The greatest Jewish intellectual of the medieval period was the philosopher-

Peter the Hermit drummed up popular support for the First Crusade, which he led, unprepared, ultimately meeting with disastrous circumstances.

scientist Moses Maimonides (1135-1204), whose work inspired such thinkers as Spinoza and Leibniz some 500 years later. Born in Córdoba, the young prodigy had to leave with his family when the city was taken by the Almohads, an intolerant Islamic sect. For a while they lived in secret in Morocco, until Moses' teacher was executed for practicing Judaism. They moved to the Jewish community of Fustat, Egypt, where Jews were allowed to practice their faith, as long as they were not former Muslims; if they had renounced Islam for Judaism, however, the penalty was death. Starting at age 16, Maimonides began writing important treatises on philosophy, law, religion, and other subjects. Supporting himself by practicing medicine, he ultimately became the sultan's personal physician. He is considered one of the greatest commentators on the Hebrew Bible of all time.

HILDEGARDE OF BINGEN

A Woman Who Dared to Be a Visionary

Hildegard was born into nobility in 1098 in Bingen, just west of today's Frankfurt, Germany. At that time, noble women were largely secluded, kept under the guarded supervision of male elders, and Hildegard was given over to a Benedictine nunnery when she was eight. By her own account, she experienced mystical visions as a child, but she was hesitant to share them, let alone write them down.

In 1141, at the age of 42, Hildegard had a vision in which she heard God instructing her to "write down that which you see and hear." A monk was assigned to help Hildegard record her prophetic and apocalyptic visions.

After more than ten years, her first work, *Scivias (Know the Ways)*, was completed. In it, Hildegard graphically describes her visions, interprets them, and reflects on potentially controversial issues such as the relationship among God, man, and woman and the true meaning of redemption.

Hildegard went on to become a prolific writer, pouring out works on myriad subjects. She wrote two additional books of visions, texts on natural history and natural healing, hagiographies, letters, a play, and upwards of 80 hymns and liturgical songs, one of the largest collections of any medieval composer. Hildegard even constructed and wrote in her own alphabet, which she named Lingua Ignota, the unknown language. Writing at a time when women were openly banned from preaching and almost any act of social participation was viewed as subversive, Hildegard amassed a cult following in her own lifetime and transcended the confinement of the cloisters in which she lived her entire life. ■

Greeted by the abbess, Hildegard of Bingen, still a child, arrives at the Benedictine Abbey of Disibodenberg, where she will spend the next 40 years of her visionary life.

THE SUFFERING OF OUTSIDERS

The lives of intellectual giants were relatively stable compared with the turmoil endured by the average Jew in these tumultuous times. Throughout Europe, Jews had in many cases become prosperous merchants, traders, tradesmen, and landowners. Along with Italians and Greeks, they had kept long-distance trade alive in the early Middle Ages, ferrying wines, spices, fabrics, and other luxury goods to the aristocracy. But when ethnic tensions flared during hard times, Jews felt the sting. They were shut out of the silk trade when Byzantine emperors banned them from Constantinople during the 10th century. Though the expulsion was ended in the 11th century, Jews were not an integral part of Byzantine society.

In western Europe the situation was similar. As non-Christians, Jews could lend money at interest, a practice that enriched Jews and enraged Christian debtors. As the Crusades proceeded, Jews were systematically persecuted.

During the People's Crusade, in 1096, Jews who could not find refuge with bishops or Christian friends were massacred in the city of Metz, France, the Frankish center of Jewish intellectual life. Though the Crusade's vanguard, led by Peter the Hermit, mostly extorted money for the onward journey to the Holy Land, this group stirred up whirlwinds of local malevolence against the Jews. Waves of marauders headed up the Rhine, unleashing pogroms on the Jewish communities of Neuss, Cologne, Mainz, Worms, Speyer, and elsewhere. Another wave spread west up the Moselle River, forcing Jews to convert, while still other pillagers went east to Bamberg and Prague.

The crusaders built large stone fortresses—such as this one in Aqaba, Jordan—as places of rest and safety and as a way to retain their advances as they moved through the eastern Mediterranean.

There were four more major Crusades up to the year 1221, then several minor ones up to 1444. Nearly all of them struck out at Jews, while Muslims, Greeks, pagans, and any others generally labeled as heretical were also singled out for torment. In the 1140s, before the official beginning of the Second Crusade, a fire-breathing monk named Radulf incited violence specifically against the Jews. He was ordered back to his monastery by Bernard of Clairvaux, who asked, "Is it not a far better triumph for the church to convince and convert the Jews than to put them all to the sword?"

By the late 12th century, crackdowns on Jews had become so commonplace they were practically an institution. The French king expelled Jews from the Ile-de-France in 1182. He let them return in 1198 but kept their property. Nobles in York organized a brutal purge of Jews in 1190 to clear themselves of debt. And kings in other places from time to time declared Jews their serfs and all Jewish property the crown's. The clergy concocted myths such as the "blood libel" charge—that Jews sacrificed Christian children in a perverse reenactment of the crucifixion. Massacres of Jews followed in England, France, Germany, and Spain. By the early 1200s Jews nearly everywhere were required to wear signifying badges. They wore a round badge in France and Spain, a pointed hat in Vienna—but in some places, Jews with money could purchase an exemption.

POGROM From the Russian for devastation, "pogrom" refers to the organized massacre of a minority people, rationalized by religious or intellectual opinions. The word entered the English language in the 19th century and would not have been used in the Middle Ages.

Decorated goblets held wine, mead, or ale for feasting. This 13th-century German chalice of silver gilt could serve wine just as easily at a banquet as at the communion table.

FEASTING IN THE MEDIEVAL WORLD

What people ate in medieval times depended, in large part, on who they were. Peasants and serfs subsisted largely on barley—a grain deemed inferior to wheat by those who could afford to choose. Peasants baked dark, heavy loaves of barley bread, sometimes adding a bit of rye. They boiled barley into porridge, and they made barley soups with cabbage, onions, and herbs. They even made barley ale. Proteins were rarely part of the diet, though beans and animal fat were added when available.

Wealthy landowners, in contrast, ate excessively, especially during celebrations. The typical medieval feast included wheat breads and puddings and meat of all kinds, from peacocks and pigs to deer and eels. The food was heavily seasoned with sauces and exotic spices—ginger, cumin, cloves, and cardamom, to name a few—especially after the Crusades, when medieval warriors returned from the east with spices and palates to match.

Presentation was everything, with roasted birds stuffed back into their plumage, beasts returned to their skins, or one animal stuffed into the body of another. Diners drank wine out of decorated goblets, used their hands as utensils, and used stale bread as plates. The metal fork made its debut at the medieval dinner table, but not for popular use.

Medieval feasts for the wealthy were, above all, unfathomably large. A feast to celebrate the marriage of Henry III's daughter in 1251, for example, took six months to prepare and included more than 1,000 deer, 7,000 hens, 170 boars, 70,000 fish and eels, 68,500 loaves of bread, and 25,000 gallons of wine.

The medieval kitchen was simple in design, with a large—and, in later times, ventilated—hearth at its center. This 14th-century illustration depicts the preparation and cooking of spleen, one of several organs considered prime for eating in the Middle Ages.

The medieval feast was an elaborate occasion. Diners were entertained with extravagantly presented dishes as well as pageants, performances, and music.

As an invention of the medieval era, the fork did not find popular use until the introduction of pasta from Italy, a cuisine for which it was well suited.

Communion represented the highest feast of all. This silver gilt paten served communion bread in church, but it also may have prompted wealthy hosts to commission fine serving platters for their own tables.

1100 — 1200

NOT UNTIL THE 1100S, THE BEGINNING OF THE HIGH, OR LATE, MIDDLE AGES, DO WE BEGIN TO see the emergence of a more civilized Europe from the dark ages of uncertainty and constant bitter struggle. Even so, brutal wars would continue in this era, and superstitions remained a way of life, but the 12th century would usher in new codes of behavior, based on the way of the chivalrous knight, and the glimmerings of rationalism would rise up from the intense intellectual ferment in new urban universities. On the peripheries of Europe, the cultures of Christians and Muslims still clashed, defining East-West boundaries and worldviews that would continue to modern times. Throughout the 12th century, new towns sprang into being, while established ones continued to grow. Italy was dominated by powerful city-states in the north and the Papal States in the south. In Germany, France, and England, power was vested in

monarchies, but the major cities grew at a fast pace as an expanding middle class of merchants and tradesmen found wider opportunities in densely populated areas. Urban universities attracted top scholars, and the most exciting lecturers enjoyed star status, with eager young students gravitating to their classes. Peter Abelard and other teachers branched beyond their clerical training into new realms of speculative thought, inspired by the rediscovery of Greek philosophy now made widely available through translations into Latin.

New forms of literary expression also developed in the 12th century. The troubadours of southern France created poems of courtly love, laying out in tightly crafted verse the mannered adoration of perfect ladies. Chivalric ideals of honor, valor, and the quest for lofty goals were further explored in romantic-

adventure epics, many of them based on tales of the legendary King Arthur of England and his court.

Legal scholarship made great strides during this period as well. Monarchies turned back to the landmark jurisprudential writings sponsored by sixth-century Emperor Justinian. Scholars pored over old texts to derive and help codify new legal systems so governments could operate on a basis that citizens would consider fair and consistent. A new class of professional lawyers came into being to interpret these laws. The church likewise set forth a body of canon law in writing for the first time, making clear that the pope was the highest ecclesiastical judge in the land. Secular and canon laws clashed in dramatic fashion when Thomas Becket, archbishop of Canterbury, challenged the authority of King Henry II.

King Frederick I Barbarossa—Italian for Redbeard—sought to dominate European politics, becoming king of Germany, Italy, and Burgundy—and Holy Roman Emperor. *PRECEDING PAGES:* Crusaders regularly battled Arab soldiers, but also at times attacked Byzantines and Turks during the war they considered holy.

Many of the century's great names were involved in crusades to the Holy Land—Eleanor of Aquitaine and her first husband, Louis VII; her son Richard the Lionheart; the charismatic Holy Roman Emperor Frederick Barbarossa (1122-1190); and the mighty Muslim warrior Saladin. The Second Crusade (1147-1149) would fail to retake lost lands in the Levant, and would make potential Christian warriors less eager to pick up the cross. The Third Crusade (1189-1192) was only a partial victory for the Latin Levant, its brutalities serving to sow further distrust between cultures.

THE GROWTH OF TOWNS

The explosion of population, agriculture, and commerce during the 12th century led to increasing urbanization—villages became towns, towns became cities, and brand-new villages mushroomed in rural areas. Central and northern Italy were the most prosperous urban zones at this time, clustering around four cities: Venice, Florence, Genoa, and Milan. These cities were really the heart of powerful city-states—Venice, ruled by doges (dukes), had gained independence from Byzantium by the ninth century; Florence with its flourishing trade belonged to the Tuscan margravate; Genoa was the chief port and commercial center on the Mediterranean; and Milan, a commercial and industrial commune in the fertile plains of northern Italy, was to become a key player in the Lombard League's 1160s struggle against Germany.

Geography and history had made the northern Italian cities the most important in western Europe. They operated under a complex political system. As independent city-states, the north Italian communes were self-governing, yet

This urn holds the remains of Frederick I Barbarossa, king and emperor, who clashed with the pope.

THE TWELFTH CENTURY

1111
Henry V of Germany becomes Holy Roman Emperor.

1122
The Concordat of Worms resolves power struggles between pope and Holy Roman Emperor.

1133
Lothair II is crowned Holy Roman Emperor by Pope Innocent II.

1146
Louis VII of France and his wife, Eleanor of Aquitaine, commit to a Second Crusade.

1192
During the Third Crusade, Richard the Lionheart and Saladin form a treaty.

1194
Cathedral of Chartres damaged by fire.

1199
King Richard the Lionheart is killed in a siege of the castle of Châlus, France.

they were also under the authority of the Holy Roman Emperor, who by tradition was the King of Germany. Frederick I Barbarossa (Redbeard) reigned as Holy Roman Emperor from 1155 to 1190, and like his great-grandfather Henry IV, who quarreled with Pope Gregory VII, he straightaway tested the papacy's hold on the empire. Cornering the pope into a treaty in 1153, Frederick guaranteed protections against the pope's enemies in northern and southern Italy in exchange for full rights to the empire. That done, he began a long campaign against the Italian city-states. He laid siege to Milan and other cities in 1158, and began establishing a system of imperial government in places he conquered. He imposed a tax on all citizens, but to gain the cooperation of the nobles, he exempted them from military service.

With their freedom severely restricted, Italian citizens began to voice outrage. A new pope excommunicated Frederick in 1160. Two years later the emperor overran Milan, scattering its citizenry to the countryside. For them, it was now time to take some action. In 1167, Milan, Venice, Mantua, and several other northern Italian cities formed the Lombard League. Eventually 20 cities were in league against the incursions of Frederick, and with papal support, they were able to stop him.

Victorious in the Battle of Legnano in 1176, the League finally won concessions from the emperor: In exchange for their fealty, he reinstated their self-governance. Milan quickly rebuilt and began a century-long economic boom. At the dawn of the 1200s, some 300 Italian towns operated as independent city-states. By creating state loans and taxing proportional property instead of individual "hearths," Italian city governments operated more efficiently than the governments of England or France. No city besides Constantinople had the combined power of those in northern Italy, and the Lombard League episode illustrated the growing influence of urban economy and culture. We will return to Frederick, one of the great Holy Roman Emperors, later in the chapter, but first let us look at the urban movement in his own Germany.

GUILDS & UNIVERSITIES

With the rise of a class of merchants and artisans, urban guilds began developing throughout Europe. Their agendas often conflicting with those of local lords, the guilds promoted tax reduction and legal control of their own jurisdictions, and they regulated working hours and wages. In Germany these guilds often found themselves at odds with bishops and abbots, who sought to control the governance of towns. Yet some princes, such as Henry the Lion, Duke of Saxony (1129-1195; r. 1142-1180), championed the move toward urban autonomy. The most potent German prince of the period, Henry supported Frederick for many years, even helping him take down Milan. Their relationship suffered, however, when Henry became the effec-

tive king of northern Germany. Along with expanding Saxony, he was keenly interested in building cities—he founded Munich in the south in 1158 and reestablished Lübeck in the north in 1159 after a devastating fire (15 years after its first founding). Both of these cities soon became key commercial centers.

Henry was able to enhance trade to his cities in northern Germany by concluding treaties with merchants and princes in Sweden and Russia. It was one of these Russian princes, Yuri Dolgoruky of Suzdal, who established Moscow in 1147. Within a decade he had fortified his town with a kremlin, or citadel—a series of

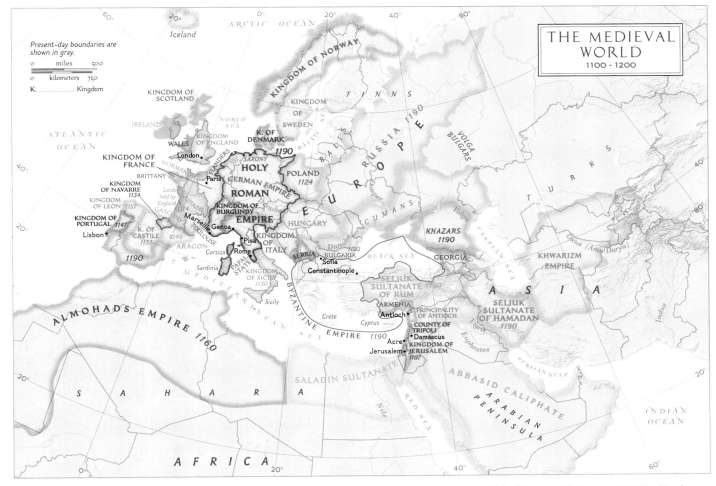

The pope unifies the Christian kingdoms in the crusader effort to regain the Holy Lands. Crusader states are established in the Middle East, and Christian kingdoms advance southward into Muslim Spain. In 1154 Henry Plantagenet, the Norman King of England, holds more land in France than the King of France.

The Krak des Chevaliers, or Fortress of the Knights, still stands in Hims, Syria, near the Lebanese border. It was used by crusaders traveling from Antioch to the Mediterranean. Some walls are 80 feet thick.

ditches, earthworks, and a wooden wall enforced by blockhouses, sited on a projection of land above the Moskva River. Moscow, too, became an important locus of trade and commerce.

In the highly developed feudal system of France, urbanization also proceeded apace during the 1100s. As in Italy, power was decentralized, in this case among the duchies. The Champagne region of northeastern France grew to its greatest prominence in the 12th and 13th centuries, its fairs making it a key player in international commerce. Situated on the trade routes between northern Europe and the Mediterranean, Champagne attracted merchants from Italy, Germany, Flanders, and England. At the fairs, northern cloth was exchanged for spices, dyes, and valuables from Mediterranean ports.

There were six annual fairs—in January, Lent, May, June, September, and October—each in a different town. Lasting up to seven weeks, the fairs altogether spanned nearly the entire year. Until war and new trade routes made the Champagne fairs obsolete in the late 14th century, they also served as banking centers, where early forms of credit were established.

England under the Normans had developed apace and had a thriving urban life in the 12th century. By 1300, the English countryside was dotted with about 650 towns, accounting for up to 15 percent of its total population, still low by European standards but growing. When

CHIVALRY The system and rules of behavior for knights, comprising bravery, honor, humility, and gallantry, especially toward women. The word comes from the French *cheval*, meaning horse, because knights were mounted soldiers.

areas became overcrowded, small landowners and free peasants cleared and drained virgin land upon which they started entire new villages.

Along with the trend to urbanization went a shift from rural monastic schools to city universities. No longer isolated from one another, intellectuals enjoyed a freer, more vigorous exchange of ideas; old dogmas were challenged and new patterns of thinking were brought forth. Students flocked to good teachers, abandoning those who were dull—the best teachers were celebrities. One of the greatest scholars and most popular teachers of the time was the French philosopher and theologian Peter Abelard (1079-1144).

Abelard studied in a number of schools in Paris and other towns, developing his own ideas and drawing the ire of his teachers. His philosophy promoted the uniqueness of the individual over the Platonic subsuming of the individual in the universal. He was branded a heretic

> IF THERE IS ANYTHING THAT MAY PROPERLY BE CALLED HAPPINESS HERE BELOW, I AM PERSUADED IT IS THE UNION OF TWO PERSONS WHO LOVE EACH OTHER WITH PERFECT LIBERTY . . . THEIR HEARTS ARE FULL AND LEAVE NO VACANCY FOR ANY OTHER PASSION; THEY ENJOY PERPETUAL TRANQUILLITY.
>
> HÉLOÏSE TO PETER ABELARD
> *Circa 1125*

for proclaiming the equal realism of both particular objects and universal concepts—that is, the seen and the unseen. Many clergy of the day took him to task for emphasizing argumentative proof over faith.

But he was best known for his tragic love affair with a private student, the niece of Canon Fulbert of Notre Dame Cathedral, Héloïse (1101-1164). After she gave birth to his son, Astrolabe, they married in secret. When her uncle discovered what had happened, he had Abelard castrated. Héloïse thereafter became a nun and Abelard joined a monastery, where he continued writing, teaching, and espousing controversial ideas. His story comes to us largely through his autobiography, *The History of My Calamities*, a no-holds-barred memoir filled with juicy details meant to grab readers and to embody his philosophy of individualism.

Abelard and Héloïse continued exchanging letters, which they published in book form in the early 1130s. She became the abbess at the Argenteuil convent outside Paris, explaining in one letter her own humble philosophy: "Riches and power are but gifts of blind fate, whereas goodness is the result of one's own merits."

ARTS & LETTERS

TROUBADOURS

Art Form for the Ladies

The troubadours of medieval France, Italy, Spain, and Germany were in the vanguard of a social revolution that changed customs, worldviews, and relations between men and women. Their name comes from the Latin meaning "to find," referring to the troubadours' ability to find, compose, or improvise poetry and song. They came from all classes of society and traveled from one court to the next, patronized by aristocratic ladies. Troubadours sang of romantic love and the code of chivalry.

Influenced by classical works such as Ovid's *Art of Love* and by the long tradition of love poetry in Islamic Spain, the troubadours first flourished in southern France, where they sang in an everyday language—known as *langue d'oc*—at a time when the vernacular was rarely used in artistic compositions. Valued for their ingenuity, troubadours enjoyed unprecedented freedom of speech in the courts of ladies such as Eleanor of Aquitaine, perhaps the most powerful woman in 12th-century Europe.

Some of the ideas in troubadours' songs were radical: For example, while marriage was in fact a strictly regimented business, they sang of women who were more than merely the property of men. In this way, the troubadours did much for the emancipation of women in Western civilization. ■

The troubadours entertained aristocratic patrons with romantic epics of courtly love and chivalry.

Originally from Bourcq, France, Baldwin II became King of Edessa, a crusader state north of Antioch, and then King of Jerusalem. Here he visits Byzantine emperor Manuel Comnenus, with whom he allied.

At Abelard's death, his body was sent to her; 20 years later she was laid to rest beside him. In 1817 they were exhumed and reburied in a single tomb in Paris, the city that had fostered Abelard's freedom of self-expression.

In the 12th century, as it turns out, urban life was creating more and more possibilities for living and thinking independently, giving rise also to a rebirth of ancient learning.

The Second Crusade

The First Crusade had established several Latinate outposts in the Holy Land. They were never so strong as at the beginning; throughout the 12th century they weakened, until they finally fell back to the Muslims in the late 13th century. None of the subsequent Crusades were as successful as the first one in creating European hegemony in the region. Under various powerful leaders, Muslims were slowly able to regain what they had lost. Local friction with Byzantine leaders accounts for some of the outposts' erosion, but more important was the apathy of European leaders. Europe may have had the manpower and wealth to wrest the Levant (the eastern Mediterranean) from the Muslims, but it lacked the will. Though marching for Christ became almost a rite of passage for kings and feudal princes, these token gestures rarely carried them all the way to the Levant—their interests lay at home. Nevertheless, the Crusades of the 12th century had important ramifications in European history.

Baldwin, brother of crusader Geoffrey, served as the first crowned King of Jerusalem from 1100 to 1118, expanding the kingdom's territory and establishing a bureaucracy that would last throughout the Frankish period in the region. His cousin Baldwin II (r. 1118-1131) was aided by two new brotherhoods of warrior monks, the Knights Templar and the Knights Hospitaller. These orders of vigilantes protected pilgrims going into and out of Jerusalem, and as they gained prestige in Europe, money flowed in to support them. Similar religious military orders sprang up elsewhere: Leper knights formed the Order of St. Lazarus, German knights formed the Teutonic Order, and a number of Spanish orders arose during the *reconquista*. The Templars and Hospitallers built numerous strongholds, including the surviving Krak des Chevaliers, a massive concentric castle constructed by the Hospitallers south of Antioch.

In 1143 Baldwin III became King of Jerusalem at age 12, and his mother, Melisende (ca 1105-1161), became co-ruler with him. That same year, the emperor of Constantinople died. A rising Seljuk leader named Imad ad Din Zengi (ca 1085-1146) decided to launch an attack on the Christian positions. Before any resistance could be organized against him, he took the city of Edessa in 1144. Zengi's lofty ambitions to take Damascus and the rest of the Frankish territory came to an end two years later when a disgruntled servant killed him.

But the fall of Edessa prompted the pope to call for another major crusade. This Second Crusade lacked the focus of the first, a novel expedition in which any conquest would have been a success. The pope's mouthpiece for this new crusade was the eloquent Bernard of Clairvaux (1090-1153), one of the most influential men of his era.

A mystic and founding member of the new Cistercian community of monks in northeastern France, Bernard's outspoken views, coupled with his zealous piety and charity, won him favor with bishops and the papacy. During one 1145 sermon he handed out cloth badges in the shape of a cross to be worn at the shoulder, then, when they were all gone, tore his own clothes into strips for use as crosses. Thousands were thus recruited into the French contingent of the Crusade, which was led by King Louis VII (1120-1180; r. 1137-1180). Later that year Bernard traveled to Germany, where by 1146 he had persuaded the German king, Conrad III (1093-1152), to join the cause.

The First Crusade was led by princes, the Second by monarchs, yet Louis and Conrad did not have the military expertise of those earlier Christian soldiers and they would suffer for it. The two armies headed out separately in 1147, Conrad in May and Louis in June. In four months, Conrad reached Constantinople and crossed into Asia Minor, where he split his forces between himself and his half brother, Bishop Otto of Freising (ca 1114-1158).

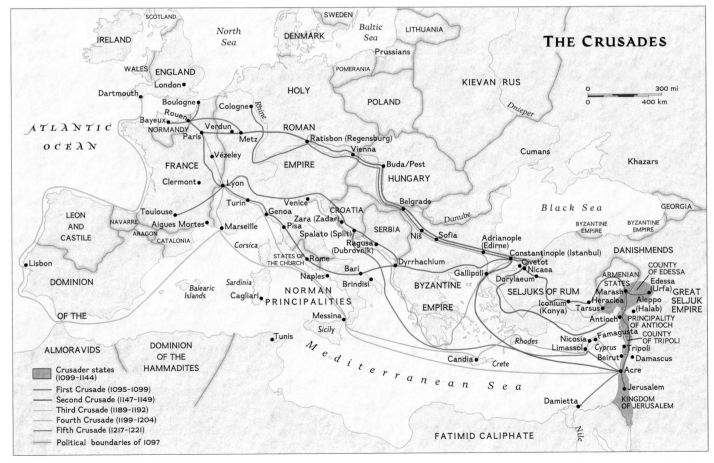

The Mediterranean world saw crusader travel and warfare through more than two centuries. Spurred on by popular devotion and zealotry, Europeans established Middle Eastern kingdoms, staging grounds for holy war and tangible proof of progress toward their goal of claiming Jerusalem for Christianity.

Notre Dame is the quintessential Gothic cathedral, with gargoyles, flying buttresses, and a rose window.

PARIS
THE CITY ON THE SEINE

Island | Devotion | Scholarship | Style

Paris—there are many reasons why it has been called *la ville-lumière*, the city of lights. Paris started as a small village on islands situated in the River Seine. A Celtic tribe called the Parisii first inhabited the site, but by the middle of the first century A.D. the Romans had taken over all of Gaul and had named the island town Lutetia. Roman occupation ended in the fifth century, as the fading empire lost its hold on outlying lands. Without a formal government, lawlessness abounded in Paris, with many tribes fighting for control of the islands and their immediate surroundings. Monasteries and bishops attempted to assert political influence, but only when the Franks arrived on the scene at the end of the fifth century was order reestablished.

The Franks easily gained control of the city, in large part thanks to the competence of their leader, Clovis. Baptized in 496, Clovis brought to Paris an alliance with the Christian Church that would long define the politics and architecture of the city as Catholic, Gothic, and elevated. By the time of his death he had conquered most of France and established Paris as its capital.

As Paris expanded, communities formed around monasteries constructed on the edge of the city, and these early neighborhoods still define the modern city's districts. In particular, St.-Denis, today a northern suburb, grew around a monastery of the same name and is the location of France's first Gothic cathedral. The Abbey Church of St.-Denis, erected in the beginning of the seventh century, became the resting place of many of France's monarchs.

When Clovis died, in 511, the city suffered tremendously. Families fought one another over land rights; murder and theft were common. In 800 Charlemagne, crowned emperor in Rome, gained control of Paris and the rest of France, but did not exert much power at such a distance. A key turning point in Parisian history came in 987, though, when Hugh Capet, the Count of Paris, became King of France, and the city began to advance in stature and culture.

In 1179 Philip II, nicknamed Augustus, took the French throne. Known as the maker of Paris, he initiated vast improvement projects in the city, the

PARIS THROUGH THE MIDDLE AGES

360
The city is named Parisea Civitas in a church document.

451
Attila the Hun attacks Gaul but spares Paris.

542
The Benedictine Abbey of Saint-Germain-des-Prés is built.

751
Pepin III (Pepin the Short) becomes King of the Franks.

885
Vikings attack Paris; raids continue for years.

987
Hugh Capet makes Paris his capital.

1163
Construction begins on Notre-Dame de Paris.

first of several centuries of activity, accomplishment, and growth. The streets were paved, fortification walls enlarged, and great churches and public buildings constructed. In 1163, on the Ile de la Cité—the historic island center of the city—the cornerstone was laid for Notre-Dame de Paris. Without a doubt one of the grandest of all Gothic cathedrals, Notre Dame is known for its flying buttresses, an architectural innovation that allowed a soaring vaulted ceiling; for its gargoyles, demonic bestial statuary intended to fend off evil spirits; and for its exquisite stained-glass windows, possible only thanks to innovations in architecture, glassmaking, paints, and ironwork. In 1248, Louis IX ordered the construction of an even grander edifice on the Ile de la Cité.

Called Sainte-Chapelle, it was built to house the exquisite gold reliquary said to contain Christ's crown of thorns and given to Louis IX by the Byzantine emperor in an effort to form an alliance. Together with Saint-Denis, built by the famous Abbot Suger north of the city, these churches represent the height of Gothic architecture and are still in use by French Catholics today.

By the early 15th century, Paris had grown to become a center of power, culture, and influence as important as London and Rome. The University of Paris was established in the middle of the 12th century on the left (or southern) bank of the Seine, in what is today called the Latin Quarter—so named because courses at the university were taught in Latin. A priest serving King Louis IX, Robert de Sorbon, founded a theological school within the new university in 1257, and out of that developed Paris's best-known center of higher learning, the Sorbonne. Scholars came to Paris excited by the new impulse to seek harmonies between classical philosophy and the Christian faith. At the same time, the city's right bank became a prosperous mercantile district.

The Hundred Years War, a long series of wars between France and England

Celts and Romans established the site of Paris, which evolved into a world center of culture and learning.

from 1337 to 1453, defined the final years of the Middle Ages for Paris. As France's capital, Paris suffered during this period. The intellectual scene all but disappeared, with little new construction due to shifts in control between the vying powers. With a truce in 1444, efforts began to restore the city. Nobles returned and built beautiful *hôtels,* or town houses.

The Hôtel de Cluny, one of the last impressive architectural monuments from this time, was built in 1490. Now a museum of the Middle Ages, it houses beautiful art, including several examples from the late 15th-century tapestry series that has become a medieval icon, *La Dame à la Licorne—* The Lady and the Unicorn.

The city of Paris began on the Ile de la Cité—the island of the city—and grew outward. Neighborhoods in medieval times were separated by concentric city walls and by the Seine River.

1190
Ramparts and a fortress are built around Paris; they become the Louvre.

1179-1223
Paris streets are paved during Philip II's reign.

1220
Duties on incoming goods and standards of measurement imposed.

1257
The Collège de Sorbonne is founded.

1348-1350
The Black Death strikes Paris and halts its growth.

1429
Joan of Arc fails to capture Paris, under English control.

1470
German printer Ulrich Gering creates Paris's first printing press.

It was not long before the Turks cut both armies to shreds.

Louis meanwhile arrived with his army and decided to try a more westerly route into the Holy Land. They found themselves struggling through the Taurus Mountains, where peaks rise above 12,000 feet, as bitter winter weather was closing in. Turkish forces took a further toll. Without the assistance of Templars, whom Louis installed as heads of each division of his disintegrating army, his forces might have perished. A much depleted army hobbled into

THE STRICKEN MARTYR BENT HIS KNEES AND ELBOWS, OFFERING HIMSELF AS A LIVING SACRIFICE, SAYING IN A LOW VOICE, "FOR THE NAME OF JESUS AND THE PROTECTION OF THE CHURCH I AM READY TO EMBRACE DEATH."

EDWARD GRIM
"THE MURDER OF THOMAS BECKET"
Cambridge, England, 1180

the Mediterranean coastal town of Attalia, where they hungrily devoured what scarce food the locals had to offer. The barons protested the idea of going forward, but Louis convinced them to continue by ship. And so, like St. Paul nearly 1,100 years earlier, they set sail west for Antioch. Bearing the sword instead of the word, their mission would prove far less fruitful.

With not enough ships for the whole army, much of the infantry had to be left in Attalia, where the majority died. After landing at Antioch, Louis decided that,

Canterbury Cathedral, one of England's oldest churches and home to the archbishop of Canterbury, head of the Anglican Church, was a popular pilgrimage destination in the Middle Ages. The colorful characters in Chaucer's *Canterbury Tales*, written in the 14th century, were traveling together from London to Canterbury.

instead of going east to relieve Edessa, he would first head south to Jerusalem, to join what remained of Conrad's army. They moved on to Damascus, which lay between Jerusalem and Edessa. In mid-summer of 1148 they camped out on the dry, treeless plains outside Damascus and began a siege. It was not long before word arrived of a Turkish relief force led by Zengi's son Nur ad Din (ca 1118-1174). Louis and Conrad called a retreat, and the Second Crusade came to a lackluster, unsuccessful end.

CRUSADING AFTERMATH

Poor planning and execution had doomed the Second Crusade from the outset, though a smaller wing fared better. A northern European fleet sailed from England to Lisbon in 1147; the crusaders and the local Portuguese then wrested the ancient Atlantic seaport from the Muslims. The following year, returning overland, crusaders helped Barcelona capture the city of Tortosa in Catalonia. And that was about all the Christians had to show for a tremendous expenditure of manpower and money.

One result of the Second Crusade was that fewer people were willing to go on later crusades. The returning crusaders complained about the lack of cooperation from the Holy Land settlers and even their possible conspiracy against the crusaders. One chronicler wrote that the crusaders "justly declined all [the settlers'] plans as treacherous and showed utter indifference to the affairs of the kingdom. Even when permitted to return to their own lands, the memory of the things they had suffered still rankled."

Another result was that Nur ad Din's status rose, and he used his new

This silver effigy of Thomas Becket, archbishop of Canterbury, was made around 1170, the time of his assassination by four knights at the instigation of King Henry II.

leverage to attack Antioch. In June 1149 he inflicted a crushing blow on the army of Antioch and killed the reigning prince, but Baldwin III of Jerusalem prevented him from actually taking the city. Nur ad Din then began raising support from other Muslim strongholds in the region, some of whom had truces with the Christians. By promoting mosques and schools, while denigrating the occupiers, he was able to change the sympathies of formerly Christian-friendly leaders. In this way Damascus became an easy conquest, many of its citizens welcoming the arrival of Nur ad Din. In the meantime, Baldwin strengthened his hold on the

Jerusalem territory, and by marrying the Byzantine emperor's niece, he formed an alliance with Byzantium that protected Christian areas beyond his ability to defend.

A final consequence of the Second Crusade was the marital strife between Louis and his wife, Eleanor of Aquitaine (1122-1204). Eleanor and her ladies-in-waiting had been outfitted in breeches and hauberks. Louis accused her of an affair with one of his generals and divorced her in 1152. When she married Henry II, a Norman duke soon to become king of England, it put a strain on relations between France and England. The tension was not resolved until the English were driven out of France in the mid-15th century, at the end of the Hundred Years War, and actually lingered on even until the Crimean War of 1850.

Headstrong and beautiful, Eleanor was the daughter of the Duke of Aquitaine. When she inherited this large duchy she held more property than the king—Aquitaine was a vast territory in southwestern France between the Loire and the Pyrenees. By feudal tradition, after her divorce she regained her duchy. Within two months she married Henry Plantagenet, Count of Anjou and Duke of Normandy; he was 19 years old, she about 30. In 1154 he became King Henry II of England and began a 35-year reign marked by conquests in the British Isles, war with France, and, to Eleanor's humiliation, serial infidelity. She gave birth to two future kings, a count, a duchess, and two queens, meanwhile managing Aquitaine and keeping an administering hand in Henry's realm, which included England and western

Archbishop Thomas Becket, having quarreled with the English king Henry II, was murdered in 1170 in a transept of Canterbury Cathedral.

and troubadours. Lyric poet-musicians, the troubadours were entertainers who sang love poems in the vernacular of southern France. Eleanor's crusader grandfather, William IX (1071-1127), Duke of Aquitaine, established the troubadour tradition and was himself a famous poet twice excommunicated for licentiousness. By the mid-1100s, troubadours in southern France and northern Italy were a standard feature of courtly life, their intricate rhymes and daring themes a sign that Europe was undergoing a lively revival, sometimes called the 12th-century Renaissance, a period of intense activity in art and literature, as well as law, government, economy, philosophy, and science.

Many writers were either employed or trained by the church, but in addition to producing church literature they began writing in vernacular languages as well as Latin. European belletristic writing—literature for entertainment, such as the student poetry of western Germany: satiric, angst-ridden verses celebrating drunkenness and debauchery—began to emerge. The goliards, the wandering clerical student-writers, often wrote on the appeal of "dropping dead in the tavern," yet they usually included a plea for forgiveness from God.

The literature of the period mixed worldly with divine themes. The vulgar, or vernacular, tongue was the language of the common people. In Norman England, vernacular literature was stunted, not to revive until the 14th century, about the time the troubadour period was ending. In France, where most of the 12th-century vernacular literature originated,

France. When their sons revolted against Henry in 1173, she provided them with military support, but was captured and imprisoned for 15 years.

She obtained her freedom when Henry died in 1189, and thereafter became the most powerful woman of her time, playing an active part in the reign of her son Richard the Lionheart (1157-1199;

r. 1189-1199). After Richard's death in 1199, she helped her son John (r. 1199-1216) hold his kingdom together. A woman of formidable will and political savvy, she died in 1204 at age 82.

THE 12TH-CENTURY RENAISSANCE
In Aquitaine, Eleanor's court consisted of vassals, knights, officials, priests, doctors,

ASCETIC A person, often a religious devotee, who chooses to practice self-denial as a discipline, believing that denial of the bodily pleasures represents a path to purity or enlightenment. Many monastic orders with origins in the Middle Ages require vows of asceticism.

the vulgar language was *langue d'oc*, from Occitan in the south, and *langue d'oïl*, from the area north of the Loire River—both of these terms mean "language of yes," but modern French would develop from the northern tongue. While the south produced troubadour lyrics, the northern trouvères wrote chansons de geste, long epic poems of heroic deeds. The *Chanson de Roland*, an account of a legendary knight in Charlemagne's army, is the most famous example. A similar poem in Spanish, *El cantar de mío Cid* (ca 1140), vividly recounts the exploits of an 11th-century Spanish warrior.

Love & Philosophy

More aristocratic and refined than the trouvères, the troubadours set their verses to music and then hired minstrels to perform them. Troubadours came from both the nobility and a class of professional artists. Cut off from the baronial wars to the north, Aquitaine and the rest of southern France devel-oped a distaste for violence and a great appreciation for manners, art, and true piety—all aspects of the "courtliness" then in vogue. It was in this cultivated atmosphere that troubadours composed poems of "courtly love," which described the delicate emotions of, and the code of conduct to be observed by, knights and their ladies.

The romantic poems of the troubadours expressed a new way of thinking and living in upper-class southern France. Warriors not at war needed a code of gentlemanly behavior that would keep their status intact; thus the concept of chivalry—that is, the way of the chevalier, or knight—arose to prescribe the knights' conduct during the many elaborate dinners, hunting and falconry events, jousting tournaments, troubadour recitals, and other ceremonies they took part in. In the poems, women were idealized in a way not seen before in Europe, with the narrator expressing courtly love for a woman to whom he was not, nor could ever hope to be, married. For some, a wife was considered a vessel for sex and childbearing, and as a business partner, hence romantic love could more easily be bestowed upon a woman outside the marriage bond. The object of the speaker's affection embodied a perfection bordering on divinity:

> *I fear the heart will melt within me*
> *if this lasts a little longer.*
> *Lady, for your love*
> *I join my hands and worship.*

How many people actually practiced courtly love is unclear, though certainly it was widely known and discussed, its complex rituals sometimes including the breathless exchange of notes, vows, and tokens. Some critics claimed the troubadour movement encouraged infidelity by perverting Latin liturgical chants into amorous poetry, while others viewed it as an outgrowth of the Virgin Mary cult and an insignificant pastime

GLASS WINDOWS

Windows That Tell Stories

Glass became more common during the Middle Ages as its manufacture became standardized and less costly, making it more practical for windows. Glass windows had adorned public architecture since classical times, but only in the 12th century did they begin to appear in private homes.

It was in cathedrals, however, that multicolored stained-glass windows became a hallmark of the Gothic style. Early stained-glass designs consisted mostly of static monumental figures, but as the technology matured, aesthetic elaborations followed, including narrative windows depicting entire stories from the Bible, with details painted on faces and clothing. To the largely illiterate populace, these windows were as educational as they were artistic.

Glass gains color when metallic oxides are added to the hot, molten glass. The glass is then blown or spun out into a plate, and pieces are broken off or cut into shapes. Those separate pieces are assembled and joined together by grooved strips of lead, called cames, that are soft enough to be molded to match the edges of each piece of glass. The completed window is then installed and reinforced with additional metal bars. Today, stained-glass windows are by and large made in the same way as they were in the 12th and 13th centuries, considered by many the golden age of this brilliant art form. ■

Stained-glass windows depicted entire parables, a kind of Bible for the illiterate.

of the idle aristocracy. The literature of courtly love revealed and encouraged the development of a gentle consideration of women. Aristocrats may have remained arrogant toward the lower classes, but they were cultivating a courtesy and gentility among themselves that reflects their longing for a less violent society. European monarchs no longer tolerated the lack of restraint once common among the warring baronial classes—the rituals of courtly love substituted for the rituals of war.

In the latter 12th century, troubadour poetry influenced the chansons de geste of the north and gave rise to a third literary form, the romantic epic. The most popular of these long, romantic adventure poems dealt with the legendary King Arthur and his court. The wellspring for this literary industry was a clerk named Geoffrey of Monmouth (ca 1100-1155), whose *History of the Kings of Britain* (1136), he claimed, perhaps tongue in cheek, to have found among old manuscripts in Oxford. Geoffrey's chronicle begins with the settlement of Britain by giant-killing Trojans, and includes the story of King Leir and his ungrateful daughters (source of Shakespeare's play), as well as the evil usurper Vortigern. Geoffrey drew upon tales from his Welsh homeland for the book, which climaxes with the sixth-century King Arthur, likely a historical British prince who was killed by invading Saxons. He may also have drawn on William of Malmesbury (ca 1080-1143), whose *Gesta regum Anglorum,* or *Deeds of the English Kings* (1120), one of the great histories of England, may have set the example.

Geoffrey introduced the magician Merlin and other well-known characters, but more complex stories were spun by later writers mining Geoffrey's book for material. The French poet Chrétien de Troyes wrote several Arthurian romantic epics in the second half of the 12th century. Two of his most famous poems, *Lancelot* and *Perceval*, emphasize different aspects of courtly love. The knight Lancelot is absurdly devoted to his lady, Guinevere, who happens to be the wife

THROUGH THIS MEMORIAL WE SHOULD EARN THE PRAYERS OF SUCCEEDING BROTHERS FOR THE SALVATION OF OUR SOUL; AND THROUGH THIS EXAMPLE WE SHOULD AROUSE IN THEM A ZEALOUS COMMITMENT TO THE PROPER MAINTENANCE OF GOD'S CHURCH.

ABBOT SUGER
ON THE CHURCH OF ST.-DENIS
Paris, 1144

of his lord, Arthur. Perceval, on the other hand, shows intense devotion to divine love on his quest for the Holy Grail—the chalice at the Last Supper of Jesus. Both knights are driven by a fervid zeal toward a perfect union whose unachievable nature makes the effort seem all the more honorable and heroic.

In the booming cultural and intellectual center of Paris, the 12th-century Renaissance generated a more scholarly contribution from such giants as Abelard and St. Bernard, whom we met earlier in the chapter. Another major figure, Abbot Suger of St.-Denis (1081-1151), was a pale intellectual of such enormous energy

and talent that Louis VII left him in charge of the kingdom when he went on the Second Crusade. Opposed to the crusade, Suger went up against Bernard and the pope, but ultimately could not persuade Louis to stay at home. Accommodating both love of God and love of worldly beauty in his outlook, Suger is best known for fostering an important new style of architecture. Believing that the most direct way to teach the faith was through pictures, he promoted stories carved in stone. Under his direction, the Abbey of St.-Denis—built in the squat, utilitarian Romanesque style—was transformed into a soaring building with pointed (instead of rounded) arches, ribbed vaults, and stained glass, including a brilliant rose window above the entrance. Gothic architecture was born.

Many late 12th-century scholars devoted their time to rediscovering the works of Aristotle and other Greek philosophers. Though few European scholars knew Greek, Latin translations were becoming widely available, and these gave Europeans increasingly abundant access to ancient Greek science and philosophy. Among the problems that kept scholars up late at night were Aristotle's interpretation of divine providence, his rejection (unlike Plato) of the immortality of the individual soul, and his belief in eternal matter instead of the creation of the world from nothing. These concepts did not square easily with Christianity, Judaism, or Islam.

Mystics and scientists in the medieval Islamic world had had considerable freedom to pursue truth. We have already mentioned the work of Avicenna; his commentaries upon Greek philosophy opened the door for the greatest Islamic thinker, Averroes, also known

The Arthurian legend grew grander and more complex as it passed through different cultures and languages. These three scenes illustrate episodes in a German manuscript of *Parsifal*, a story of one of King Arthur's knights and his adventures during the Crusades.

as Ibn Rushd (1126-1198). Working mainly in Córdoba, Averroes came up with an expansive worldview that reconciled Aristotelian scientific truth and Islamic religious faith, even though they seemed sometimes to contradict each other. Though North African–based Islam would repudiate the dichotomies Averroes posited, thus killing off Muslim scientific investigation in the 13th century, his work was to have a profound impact on Christian philosophy. European speculative thought developed under the watchful eye of the church, and, strengthened by the infusion of ancient Greek philosophy, it began to expand.

THE THIRD CRUSADE

While the chivalric ideal was developing in Europe, the counterpart in the Muslim world was coming to perfection in the person of a Kurdish sultan from Mesopotamia. Born about 1137, Saladin, or Salah ad Din, was the most talented military leader serving under Nur ad Din; by 1169 he was commander of Syrian troops and vizier of Egypt. Two years later he overthrew the Fatimids and was on his way to uniting Syria, Palestine, northern Mesopotamia, and Egypt. In 1187 he took on the Frankish kingdom of Jerusalem, conquering several of the outlying towns before capturing the big prize, Jerusalem city. The inhabitants might well have feared a recurrence of the massacre of 1099, but, unlike the conquering Christians, Saladin was generous and kind to the city dwellers. Broad-minded and bold, Saladin was also highly emotional, subject to bouts of depression and easily moved to tears. To the people back in Europe, his capture of the Holy Land capital did not sit well.

PERSONAE

TAMAR OF GEORGIA

The Woman Who Would Be King

Tamar, born around 1160, was the daughter of King George III of Georgia. She became co-ruler when she was 18. Her father died in 1184, and she became the first woman to rule Georgia. She faced immediate political opposition, which she rebuffed with help from her aunt and advisers.

With her reign secured, Tamar took advantage of declining Byzantine and Turkish authority. Through successful military campaigns and thanks to powerful allies, she brought the kingdom of Georgia to the peak of its power. She controlled lands from the Caspian to the Black Seas and from modern-day Azerbaijan to southern Russia.

After Constantinople fell to European invaders of the Fourth Crusade in 1204, Tamar supported her nephews, the Byzantine princes Alexius and David Comnenus, in establishing the buffer empire of Trebizond on the southern shores of the Black Sea. She commissioned works of art, architecture, poetry, and prose. She died around 1213, and a Mongolian invasion seven years later brought her pan-Caucasian empire to an end. ■

Queen Tamar, the first woman to rule Georgia, reigned over her prosperous empire for 35 years.

As a king of England, Richard I the Lionheart would not measure up against his father, Henry II. After all, in his ten-year reign (1189-1199), he spent but six months in England. He would make his mark as a fighter and as the embodiment of noble knighthood, both in his time and in subsequent legends. A complex personality, Richard was more than simply the paragon of knightly virtues. He was by turns selfless, driven, passionate, and cruel. And he left no heirs. After the death of his father, whom he had relentlessly warred against, Richard at age 32 was heir to England and most of western France—Aquitaine, Normandy, and Anjou. Yet his overriding interest was to lead a Crusade to take back Jerusalem. In Saladin he was to meet his match, and by the end these two great medieval heroes would each earn the other's respect.

Richard hastened from France, where he spent most of his time, to England in 1189 to raise money for the Crusade. He went about selling everything he could. "I would sell London itself if I could find a buyer," he said. His coronation in London was marred when the crowd attacked a group of Jews who had come to offer gifts to the king; Richard punished the instigators, but crusading fever was loose in England. By December the king was ready to embark for the east. He would travel by sea with a fleet of 114 ships, making port in Lisbon, Marseilles, Genoa, Ostia (port of Rome), Naples, and Salerno, site of Europe's first medical school.

Richard's tour next stopped at Messina on the northeast tip of Sicily, one of the richest of Mediterranean kingdoms. The ancient seaport, founded by Greeks in the eighth century B.C., was captured by the Saracens in 831, but the

For more than a thousand years, a castle has stood atop this hill near Dunster, Somerset, in England. It was the family home of the Luttrells for 600 years, from 1376 to 1976. Castle building reached a peak in the last centuries of the Middle Ages as nobles sought to outbuild the towers, turrets, and fortifications of their neighbors.

Normans, raiding down the boot of Italy, had taken over in the mid-1000s. Richard's sister Joanna had married the King of Sicily, and they ruled over a mixture of Latins, Greeks, Muslims, and Jews. The king had recently died, and Richard found his sister in prison and the throne occupied by an illegitimate grandson of Sicily's first Norman ruler. Outraged, Richard, according to one report, "took Messina more quickly than a priest could say his matins."

From Sicily, the fleet sailed east across the Mediterranean, stopping briefly on the castle-studded island of Cyprus, where a tyrant named Isaac Comnenus (ca 1155-1196) tried to seize them.

Richard overran the island and captured Isaac, who begged not to be put in irons. Always one for a dark joke, Richard had him placed in silver chains, and took his horse to ride on the Crusade. He took time out to marry a Spanish noblewoman, whom his indefatigable 69-year-old mother, Eleanor, had brought on a separate expedition. Eleanor was desperate for Richard to have an heir.

Now a married man, Richard landed in the Holy Land in June 1191 at the port of Acre, one of the towns Saladin had taken. Situated about halfway between Jerusalem and Tripoli, Acre was protected on the sea side by a great iron chain and on the land side by walls and a ditch.

Another army of crusaders, led by French King Philip II Augustus (1165-1223), was already there doing reconnaissance. Philip had warred with Richard's father over the latter's French holdings, adroitly playing off father against son. At home Philip and Richard were adversaries, but here at Acre they formed an alliance to try to topple Saladin.

Philip would go on to become the most powerful man in Europe and one of the great French kings, but on the Crusade he was brought down by camp fever. Richard was even sicker with ague, yet he had his assistants carry him to where he could join his crossbowmen. The crossbow was a relatively new European invention, and

THE WORLD IN THE TWELFTH CENTURY

The fight for the Holy Land gained new momentum as crusaders secured and then lost control of Jerusalem to the sultan Saladin, who had earlier taken Egypt from the Fatimids. Crusaders never regained control of the Holy Land and turned instead to Constantinople, where they waged war on Orthodox Christians. The newly weakened Byzantine Empire later became prized territory for Turkish invaders. Meanwhile, as the Seljuk empire expanded westward, its eastern territories grew vulnerable; the death of Iraq's last Seljuk ruler resulted in a deeply divided kingdom.

South Asia enjoyed a period of stability and cultural expansion. With the construction of Angkor Wat, the capital of the Khmer empire became one of Asia's most splendid cities. In nearby Burma, the golden age of Buddhist art generated magnificent temples and statues. Chinese innovations include gunpowder, porcelain, and the empire's greatest segmental arch bridge, now known as the Marco Polo Bridge, near Beijing. In Japan, the samurai began to take hold of society, ushering lasting changes.

In North America, the Anasazi continued to thrive in New Mexico's Chaco Canyon. Farther south, the Toltec began to decline; the Mixtec continued to flourish, producing fine art and written records; and the Aztec moved into central Mexico. In South America, the rise of the Chimu empire in Peru marked the region's first coastal settlement in over 500 years. ∎

Arctic

North America

Pacific Ocean

EQUATOR

South America

Atlantic Ocean

CHIMU PEOPLE **With an empire that spans 625 miles along the Peruvian coast, the Chimu prosper from the mid-12th century on. Irrigation systems help grow food in the dry climate, and surpluses support the rapidly expanding population.**

RAPA NUI **Isolated in the Pacific Ocean, 1,200 miles from the next inhabited island, Rapa Nui—Easter Island—has been settled for centuries. Artisans now develop the massive stone monuments, or** *moai,* **for which the island is known.**

SAMURAI CULTURE As warrior aristocrats model an ethic of courage and stoicism, Minamoto Yoritomo establishes military rule in Kamakura, a town that gives its name to his shogunate, or reign, and to this period of Japanese history.

GHAZNAVIDS FALL After more than a century in power, the Ghaznavid empire in Afghanistan and northern India falls to the Ghurids. The short-lived Ghaznavid period exerts a great influence on Islamic culture, particularly in the arts.

KANEM KINGS Kanem, in west Sudan, is one of many empires on the rise in sub-Saharan Africa. The Kanem kings, like other African rulers, convert to Islam; their connection to the Muslim empire provides significant trading advantages.

ANGKOR WAT King Suryavarman II achieves sole rule over Cambodia and begins construction of Angkor Wat, a temple honoring the Hindu god Vishnu. He dies before the temple is completed, and it becomes his funerary vault.

Bernard, a French abbot, symbolized a life of ascetic monasticism, and yet he stood at the center of controversies involving papal succession, the punishment of heretics, and the failed Second Crusade.

While Richard picked off defenders, his sappers tunneled under a defense tower and set fire to it. Stone-throwing catapults brought the flaming tower to the ground, and after some fierce fighting in the breach, Acre surrendered to the two kings. A chronicler recorded the Europeans' respect for their enemies: "And when the day came that the Turks, so renowned for their courage and valor . . . and famous for their magnificence, appeared on the walls ready to leave the city, the Christians went forth to look at them, and were struck with admiration when they remembered the deeds they had done." And yet the Franks were shocked by the degree to which Christians and Muslims mingled in the Holy Land.

Not in Acre when it fell, Saladin had sent Richard fresh fruit and snow on hearing of his illness. Richard later reputedly returned the courtesy by knighting one of Saladin's sons. Philip, on the other hand, fell from chivalric grace when he used his own sickness as an excuse to go home, where he soon broke his promises and began attacking Richard's ancestral Plantagenet lands. And Richard himself dishonored the knightly code when, impatient for surrender terms to be carried out, he slaughtered 2,700 hostages. The clemency Saladin had shown the Christians would hereafter dry up. Muslim mothers would later quiet their children by invoking Richard's name.

Richard pressed south, outnumbered three to one. He took back Joffa, an Old Testament–era town, then pushed on, fighting even with arrows sticking out of him "like the bristles of a hedgehog." Armed to the teeth, Saladin was waiting for him in fortified Jerusalem.

Realizing he was stalemated, Richard could only turn back home in regret. He

for a while it was the most feared weapon on the continent. The short, metal bow had a cranking mechanism for the string, which was then trigger-released. Arrows or small missiles shot by a crossbow could travel up to one thousand feet.

Some decried the newly designed weapon as unchivalrous, and in 1139 the Second Lateran Council (held by the Catholic Church in Rome's Lateran Palace) banned its use against Christians. But against Muslims it was okay, joining long hooks and knives in the arsenal of weapons that could rip through chain mail. Crossbows eventually necessitated the use of unwieldy iron-plate armor.

had saved the kingdom of Jerusalem, though it was much diminished and its capital was moved to Acre. On his return, he was driven ashore by a storm in the Adriatic Sea, and he decided to continue overland in disguise. He took this precaution because he was traversing the lands of Leopold of Austria, whom he had insulted at Acre by tearing his ducal banner off a castle Richard had claimed. Richard's large contingent could hardly go unnoticed—he was captured and imprisoned near Vienna. He was transferred to Germany and held there by Emperor Henry VI from 1193 to 1194.

Richard's mother enlisted the pope's help to gain his release, signing herself "Eleanor, by the wrath of God, Queen of England." She finally paid a staggering ransom of 150,000 silver marks—more than a year's royal revenues from England and Normandy. Eleanor herself took the money up the Rhine to the emperor's court. Richard was welcomed home as a hero, but immediately had to suppress his brother John, who had been scheming with Philip. Then the match with Philip continued over the chessboard of France. "If its walls were made of solid iron, yet would I take them," Philip sneered about Richard's Norman stronghold. "By the throat of God," the Lionheart roared back, "if its walls were made of butter, yet would I hold them." At one point Philip found himself hurrying over a bridge, pursued by Richard's men; falling in the river when the bridge gave way, he nonetheless escaped.

Richard's high-handedness caught up with him in 1199, when, at age 42, he insisted on taking some Roman treasure found by a peasant in Aquitaine. The peasant's lord refused to hand it over, so

YOU WANT ME TO TELL YOU WHY GOD IS TO BE LOVED AND HOW MUCH. I ANSWER, THE REASON FOR LOVING GOD IS GOD HIMSELF; AND THE MEASURE OF LOVE DUE TO HIM IS IMMEASURABLE LOVE.

ST. BERNARD OF CLAIRVAUX
DE AMORE DEI (ON LOVING GOD)
Circa 1130

PERSONAE

SAINT BERNARD

A True Ascetic and a New Monastic Order

Within two centuries of its founding, the Cluniac order fell into the very luxuries that it had once opposed. In response, a new monastic movement emerged that emphasized poverty and sustainability and attracted many new converts, including a French ascetic of noble birth named Bernard. He ultimately founded his own monastery in a town that came to be called Clairvaux.

Bernard and his companions spent more than a decade in extreme deprivation before their monastery became self-sufficient. The roof of Bernard's bare cell was so low, he was unable to stand upright in it; he was plagued by bad health most of his life. He wrote avidly, both on his mystical connection with God and on matters of church doctrine, over which he clashed with his rationalist contemporary, Peter Abelard.

An adviser to five popes and the driving force behind the Cistercian order, Bernard de Clairvaux was one of the most influential figures of the 12th century, in large part responsible for a spiritual revival that swept much of Europe. ■

Richard laid siege to his castle. Riding recklessly close to the castle without his armor, Richard was hit in the shoulder by an arrow. He pulled it out, but the barb had to be surgically removed; infection followed. The castle was stormed, its defenders hanged—except the crossbowman who shot the king. The unrepentant soldier told him, "You slew my father and my two brothers, now devise what torments you may for me." Richard pardoned him, granted him 100 shillings, and later died in his mother's arms. Saladin had died six years earlier at age 56. An era of great warriors was over, but the legends were just beginning.

NATURAL LAW

Besides literature, the main advance of the 12th-century Renaissance was in the area of law. With the emergence of stable European states, controlled by increasingly centralized governments, an efficient and widely accepted legal system became vitally important. A secular, well-educated class of professional lawyers began to develop. In order for peace and harmony to exist—and lawyers to have work—governments had to have laws on the books. The hugely important task of reforming and codifying the law of the land fell to scholars, and it began in northern Italy with a look backward to ancient Roman law.

Although the tradition of Roman law had survived in Italy, no one for almost five centuries appears to have studied the full text of Justinian's Code (imperial legislation from the second century to the sixth) and Digest (more than 9,000 extracts from 39 imperial jurists). Justinian's Code, the *Corpus Juris Civilis*, is the most comprehensive legal code ever recorded, and is one of the foundations

Clergy, such as the bishop sermonizing in the manuscript illumination above, wielded considerable power in the medieval world. They had the ability to influence the lives of peasants and nobles alike both spiritually and tangibly, through sermons, confessions, and canon law.

of all western law. One of its underlying principles is that written law should be based upon natural law—that is, principles of justice derived from reason. But in order for equity to prevail, the final arbiter—the emperor—could decide a particular case based on ethical principles outside the written statutes. Though the system does not account for the possible corruption of jurists and tyranny of the emperor, it worked well for ordinary cases and was a starting point for European states.

The growth of town governments and the increasing complexity of Italian politics in the late 12th century created a demand for administrators trained in Roman law. Hundreds of young men flocked to "learned Bologna" at the foot of the Apennines to hear the renowned Irnerius (ca 1055-1125) lecture on Roman law in the first European university (founded 1088). Around 1160 Emperor Frederick Barbarossa, delighted with the revival of a system of law that exalted imperial power, granted students in northern Italy a charter of rights and privileges.

Frederick was one of two extremely powerful and charismatic monarchs in the 12th century, the other being Henry II of England. From 1155 to 1190, Frederick ruled and expanded his empire, encouraged education and the development of cities, and kept interior conflict to a minimum; for these accomplishments he became a folk hero. We saw earlier in this chapter how he struggled, and later settled, with the cities of northern Italy. While Frederick was distracted with Italy, the German princes were pushing east into Slavic territory. The new settlements of eastern Germany could enrich the empire, and Frederick gained concessions by feudal right over the strongest of the princes, Henry the Lion of Saxony.

Finally, about 67 years old, Frederick took up the cross and joined the Second Crusade. He never met up with Richard

CANON LAW Rules established by a council of the church and incorporated into the church's ecclesiastical law. In the Middle Ages, canon law often exerted more power than civil law. Many laws in modern legal systems originated in canon law of the Middle Ages.

and Philip, for he drowned while crossing a river in Asia Minor in 1190. His son was an overbearing bully, but was able by marriage to take Sicily; his early death seven years after assuming the throne precipitated the temporary collapse of the German empire. But his father's legacy remained. Frederick's early acceptance of Roman law, albeit for his own imperial aims, started reforms in civil law that would take hold by the 1300s.

CANONIC DEVELOPMENTS

The state was not the only body interested in the law in the 12th century. Canon, or church, law underwent great scrutiny and reform during this period. The fact that there were separate legal codes for church and state indicates that each was developing separately, yet the two legal systems could not help but affect each other. Since the mid-11th century, clerical scholars had been working to systematize church law from the reams of council pronouncements, papal edicts, and biblical and other sacred literature. During the 12th century, the work of lay legal scholars inspired the church to come up with a similar code based on precepts that would establish the pope as the church's highest judge, just as the emperor was the supreme authority in civil law.

The culmination of several decades of church legal scholarship was the *Decretum*, a collection of some 4,000 texts compiled around 1140 by Gratian, an Italian monk. His alternative title was *The Concordance of Discordant Canons*, because of his use of the dialectic method of scholarship recently popularized by French philosophers. By this method, he harmonized contradictory principles by presenting them side by side. Gratian placed a principle (thesis) in juxtaposition to a contradictory principle (antithesis); his resolution of them was the synthesis. Logic was the operative rule, with papal wisdom as the ultimate authority. Ecclesiastical courts followed the procedure of the civil courts. The Inquisition of the 13th century was a natural outgrowth—the pope simply commissioned a court to try heretics, and torture was part of the old Roman law.

Whereas Italy, Germany, and later France adapted the Justinian Code to their political systems, England for the most part did not. Under the Normans

The energetic and visionary Abbot Suger, friend to two French kings, started with the Romanesque Church of St.-Denis in Paris and renovated it in Gothic style, signaling a new era of architecture.

St. John's Hospital in Bruges, Belgium, a city traversed by canals, is one of Europe's oldest hospital buildings. It dates to the 12th century, when Bruges was a bustling town built on the success of a local wool and weaving industry. Today the building houses an art museum.

Although hospitals of a sort had existed in the Roman Empire, it was not until the widespread adoption of Christianity that they became places for treating illness and not simply isolating the ill. In the early Christian tradition, it was one's social obligation to care for those who suffered, and by the fourth century, buildings designated for the care of the poor, the sick, and the elderly became a standard feature of monasteries. In these hospitals, learned monks used medicinal herbs, spiritual advice, and physical treatments such as bloodletting to treat everything from blindness to bubonic plague.

By the fifth century, church law required that bishops spend a portion of their revenue on those who were suffering. Some clerics went on to found and support multiple hospitals in a diocese. The spiritual revival of the

THE HOSPITAL

Care for Those in Need

twelfth century brought a renewed sense of charity for the poor and the sick, resulting in purpose-built hospitals such as the Hospital of the Holy Ghost in Montpellier, France; the Hospital of the Holy Spirit in Rome; and St. Bartholomew's Hospital in London. The knightly Order of the Hospitallers of St. John began in 1113 to establish hospitals along much-traveled pilgrimage routes to Jerusalem, disease being as fatal an opponent as the Muslims during the Crusades.

The urge to build hospitals was not exclusively Christian by any means—Islam, too, expected its faithful to tend the sick, poor, and aging. By 1300 hospitals in Baghdad, Damascus, Cairo, Córdoba, and elsewhere had achieved a high standard of care and treated patients regardless of class, race, or religion— unlike the Christian hospitals, which often did not treat Jews or Arabs.

The largest of the Muslim hospitals had separate wards for different ailments, heated and cooled rooms, laboratories, pharmacies, kitchens, baths, and lecture halls for medical classes. Life expectancy was considerably higher in the Muslim world, in large part due to this high standard of medical care. Many medical innovations of the Middle Ages and Renaissance began with Muslim practitioners who influenced European medical schools. ▪

and Angevins, England had galloped ahead of the continent economically and politically; thus while Frederick was using legal reform to consolidate power, the other great charismatic leader of the day felt that England's legal system needed no retooling. Henry II, whose reign (1154-1189) fell a year short of coinciding perfectly with Frederick's, was content to let the English system of oral pleadings and verdict by ordeal stand.

English law was derived from the moot courts of the Anglo-Saxons, in which legal matters were handled by the community instead of the central government. By letting local leaders run their own trials in the shire courts, Henry saved money on professional jurists—his agents merely stood by and collected the appropriate fees and taxes. In practice, the English common, or unwritten, law was woefully prejudiced against defendants, but it remained popular. Henry did extend the use of juries in civil suits, and added grand juries for indictments in criminal cases. And the Fourth Lateran Council forbade ordeals in 1215. What remained was a unique system in which, at least in theory, the law and not the king was the highest authority.

THE MAN FOR ALL SEASONS

Henry's England became the backdrop for a collision of civil and canon law in one of the great medieval tragedies. Like Frederick, Henry was handsome, ambitious, and gifted as a leader; strong and just, he met with almost no internal opposition. The lone exception was no doubt a surprise. Henry appointed his chancellor, Thomas Becket, to be archbishop of Canterbury. Some 22 years Henry's senior, Becket had always been

> AT THE FIRST, THE KING ATTEMPTED TO WIN THE ARCHBISHOP OVER TO HIS WILL BY FLATTERIES, IN ORDER THAT THEREBY HE MIGHT WANDER FROM THE PATH OF JUSTICE; BUT THE MAN OF GOD, FOUNDED UPON THE ROCK, WOULD NEITHER BE CAJOLED BY FAIR WORDS, NOR TERRIFIED BY FOUL.

> GERVASE OF CANTERBURY
> *THOMAS BECKET'S LIFE*
> **Circa 1200**

friendly and cooperative with his patron, but in his new post he began a quarrel that he could not drop. Becket insisted that the clergy were exempt from civil law, that only courts of canon law could try churchmen. To Henry, this was a slap in the face, a blatant abuse of power on the part of his protégé.

Born in Cheapside, a market district in London, Becket was the son of merchant-class parents. The rise to prominence of a member of the bourgeoisie was a new phenomenon north of Italy. And he was an unlikely candidate. Historians analyzing Becket's personality have found mental instability, erratic behavior, and overcompensation for feelings of inferiority among the gentry. One thing is certain—he was determined to defend his position as a servant of God to the death. For eight years he was a thorn in Henry's side. Turning to reformist ideas of the previous century, he had a hard time enlisting even the help of the papacy, which was interested in keeping strong ties with Henry while it struggled with Frederick.

For a while, Becket found refuge in France, but when he returned to England he excommunicated some of Henry's bishops. At wit's end, Henry remarked to his court, "Who will free me from this meddlesome priest?" Four zealous knights took the words literally and rode out to Canterbury Cathedral to pay a visit to Becket. He was waiting for them on the high altar, as though martyrdom were his wish all along. One of the knights called out, "Where is Thomas Becket, traitor to the king and realm?" Becket replied that he was no traitor, and he refused to lift the excommunications. According to a contemporary account, the knights then struck him with their swords, Becket falling to his elbows and knees after the third blow. A final blow opened his head "so that the blood white with the brain, and the brain red with blood, dyed the surface of the virgin mother church . . . in the colors of the lily and the rose."

Becket became an instant martyr (Chaucer's "holy blisful martyr") and Canterbury a shrine visited by thousands of pilgrims for three centuries. Miracles were attributed to his spirit. Henry was shamed into public penance—he knelt at Becket's tomb while clergymen flailed him. And, even more humiliating, he had to retreat on the issue of ecclesiastical courts; churchmen could plead "benefit of clergy" to obtain trials outside royal courts. Yet Henry continued to appoint bishops and to receive the loyalty of his clergy as before. Becket remained a hero in England until the Reformation of the 1500s, when Henry VIII burned his bones and erased his name from church records. Catholics continued to venerate him as a saint.

Wielding a lance and sporting heavy protective armor, the medieval cavalryman was no match for the warrior on foot. The introduction of the stirrup further increased the horseback warrior's efficiency and power.

WARFARE & WEAPONRY

The iconic image of the courageous, chivalrous knight in armor, handed down to us from such stories as *Don Quixote* and the legends of King Arthur, is not too far from the truth. Knights did ride heavily armored and decorated horses, beneath colorful banners that bore the family's coats of arms. They jousted with lances, and they sometimes carried the sleeve or scarf of a worthy lady. Knights, above all, were noblemen, descendents of gentry who had proved their ability to fight. They valued honor and service and took pride in protecting their lord and land.

Battle on horseback became more nimble with the introduction of the stirrup. Brought to Europe from the east, stirrups allowed the rider to brace himself on the horse while engaging in combat. A soldier on foot was no match for a knight on horseback, wielding shield and sword, and cavalries became central to medieval warfare. From intercity battles to the campaigns of the Crusades, the cavalry proved its might and influenced warfare for centuries to come.

The iron horseshoe was equally important to the growth of cavalries, enabling horses to traverse difficult terrain with ease. Iron, a relatively new material, had emerged as the preferred metal of the era, used not only in the making of horseshoes but also in the smelting of armor and weapons. Stronger than bronze and more readily available, iron required difficult smelting techniques, but once forged, iron weapons and armor survived significantly longer than their bronze counterparts.

Gunpowder changed the scope of warfare in the late Middle Ages, providing fodder for cannons—which were often large and had to be wheeled from battle to battle—as well as primitive types of gun. Guns, however, would not come into use until much later, and the weapons of choice for medieval warriors remained crossbows, swords, and lances.

Knights often rode to battle carrying banners with coats of arms that followed a complex set of heraldic symbols and denoted certain noble families.

Early medieval battles were a clash of lances, of sword and shield. Without the long-range weaponry of the modern age, hand-to-hand combat remained the primary style of warfare.

When not fighting in defense of their lord or land, knights often competed in jousting tournaments. For such matches, both knight and horse donned colorful—and often coordinating—armor.

The metal crossbow was new to Europe and became one of medieval warfare's most valuable weapons. More efficient than a traditional bow and arrow, the crossbow allowed warriors to shoot with greater precision and a range of up to a thousand feet.

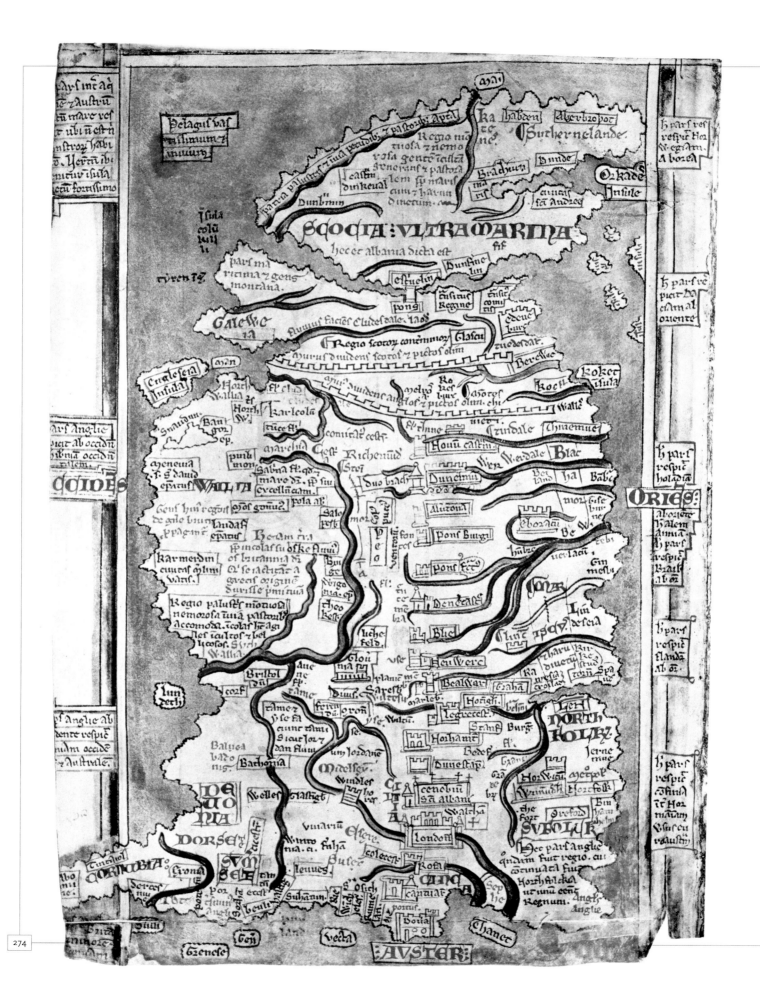

1200 – 1300

EVERAL UNUSUAL DEVELOPMENTS OCCURRED IN 13TH-CENTURY EUROPEAN CIVILIZATION ALONG its way toward the modern era. The lack of major wars for most of the century shifted the role of the nobility from a warrior class to a more strictly ruling class, with elaborate rituals and codes of conduct. While lineage was still highly important, a developing middle or merchant class made clear that money was becoming at least as important as birth. The expansion from the middle was accompanied by an overall growth in population and inflation. Finally, owing to these and other factors, the 13th century saw the development of important new governmental and legal institutions that served to restrain the excesses of the ruling class. The largest class of society, the peasantry, continued working the land as they had throughout the early medieval era—and would up to modern times—yet the boom years of the 1200s improved the peasants'

economic condition. Irascible, unpredictable King John ushered the 13th century in for England. Though considered a bad ruler, he unintentionally left his country a lasting mark in Magna Carta, a document the nobility forced him to sign. It limited the power of the king to the written laws of the land, thus putting a brake on absolute monarchy and setting a precedent for representative government. By the end of the century, meetings of Parliament—including members of both noble and merchant classes—had become a routine way for English kings to direct national policy, levy taxes, and handle legislative matters.

A completely different kind of king ruled France in the mid-1200s. Though a feudal monarch, Louis IX brought about popular reforms in law and government, and learning and

the arts thrived during his reign. Notre Dame and Chartres Cathedrals were but two among hundreds of splendid Gothic churches erected in the 13th century. St. Louis, as he became known, is perhaps best remembered for his contributions to the welfare of the poor and unfortunate. Making up for a youthful revulsion to lepers, he established a number of institutions for sufferers of all stripes.

Germany and Italy were dominated by the brilliant Holy Roman Emperor Frederick II, an eccentric autocrat who continued the tradition of emperors challenging papal authority. The fact that he ultimately lost the struggle, while a pious ruler such as Louis enjoyed a successful reign, was living proof of the political philosophy of Thomas Aquinas, the century's greatest thinker. Thomas advocated a system of government legislation

By the 13th century, European mapmaking had became more geographically accurate and less symbolic, as evidenced by this map of Great Britain created around 1250. *PRECEDING PAGES:* This fresco adorns a 1295 church in Macedonia where Christian treasures were hidden two centuries later, brought when Hagia Sofia became a mosque.

that conformed to natural or moral law. Best known as a theologian, he was in the forefront of practical thinkers who were busily trying to bring in line the vast body of Aristotle's work—newly available in translation—with Christian theology. The greatest minds understood that a revolution in thought was taking place, and the new demands of logic and reason had to somehow be wrestled into compliance with the old doctrines of faith.

Life was still hard and demanding, but the 13th century was full of growth and the possibilities of change for the better.

Magna Carta: King versus Barons

In England the 12th century closed with the death of Richard in 1199 and the succession of his brother John, one of the most complex monarchs in English history. Subject to bouts of manic depression, John was at times a brilliant administrator and fighter and at other times a paranoiac, intent on subverting the law to punish suspected traitors. Historians have used a number of adjectives to describe him, most of them bad— erratic, unscrupulous, astute, cruel, lecherous, unpopular, unprincipled, and vengeful. The favorite of his father, Henry II, John was called Lackland because his older brothers inherited lands intended for him.

In 1200, the 33-year-old king offended the French by marrying the daughter of a minor French nobleman who had betrothed her to someone else. The claimant to her hand was irate, and John was called to the French court to settle the matter, since by feudal custom he was a vassal to the

THE THIRTEENTH CENTURY

1202
Pope Innocent III begins the Fourth Crusade.

1204
Crusaders capture Constantinople and establish the Latin Empire.

1215
Magna Carta is issued.

1219
Damietta, Egypt, falls to the Fifth Crusade.

1220
England's King Henry III is crowned at Westminster Abbey.

1228-1229
Frederick II, Holy Roman Emperor, spearheads the Sixth Crusade.

1244
Khwarezmian forces raze Jerusalem, prompting the Seventh Crusade.

1273
Rudolf I is crowned Holy Roman Emperor, first since the great interregnum, beginning in 1250.

1300
Europe's population is approximately 73 million.

King Louis IX of France, who ruled from 1226 until 1270, donned this gem-encrusted crown of gilt silver.

French king for the territories—Normandy, Anjou, and Aquitaine—that he held in France. John could not be bothered with the niceties of showing up. The French court then declared John a rebellious vassal, and it ordered the seizure of Normandy and Anjou. A sluggish military response cost John not only the homeland of the Angevin English kings but the respect of his people.

The death of the archbishop of Canterbury in 1205 precipitated another crisis in the growing rift between the king and his subjects. The monks at Canterbury overlooked John's choice of a replacement and secretly chose another. As a compromise, the pope offered a third alternative, an English cardinal named Stephen Langton. After John's refusal to accept Langton as archbishop, the pope excommunicated the king and placed England under interdict, so that priests were prohibited from performing most sacraments, including Christian burial services. The quarrel continued for seven years, until English barons threatened to depose John if he did not give in.

The barons were also fed up with John's high-handed conduct in several other arenas, particularly revenue collection. In a delayed reaction to the lost French provinces, John had decided to fight the French. But to do so he needed money, and he began bearing down on his subjects, digging out every farthing of tax possible and exercising tyrannical royal authority. He collected heavy and frequent scutage (payment in lieu of military service), extorted taxes on top of those regularly paid by

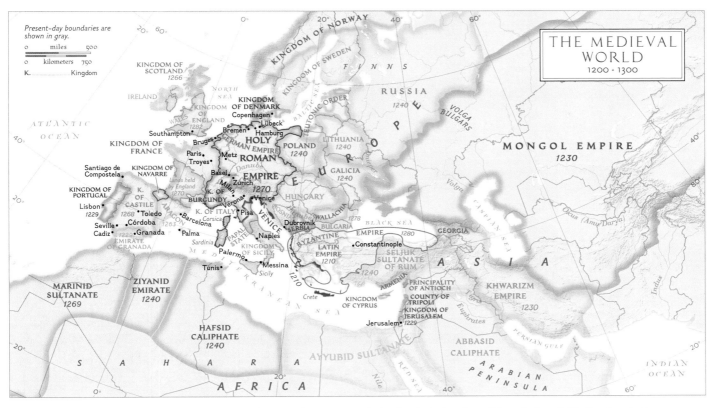

During this century the Almohads, or North African Muslims, vacate Spain, leaving the Arab emirate of Granada the only Muslim stronghold in western Europe. The Papal States revive, while crusader states in the Middle East diminish in size and stature to the point of disappearance.

the barons, and collected a special tax on widows who did not marry the men he chose for them.

Not pleased with their king's creative methods for filling royal coffers, the barons finally revolted after his army was soundly beaten at the 1214 Battle of Bouvines in northern France. It was Archbishop Langton who organized the rebellion, proposing that the barons present their demands to the king in a "great charter" similar to the coronation charter Henry I presented to the church and laity in 1100.

The nobles began drawing up a list of grievances that would take the form of a contract between the king and the nobility, guaranteeing the latter certain customary feudal rights. The barons sent the king a draft, along with the message that his failure to sign would result in

their seizing his fortresses and demanding satisfaction.

Indignant, John replied, "Why, amongst these unjust demands, did not the barons ask for my kingdom also?" He swore that he would never grant the kind of liberties that would effectively make him their vassal. But the nobles had by now assembled an army of some 2,000 knights, as well as foot soldiers and attendants, and when they moved out against the king his support evaporated.

The cornered king met with his aggrieved subjects at Runnymede, a meadow on the Thames River 20 miles west of London, on June 15, 1215. Here he signed and put his seal to the Magna Carta, a list of more than 60 privileges that the king was supposedly granting freely. The provisions read more like a list of grievances that needed redress:

"No scutage or aid shall be imposed in our kingdom save by the common council of our kingdom. . . . To no one will we sell, to no one will we deny, or delay right or justice." Peasants were not mentioned in Magna Carta, which was a charter specifically between the king and the nobility. But the document was to become a historical landmark, a forerunner to the Declaration of Independence of the United States of America and other charters of democratic rights, because it spelled out on parchment the limits of a ruler's power. He was to govern by the rule of law rather than his own will.

Written in Latin, Magna Carta was copied and sent to cathedrals across the land for safeguarding. Local sheriffs were expected to read the document out loud in public four times a year. Barons were required to enforce it, and bishops were expected to condemn those who broke its tenets. Though the majority of the provisions are now obsolete, many have evolved into laws still on the books.

Article 12 outlawed scutage except by "general consent," which later meant the consent of commoners in Parliament. Article 28 forbade government officials from seizing "grain or other chattels, without immediately paying for them in money." (The Fifth Amendment to the United States Constitution states, "nor shall private property be taken for public use without just compensation.") Article 39 stipulates that "no free man shall be taken or imprisoned . . . except by the legal judgment of his peers"—a forerunner to the requirement of trial by jury.

The immediate impact of Magna Carta was less than legal. John turned to Pope Innocent III as his overlord, declaring that he had been forced to sign. The pope sided with the king and suspended Langton for rebelling. He then annulled the charter, which precipitated a civil war. John went on the attack, ravaging counties along the border of Scotland and capturing the castle at Rochester in southeastern England.

The barons meanwhile enlisted the help of France to overthrow a king who now seemed clearly a tyrant. A wider national emergency was averted by the timely death of both king and pope in 1216. John's nine-year-old son became King Henry III (r. 1216-1272), and Langton organized a reissue of Magna Carta, ensuring its survival.

By the time Henry III came of age the barons had even more political power, and since he was as ineffective a leader as his father, the country suffered one crisis after another. Cultured but lacking in savvy and will, Henry had a long but

PERSONAE

HENRY III

The Fading Powers of the Throne of England

Henry III was the son and heir of King John of England, who was forced to sign Magna Carta in 1215 but who soon afterward overthrew it and refused to abide by its rules. Young Henry took the throne at the age of nine, but he was pliable and docile and did not come to actual power as King of England until 18 years later, in 1234.

Even at that distance in time, his father's past continued to plague him. As early as 1237, England's land-owning barons clashed with Henry over the foreign influence in his court and later over ill-advised military ventures overseas. In debt and at risk of excommunication, Henry was forced in 1258 to sign the Provisions of Oxford, which, like Magna Carta, asserted the Germanic constitutional principle of limits to the powers of the king.

The English government was put under the joint rule of the king and a baronial council, and a Parliament of secular and church magnates was to meet three times a year to discuss policy. Though overturned within three years, the Provisions of Oxford effectively ended Henry's rule and contributed to the decline of absolute monarchy in England. ∎

The pliable nature of King Henry III contributed to the weakening of absolute monarchy in medieval England.

undistinguished reign. Early on he got financially embroiled in a papal war, for which he expected help from the English barons. Out of patience, a "parliament," or committee of barons, took control of the government in 1258. Henry tried to regain his power six years later, but the struggle degenerated into an actual battle, in which he was captured.

The leader of the rebels, Simon de Montfort, was an English earl and Henry's brother-in-law. Far more capable than Henry, he became, in effect, England's ruler. During this time, a rising merchant class known as knights of the shire was elbowing its way into the upper classes by serving as coroners, sheriffs, and justices of the peace. Montfort recognized the influence of this early gentry by including them—four from each shire—in a 1264 Parliament, an assembly of leaders to set up a new government. He called another Parliament the next year, adding representatives from the towns, or commons.

Despite the progress made in representative government, the dispute between the royals and the barons was unresolved, and in 1265 Montfort was killed in a battle at Evesham, on the Avon in west central England. Henry's son Edward led the victorious troops, after which the now-senile king turned over the government to him. Montfort's supporters continued a sporadic guerilla war from forest strongholds, reminiscent of the legends of Robin Hood.

On Henry's death seven years later, his son became King Edward I (r. 1272-1307). Henry's inglorious reign was over, but the give-and-take between himself and the nobility had left Parliament as an enduring legacy to the world. Edward continued to convene parliamentary meetings, primarily to help fund his

John, king of England from 1199 to 1216—here shown with his two dogs—earned the name "Lackland" because, as the youngest son, he did not inherit family land, and also because he lost land to France. Formulated during his reign, Magna Carta dissipated the power of the English throne.

military ventures against France, Wales, and Scotland. By century's end Parliament had become the arbiter of national policy, the tax-levying authority, and the main body of public opinion.

A NEW KIND OF MONARCH

The other European power of the 13th century was France, and by the end of the century it would be the wealthiest and strongest country. While England was spreading government control outward from the crown, the French nobility were fighting among themselves, allowing the king to assume legal power.

Under Philip Augustus in the early 1200s, the authority of the French monarch began expanding well beyond the traditional confines of the Ile de France (Paris and surrounds) into the duchies. By marriage, diplomacy, and war, he pushed out into the surrounding provinces of Vernandois, Artois, Normandy, Maine, Anjou, and most of Pitou.

Philip Augustus also built up a huge treasury, paved the streets of Paris, and erected the Louvre Palace as a fortification on the River Seine. He centralized power by authorizing royal *baillis,* or bailiffs, to collect taxes and to try cases that had formerly been judged by feudal lords. Unlike the itinerant circuit judges in England, these civil servants remained in one jurisdiction, receiving promotion for good work.

On Philip's death in 1223, his son Louis VIII took over and continued efforts to enlarge the kingdom, warring against the Plantagenets in the south. Dying only three years later, he was succeeded by his 12-year-old son, Louis IX (r. 1226-1270).

Magna Carta, one of England's first constitutional documents, was signed into law by King John on June 19, 1215.

The boy's mother, Blanche of Castile, assumed the role of French monarch for the next 12 years, becoming the first in a long string of redoubtable Spanish princesses. A granddaughter of Eleanor of Aquitaine, Blanche was a product of European royal matchmaking. She had already shown her mettle by trying to take the English throne after John's death. Now she went about protecting her son against rebel contenders to the French throne—dressed in white, riding a white horse, she led troops into battle.

Blanche gets the credit for ending the Albigensian revolt in the province of Languedoc, around Toulouse in southern France. In 1209, the pope had ordered a crusade against the heretical Albigensians (named for the town of Albi), ascetics who believed in two gods—one good, one evil. The Albigensians were likely disenchanted with their corrupt Catholic priests, and so they came up with a seemingly more virtuous religion.

The pope's decree came after years of unsuccessful nonviolent attempts to bring the Albigensians into line, and it was the first time that the pope gave full backing to a crusade within Europe. In response, some 20,000 French, English, and German knights took up the cross and sword and marched on Languedoc. But the crusade quickly got out of hand when whole villages of Catholics and heretics alike were brutally massacred. Locals viewed the attacks as territorial aggression instead of religious war. After 20 years of stout resistance, Languedoc finally gave in to Blanche's deal making and submitted.

THE REIGN OF LOUIS IX

Owing partly to luck and partly to skill, Louis IX reigned during a period

King John of England unwillingly signs Magna Carta by demand of the English barons, guaranteeing them certain rights and liberties. Some monarchs thereafter ignored it, but its effect lasts to this day.

of widespread peace and prosperity, thus becoming the most successful and beloved of all the Capetians, the house that ruled France from 987 to 1328. His piety, concern for justice, and charity toward the poor and infirm won him the nickname St. Louis—all traits he learned at his mother's knee. She often told him, according to a knight who accompanied him on the Crusade, that "she would rather he were dead than that he should commit a mortal sin."

His court groaned at the amount he lavished on charity instead of on festivities, but he was swift to put down any hint of insurrection. Meanwhile he went on building homes for the elderly, the blind, abandoned women, and orphans. He personally waited on beggars and even served food to lepers.

For all his piety, Louis was not quite enlightened enough to extend his charity to Jews. Christian devotion meant viewing Jews as enemies of Christ. Louis's anti-Semitism was limited to burning the Torah rather than people. He also publicly offered benefits to Jews who chose to convert to Christianity. In attempting to reform the clergy he could be brutally imperative, but in general he was kind, trustworthy, and of a generous spirit.

Tall and outgoing, Louis married a woman his mother picked for him, the daughter of the Count of Provence, and when he proved himself a devoted husband his mother became jealous. Yet with his strength of personality there was little she could do to interfere. She remained an ardent defender of his policies. After fending off Henry III's halfhearted incursions into southwestern France in the early 1240s, Louis decided to take up the cross and crusade in quest of freeing the Holy Land once again.

SHIRE An administrative subdivision within Britain, established during Anglo-Saxon times as a system of tax collection. Each shire had a fortressed town as its seat. Today's counties evolved from the old shires, as indicated by names such as Lancashire and Leicestershire.

The Palace of Westminster served as the King of England's residence for much of the Middle Ages.

LONDON
THE RISE OF COMMERCE

River | Royalty | Trade | Finance

Romans moved into the area of today's London in A.D. 43, establishing a farming settlement along the River Thames. Within a few centuries the city, known then as Londinium, had grown substantially in size and importance. It was the capital of a portion of Roman Britain, and fortification walls were built around the city to protect against invaders.

With the collapse of the Roman Empire around A.D. 400, however, Roman London was virtually abandoned. Few people remained during the next half century.

Life was slowly pumped back into London after the Saxon takeover of Britain in the late fifth century. Over the course of the next 200 years, the port of London developed into a major hub for trade and travel, its location influenced by the Thames, a river deep enough to carry seagoing vessels from the English Channel inland.

It was during this time that Christian missionaries were traveling northward, and the new religion gained in influence in the city on the Thames. St. Augustine, sent from Rome to convert the Anglo-Saxon pagans, was well received by King Aethelbert of Kent who, in 604, built the city's first church, St. Paul's Cathedral, on Ludgate Hill—and possibly on top of the ruins of a Roman temple to Diana.

A Benedictine monastery was founded in 960 on a small island in the Thames, called Thorney Island, with a population of 12 monks to begin with. The abbey received support and more land from the crown, and eventually it became London's Westminster Abbey, the site for coronations from William the Conqueror on. Many kings and queens are buried there, too.

The city's importance grew drastically after 1066. In order to secure Norman power, William the Conqueror began an extensive building program throughout England. He built castles and forts, including the White Tower in London.

Built in 1078 of limestone imported from Normandy, the tower stood on the river's edge to control trade. The White Tower became the central keep of the larger and more complex Tower of London—a fortress, armory, and prison that was expanded many times, particularly during the 12th and 13th centuries.

CITY OF LONDON TIME LINE

407
The Roman army leaves Britain.

600
Saxons build a port town, Lundenwic.

604
St. Paul's Cathedral opens.

670-870
London is controlled by the Anglo-Saxons of Mercia.

871
Danes invade England and take London.

886
Alfred, King of Wessex, recaptures the city.

1065
Edward the Confessor expands and consecrates Westminster Abbey.

William originally held court in the tower but eventually moved it upstream to Westminster, the royal residence through the medieval period. Originally two cities, London and Westminster ultimately merged, with London becoming the city's center for trade and commerce and Westminster the royal capital.

By the 1200s London was the largest city in northern Europe, with a population well over 30,000, nearly double what it had been a century before. Agricultural expansion in the country supported an urban population boom. Increased productivity led to specialization of labor, and a class of artisans emerged.

Specialized workers coalesced into trade organizations called guilds to protect the integrity of their work. London's Weavers' Guild, first to form, dates to 1155. Guild members carefully tapped new masters of the trade, established monopolies, and set and maintained standards for price and quality.

Guilds originated first for merchants but before long, every type of occupation had an associated guild, from bell ringing to begging. Well-established guilds built their own buildings, and London's Guildhall—erected in the 15th century on the site of an older medieval guildhall—is still the administrative center for the city.

London steadily expanded into a major port city. Local trade and travel moved up and down the Thames, but during the 12th and 13th centuries, international merchants became an important part of London's economy, unloading goods at wharves downriver from the city. Records of the city's first mayor, Henry Fitz Ailwyn, date from 1193.

As trade increased, the population diversified to include Danes, Germans, Italians, and Jews. Imports came into London and from there were distributed to the rest of the country; goods from the countryside were loaded onto ships for export from the London wharves. Business increased, and the old wharves had to be replaced with bigger ones. Warehouses were also built on the bank of the river to store goods before distribution.

Originally a Roman settlement, London became a thriving metropolis in the 13th century.

London's medieval growth reached its peak around 1300. The city's population totaled nearly 80,000, and profits from the wool trade had made many people rich. Disaster followed good fortune, however, as poor harvests and wet summers ruined crops and caused widespread famine, causing the markets to plunge. By 1340 large parcels of land in England, Wales, and Scotland that had been under cultivation a century earlier had been reclaimed by wetlands.

Then the bubonic plague arrived. By 1349 nearly half of the population had fallen victim to it. The city did not recover for more than a century, but by 1500 the population was growing again. New industries, such as glassblowing and shipbuilding, launched the next phase of London's history.

Merchant vessels brought goods from the Hanseatic League on the North and Baltic Seas into medieval London. The cities of London and Westminster developed north of the Thames; Southwark, south.

1066
The Normans invade England but spare London.

1087
London is the largest city in northern Europe, population 30,000.

1176
Old London Bridge, made of stone, replaces a wooden bridge.

1189
Henry Fitz Ailwyn becomes the first mayor.

1348-1349
Thousands die during the Black Death.

1381
Farm workers revolt.

1485
Henry Tudor defeats Richard III—first in the Tudor line.

A food surplus in the 13th century brought increased trade and spurred the growth of medieval Europe's towns and cities. Shops like the pharmacy above enjoyed a healthy business.

istrative reforms. He sent officials called *enchêteurs* out to examine complaints about corrupt bailiffs and foresters. Professional judges heard cases in the *parlement*, a new branch of the royal court; ordinances defined stiff penalties for government corruption and counterfeiting. A mix of both royal officials and citizens comprised the new government of Paris. Royal officials could not gamble or visit taverns. Prostitution was outlawed, as were judicial ordeals by battle or duel. Arts and literature flourished under Louis, and the budding University of

> WE PROHIBIT . . .
> THE STUDENTS FROM
> CARRYING WEAPONS
> IN THE CITY, . . .
> AND THOSE WHO CALL
> THEMSELVES STUDENTS
> BUT DO NOT FREQUENT
> THE SCHOOLS, OR
> ACKNOWLEDGE ANY MASTER,
> ARE IN NO WAY TO ENJOY
> THE LIBERTIES OF
> THE STUDENTS.
>
> ———————————
>
> STATUTES OF GREGORY IX
> FOR THE UNIVERSITY OF PARIS
> *France, 1253*

With the loss of Jerusalem to Egypt in 1244, the pope declared yet another Crusade in the vain hope of wresting it from the infidels. Most of Europe was too preoccupied to be concerned, but Louis, against the wishes of his mother and advisers, decided to heed the call. After about four years of preparation, he put together an impressive army of more than 25,000 soldiers, including 1,500 knights and 5,000 crossbowmen, and they set sail for Egypt. He was able to advance his army by land and water about 50 miles inland, or about half the distance to Cairo, winning little victories along the way. But the sultan then positioned ships in the Nile to cut off Louis's retreat route. Bogged down for months, Louis's army was ravaged by disease—thousands of bodies floated down the river, and Louis himself took sick. He finally surrendered and was captured; he had to pay nearly an annual revenue's worth of ransom for his release. He was supposed to pay additional ransom later, but he never did. He spent the next four years at Acre, shoring up what was left of the kingdom of Jerusalem.

THE FRUITS OF LOUIS'S LABORS

In his later years Louis IX enacted a number of important legal and admin-

Paris attracted hordes of students. Louis's chaplain, Robert de Sorbon, founded the famous Collège de Sorbonne in 1257.

The building of the great Gothic churches reached a pinnacle in mid-13th-century France. Altogether more than 500 such churches were built in France in the hundred years before 1270. The best-known cathedral, Notre-Dame de Paris, was begun in the mid-12th century; work proceeded slowly and steadily, with the choir, west front, nave, and rose windows completed by around 1250. Work also began on another massive cathedral that would exceed even Notre-Dame de Paris in size, grace, and magnificence.

Notre-Dame de Chartres arose from the wheat-rich plains southwest of Paris in a mere 30 years in the mid-1200s, an astounding feat considering that everything from the largest stone pier to the smallest stone angel and piece of stained glass was shaped by hand and erected without the aid of engines, which were 600 years in the future.

A town of 10,000 people put its full energy into the cathedral, many of them helping haul tremendous blocks of stone from a quarry 7 miles away. An army of builders, masons, stone carvers, woodworkers, glassmakers, and blacksmiths went to work. When the cathedral was consecrated in 1260, thousands of people attended, staring in awe, the vaulted roof soaring 123 feet above the floor.

As if determined to give his life for his religion, Louis went on crusade again in 1269 at age 55. This time he landed west of Egypt, at the Mediterranean port of Tunis. He took the ancient city of Carthage but was again stricken by some form of plague; he died in August 1270, and the Crusade dissolved. All along the route home through Italy and France, people lined the way to pay respects to the man whom historians would dub the "ideal feudal monarch." Before the century was out he would become the only French king canonized as a saint.

The Holy Roman Empire

In marked contrast to Louis was the autocratic Holy Roman Emperor Frederick II

(r. 1220-1250), one of the strangest figures in all the Middle Ages. The grandson of Frederick Barbarossa, Frederick II was king of both Sicily and Germany by the time he was 18 in 1212. Over the next four decades he would exhibit qualities that might have made him a great leader, and actions that caused the pope to dub him the Anti-Christ. Instead of strengthening Germany, he did his part to let it disintegrate and leave it a non-player in European politics by the late 13th century. Refined and intellectual, he could also be a megalomaniac and a brutal despot. He modeled his court and administration after that of the Greeks and the Arabs.

"Of faith in God he had none," wrote a contemporary of Frederick II. "He was a crafty man, deceitful, a voluptuary, malicious, and wrathful. And yet at times he could be a worthy man when he wished to show his benevolence and good will." He showed interest in his three successive wives only for childbearing purposes; otherwise, they were sequestered away in southern Italy, guarded by eunuchs. He devised special cruelties for his enemies—some were sewn into bags with poisonous snakes and thrown into the sea. On the other hand, he was an avid patron of the arts and the sciences, and he was himself a scholar who wrote poetry and knew six languages. He also

INNOVATION

TALLY STICKS

Calculators of the Middle Ages

Tally sticks were invented in the absence of hard currency as a way to keep financial records. While coins of precious metals were not practical for day-to-day business, simple sticks were abundant. People could easily make marks or notches on them with blades or sharpened stones. One could record different values with different markings on a tally stick and then split the wood lengthwise down the middle, resulting in two identical halves, one for the debtor and one for the creditor. Thus the tally sticks amounted to durable duplicate proof of the transaction.

Once the practice of using tally sticks was exported from continental Europe to England, it became integral to the national system of taxation there. In the 12th century, the monarchy set up the Office of the Exchequer to oversee matters of taxation, and tally sticks were critical to the system. One stick went to a local sheriff; the other stayed with the royal exchequer. The sheriff would travel through his locale, collecting what was due, and return to the exchequer with the currency and his revised tally stick.

Some English kings, needing to raise capital, sold their tally sticks at discounted rates, a kind of governmental bond. The holder of the discounted tally stick could then sell it again or else could cash it in when local taxes had been collected. ∎

Tally sticks—a common, simple, and convenient form of accounting and record keeping in the Middle Ages—were used in some rural areas of Europe even into the 20th century.

authored a definitive book on falconry, based on his own research. Widely considered a genius, he was known as *Stupor mundi*, "the wonder of the world."

By tradition, the German king was also emperor of the Holy Roman Empire, which included both Italy and Germany. Complicating this political arrangement was the fact that the northern Italian city-states were fiercely independent, and the pope, based in Rome, was the spiritual head of the empire.

The Lombard League had prevented Frederick II's grandfather from making any real headway in northern Italy. But Frederick II, unlike his grandfather, was an Italian by birth—the son of Constance of Sicily and Emperor Henry VI, he was born in the central Italian town of Jesi and raised in Sicily, which accounts for his lack of interest in Germany. He allowed the region to disintegrate into separate German principalities and towns.

By inheriting Sicily and Naples, Frederick controlled most of southern Italy and wanted to expand his claim to northern Italy. Pope Innocent III thought he could stop him and buy Frederick off by crowning him emperor, but he was mistaken. Frederick was determined to succeed in northern Italy, where his grandfather had failed.

He tried to placate the pope by claiming that a conquest in the north would not threaten the independence of the papacy. Meanwhile, he ignored promises to give up Sicily and instead began building up his defenses there—adding

This ciborium, which held communion wafers, was made of gold and precious stones in Limoges, France—a sign of the wealth of the medieval church.

castles, a navy, and a merchant marine. He also initiated the training of a corps of civil servants at a new state university in Naples, which he founded in 1224, and he established trade and production monopolies over iron, steel, salt, hemp, tar, and silk. In 1232 he began minting gold coins—a first in Europe.

Earlier, the multitalented emperor had made a vow to go on a Crusade; his delay of the journey worried the pope. His offhand statements and careless attitude about the church made it clear that he thought himself above the moral code of ordinary humans. Gregory IX, pope from 1227 to 1241, was not so willing to make concessions as his predecessor, and in his first year he excommunicated Frederick.

Reserved and serious, Gregory was one of the most powerful popes during a century that saw the church at its apex of influence. He had been a personal friend of St. Dominic and St. Francis of Assisi, founders of the mendicant preaching orders, who took vows of poverty. An early champion of Frederick, Gregory became distrustful as the emperor accumulated more and more power and prestige.

"In your empire," Pope Gregory complained of Frederick, "no one may dare, without your leave, to move hand or foot." His excommunication of the emperor fell on deaf ears—Frederick simply turned around and denounced the papacy.

Yet he still decided to go to the Holy Land in 1228, independent of any papal sanction, which infuriated Gregory. Nor could the pope take any private schadenfreude in the wayward emperor's folly, for Frederick was both a capable warrior and diplomat.

On his Crusade, Frederick II convinced the sultan of Egypt to give up Jerusalem, Bethlehem, and Nazareth. Then, like the risen Christ he had come to believe himself, he made a triumphal entry into

EXCOMMUNICATION The formal exclusion of an individual from church membership, based on the judgment of church leaders. In the Roman Catholic tradition, a person who has been excommunicated may not receive communion or be buried in a church cemetery.

Jerusalem and had himself crowned in the Church of the Holy Sepulchre.

POPE & EMPEROR AT ODDS

The pope used Frederick's absence to send his armies down to Sicily. When Frederick got wind of this action, he hurried home and retook the lost ground, but tactfully restrained himself from attacking the Papal States. The pope rewarded him by lifting the excommunication.

It was not long, however, before Frederick was carrying out his plan of action against northern Italy—and the pope excommunicated him again. Frederick countered with what amounted to a declaration of war against the papacy, ordering the sinking of ships that were bringing clergymen to a papal council. With the emperor now considered beyond the pale even of a heretic, the Pope felt he had no choice but to preach a Crusade against Frederick himself.

The problem with this Crusade was that no European leader was willing to go up against Frederick, who meanwhile was making inroads against the Lombard League. The municipality of Milan, distrustful of the emperor, refused to surrender, sending this message: "We fear your cruelty, which we have experienced; so we prefer to die under our shields by sword, spear, and dart than by trickery, starvation, and fire."

For about the last 13 years of his life, Frederick pursued his brutal war in northern Italy, destroying villages and lives but never ultimately winning. The pope's Crusade against him amounted to little more than a war of words, but after Frederick's death in 1250 of dysentery, the papacy insured that no one from his family would ever again trouble the world.

Frederick's son Conrad IV ruled Germany for only four years until his own death. In Sicily, Frederick's illegitimate son Manfred ruled until 1266. Both Manfred and a son of Conrad's were killed at the pope's bidding—one in battle, the other by execution. The century-long

The English Parliament, first established in 1295, has for more than 700 years convened in Westminster Palace, built around William the Conqueror's residence on London's Thorney Island. Old and new sit side by side; the chamber of the House of Commons, shown above, is one of the newer wings of the government complex.

Hohenstaufen dynasty, which began with Frederick Barbarossa, had now ended.

MEDIEVAL MERCHANTS UNITE

The conflict between Frederick and Gregory had weakened both Germany and Italy: Germany remained a disjointed nation of principalities for the next two centuries, and the prestige of the papacy was tarnished by a campaign of vengeance almost as violent as that of the emperor.

While its king was spending his capital and energy fighting Italian wars, Germany went about the business of commercial expansion on its own. A group of cities in northern Germany founded the Hanseatic League (from *Hanse*, merchant association) to protect their trading concerns in the Baltic Sea region. As part of a vast trade network stretching from England to the hinterlands of Russia, the League provided military and political support to German merchants to prevent Scandinavian rulers from

> WE WILL APPOINT AS JUSTICES, CONSTABLES, SHERIFFS, OR OTHER OFFICIALS ONLY MEN THAT KNOW THE LAW OF THE REALM AND ARE MINDED TO KEEP IT WELL.
>
> MAGNA CARTA
> *London, 1215*

gaining control. By the late 1200s this northern alliance had joined with German merchants along the Rhineland to the south to defend against piracy, build lighthouses, and establish trading posts all the way to the Mediterranean.

The center of the League was the Baltic port of Lübeck, its position on the Trave River giving it inland access. Raw materials from the northeast such as tar, pitch, lumber, furs, and herring flowed

through this crossroads, as did goods manufactured in western Europe. During the 13th century, Lübeck formed its own government and anchored the German colonization of the eastern Baltic Sea. Other members of the League included the northeastern port of Rostock (in today's Germany), Danzig (today's Gdansk, Poland), the port of Riga (in today's Latvia), and Reval (today's Tallinn, Estonia) along the Baltic.

Despite the incursions of Frederick, brisk trade continued in Italy as well, but here the city-states were rivals instead of partners. The Lombard League had disbanded by 1250, and in any case, its primary purpose had been mutual defense, not trade.

Genoa had North African trading outposts on both the Atlantic and Mediterranean coasts, while its rival Pisa held firm to Tunis. Venice continued expanding its commercial and colonial empire, which now included Crete, Euboea, and other Aegean and

THE GREAT EXPANSION

An Ever More Interconnected World

Economic, political, and religious change leading up to the 13th century allowed Europe to expand its influence. Crop diversification and agricultural improvements, including the water mill and the windmill, led to a population boom in Europe: 44 million in 1100; 58 million in 1200; 79 million in 1300.

Cities thrived, from Norway to Italy. Business practices improved; advances in silver mining increased coinage. Merchants traveled widely with less risk. Missionaries such as the Cistercians cleared frontier lands for cultivation and sheep farming while semireligious military orders pushed the boundaries

of Christendom into Scandinavia, the Baltic, and the Mediterranean Basin.

At the same time, popes and the clergy were encouraging military campaigns against the Muslims, trying to win territory for Christianity. Two Norman brothers, Robert and Roger Guiscard, captured Sicily from the Muslims. Spain took more time and bloodshed, but it was largely claimed in the first half of the 13th century. The Crusades evolved out of this spirit of land reclamation. By 1250, five major thrusts into the Middle East had been attempted.

In the end military failures, the Crusades had other long-lasting effects. They brought

the ideas, technologies, and trade goods of the East to western Europe. Increasing demand for exotic goods drove Italian merchants to establish commercial ties with cities like Constantinople, Alexandria, Cairo, Beirut, Damascus, and Samarkand.

By the 13th century, certain adventurous Italians, such as Marco Polo, were bypassing Muslim intermediaries and traveling directly to markets in India, China, and southeast Asia. Powerful cities and states supported all these developments, ultimately leading to lively trade and intellectual connections between western Europe and the Eastern Hemisphere. ∎

Mediterranean islands. And the up-and-coming region of Catalonia in northeastern Spain vaulted Barcelona to a major-player position in the growing network of trade in the Mediterranean world.

THE FINAL CRUSADES

Ten years after the Third Crusade failed to capture Jerusalem, ending in 1192, a vigorous new pope was calling for yet another Crusade. One of the strongest medieval popes, Innocent III (r. 1198-1216) shrewdly extended his authority to manipulate European politics more effectively than any previous pontiff. He intervened early in French and English

Trade goods flowed through the harbors of medieval cities, such as Rostock, in northern Germany. Peasants working the countryside produced a valuable food surplus in the 13th century, spurring commerce.

affairs by deciding to excommunicate King John. An early supporter of Frederick II, he eventually turned against him, at the same time strengthening the papal Curia, or administration, and codifying the first official set of canons, or church laws. His plan with the Fourth Crusade (1202-1204) was to take back Jerusalem, currently under Muslim control, having been conquered by the Egyptians under Saladin in 1187.

In fact, the Crusade would get sidetracked to another goal.

No other kings were interested in this Crusade, but plenty of knights took the opportunity to prove themselves worthy Christian warriors. The staging point was Venice, which was under contract to transport the 35,000 expected soldiers. But as it turned out, only about a third of the soldiers arrived, the rest heading to other ports.

Venetian merchants and captains refused to get the expedition under way until the full payment was in hand—some nine tons of pure silver. In the meantime, hundreds of vessels stood waiting in the harbor, along with thousands of tons of provisions. After a great deal of heated wrangling, the crusaders

German friar Albertus Magnus, considered the first scholastic, helped to spread knowledge of Aristotle and classical Greek thought to the scholars of medieval Europe.

gave them, but by now they were running out of food and money.

A new expedient arrived in the form of a disinherited Byzantine prince. It seems that his emperor father had been blinded and deposed by his uncle, and he needed help rooting out the usurper. Offering large amounts of food, money, and military support, Alexius Angelus convinced the crusaders to detour to Constantinople. After two months of sailing, the fleet arrived at the great center of Eastern Christianity in June 1203.

Though no army had ever breached its walls, Constantinople was in a weakened state, its navy small and its populace poor. After negotiations failed, the crusaders attacked from the northeast by land and sea. The defenders held firm, but the usurping emperor feared a coup and fled the city. Without a great deal of fighting, then, Alexius entered the city and was crowned emperor. His reign would be short.

Alexius was now in the untenable position of reconciling the crusaders' demand for the balance of their payment with his subjects' resistance to paying taxes in support of the much-hated Westerners. While trying to come up with the money, he offered to put the crusaders up for the winter in the suburb of Galata, across the harbor. But after a while, the crusaders felt betrayed and began exacting payment by pillaging the countryside. Now Alexius had an internal revolt on his hands as well—a coup resulted in the emperor's death in January 1204, and a palace factotum took over as emperor. He too would soon pay with his life.

The crusaders began putting all their resources into attacking Constantinople, and in April they broke through. What followed was ugly, but unsurprising,

made a deal with Venice. In exchange for transport, they would stop along the way and capture Zara, a Dalmatian coastal city formerly under Venetian control.

So off the Crusade went, southward in the Adriatic Sea to Zara, which happened to be under papal protection, a detail the crusaders figured they could deal with later. When Zara refused to surrender,

the crusaders sacked it, knowing they were risking excommunication. Yet the crusaders decided that God wanted them to continue, and the only way to do so was by honoring their commitment to Venice. The pope promptly followed through, excommunicating the Crusade and Venice. Following a humble letter of apology from the Crusade leaders, the pope forgiven the traditions of medieval warfare. Since the city had resisted attack, the crusaders felt free to ransack it, and so for three days they vented their battle-lust in a rampage of looting, ravaging, and destroying. Churches and women were supposed to be off limits, but few crusaders kept their vows.

The despoilers went home loaded down with an enviable quantity of treasures and holy relics, enough to make up for the frustrations of the trip. Among the relics were the reputed head of John the Baptist, a hair from the head of the Virgin Mary, body parts of saints, pieces of the True Cross on which Jesus was crucified, and possibly the Shroud of Turin.

The pope had not authorized the capture of Constantinople, but he hoped it might heal the schism between East and West. In fact, the rift only widened after Constantinople was destroyed by the very people who started out to rescue it. From a population of half a million,

ALTHOUGH THOSE THINGS WHICH ARE BEYOND MAN'S KNOWLEDGE MAY NOT BE SOUGHT FOR BY MAN THROUGH HIS REASON, NEVERTHELESS, ONCE THEY ARE REVEALED BY GOD, THEY MUST BE ACCEPTED BY FAITH. . . . AND IN THIS, THE SACRED SCIENCE CONSISTS.

ST. THOMAS AQUINAS
SUMMA THEOLOGICA
Rome, circa 1250

it had declined to 35,000 by the time it was retaken by the Byzantines in 1261. It never regained its former glory, and was finally conquered by the Ottoman Turks in 1453.

A number of popular Crusades, led by commoners, took place in the 13th and early 14th centuries. Among the most well known are the Children's Crusades.

One such Crusade was led by a boy claiming that angels had told him to free the Holy Sepulchre from the Saracens. He and several thousand unarmed young people headed south from Cologne, Germany, in the spring of 1212—they traveled up the Rhine Valley and over the Alps, arriving in Genoa in late summer. Here the Crusade ended, some youths possibly going to Rome to try to meet the pope, others finding jobs in the area, still others perhaps lured onto ships and then sold into slavery. A few straggled back to Germany, where outraged parents hanged the leader's father.

Another Crusade arose in north-central France, led by a shepherd boy who wanted to deliver a letter from Christ to the king. He and about 30,000 followers made their way to Paris to seek an

SCHOLASTICISM

Applying Reason to Faith

In the early Middle Ages only a few of Aristotle's works—and minor works at that—were available to Europeans, translated into Latin. As additional texts became available, thanks to the Spanish philosopher and Islamic intellectual of the 12th century, Averroes, scholars put their minds to the task of synthesizing the ancient Greek worldview with that of Roman Catholicism. This intellectual endeavor came to be known as scholasticism.

The first scholastic theologian was a 13th-century Dominican friar, Albertus Magnus, who was associated with the University of Paris. He spread knowledge of the works of Aristotle but stopped short of synthesizing Aristotelian

reason with Catholic faith. That task would be left to his pupil Thomas Aquinas.

Taking Aristotle's metaphysical analysis of the world as his base, Aquinas systematically rationalized and justified Catholic ideas, resulting in his *Summa Theologica*. He considered the work a comprehensive view of the whole of attainable truth, but it went against all other strains of thought in 13th-century Europe. In 1277 Aristotle's texts, along with many of Aquinas's teachings, were banned by the church. In time, new lines of thought and "dangerous discussions" were altogether prohibited, as conservative theologians preferred refining prevailing dogma and repressing heresy. ▨

Classical and Christian thought—temple and Bible—influenced Thomas Aquinas.

THE WORLD IN THE THIRTEENTH CENTURY

After uniting disparate warrior tribes, the chieftain Temujin was chosen as ruler, or khan, of a new Mongol confederation in 1206; he eventually became known as Genghis Khan. Under him Mongol warriors, gifted at fighting on horseback, moved first into northern China and then conquered central Asia all the way to the Caspian Sea. Though Genghis Khan died in 1227, his military campaigns were carried on by his heirs. By 1300 the Mongol Empire stretched from China to eastern Europe.

In Japan, typhoons thwarted a naval invasion by the Mongols, while the skilled samurai warriors defeated them on land. India, too, stayed free of the Mongols, but began to feel the effects of previous invasions; by the 13th century, Islam was exerting influence over Indian society, especially in the north. Jainism rose in prominence in the region of Rajasthan, and several magnificent temples were constructed at Mount Abu.

Some of the great American civilizations arose in this century, from the Inca in Peru to the Aztec in Mexico. The Inca replaced the collapsed Tiahuanaco civilization in the Andes, founding the magnificent city of Cuzco as their capital, while along the coast, the Chimu civilization grew in prosperity. Meanwhile, the Aztecs settled central Mexico and became prized mercenaries for the city-state of Culhuacan. In North America, the Anasazi continued to flourish, settling new regions of the southwest and advancing their knowledge of the natural world. ∎

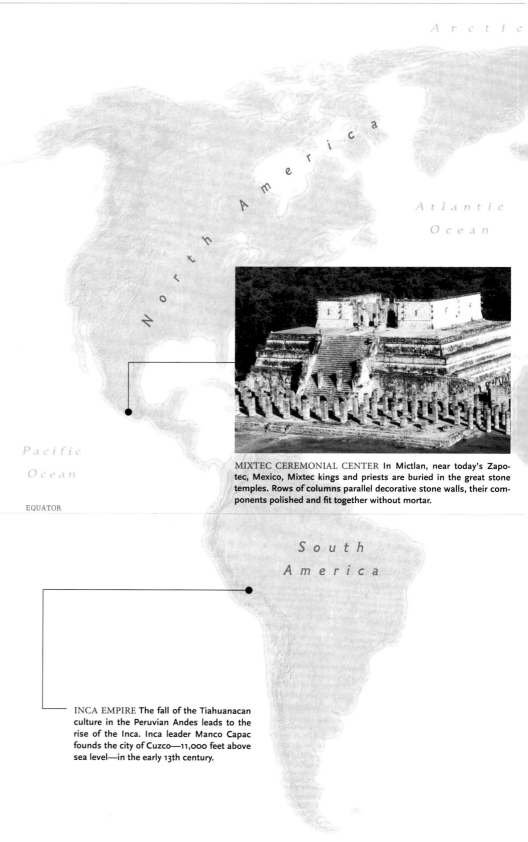

MIXTEC CEREMONIAL CENTER In Mictlan, near today's Zapotec, Mexico, Mixtec kings and priests are buried in the great stone temples. Rows of columns parallel decorative stone walls, their components polished and fit together without mortar.

INCA EMPIRE The fall of the Tiahuanacan culture in the Peruvian Andes leads to the rise of the Inca. Inca leader Manco Capac founds the city of Cuzco—11,000 feet above sea level—in the early 13th century.

Ocean

Europe

Africa

Asia

Pacific Ocean

Indian Ocean

Australia

EQUATOR

GENGISKAN

GENGHIS KHAN As chief ruler of the Mongols, Genghis Khan unites nomadic tribes into a vast military empire. By 1218, his campaigns into Persia, Turkistan, and China as far as Beijing stretch Mongolia from Asia to the Adriatic Sea.

SELJUK TURKEY Konya, on the central Anatolian Plateau, becomes one of the world's most magnificent cities under the Seljuk sultans, who support the arts and build temples and schools still revered as examples of Seljuk culture today.

SANJUSANGENDO, KYOTO Commissioned by Emperor Go-Shirakawa in 1164, Kyoto's Sanjusangendo Temple burns down in 1249 and is rebuilt in 1266. The temple's deity is represented by 1,000 life-size statues in the main hall.

CHURCH OF BETA MARYAM King Lalibela of Ethiopia's Zagwe dynasty builds churches in Roha (now Lalibela, after the king). Each church is carved from a single granite block. They become among the holiest of all Christian sites in Africa.

Medieval students attend a lecture on theology at the Sorbonne, a college within one of Europe's oldest universities, the University of Paris.

audience with Philip Augustus, himself a former crusader. They wanted him to pick up the cross again, but he just told them to go home; a few may have joined the Crusade against the Albigensians.

The religious zealotry of the time continued to give rise to similar Crusades. A Shepherds' Crusade in 1251 pitted peasants against nobility and was quelled by Blanche of Castile. A second Shepherds' Crusade, in 1320, turned into persecution of Jewish communities. Riots resulted in the massacre of hundreds of Jews.

After the Fourth Crusade, the Byzantine Empire was in an even weaker state than before. The establishment of a Latin Empire in Byzantium was but a temporary measure—a new administration was

laid out, but the territories were defended by crusaders who were not interested in staying more than a year. After they left, the Byzantines made alliances with Bulgarians and others who wanted to take back the lost lands. Pope Innocent III called for a new Crusade to accomplish what the Fourth had failed to do—actually go to the Holy Lands.

The Fifth Crusade (1217-1221), the last major Crusade, did not get underway until a year after Innocent's death. The Ayyubid sultans who occupied most of the Holy Lands in the decades after Saladin's death (1193) were subject to political instability and were less interested in expansion than in simply defending what they already had—of this, they were quite

capable. In 1218 crusaders from England, Germany, and the Netherlands arrived in Acre, the capital of the Latin kingdom of Jerusalem now that Jerusalem itself was in Muslim hands. Other contingents landed later and the forces combined for a joint campaign on the Nile Delta, the quickest route to Cairo, the Ayyubids' home base.

After a year and a half, the city of Damietta on the eastern mouth of the Nile finally fell to the crusaders. An Iraqi chronicler described the siege: "After a prolonged struggle the defenders reached the end of their resources. They were almost without food, and exhausted by unending battle. . . . In spite of this they held out amazingly and suffered great

SULTAN A king or leader of a Muslim state. The term originated in the Middle Ages and came into greater use during the Ottoman Empire. Caliphs were religious and spiritual leaders, while sultans were worldly leaders, and therefore expected to be obedient to a caliph.

losses from death in battle, wounds, and sickness." The city of 60,000 had dwindled to 10,000. At this point the sultan was willing to trade Jerusalem and other holy sites for Damietta, but the crusaders, expecting the arrival of reinforcements under Frederick II, rejected the offer.

MISSIONARY ZEAL

One of the Europeans' negotiators was a monk named Francis of Assisi (ca 1181-1226), who founded the Franciscan order in 1209. He and his disciples took the radical approach of living in total poverty, to free themselves from the corrupting influences most clergymen were subject to. In practicing self-denial, he tried as much as possible to model his life after that of Jesus.

A Spanish preacher named Dominic (ca 1170-1221) founded the Dominican order in 1216. These two itinerant preachers later became venerated saints, and their mendicant orders instituted lasting changes in the methods and outlook of the clergy. Dominican and Franciscan friars staffed the earliest papal Inquisition, which was set up during the Albigensian Crusade.

Recent research indicates that these early courts of inquiry were among the most humane to be found in medieval Europe; the cruelties associated with the institution mainly derive from the Spanish Inquisition, which occurred more than two centuries later. Although negotiations with the Egyptian sultan ultimately broke down, he was evidently impressed with Francis and allowed him to visit holy sites in Palestine.

In the meantime, the crusaders continued trying to make their way to Cairo. But Frederick's contingent never showed up, and the annual Nile floods came in especially high, cutting off the crusaders' route of retreat. They were forced to surrender, giving up Damietta and returning home in dejection and defeat. By the late 1200s, Crusades had lost their spiritual significance. Employed only for political purposes, they not only failed to generate much support, they also hurt the image of the popes who called them. After generations of accepting the existence of the Muslim culture, Europeans had lost their enthusiasm for fighting against infidels. Proselytizing was much more palatable, and the Franciscans were among those who took on the challenge.

Some interest was taken in converting the Mongols—who were pressing against the eastern Mediterranean—before they succumbed to the influence of Islam. But for the most part, conversion became an inward-focused, European affair, and persecution of Jews and heretics thus became an unfortunate legacy of the crusader movement. On the other hand, for the development of Europe, the Crusades (in particular, the First) had prevented a Muslim hegemony in the Mediterranean, and they propelled the *reconquista* of Iberia, which would become the leader of European imperialism in the 15th and 16th centuries.

As for the Holy Land itself, it slipped away from European hands: Antioch fell in 1268, Tripoli in 1289. Two years later, the last European defenders of Acre packed up and left. Yet contact with the advanced civilizations of the Muslims and the Byzantines had had a beneficial impact on Europe. Exposure to goods from the East—rugs, tapestries, spices, and exotic foods—opened trade routes, and Europe began to play a bigger role on the world stage.

RELIGION AND REASON

The expansion of speculative thought in the 12th century led to the scholastic system of theology and philosophy

ENGLAND'S TRILINGUAL SOCIETY

English, French, and Latin

Learned scribes of late 13th-century England were expected to know three different languages: Latin, Anglo-French, and Middle English.

In most of medieval Europe, Latin was the predominant language of the church, government, and systems of education and the law. The Norman Conquest of England in 1066 subjected the Anglo-Saxon majority to rule by French nobility, who in time produced a new dialect of French specific to England called Anglo-French or Anglo-Norman. Although it never became England's primary administrative language, Anglo-French appeared in certain governmental, legal, and commercial documents by the late 13th century. Viewed as a mark of gentility, Anglo-French became a second language to many. Literary and historical works were produced in Anglo-French, while within the Universities of Oxford and Cambridge, founded at the turn of the 13th century, scholars still wrote in Latin.

So the published languages of 13th-century England were Latin and Anglo-French, but Middle English was still the mother tongue for most of the population. Middle English borrowed words and phrases from the lexicon of Anglo-Norman but never lost its intrinsic character. It came into wider literary use in the 14th century, as shown by the best-known work in Middle English, Geoffrey Chaucer's *Canterbury Tales*. ■

in the 13th century. The great problem for the scholastics was to reconcile the conflicting tenets of Christianity and of Aristotle, whose works were now widely available in Latin translations. Recognizing the brilliance of Aristotle, who had tried to prove the existence of God through logic, thinkers now added the tools of reason and experience to the truths gleaned from the Bible and other theological writings. The proliferation of universities in western Europe brought the scholastic movement to its zenith in the 1200s.

Building upon the work of Peter Abelard and other 12th-century writers, German philosopher Albertus Magnus (ca 1200-1280) devoted much of his extensive writing to Aristotelianism. Albertus proposed that truth could be arrived at by two avenues—faith and reason—and that these two, instead of contradicting each other, were in fact harmonious. Thus revelation need not oppose science as espoused in the intellectual disciplines of mathematics, astronomy, economics, politics, ethics, metaphysics, logic, and rhetoric. At times, the writings of Albertus could be unclear and vague, unlike those of his most famous student, Thomas Aquinas (1225-1274).

THE INTELLECTUAL SAINT

Born into an aristocratic family near Aquino in southern Italy, Thomas entered the Dominican order in his late teens. His parents had envisioned a contemplative life of prayer for their son, not the peripatetic preaching of the radical new order. When he was on the way to Paris, they had him abducted, then detained him for a year. Undeterred, he went on to the University of Paris and studied under Albertus and others stimulated by the

recent work of Islamic philosopher Averroes, whose commentaries on Aristotle were impossible to dismiss yet difficult to square with Christian dogma.

Averroes posited a deterministic universe made of eternal matter. This position went against both Islamic and Christian teachings, because it precluded God's having created the universe *ex nihilo*—out of nothing. The solution for Averroes was a dual truth—spiritual faith and scientific reason are both valid. Thomas, on the other hand, wanted to join faith and

> THERE SHALL BE
> STANDARD MEASURES
> OF WINE, ALE, AND CORN . . .
> THROUGHOUT THE
> KINGDOM . . . THERE SHALL BE
> A STANDARD WIDTH
> OF DYED CLOTH, . . .
> WEIGHTS ARE TO BE
> STANDARDIZED SIMILARLY.
>
> MAGNA CARTA
> *London, 1215*

reason in one grand system, as Albertus had tried to do.

In 1248 Thomas went with Albertus to teach in Cologne, Germany, returning to Paris seven years later; for the rest of his life he taught in Paris and Italy. Obese, self-confident, and highly intelligent, Thomas was both a great lecturer and writer. His magnum opus, the *Summa Theologica*, would become a pillar of Western thought, though at the time it was too controversial to gain wide acceptance.

He argued that indeed there are two paths to truth—faith and reason—

but they are not separate. Faith brings understanding or illumination through revelation, while reason brings knowledge by logic or experimentation. But since faith uses knowledge—that is, Christian theology can be proved by rational logic—faith cannot be in conflict with reason, especially since both faith and reason reveal God as the source of all truth.

By yoking philosophy and theology, Thomas was also bridging the views of the new mendicant orders. His own Dominican order stressed the validity of the budding natural sciences of optics and mechanics, while the evangelical Franciscans tended toward a more faith-based outlook.

For about another 200 years beyond this point, the prevailing Christian theology was based on the doctrines of St. Augustine (354-430), who believed that knowledge was divinely granted. Thomas challenged that view, advocating knowledge as an accumulation of sensory experience. He admitted that reason could take one only so far—some miracles could not be proved by logic. On the other hand, Aristotelian logic could prove other Christian principles, such as creation ex nihilo and the immortality of the individual soul.

Critics assailed what became known as Thomism from both sides. The strict Averroists claimed he was falsely using Aristotelian causality and logic, while the Augustinians argued that his Christian conclusions were wrongly derived—he had not gone beyond Aristotle at all, but had instead conjured a mechanistic God. This latter camp was dominated by the Franciscans, who believed Thomas erred by emphasizing the intellect over the will.

Louis IX of France and his mother dictate to scribes in this illustration from the Bible of St. Louis, one of the world's most precious illuminated books.

BELIEF

It took a village, and more, to build a medieval city's cathedral like this one in Chartres, France. From afar, their steeples welcomed weary pilgrims.

THE CATHEDRAL

Sacred and Symbolic Space

Construction of a Gothic cathedral was a massive undertaking of time, money, and labor, involving hundreds of people over decades. During the boom of cathedral construction in Europe, in the 12th and 13th centuries, competition was fierce, as planners designed each new cathedral to surpass the old in height, breadth, and splendor—sometimes with disastrous results.

What first made this flurry of innovation possible was the introduction into Europe of the pointed arch of Muslim architecture. What turned the pointed arch into the high, soaring vaults of the Gothic cathedrals was the flying buttress. Used, for example, in the Cathedral of Notre-Dame de Paris, the flying buttress worked like a permanent stone scaffold and propped up a cathedral's upper walls and vaults.

On a cathedral construction site, guilds of paid craftsmen were organized into teams of stonecutters, carpenters, mortar layers, glaziers, and laborers, all overseen by a master mason and a master carpenter. Using simple hand tools, geometric know-how, and the newly reintroduced wheelbarrow, these teams of workers erected the largest buildings in Europe since Roman times, some as tall as 150 feet.

First, foundations were dug and the bases of the walls, buttresses, and columns were laid out. The structure was then built upward, using wooden scaffolding and man-powered devices for lifting heavy stones. The massive timbers of the exterior roof were lifted and fitted into place once the prescribed height was reached. Then came the ceiling's arches and ribs. Finishing touches included stained-glass windows and stone-cut gargoyles.

One of the most modern achievements of the cathedral builders was their success without depending on slave labor. Construction was costly and often strained the resources not just of the commissioning bishop but of local kings, nobility, and merchants alike, but cathedrals were the creation of community. Municipal pride spurred on these endeavors, the end result being a public space of awe-inspiring proportions that symbolized divinity to all who entered. ■

Among those less interested in criticizing than in pushing intellectual investigation forward in the beam cast by Aristotle was Robert Grosseteste (ca 1175-1253), bishop of Lincoln and protector of the English Franciscans.

It was ironic that a Franciscan—a member of the evangelical order—should also be a translator and commentator on Aristotle and a champion of natural science. Yet early Franciscan philosophy had much in common with Platonism, which suggested an ideal, mathematically constructed cosmos. Hence it was Greek philosophy, albeit not that of Aristotle, which influenced Grosseteste's theory on the quantification of nature.

Another English Franciscan, Roger Bacon (ca 1220-1292), was ahead of his time. He did not just theorize; he actually conducted experiments in optics and alchemy. At the pope's request, Bacon also wrote an encyclopedia with essays on mathematics, physics, philosophy, logic, and grammar. He studied the physics of lenses and mirrors, made a camera obscura for observing eclipses, and recorded the first Western recipe for gunpowder.

His experimentation may not have yielded important scientific findings, but his rigorous approach and insistence on empirical evidence set a standard more than three centuries before the arrival of modern science. Accused at various times of black magic and heresy, Roger Bacon was even imprisoned for a while by his fellow Franciscans, partly because of his vituperative criticism of other theologians.

POLITICAL THOUGHT IN THE MIDDLE AGES

In addition to philosophy and theology, the great thinkers of the 13th century spent time on political theory, and the most original voice was, again, Thomas Aquinas. St. Augustine had promoted

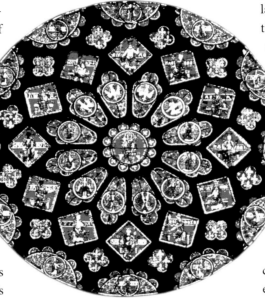

Chemistry and physics, geometry and color, symbol and light: Science, art, and faith meet in the exquisite rose window that lights the interior of Chartres Cathedral, outside Paris, France.

the primacy of the individual soul's relationship with God above all other relationships. The organized state, Augustine argued, with its demands of allegiance, could only get in the way of that higher spiritual union with the divine. Philosophers in the 12th and 13th centuries, living in feudal societies that were more and more controlled from the center, had to reconfigure their thinking based on current systems of government.

The political philosophy of Aquinas carried forward Aristotle's belief in man as a political being—and thus the possibility of a moral state—but he also integrated that concept with the Augustinian demand for the supremacy of the church. He did this by proposing a philosophy of legislation whereby man's laws would conform to natural laws and therefore keep man under the guidance of divine will.

Thomas's vision of moral authority vested within the state was borne out almost to perfection in his contemporary Louis IX of France. Piety was central to Louis's life and reign—his concern for the less fortunate, his Crusades, and his maintenance of peace. Louis was known to sit under an oak tree, seeking divine guidance, when dispensing justice in legal cases. His canonization was already under consideration in Rome before his death. As a counterexample, the acquisitive Frederick II challenged papal authority and failed. His dynasty came to an abrupt end—an indication that his governance did not harmonize with the divine will.

A third example of real-life politics was troubling to the church, for it did not mesh with feudal political philosophy. Even if King John were willing to submit to the demands of the pope, he could do so only at the behest of his people. Government in England seemed to be turning the world order upside down: Here was an accepted monarch of a major power who did not have absolute authority over his own kingdom. The future of such a system was unclear.

FLYING BUTTRESS A buttress is a stone prop that supports a wall built to significant height; a flying buttress stands apart from the wall it supports, joined by arches. Flying buttresses were significant architectural developments that allowed vaulted cathedral ceilings.

TELLING TIME IN THE MEDIEVAL WORLD

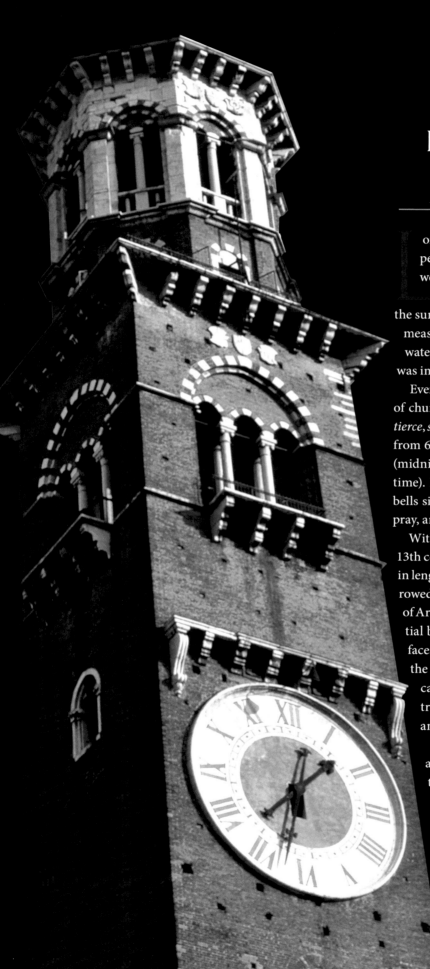

ong before the first clocks ever loomed over public squares, people kept time by sundials. The hours of the day, therefore, were not fixed. They passed in accordance with the sun, which meant that in the winter, hours were very short, and in the summer, very long. When the sun was not shining, time was measured by a variety of other means: hourglasses filled with water or sand, calibrated candles, and water clocks. The system was imperfect, and time was often disputed.

Even more important than the sundial, however, was the system of church bells that divided the day into four segments: *prime*, *tierce*, *sext*, and *none*, corresponding roughly to three-hour periods from 6 a.m. to 3 p.m. The church later added four more: *matins* (midnight), *lauds* (dawn), *vespers* (evening), and *compline* (bedtime). Heard throughout the town and surrounding lands, the bells signified when one should wake, begin work, finish work, pray, and sleep.

With the development of the mechanical clock at the end of the 13th century, time became fixed: Hours were now roughly equal in length, no longer governed by the sun. These early clocks borrowed their technology from the astrolabe, a mechanical device of Arab origin that computed the height and movement of celestial bodies. The astrolabe eventually found its way onto clock faces, so that the era's more impressive timepieces tracked both the hours and the movement of the heavens. The astronomical clock in Prague, for example, built in the 15th century, traces the independent revolutions of the sun, the moon, and the stars.

The early popularity of clocks also stemmed from automatons—mechanical figures that moved around the clock at the change of hours or days. These automatons, like the clocks themselves, grew more sophisticated through the centuries and often reflected the artistic and cultural sensibilities of their locale.

Like many medieval cities, the north-central Italian town of Verona rises to its highest point with a grand stone clock tower. Originally built in the 12th century, it was reconstructed in the 15th after lightning struck.

Still in use today, the 15th-century Prague *orloj*, or astronomical clock, tracks the sun and moon on one dial and the zodiac months on another.

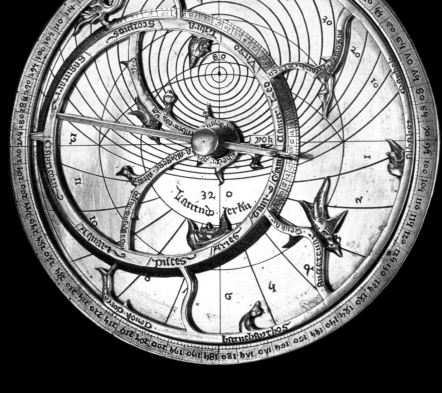

Like the Arabic examples that inspired it, the oldest-known European astrolabe, dating to 1326, tracked the movement of the sun, moon, and stars. It became an essential tool for navigation as Europeans plied the world's waters.

From a page of a 14th-century Arabic manuscript, *Book of Knowledge of Ingenious Mechanical Devices*, this gateway is also a water-driven clock. Zodiac signs representing months cycle above it.

PILGRIMS AND PALMERS PLEDGED THEM TOGETHER
TO SEEK SAINT JAMES AND SAINTS IN ROME.

WILLIAM LANGLAND, VISION OF PIERS PLOWMAN, *CIRCA 1360*

1300 — 1400

AFTER A CENTURY OF RELATIVE PEACE, A CENTURY OF WAR AND CALAMITY TOOK HOLD OF Europe. Western civilization was nearing the modern age in many ways during the 1300s, yet science and technology were still a long way from keeping pace with population growth. Storms large and small were about to erupt over the embattled medieval landscape, the culmination of troubles that had been brewing for too long. The 14th century began with a classic church-state imbroglio, this one centered on Philip IV of France and a testy Pope Boniface VIII. Philip wanted to raise money by taxing that richest of institutions, the church. The pope maintained that he had no right to do so. A heated war of words turned into a test of brinkmanship as well as ideology. The church, which had stood at the peak of its influence in the 13th century, would see its most powerful office humbled and seeking direction.

In the 1320s, the Capetian line of French kings ended and English King Edward III, grandson of Philip, claimed the French throne. The marriage of France and England, forged by William the Conqueror more than 250 years earlier, was about to enter a long and bitter battle of divorce. The simple fact was that even though France was still a nation of duchies, the English holdings in France were there—in France. They were not within the British Isles, but across the channel. The French people, bound by language and culture, were more and more offended by this awkward arrangement. But it would take the Hundred Years War (1337-1453), an intermittent struggle, to finally settle the matter.

In the midst of this war, disaster spread across Europe in the form of the bubonic plague. Urban crowding and poor sanitation made conditions perfect for the worst pandemic known to history. The loss of nearly one-third of Europe's population led to labor shortages and unrest, as well as violence against minorities. Civilization teetered, yet held together, as Italy and other countries began building monumental hospitals and enacting new public health laws.

By the second half of the century, church corruption had risen to intolerable levels as the church struggled to raise money, while disenchanted Christians, influenced by John Wycliffe and other progressive theologians, refused to give as much as they had in the past. With better education, citizens were beginning to challenge Rome's leadership. The crisis came to a head with a papal schism (1378-1417), during which two popes reigned, one in Rome and one in Avignon, France.

Members of the royal court listen as Geoffrey Chaucer, author of the *Canterbury Tales,* reads his poetry to them. Chaucer served as a diplomat and clerk to Richard II. *PRECEDING PAGES:* England's Edward III pays homage to Philip VI, ending his claim to France's throne in exchange for Aquitaine, a southwestern region of France.

In the east, the Ottoman Turks rapidly spread from Anatolia into southeastern Europe—the Balkans and Greece—hastening the demise of the Byzantine Empire. The fierce nomadic warlord Tamerlane would sweep down from the Central Asian plains, checking the Ottoman momentum. But Tamerlane was merely a tidal wave in an inexorable ocean. The Ottomans were systematic in their advance, not solely destructive. They occupied cities with an eye to the future, endowing them with Ottoman political and social systems. Their empire would soon become the greatest in the world.

THE LITTLE ICE AGE

Before the 14th century, Europe had enjoyed a relatively warm climate, enabling farmers to produce abundant and varied crops. Lack of summer ice in the North Atlantic allowed the Vikings to explore the northern realms of the ocean from Iceland to Greenland and North America. Thereafter, the climate underwent a change. From about 1300 to 1800, the Little Ice Age—probably caused by complex interactions between atmospheric pressure and ocean currents—brought lower than average temperatures. Sea ice locked up formerly passable lanes in the north, while early frosts spelled crop failures in Russia and Poland. Glaciers began advancing in Scandinavia and the Alps.

At the beginning of this period, most of Europe benefited from unusually dry, warm summers, owing to low pressure over Greenland. But by the end of the 14th century, unpredictable weather wreaked havoc on food production and trade—in some years rivers froze, in other years flooding rains brought wide-

This jug, decorated with a man's face, is typical of the ceramics made in London during the 14th century, until the Black Death. Copper makes the glaze green.

THE FOURTEENTH CENTURY

ca 1300
Paris's Cathedral of Notre Dame is completed.

1302
Pope Boniface VIII proclaims the primacy of papal power over secular kingship.

1307
Dante Alighieri begins his epic poem, *La Divina Commedia (The Divine Comedy)*.

1314
In the Battle of Bannockburn, Scotland wins independence from England.

1326
The Florentine army uses the first cannons.

1337
The Hundred Years War between France and England begins.

1360
The Treaty of Brétigny marks a temporary peace between France and England.

1375-1378
Florence leads Italian city-states in the War of the Eight Saints against Pope Gregory XI.

spread devastation. Bitterly cold, snowy winters followed blazing hot summers. Previously reliable weather patterns shifted, and adjacent regions suffered diverse effects. Though it is nearly impossible to tease out the precise impact of the environment on large historical movements, certainly local crop failures led to famine and disease, which contributed to political instability. Since people relied on subsistence farming, they had to adjust. In England and the Low Countries, for example, clover and root crops augmented the standard cereal crops that depended on reliable weather.

On the political front, the 1300s ushered in a frosty period in church-state relations. The century began with great festivities when Pope Boniface VIII proclaimed a jubilee in celebration of the 1,300th anniversary of Christ's birth. Some two million people jammed into the streets of Rome, their pockets full of money as offerings for churches. All seemed well. The pope in particular had every reason to celebrate. Elected six years earlier, he had become the vicar of Christ, some claimed, by forcing his predecessor into an early retirement, and he fully expected to continue showing the tradition of papal strength. Instead, he would end in ignominy, and with him the papacy would tumble to its lowest prestige in history. Given the circumstances, the stubborn and impolitic Boniface might have failed even with a different personality, but in forcing the issues, he made unnecessary trouble for himself.

In the 200 years since the face-off between Pope Gregory VII and Emperor Henry IV at Canossa, European states had grown stronger and more confident. The church was still important, but the new states could

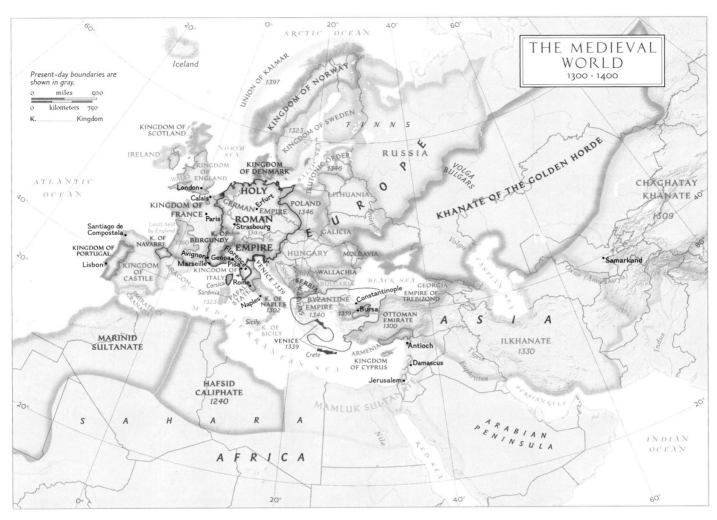

The Medieval World 1300 – 1400

The Kingdom of Sicily gets split in two: Aragon supported a rebellion on the island, and the mainland remainder under French rule is called the Kingdom of Naples (1302). The Ottoman emirate threatens the Byzantine Empire, and Mongol raiders sweep in from the east.

not easily be checked. The largest controversy in political relations was the growing tension between France and England over French turf. To pay for war—and to simply keep themselves at the top of the heap—the monarchs had to increase taxes. Edward I in England and Philip IV in France both came up with the same idea—tax the clergy. The church had given monetary support to aggression in the past, most notably for the Crusades. But that was different, according to canon law, from assessing a tax for any old war.

The pope had not authorized any new taxes, and according to canon law only the church could tax the church. Boniface could not help wading into this conflict, but he got in up to his knees when in 1296 he issued a bull called *Clericis Laicos*, after the initial words of the edict, warning that emperors and kings "who shall impose, exact, or receive" payments from the clergy without papal consent "shall incur the sentence of excommunication." Impassioned rhetoric had become commonplace, but the vehemence of the bull left no room for negotiation; the penalty was automatic.

Unbowed, Edward simply took over church property and declared that clergy who did not pay were operating illegally. Philip embargoed shipments of gold, silver, and jewels to the Italian banks that propped up the papacy. In response, Boniface seemed to surrender almost immediately, and thereby made a tactical error. His new bull clarified that the state actually *could* tax the clergy, but only when, in the judgment of the kings, there was "dire need." Satisfied with the concession, Edward turned his attention to other matters.

But Philip, when later challenged by Boniface, would see the pope's about-face as a weakness to be exploited.

FACE-OFF WITH A POPE

Named for his good looks, Philip the Fair (r. 1285-1314) took the throne at age 17, determined to live up to the high standards of his grandfather Louis IX. Louis's long reign had been generally peaceful, and he was canonized in 1297. But for Philip, being a good Catholic seemed to clash with being a good king, thanks to the injudicious policies of Boniface. Ebullient and confident after the terrific success of the jubilee, Boniface was ready to test his powers. Pope and king found a casus belli in 1301 when Philip took some church money intended for Rome, and Boniface asked a French bishop to find out why. Philip had the bishop arrested and put in prison, then requested Boniface to defrock him.

Boniface responded by revoking the previous order allowing church taxation. He then rebuked Philip for his immoral administration, and summoned the French clergy to Rome for a special council on church reform in France. Philip likewise overreacted by calling an assembly of the French nobility, clergy, and bourgeoisie—the first meeting of the Estates-General (the general assembly)—to garner support for his cause.

The pope countered by issuing another incendiary bull in 1302, the famous *Unam Sanctum* ("One Holy," i.e., the church), which held that since the pope, as God's agent, wielded spiritual authority—higher than

In a power struggle, Pope Boniface VIII sparred with France's Philip IV: Boniface was denounced as a heretic; Philip was excommunicated.

temporal power, which would be subject to him—he could dethrone a king: "We declare, proclaim, and define that subjection to the Roman Pontiff is absolutely necessary for the salvation of every human creature."

> WE MUST RECOGNIZE THE MORE CLEARLY THAT SPIRITUAL POWER SURPASSES IN DIGNITY AND IN NOBILITY ANY TEMPORAL POWER WHATEVER, AS SPIRITUAL THINGS SURPASS THE TEMPORAL.
>
> POPE BONIFACE VIII
> *UNAM SANCTAM*
> *Rome, circa 1302*

One of Philip's ministers retorted, "My master's sword is made of steel. The pope's is made of verbiage." With that threat hanging in the air, the ministers first went to work by deceit. Philip's head lawyer, William de Nogaret, had become virulently antipapal because of the Inquisition. His parents had been executed for heresy. At the Estates-General meeting he denounced the pope as a heretic and murderer, reviving rumors that Boniface had ordered the poisoning of his predecessor.

Nogaret's own hands were none too clean—he had approved the extortion of testimony by suspending a honey-smeared witness over a beehive. Now his smear tactics against the pope included trumped-up charges, hyperbole, and outright lies, and they succeeded in stirring up fear and resentment. Nogaret argued, for example, that the pope had to be a heretic for remarking that he would rather be a dog than a Frenchman, for it meant that Boniface did not believe in the soul.

Having employed threats and calumny, the French government's next move was violence. Nogaret was happy to lead a secret mission in 1303 to arrest Boniface and bring him to France for trial. The elderly pope had taken refuge from the summer heat at his family palace in Anagni, in the Apennine foothills of central Italy. Nogaret and his henchmen burst into the pope's bedroom and seized him. How roughly they handled him is unclear, but the language they used was anything but kind. The pope never left Italy. After a couple of days, villagers and relatives came to his rescue and escorted him back to Rome. A few weeks later, physically and emotionally drained, Boniface died.

Christians across Europe were shocked by the French government's use of brute force against their holy man. The Italian poet Dante (1265-1321), a critic of Boniface, now likened him to the crucified Christ. Nevertheless, the pope's humiliation at Anagni brought the papal see to a nadir of influence, just as Emperor Henry IV's pardon at Canossa in 1077 had been a high point. The rising prestige of French cardinals resulted in the election of a French archbishop as the next pope, Clement V, who moved the seat of the papacy to Avignon, just across the Rhone River in France. It remained there for the next 70 years.

The power and prestige of France grew considerably under Philip the Fair and his ministers. In addition to establishing the monarchy as more powerful than the church, he created an efficient bureaucracy, capable of raising vast revenues

and armed forces. With Clement's help, he brought down the Knights Templar, the service organization that ran a huge bank for the papacy, and seized their assets. A bulked-up France was now ready to take on England in what would become the Hundred Years War.

England under Edward I (r. 1272-1307) had also been attempting to expand its sphere of influence. Edward made successful campaigns into Wales, and he introduced the parliamentary system of government. His efforts to take Scotland, however, proved less than successful. Insurgents led by Sir William Wallace, a Scottish knight and landowner, won a string of victories against the English around the turn of the century. Arrested in 1305, Wallace was taken to London, where he was hanged, disemboweled, beheaded, and quartered. The Scottish independence movement continued under Robert I the Bruce, descendant of a Scottish royal family.

Robert started his career as an ally of Edward I, but in 1306 he decided to seize the Scottish crown, once worn by his grandfather and appointed as a feudal right by the English king. Edward tried to crush the usurper, winning early victories and killing three of Robert's brothers. Edward's death the following year led to vain attempts by Edward II to overtake Robert, and not until near the end of Robert's life, in 1329, did the English government, under Edward III, make a settlement. Both Wallace and Robert the Bruce became Scottish national heroes.

THE BLACK DEATH

By the 1300s Europe had grown more prosperous than ever, but two catastrophes would set it back. One, the Hundred Years War, was of man's devising; the other was a scourge of nature. The Black Death, a series of devastating plagues at mid-century, reduced Europe's population by nearly one-third in just 20 years.

LOCUS

THE GREAT FAMINE

The Social Consequences of Climate Change

A string of cool summers, hard winters, and heavy rainfall beginning in 1315 brought about such extraordinary conditions that grain in northern Europe did not ripen. With wheat the primary food for peasants and nobility alike, the failed harvests produced widespread famine and even starvation. With so little food available, domesticated animals suffered, and disease spread rampantly. Prices rose steeply for both bread and salt. Between 10 and 25 percent of some areas were decimated, bringing the progress of previous centuries to a grinding halt.

The social implications of what came to be known as the great famine of 1315-1322 were many. Crime rates rose, infanticide and child abandonment became more common, faith in institutionalized religion was shaken, and the health of society weakened in 1338, just as the Black Death approached.

We now recognize that climate change was occurring on a near-global level. Europe was nearing the end of a warm period and entering what became known as the Little Ice Age. A long-term cooling trend meant shorter growing seasons and less crop diversification. Some northern settlements could no longer support agriculture.

As populations waned, greater value was placed on human labor, steering European society in the new direction it would follow for centuries. ■

Finding himself in a metaphorical dark woods, Dante Alighieri says he accepted the Roman poet Virgil as his guide through the underworld of hell, as described in his masterpiece, *La Divina Commedia*.

From Messina the contagion spread to the rival cities of Genoa and Pisa by early 1348, claiming victims in both. By year's end, it surfaced all over Italy and reached Paris, the Low Countries, and southern England. In 1349 the plague swept into Germany, Austria, and Scandinavia, and within two years victims were falling as far away as Moscow. For a while the infection seemed to disappear, only to recur, in somewhat less potent form, off and on until well into the next century.

The bubonic plague was named for the telltale buboes, or swellings, that appeared in the victim's armpits or groin. The buboes, now understood as swellings of the lymph glands, would grow as large as apples. Black splotches then spread over the victim's limbs, giving the pestilence its descriptive name. Convulsions, vomiting of blood, and delirium followed, and within three days the sufferer was dead.

The Black Death was also highly contagious; it could be spread by inhaling a victim's breath or by handling his clothing or bedding. Doctors, nurses, and grave diggers wore protective masks; infected clothing was burned; and since blackened corpses remained infectious for 24 hours, they were sprinkled with lime. Some people held nosegays of flowers to their faces as they walked the streets, believing that the stench of carcasses carried the infection and that smelling something pleasant could avert the problem.

Cities were hit the worst, particularly in France and England. In areas where thousands of destitute and malnourished people crowded together, the statistics

In early October 1347 ships plying the Mediterranean made a routine stop at the port of Messina, Sicily, where cargo and passengers were unloaded. Some of the passengers were sick with the bacillus *Yersinia pestis,* which probably originated in China more than a hundred years earlier. Carried by fleas on rats, it had journeyed overland with travelers and arrived in the Crimea in the 1340s, where Mongols may have spread it by catapulting diseased corpses into besieged towns.

Europe had been hit by outbreaks of plague in the past, but what was in store now was unlike any disaster yet known or heard of. Urban crowding and unsanitary conditions were a perfect recipe for a pandemic.

BUBONIC PLAGUE A highly infectious disease caused by the bacterium *Yersinia pestis,* carried by fleas on rats and easily transmitted to humans. It is named for the buboes, or swollen lymph nodes, that those stricken with the disease suffer in armpits, groin, and neck.

were staggering. About half of Paris succumbed, mostly children and the poor. Some villages were nearly wiped out. Normandy lost 70 to 80 percent of its population; Provence 60 percent.

LIFE IN PLAGUE TIMES

Reactions to the epidemic varied widely, according to writer Giovanni Boccaccio (1313-1375), whose *Decameron* characters entertained one another with stories during the plague. Those who could, fled the cities. Some people shut themselves up in their homes, like the characters of the *Decameron,* while others partied wildly, singing and drinking their way from one vacant house to another.

A sick woman would with no shame "show any part of her body"—presumably the affected part—to a man if she thought he could help her, wrote Boccaccio. Some preferred death to such immodesty. Those who took care of the sick or buried their loved ones risked contagion, causing many families to abandon the stricken in

their direst hour: "Incredible as it seems, fathers and mothers fled away from their own children," Boccaccio recounted. Still others were left to the mercy of servants who extorted high wages.

Many people saw the Black Death as a sign of God's wrath. Groups known as flagellants would whip their own backs with spike-tipped thongs, trying to purge their bodies of sin before the plague did. Weird cults of death and mysticism sprang into being, and art and literature became suffused with morbid, even necrophiliac imagery.

A macabre genre known as the Dance of Death proliferated—grinning skeletons partnered with bishops and nobles, a reminder that death spared no one. Skulls began to appear in artwork and as decorative motifs. The meaning of the death's-head, or memento mori (reminder of death), was twofold. It reminded people of their mortality and thus their need to prepare themselves to meet God, but it could also—especially

when adorning a pub or drinking cup—express the idea that since life is short, one had best make the most of it. In other words: Eat, drink, and be merry, for tomorrow we die.

Scholars are still trying to piece together the complex economic and political patterns created by the plague. Certainly the decline in European population led to labor shortages in both rural and urban areas. England teetered on collapse when peasants realized they had the power to demand higher wages; when refused, they simply moved on to another location. In 1351 Parliament passed the Statute of Laborers, forbidding workers to charge more than they had earned before the plague. Attempts at enforcement only created more unrest.

The ugliest spin-off of the plague was a renewed suspicion and hatred toward Jews. As the uneducated looked about for the cause of so much suffering, they too often turned against communities of a different faith.

ARTS & LETTERS

GIOVANNI BOCCACCIO

Poet of the Plague

Giovanni Boccaccio was born in 1313 to a prosperous Florentine banker, but he spent much of his youth and early manhood in the courtly circles of Naples, a major intellectual and cultural center at the time. Returning to Florence around 1341, he had already gained a reputation for eloquence in letters. He saw himself primarily as a poet who wrote in Latin, yet one of Boccaccio's greatest contributions was to elevate Italian vernacular literature to classic status.

Inspired by Dante's *Divina Commedia,* Boccaccio set out in 1348 to write his own human comedy, the *Decameron.* Set against the backdrop of plague-ravaged Florence, it follows ten young women and men as they escape into the countryside and pass ten days in leisure and conversation. Somber descriptions of the plague open the book, in sharp contrast to the levity of the rest of the work, which does not express any grand moral message so much as it ennobles the human condition in an entertaining way.

Boccaccio was also an avid collector of classical texts and a writer of encyclopedic compendia. A true humanist, he rejected the idea of divine intervention and insisted on the independence of men and women on earth, in effect laying the groundwork for the Italian Renaissance of the 15th century. ∎

Boccaccio wrote the widely popular *Decameron,* which inspired Chaucer and many others.

The Duomo of Filippo Brunelleschi rises above the streetscape of Florence, the cradle of the Renaissance.

FLORENCE
CITY OF NEW IDEAS

Landscape | *Finery* | *Currency* | *The Arts*

Florence is often called the birthplace of the Renaissance, where renewed appreciation for classical learning flourished in the 14th and 15th centuries. Originally an Etruscan city, Florence was conquered by the Romans as they expanded their reach through the Italian peninsula. It was built along the Arno River and expanded in a grid pattern, like other Roman cities.

With the decline of the Roman Empire, cities had to fend off invaders previously held at bay by Roman troops. Despite several attacks, Florence was not taken, although some scholars speculate that the population had dwindled to around 1,000 by the sixth century. The Lombards, a Germanic people entering from the north, took control, yet the city remained tiny until Charlemagne and the Franks drove the Lombards out of Italy in 774.

Charlemagne ordered new fortifications built around Florence. Under the Franks, Florence began to grow again, supported economically by the fertile Tuscan hills that surrounded it. By the 11th century, the city was largely self-governing, with a population as large as 20,000. A textile industry proved profitable, renowned for its velvet.

The attention Florence received from La Gran Contessa—Matilda, the Countess of Tuscany—helped the city as well. When power struggles erupted between Pope Gregory and Henry IV, the Holy Roman Emperor, Matilda sided with the pope, and it was at her residence that Henry capitulated to Gregory.

The quarrels between the pope and the emperor spilled over into Florentine daily life: Supporters of the emperor, mostly descendants of feudal lords, were called the Ghibellines; those who supported the pope, the descendants of rich merchants, were called the Guelphs. Under Matilda's patronage, the city sided with the pope, but disputes between the Ghibellines and the Guelphs lasted for centuries.

Despite the divide, the city's textile industry burgeoned during the 12th century. Guilds, bankers, and merchants all prospered, and Florence quickly grew into a leading mercantile center. By 1252, the city was producing its own gold coin, the florin, which became an accepted currency across Europe. The influx of money prompted many architectural projects,

FLORENCE THROUGH THE MIDDLE AGES

401
The Ostrogoths attack and are defeated by Roman soldiers.

542
The Goths attack and fail to capture the city.

568
The Lombards become the city's influential family.

774
Charlemagne captures Florence and drives out the Lombards.

1100
Powerful guilds develop; Florentine goods sold across Europe

1207
Florence temporarily triumphs over rival city Siena.

1215
Guelphs and Ghibellines feud over whether pope or emperor rules.

and many constructions from the 13th and 14th century still stand today, most famously the Ponte Vecchio and the Church of Santa Maria del Fiore.

The Ponte Vecchio—Old Bridge—crosses the Arno at its narrowest point. Built and rebuilt, it originated as a Roman bridge. Disastrous floods destroyed it in the 14th century, and it was rebuilt in its present form in 1345, following a breakthrough design that moved away from the Roman arch and allowed for fewer piers in its construction. Its two-story gallery houses an array of shops.

The Church of Santa Maria del Fiore was begun in 1296, but its most important feature—its massive dome, designed by Filippo Brunelleschi—dates to 1420. The *duomo* remains the dominant feature in the city's skyline, paired with the nearby *campanile* (bell tower), designed in part by the painter Giotto.

One family, the Medici, exerted tremendous influence as Florence evolved from a medieval to a Renaissance city. Their astute and artful use of wealth allowed them to gain and maintain political control for more than a century.

Giovanni de' Medici inherited his family's silk and cloth business, and his shrewd business skills led his company to profit. His son Cosimo expanded the business by sending representatives to cities around Europe. A major political force within Florence and the first Grand Duke of Tuscany, he built the Uffizi (offices) as administrative buildings, now a museum holding one of the world's most extensive art collections.

A major patron of the arts, Cosimo de' Medici offered his home as a safe haven for exiled Greek scholars and artists. Before long, the city became known as a center for the arts. Medici patronage continued thanks to Lorenzo the Magnificent, Cosimo's grandson, during whose rule, from 1469 to 1492, the family reached its peak of power.

Florence, seat of agricultural Tuscany, was a regional power among the city-states of medieval Italy.

A poet himself, Lorenzo de' Medici surrounded himself with artists and intellectuals, perhaps most notably the sculptor and painter Michelangelo di Buonarroti. The Medici Chapel in Florence, designed by Michelangelo, was completed in 1527. It is one of the best examples of how he respected classical styles and yet innovated, an aesthetic impulse central to the Renaissance.

This energetic revival of classicism, led by the artists of Florence, ultimately swept all of Europe, as the Middle Ages evolved into the Renaissance. The art, opulence, and ideas central to this intellectual rebirth still enliven the city of Florence today.

The Arno River wends through the city of Florence. At its narrowest point it is traversed by the Ponte Vecchio—Old Bridge—which is still lined with shops, as it was in the Middle Ages.

1252
The city mints its first coin, the florin, soon accepted throughout Europe.

1265
Dante Alighieri is born in Florence.

1296-1436
Construction proceeds on the Cathedral of Santa Maria del Fiore.

1348
The Black Death strikes Florence.

1420
Construction begins on Brunelleschi's dome for the cathedral.

1469
Lorenzo de' Medici assumes leadership of Florence.

1472
Leonardo da Vinci is accepted into the painters' guild.

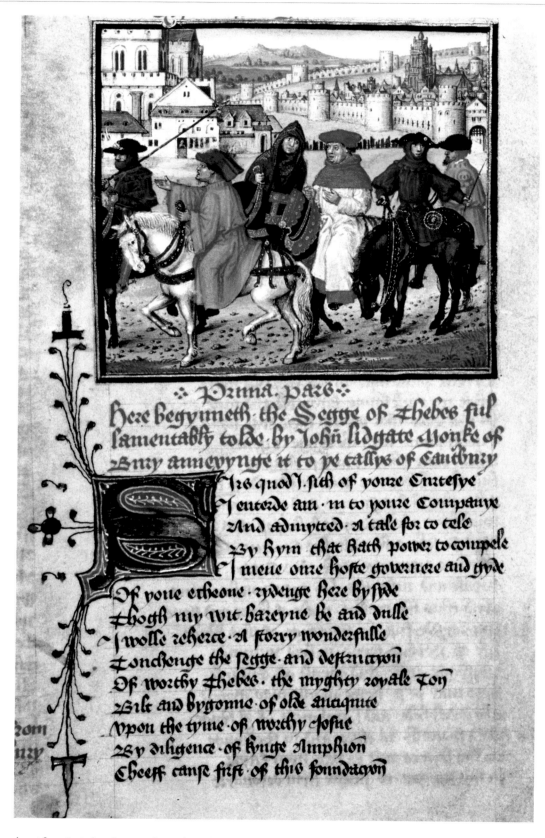

Pilgrims depart from Canterbury in a page from John Lydgate's *Troy Book*, inspired by the *Canterbury Tales* of Chaucer, whom Lydgate admired.

Rumors that Jews had caused the plague by poisoning the wells spread from southern France and northern Spain into Switzerland and Germany, few people pausing to consider the fact that Jews had contracted plague at the same rate as Christians. A historian from Strasbourg, France, and apparently an eyewitness, Fritsche Closener noted that "Jews were burnt all the way from the Mediterranean into Germany, but not in Avignon, for the pope protected them there." In some cities Jews burned themselves before the mob could get to them.

In 1349 the leaders of Strasbourg held a conference to decide what to do about the Jews. The city deputies maintained the Jews were blameless, but when the topic of wells came up, a huge argument erupted. The bishop of Strasbourg and the feudal lords decided the Jews had to be killed.

"The result was that they were burnt in many cities, and wherever they were expelled they were caught by the peasants and stabbed to death or drowned," according to Closener. Some 2,000 Jews were put on a wooden platform in the Jewish cemetery in Strasbourg. About half of them decided to accept baptism; the rest were burned. All the debts owed the Jews were then canceled, and all their money was confiscated and divided among the workingmen.

"The money was indeed the thing that killed the Jews. If they had been poor and if the feudal lords had not been in debt to them, they would not have been burnt," wrote Closener. It was decreed that no Jew should enter the city for 100 years, but after 20 years the council and magistrates lifted the ban.

Jews in some cities hid their wealth from the frenzied mobs. In Erfurt, in central Germany, a large hoard of gold and silver coins, ingots, tableware, and jewelry was stashed in the walls of a house in the Jewish quarter. There it sat for 649 years, until it was discovered in 1998. Recognized as a cache of rare and exquisite medieval metalwork, it was also a startling piece of tangible history.

THE YEARE OF OUR BLESSED SAVIOUR'S INCARNATION, 1348, THAT MEMORABLE MORTALITY HAPPENED IN THE EXCELLENT CITY, FARRE BEYOND ALL THE REST IN ITALY; WHICH PLAGUE, . . . BY THE JUST ANGER OF GOD WAS SENT UPON US MORTALS.

GIOVANNI BOCCACCIO
"THE INDUCTION OF THE AUTHOR"
THE DECAMERON
Circa 1350

Though the Black Death was a time of turmoil and misery, it also resulted in some improvements in medieval life. The working class, now with thinner ranks, became more enterprising; crafts guilds recruited people who had been mired in poverty; textile and other commercial markets began to expand. And cities began to develop better systems of public health. Municipalities passed sanitation laws, requiring that streets be clean of human and animal waste, and appointed physicians to provide free health care to those in need. Health boards were set up, and quarantines were initiated.

One of the greatest new institutions was the hospital, which evolved into a place for the impoverished sick to receive medicine and care. Earlier "hospitals," or places of hospitality, such as those established by the Knights of St. John (Hospitallers), existed for pilgrims. These places of refuge evolved into charitable institutions for the needy and infirm of major cities. The largest hospitals could care for hundreds of patients at a time. In the forefront of the movement, Italy built several innovative hospitals.

A CENTURY OF WAR

In addition to the Black Death, war plagued western Europe in the 1300s. The Hundred Years War actually lasted 116 years, and it was not a continuous war. It began in 1337 when Philip of France laid claim to Guienne, that rich province in southwestern France which roughly corresponded with the old duchy of Aquitaine.

Ever since Aquitaine had been joined with the fortunes of England, there had been tension across the English Channel. England was the more unified and centrally controlled nation of the two, and it had kept control of its French holdings now for some 200 years, although the territory had shrunk somewhat since the days of Henry II. Still, the English considered the large fiefdom in the southwest of France theirs, and English nobles had grown accustomed to the fine Bordeaux wines that the region produced. The French monarchy, though, was growing more powerful, and the time seemed propitious to rid the nation once and for all of its cross-channel parasite.

France was now the most powerful and wealthy state in Europe, but its overconfidence, poor military strategy, and lack of new technology resulted in the failure of three major battles to drive

An unknown writer invented the identity of Sir John Mandeville (shown above, center, in white) and published travel writings claimed to be by him. Above, he greets King Edward II of England.

He had, seven years earlier, seized the government being held in his name by his mother and her lover, Roger Mortimer. Entering the castle where they were staying by an underground passageway, he had Mortimer arrested, hanged, drawn, and quartered. He then invaded Scotland and, not long after, declared war on France. Though military action was slow at first, Edward won a tremendous naval victory in 1340, nearly destroying the French fleet at Sluis in the disputed territory of Flanders.

Edward added the French fleur-de-lis to the lions on his coat of arms, and then led an invasion of Normandy, on the northwest coast of France. In 1346 the English won a decisive battle at Crécy, a small town north of Paris. It was here that the English proved themselves a military powerhouse by the use of the longbow, a new weapon.

At that time, the longbow could shoot farther than the crossbow and was much quicker and easier to use—a longbow archer could shoot five to six arrows in a minute, the same time it took a crossbowman to shoot one. The English shot forth such a torrent of deadly fire, the arrows fell like snow, as tradition puts it. English pride swelled after Crécy, while the average Frenchman lost patience with the war. Adding to the insult, mercenaries hired by both sides spent their between-battle free time plundering the countryside, and the ravages of the plague were shortly to hit as well.

More English victories followed. The port of Calais, on the Strait of Dover, fell in 1347. And at the 1356 Battle of Poitiers in west-central France, the English captured French King John II, who had succeeded Philip VI in 1350. Edward's son, Edward the Black Prince (named

the English off the continent. Yet the French had three times the population of England, and they gradually managed to erode the English presence.

In 1328, 14 years after the death of Philip the Fair, the 300-year-old line of Capetian kings of France came to an end as one by one Philip's sons died off. His daughter Isabella had married Edward II, king of England, and so their son Edward III (r. 1327-1377) claimed France as his domain. French nobles had no desire to

be governed by an English ruler, despite his French connections. They chose a nephew of Philip the Fair as their king, and Philip VI (r. 1328-1350), son of Charles of Valois, became the first Valois ruler of France.

French monarchical aggression under Philip VI met with English expansionism in the person of Edward III to initiate what would prove to be a very long war. Talented and energetic, Edward was but 25 years old at the outset of hostilities.

for his armor), scored the win, and took his prize off to London.

In the Treaty of Brétigny and the subsequent Treaty of Calais, France agreed to give up claims to Aquitaine in return for their king. In turn, King Edward agreed to drop his claim to the French crown. By 1360, England held about one-third of France, the same as it had two centuries earlier. But France would shortly go to work undermining those holdings.

THE PEOPLE REBEL

Throughout the French and English countryside, people had grown restless under the constant threats of violence, plague, and famine. Uprisings led by peasants or petty knights rocked the land. In the 1320s Flemish peasants revolted against new taxes, forcing the nobles out and taking their land. Setting up their own armies and courts, the peasants reestablished the government. Armed forces from France and Navarre (northern Spain) finally wrested the

territory away in 1328. Unrest continued as England tried to manipulate Flanders against France at the beginning of the Hundred Years War.

After the Battle of Poitiers, armies of peasants in northern France rose up to fight bands of marauding mercenaries. In 1358 a peasant group derisively called the Jacquerie (after their leader's nickname, Jacques Bonhomme—Jack Goodfellow) went a step further—they began going after the nobility for their failure to shield the countryside from the ravages of war. Not only did the nobles no longer provide protection, they continued to exact the usual rents and fees.

Roused to murderous fury, the peasants burned manor houses and lashed out at nobles with sticks and scythes. When the reprisal came, it was swift and brutal: The swords and lances of mounted knights fell upon the peasants with avenging wrath; whole villages were razed, and peasant leaders were hanged outside their cottages.

Similar insurrections flared up in England, most notably during the Peasants' Revolt of 1381 led by former soldier Wat Tyler. The inciting cause was a new tax to cover war expenses, but underlying the revolt was a general reaction against years of serfdom. Labor shortages after the Black Death had given peasants a new sense of their worth, and they were no longer so inclined to accept repression as their lot. Instead of simply trying to kill nobles, Tyler and his Essex and Kent rebels marched on London with specific demands—they wanted an end to serfdom, fairer rents and taxes, no restrictions on free trade, and amnesty for the rebels.

Edward III's grandson Richard II (1367-1400) now held the throne, and at age 14 he himself went out into the mob and promised to meet their demands. At a parley the following day, Tyler presented more demands. A fight broke out, and Tyler was wounded and taken to a local hospital. The lord mayor of London had

JOHN WYCLIFFE AND HIS BIBLE

Belief in the Word over the Wealth of the World

John Wycliffe was a learned man who studied divinity at the University of Oxford in 1372. He soon became involved in church politics by asserting that ecclesiastical authority was derived not from priesthood but from the Bible. He criticized the papal church for its corruption and called on its leaders to renounce wealth and material possessions and to choose poverty—which was not very likely.

Wycliffe could count on protection from the English nobility, who were also distrustful of the land holdings and power of the church. He was also something of a tool in their hands, however. Sincere in his desire to reform the church, Wycliffe could also be bitter and vitriolic.

Holding the Bible as so important, Wycliffe organized its first translation into the English language. His followers, called the Lollards, disseminated copies of it and preached a faith based on personal experience.

The Lollards may have had a hand in inspiring the Peasants' Revolt of 1381, which resulted in the murder of the archbishop of Canterbury. The next archbishop took a strong stand against the influence of Wycliffe, condemning his works and banning his teachings.

Wycliffe continued to write until his death, in 1384. His works found a new audience in the 16th century. He has been called the "morning star" of the Protestant Reformation. ∎

John Wycliffe railed against church abuses in the 14th century. His antipapal belief in Bible readings as the source of revelation presaged the Protestant Reformation of the 16th century.

The Battle of Poitiers of September 1356 won the English a temporary upper hand over the French in the Hundred Years War. Soldiers both mounted and on foot followed Edward, the Black Prince, to victory, even though their swords and spears could not pierce the curved metal armor worn by the French.

him abducted and beheaded. At that, the rebellion fizzled out, and, as in France, there was some retaliation. But the English peasants had also gained recognition and won some bargaining power with their landlords.

In Florence, Italy, cloth workers caught the spirit of rebellion in 1378 when they combined with small business owners to protest the restrictions of the ruling class. The Ciompi (wool carders) Rebellion gained control of local government, but three years later the old elites were back in power. By the early 1400s Florence began to be controlled by the mighty Medici family.

The second phase of the Hundred Years War got under way during the period of the peasant revolts. This phase favored the French, though they did not score any major battlefield victories. Charles V of France (r. 1364-1380), nicknamed the Wise, wanted to avoid massive battles, and the guerilla warfare of the French during this time worked more to their advantage. Richard II was King of England during Charles's reign, yet he was just a boy, and the English government was dominated by his inept uncle John of Gaunt, Duke of Lancaster.

Thus England in the late 1300s was not sufficiently unified for big military operations, and when Richard came of age and took over, he was distracted with other problems at home. Luckily for France, Charles V was a strong and capable leader who capitalized on England's momentary weakness with a reformed army that employed a hit-and-run strategy. By 1380 English holdings in France were trimmed to Calais and part of Aquitaine.

Charles was succeeded in 1380 by his son Charles VI, who ruled for 42 years.

PERSONAE

WILLIAM WALLACE

Fighting for a Scotland Ruled by Scots

I n 1296 England's Edward I imprisoned the King of Scotland and took control. In response, William Wallace and some 30 other Scottish landholders stormed the English garrison in the market town of Lanark and killed the English sheriff.

An army organized around Wallace, and on September 11, 1297, they faced the English at the Battle of Stirling Bridge. The Scots slaughtered the English as they crossed the narrow bridge, and in December 1297, Wallace was named guardian of the kingdom of Scotland.

In 1298 a reinforced English army invaded Scotland, defeating Wallace at the Battle of Falkirk. Wallace likely continued with small-scale guerilla warfare from this point on, but the tide was turning, and by 1304 most members of the Scottish nobility had submitted to English rule.

Wallace still had a bounty on his head. Arrested in 1305, he was brought to London, hanged and quartered, his head displayed on London Bridge.

A year later, one of Wallace's early supporters, Robert the Bruce, fomented the rebellion that ultimately led to Scottish independence. ■

William Wallace led a popular revolt against the English occupation of Scotland, a cause for which he was martyred in 1305.

Known both as Charles the Mad and Charles the Well-Beloved, he was 12 on ascending the throne, but by 1392 he was involved in peace negotiations with the other young king, Richard II. The effort stalled when Charles suffered the first of several bouts of insanity, each lasting several months and characterized by fever, convulsions, smashing of furniture, and rending of clothes. Sometimes he could not recognize his queen; other times he thought he was made of fragile glass. During his lucid periods he made valiant attempts to reestablish his rule, but as his bouts of madness became longer he became more irrelevant and France slipped into political confusion, suspending the war for a time.

THE PAPAL SCHISM

The late 1300s were marked by upheavals in the Catholic Church, affecting the course of the Hundred Years War and the future of Christendom. A radical new movement was loose in western Europe, promoting social equality through reform of the church. One of the leaders of this intellectual groundswell was Oxford philosopher and theologian John Wycliffe (ca 1330-1384), a precursor of the Protestant Reformation.

Wycliffe challenged the clergy's position as spiritual leaders—each person, he claimed, was responsible for his own salvation. He took apart the doctrine of transubstantiation, arguing that the faithful were not partaking of the actual body of Christ during communion but of his spirit through their own faith. This argument attacked the mystical power of the priesthood, which claimed the sole authority to provide the Eucharist and other sacraments. His urging that the church be divested of secular wealth—

and that the laity should take church lands—was approved by the English, for they knew that church support of the papacy at Avignon was likely helping fund the French war effort.

Furthermore, Wycliffe asserted that the Bible was a sufficient guide to spiritual matters; the church was not required for faith. He and his followers were preparing an English translation of the Bible so that it could be read by all, when his works were condemned for, among other things, helping foment the Peasants' Revolt. "I believe that in the end the truth will conquer," he wrote to the Duke of Lancaster. Although he was summoned before a synod to respond to allegations of heresy in 1382, he was let free. It was not until 31 years after his death in 1384 that his bones were exhumed and burned to ashes as a heretic's.

In 1377 the church began to realize that reform had to come, and Pope Gregory XI, the last of the Avignon popes, decided it was time to return the papacy to Rome. But when he died the next year, the papacy underwent a schism that lasted until 1417, and the church never fully recovered. The Western or Great Schism (not to be confused with the schism between the Greek and Roman

This seal stamped official documents of Robert the Bruce, champion of Scottish independence. The reverse side of the seal shows Bruce mounted, in full battle armor, sword and shield drawn.

Catholic Churches in 1054) came about in the following way.

In 1378 the College of Cardinals elected an Italian, Urban VI (1318-1389), as the new pope. Within months, Urban made clear that he was to be a brusque and antagonistic reformer, prompting the many French cardinals to claim that his election was invalid "because it was not made freely but under fear." They chose one of their own as Pope Clement VII (1342-1394), and he moved to Avignon. Now under dual popes and papal

sees, the Catholic Church lurched into a troubled future.

Nations lined up behind the two rival popes: France sided with Clement, the so-called antipope, as did Scotland, northern Spain, and Portugal—which switched allegiance four times. England sided with Urban, joined by Germany, Poland, Hungary, Flanders, northern and central Italy, and Bohemia (between Germany and Poland).

The schism heightened existing political tensions between France and England, and it also sparked brutalities of its own. For example, prelates found guilty of conspiring against Urban were arrested and executed. Anarchy broke out in the Papal States, and Urban himself died of a possible poisoning in 1389.

Attempts to heal the rift broke down over the very question of whether the pope had the authority to convene a council. Then in 1409 cardinals gathered for a conclave in Pisa. They deposed the two rival popes and elected a new one. But since the incumbent popes refused to step down, there were now three popes.

Finally Europe's secular rulers had had enough of this foolishness. Representatives of several states met with prelates in the mid-1410s in the German city of Constance to find a solution. The Council of Constance secured one pontiff's abdication, deposed the other two, chose a new

PAPACY The office and powers held by the pope, the bishop of Rome, who serves as spiritual and administrative leader of the Roman Catholic Church worldwide. This definition originated with Pope Gregory I around A.D. 600. Its interpretation has long provoked debate.

With the revival of commerce and trade, merchant guilds and their attendant guildhalls appeared in many of the major cities of medieval Europe. The 16th-century butchers' guildhall, or Knochenhauer-Amtshaus, of Hildesheim, Germany, took guildhall architecture to extremes.

Throughout the towns and cities of medieval Europe, merchants and craftsmen banded together to protect their interests and regulate commerce and industry. Craft guilds were dominated by a master craftsman who oversaw the advancement of apprentices and journeymen, licensing them to work in a trade. The masters of the craft guilds also set standards and fixed minimum prices for their manufactured goods. Sometimes they fixed wages, hours, tools, and the entire production process.

Guilds had a social function as well, and they often had the wealth required to build large halls to host meetings, banquets, and parties. Guildhalls built in towns and cities of Flanders, Belgium, and northern Italy were adorned with ornate architectural decoration, marble paneling, and masterpieces of art. Communes

THE GUILDHALL

Tradesmen & Merchants Gather

maintained their independence in parts of northern Germany, where they comprised the Hanseatic League, trading goods along Baltic Sea routes from London to Russia.

The wealthy guilds came to control local governments, and their guildhalls became town halls. In some cases, merchants banded together to found a new self-governing town, or commune. Town councils composed of merchants were able to pass legislative measures to achieve monopolies on local commerce.

The merchant guilds controlled many aspects of urban life in Europe from the 12th to 15th centuries. They built schools, roads, and churches. They expanded the economic base that made their class powerful. They developed banking institutions that became increasingly wealthy. In general, they established a social infrastructure that allowed the slow transition away from feudalism.

Some went outside town walls to conduct business free from guild regulations. In the countryside, they sought to exploit the cheap labor of peasants, and landowning lords leased their land to Europe's first capitalists. In the larger industrial cities, such as Florence, where wealth was amassed by a small oligarchy and a proletariat of factory workers emerged, class conflicts ensued and social systems collapsed. ■

THE WORLD IN THE FOURTEENTH CENTURY

The Ottoman Turks swept through Anatolia and southeastern Europe and seized the Byzantine Empire, weakened by the bubonic plague. A few rulers continued for a while longer, such as the Mamluks in Egypt and Tamerlane in Uzbekistan, but the Ottomans soon ruled supreme.

The new Ming dynasty—China's only native rule between the Mongols and the Manchu—brought strict but stable autocratic rule and elevated the arts, especially theater. Japan's Noh theater tradition was emerging, and samurai culture continued to wield influence.

While northern Africa remained caught up in the affairs of the Middle East, sub-Saharan Africa—especially in the gold- and salt-laden west—emerged as a powerful commercial center. Mali, Ghana, and Songhai built lasting empires on the gold trade, and contact with Arab merchants made Mali an important center of Islamic scholarship.

In the Americas, trade brought wealth and contact between cultures. The Inca and the Aztec flourished, developing sophisticated governments. More than 10,000 traders exchanged goods daily in the grand Aztec capital of Tenochtitlán; some historians speculate that goods came from as far away as Peru.

Farther north, drought forced the once thriving Anasazi to scatter through the southwest, abandoning their large pueblos. The Hohokam devised irrigation systems. The Mississippi mound-building societies regressed into smaller tribes that traded with people of the eastern woodlands. ▪

MAMLUK DYNASTY The Mamluk Bahrite dynasty, which began in Egypt and Syria in 1250, achieves military and commercial success. The sultanate survives until 1517, when the Ottomans take over. This exquisite Egyptian Mamluk Koran shows the culture's artistry.

Arctic

North America

Pacific Ocean

EQUATOR

TENOCHTITLAN Founded in 1325 on an island in Lake Texcoco, the magnificent Aztec capital of Tenochtitlán becomes one of the most vibrant cities in the Americas. The city is divided into carefully planned districts; its central marketplace is the largest of its kind.

Atlantic Ocean

South America

CASA GRANDE Along the Gila River in today's Arizona, Hohokam Indians build a compound of unreinforced clay; at its center rises a four-story structure known today as Casa Grande. The first story is filled with dirt to support the top three stories, probably living spaces.

Ocean

Europe

NOH THEATER **Derived from earlier forms of dance and spiritual rituals, Noh emerges as a distinct dramatic form in Japan. Storytellers often wear masks and interpret legends well known to their audience. Noh is one of the oldest surviving theatrical traditions in the world.**

A   s   i   a

Pacific Ocean

Africa

Indian Ocean

EQUATOR

MING DYNASTY **Zhu Yuanzhang takes Dadu, or Beijing, from the Mongols in 1368, establishing the Ming dynasty, which thrives on autocratic rule and civil service. Its style of government persists in China until the fall of imperial rule in the early 20th century.**

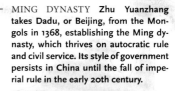

Australia

OSMAN I **First ruler of the Ottoman Turks, Osman I leads successful military campaigns and founds one of modern history's most formidable empires. Taking advantage of a weakened Byzantine Empire, the Ottomans swiftly conquer Anatolia.**

pope, and along the way condemned the doctrines of Wycliffe and his followers. The year 1417 brought an end to the Great Schism, but the 39-year period of nine popes and antipopes had done irreparable damage to papal prestige and church authority.

RENOVATING THE CHURCH

After the disgrace of Avignon and the Great Schism, the Roman Catholic Church floundered for direction, and the Catholic Church slid into a morass of corruption. In the early 1200s, Pope Innocent III had made serious efforts to curb moral laxity in the church, but with the practice of lay investiture still predominant, it was difficult to control what were essentially political appointments. With the papacy in ruins in the 14th century, the system of visitation, whereby bishops kept tabs on local parishes, was haphazard at best.

INSTEAD OF THE BARE FEET
OF THE APOSTLES,
THE SNOWY COURSERS
OF BRIGANDS FLY PAST US,
THE HORSES DECKED IN GOLD
AND FED ON GOLD,
SOON TO BE SHOD WITH GOLD,
IF THE LORD DOES NOT
CHECK THIS
SLAVISH LUXURY.

**PETRARCH TO A FRIEND
REGARDING THE PAPACY**
Avignon, circa 1340

The lack of supervision allowed greed and incompetence to flourish in churches as never before. Families with influence often had their eye on church property and income; getting a son into high church office gave the family insurance against future tribulations,

whether or not that son was fit for such office. Dukes and princes sometimes simply took over church property, or manipulated the law to acquire it, and then appointed an uneducated relative as bishop.

Under the spiritual care of ignorant or grasping clergy, a better-educated middle class recoiled at the obvious mismanagement. A desperate cycle of corruption, leading to underfunding, was now in place. The practice of paying for indulgences—ridiculed by Chaucer and other writers—arose as a means to shake down money from the populace.

The church had long ago instilled the notion that a person who committed a sin could gain remission of the punishment due that sin by an act of piety, such as a pilgrimage, viewing a holy relic, or going to a special church celebration. The more serious the sin, the greater the action a sinner had to perform; thus a pilgrimage might give a murderer only a limited

---

THE COMPASS AND ITS ROSE

A Guide to Navigation in the Open Sea

The compass arrived in European ports by 1187, carried by the Chinese and Arab mariners who already used it. Italian and Spanish navigators combined this innovation with the wind rose, a hand-painted chart of the directions of the winds, and the result came to be known as the compass rose.

The compass rose envisions winds coming from every possible direction, and divides the horizon into 32 points, indicating 8 cardinal winds, 8 half winds, and 16 quarter winds. With compass and map on hand, and the compass rose drawn onto both of them, seafaring merchants from Venice, Genoa, Pisa, Barcelona, and Majorca no longer had to set their course

by visible landmarks but could chart direct pathways to distant harbors of the Mediterranean. Sea charts were drawn for the Atlantic, north to Ireland and south to Africa.

Hand-drawn compass roses became detailed and ornate, with a fleur-de-lis pointing north, a cross toward the Holy Land in the east, and color-coded lines in between that charted shortest possible navigational routes.

Still unsolved questions of latitude, curvature of the Earth, and other variations made the compass rose less accurate the farther from its place of origin, yet it nevertheless facilitated a boom in commerce and exploration from Asia to Scandinavia. ∎

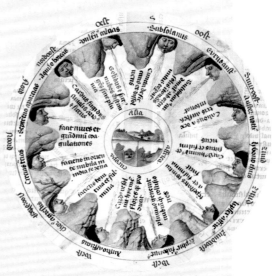

**The compass rose envisioned—and sometimes
animated—winds from all directions.**

reprieve from purgatory, the place where sinners are punished for, and purged of, their sins.

Pope Urban II had declared that going on the First Crusade in 1095 gave one a totally clean slate. Later, simply providing monetary support to a Crusade was considered almost as worthy, earning the contributor a certificate of indulgence. This easy-pay method saved people a lot of trouble and became especially popular during the 14th century, a time of widespread war and economic downturn. The idea of the afterlife was a great comfort, but few people had the money for, say, a thousand-mile pilgrimage to the shrine of Santiago de Compostela in Spain. Friars and other mendicants went about selling indulgences to collect money for the church. Many people paid, not just for themselves but for their dead relatives as well, while others saw the practice as blatant extortion. The massive loss of confidence led to further church disintegration.

The late medieval church actually did make progress in modifying the sexual behavior of its clergy. By the end of the 14th century, clerical celibacy was an established and growing tradition, with common-law marriages (cohabitation) in the priesthood becoming rare. Mistresses and visits to prostitutes were also on the decline among the clergy. Early 16th-century reformers would complain that clerical celibacy was more a weakness than a cleansing influence in the church. In any event, the Roman Catholic Church and the leadership of the pope had begun to slip in influence. The coming Protestant revolution would

Pope Clement V and King Philip IV of France receive members of the Knights Templar, whose power had grown so great by the 13th century that both church and state wanted the order crushed.

react against every perceived Catholic excess, from papal indulgences to fancy church architecture.

ISLAM ADVANCES

Southeastern Europe went through a profound transformation in the 14th century when the Ottoman Empire spread out from northwestern Anatolia (in present-day Turkey), bringing Islam to formerly Christian territories and shrinking the size of the Byzantine Empire. A confederation of Turkic nomads, the Ottomans were named for their first leader, the charismatic Osman I (also called Uthman).

In the late 11th century, the Ottomans' descendants moved from the steppes, the vast plains of Central Asia, to Anatolia, organizing themselves around regional leaders known as *ghazis*. As a ghazi who was both a capable administrator and

CRUSADE Those first using this word, in the 12th and 13th centuries, specifically referred to zealous activities furthering the goals of Christianity: The root of the word comes from the Latin for cross. It has since broadened to mean any shared effort for a perceived cause.

The campaigns and raids of Turkish conqueror Timur financed the construction of an intricate mausoleum in which he and his family are buried: the Shah-i-Zindeh, or Tomb of the Living King, still standing in Samarkand, Uzbekistan.

devout Muslim, Osman consolidated power in the late 13th century and began to grow restless. In 1299 he declared independence from the ruling Seljuk Turks and embarked upon a war of conquest.

In 1301 he captured the ancient Anatolian city of Nicaea, and near the end of his life, in 1326, he claimed the Byzantine city of Bursa. Situated at the foot of Mount Olympus in what is now northwestern Turkey, this former seat of Bithynian kings and stronghold of Roman and Byzantine Empires would serve as the Ottoman capital from 1327 to 1361.

After the death of Osman, his heirs continued to expand the empire westward into Byzantium and eastward against smaller Turkish principalities. Taking the emirate of Karasi east of Bursa in 1345 brought them to the shores of the Mediterranean.

THE OTTOMANS UNDER MURAD

Crossing the strait known as the Dardanelles, Ottoman conquerors gained their first foothold in Europe in 1354 by capturing Gelibolu (Gallipoli), an ancient Greek port and medieval trading center.

After taking Thrace, a region in Europe's southeastern corner, in the 1360s, the Ottomans under the inspired leadership of Sultan Murad I (r. 1360-1389) won a major battle in 1371 against a coalition of Serbian rulers along the Maritsa River (between Greece and Turkey), opening the Balkans to Ottoman penetration. Towns in Macedonia and beyond fell quickly

to Ottoman determination and ability. The sheer speed with which Murad and his forces—including dedicated fighters such as his second lieutenant Lala Shahin Pasha—occupied such a vast territory was staggering. By the 1370s he had forced the Byzantine emperor, as well as regional

This lamp, inscribed with three quotations from the Koran and a dedication to Beybars II, an Egyptian sultan, was made in the 14th century to light the interior of a mosque.

princes, into a state of vassalage. The Ottomans had yet to take Constantinople, but danger was extremely near.

Now Murad made a deep thrust into Europe, winning the Battle of Kosovo in 1389 against Serbs, Albanians, and Bosnians. He was killed in the battle, but his son Bayezid I (1389-1402), called the

Thunderbolt, assumed command. Four years later Bulgaria became part of the expanding Ottoman Empire.

Under Murad, the Ottoman culture developed some of the institutions that would carry it through nearly four centuries of expansion. Administrative military offices became regulated and were sometimes given to men outside the royal family, and a land-tenure system was put in practice in the Balkans. Most important, the elite fighting corps known as the Janissaries was born during Murad's rule.

The first Janissaries were Christian youths taken from conquered Balkan villages. A seven-year training period honed them into ardent and disciplined Muslim fighters. They were ranked in three divisions and were required to observe strict celibacy. The Janissaries later became an important political entity. The celibacy rule was dropped later in the 16th century.

Bayezid solidified the Ottomans' vast holdings, while pushing out in all directions. He advanced farther east against Anatolian Turks in the early 1390s, captured the Macedonia seaport of Salonika in 1394, and invaded Hungary in 1395. A Hungarian-Venetian crusade of French, English, and German forces tried to stop Bayezid's army at Nicopolis on the Danube River in northern Bulgaria in 1396, and suffered a bruising defeat. But Bayezid finally met his match in a cyclonic invader from the east who would put the Ottoman Empire on hold—thus delaying Byzantium's death throes—for half a century.

VASSAL A vassal was a person who vowed loyalty and homage to the lord of the estate on which he lived. In exchange, a vassal usually received a home for his family and land to work for food. The land on which he lived was called a fief. Intricate laws of inheritance evolved.

TIMUR'S REIGN OF TERROR

He was called Timur the Lame, though not to his face. Born in 1336 in a Central Asian valley between Samarkand and the Hindu Kush mountains, Timur (or Tamerlane) was a Muslim of a Turkic clan, and although he was not an imperial Mongol, he fancied himself a leader in the mold of the great Mongol warrior Genghis Khan (r. 1206-1227), from whom he claimed descent. The Mongols still ruled in China, but the old-style nomadic conquerors had all but disappeared. Timur would be the last. His Persian enemies nicknamed him for his lame right leg and arm, but he was tall and strong and few of his enemies lived long enough to lay eyes on him.

He started out in the 1360s by organizing a band of warriors to take over Transoxania (roughly equivalent to today's Uzbekistan). That done, he set up his capital in Samarkand and moved on.

One of the oldest Central Asian cities, Samarkand became the region's cultural and economic center, and the arts and sciences flourished under Timur's patronage. Other cities he left in smoking ruins.

Unlike the Ottomans, Timur moved like a ferocious beast, not worrying about holding territory he conquered, only intent on leaving a trail of brutal devastation. He lived the life of a nomad, even in his brilliant capital city—he would visit for a few days, then move back out to his encampment on the plains. His was a life in the saddle, on the go with his mounted archers, in the most searing desert heat and the bitterest cold. His court and at least one of his nine wives and concubines traveled along, moving with the seasonal pasturage.

PERSONAE

CHRISTINE DE PISAN

Poetry from a Woman's Point of View

Christine de Pisan, born in Venice in 1364, moved as a child to Paris, where her father had been appointed royal astrologer and where she received her education. She married at the age of 15, gave birth to three children, and lost her husband, who died on campaign. She took up writing at 24 in order to support her family.

Her early poems of love lost met with success. She continued writing ballads, romantic poems, and biographies for noble patrons—dukes, queens, and earls—and her writing eventually carried her to a position of prominence and fame. Once there, she used this position to criticize representations of women in medieval literature.

Her *Letter to the God of Loves* of 1399 defended women and their angry response to the popular *Romance of the Rose*, a bitter satire on marriage and courtly love. Her later works challenged traditional attitudes on the role of women in society, prompting some to call her one of the world's first feminists. ∎

Poet Christine de Pisan was one of the few writers of the Middle Ages to champion women and question their role in society.

Over the course of three decades he thundered across the land from Mongolia to the Mediterranean, randomly taking states along the way. He captured Persia, Iraq, Syria, Afghanistan, and parts of Russia. He attacked India, sacking Delhi in 1398 and killing most of its people. Reports of his brutality spread panic far and wide—he was known to execute all males in a conquered city, killing Muslims as readily as Christians. In one place he left 70,000 beheaded bodies. Even places that submitted in fear sometimes felt his fury—he buried 4,000 Christians alive in 1400 on his way to Damascus, which he almost completely destroyed. A skilled chess player, Timur used every tactic imaginable, including propaganda, espionage, treachery, and surprise attacks.

Since he left almost nothing in the way of occupying forces other than menacing towers of skulls, revolts were a natural aftermath. After Timur had left Asia Minor, Bayezid led a campaign to stop him. The decisive confrontation between the two warriors came on July 20, 1402, in Ankara. It was no contest—the Ottomans were crushed, and Bayezid was captured, tortured, and jailed in a pit, where he died a few months later.

Western Europe rejoiced in the victories of the man they called Tamerlane, hoping that he was the key to throwing off the Ottoman Empire and allowing for a rebuilding of Byzantium. A delegation of Franciscan monks was sent out to parley with him, but they had a hard time finding him. Timur had shifted his interests away from the west. The envoys caught up with him in Persia, and, after being roughly handled, they were brought before his majesty. Nothing was accomplished—

expecting a Mongol, they found instead a Muslim, and a Turk at that. They had been misinformed.

In 1404 Timur returned to Samarkand to celebrate his victories. The city was enriched with the spoils of war—gold and ostriches from Egypt, caravans of elephants from the Punjab, master craftsmen from Damascus, scholars from Baghdad.

> BE WELL-INFORMED IN ALL THINGS AND CAUTIOUS IN DEFENDING YOUR HONOR AND CHASTITY AGAINST YOUR ENEMIES! MY LADIES, SEE HOW THESE MEN ACCUSE YOU OF SO MANY VICES IN EVERYTHING. MAKE LIARS OF THEM ALL BY SHOWING FORTH YOUR VIRTUE.

> CHRISTINE DE PISAN
> *LIVRE DE LA CITÉ DES DAMES*
> *(BOOK OF THE CITY OF LADIES)*
> **Paris, 1404**

But Timur was set on further conquests and prepared for a campaign against the Ming dynasty of China. A huge expedition set out for the crowning achievement of incorporating China to his realm, but on the way Timur took a fever and died in 1405.

Thus ended the era of nomadic conquests. With his death, the lands he conquered were split among his heirs. His Timurid dynasty governed Central Asia and Iran for another hundred years. One man of his lineage, Babur, founded the Mughal Empire of India in 1526.

The last of the Knights Templar, Jacques de Molay, was burned at the stake as a heretic—an all too common fate for political dissidents and for those who challenged convention in the late Middle Ages.

One thing Timur's reign of terror did was to bring disarray to the newly established Ottoman Empire. With the loss of most of their Asian territories, the sons of Bayezid fell into waging civil wars against one another. Surprisingly, none of the Ottoman states in southeastern Europe formed an organized resistance against Timur during this period. They either had no strength or leadership or were intimidated by or perhaps even content under Ottoman rule.

Yet earlier Ottomans had laid sufficient groundwork so that once reunified under Sultan Mehmed I (r. 1402-1421), the state continued on its former course. The Ottoman rulers held absolute authority over the state; religious leaders were considered subservient to secular rulers; taxes from a prosperous peasantry supported roads, troops, and a navy; and rebellion was harshly suppressed.

But Timur had only stalled Byzantium's inevitable demise. Constantinople would fall to the Ottomans in 1453. By 1500 the Ottomans had regained total control of Anatolia, the Peloponnese, and the Balkan Peninsula south of the Danube River. During the 16th and 17th centuries, the Ottoman Empire would be the world's superpower, its reach extending from northern Africa to southeastern Europe and across to southwestern Asia. Not until the 20th century and the First World War would this mighty empire fall.

MUSIC OF THE
MIDDLE AGES

he simple, meandering strains of liturgical chant emerged in the ninth century as the dominant musical tradition of medieval Europe. Sung in complete unison, without harmony or accompanying instrumentation, the early liturgical chants are well documented in musical treatises and in manuscripts using rudimentary forms of musical notation. The later ninth and tenth centuries saw a flourishing of form and creativity, evident in the development of the popular Gregorian chant, which drew from older Roman and Frankish traditions. Despite these advances in melody and composition, however, the monophonic tradition would persist well into the 12th century, when the influences of eastern music—especially Arab—and other secular traditions led to a richer, polyphonic sound.

The diverse range of medieval instruments included those made of wood and string—lutes and harps—along with brass horns, tuned bells, pipes, and reeds. Around the eighth century, the organ added a new sound to the musical landscape. Byzantine emperor Constantine famously presented Pepin, the Frankish ruler, with an organ in 757. Other advances of the period include theories and practice of musical notation. In the 11th century, building on the recently devised system of neumes, from the Greek *pneuma,* or breath, for a basic system of musical notation, the Benedictine monk Guido d'Arezzo developed the musical scale and notation symbols still used today.

Medieval music, on the whole, provided a vibrant and culturally distinct form of entertainment. Beginning in the tenth century, liturgical dramas with instrumentation and ecclesiastic chant were frequently performed at Christmas, Easter, Pentecost, and Epiphany. Eventually these dramas moved out of the church and into the public square.

Secular traditions, too—from court music to French troubadours and goliards, or clerical student performers, and traveling professionals—expanded in popularity and differed vastly from one culture to another. By the 13th and 14th centuries, the continued convergence of ecclesiastic and secular music had inspired an abundance of rich, polyphonic compositions—sounds that would ultimately give rise to the classical music of the Renaissance.

Musicians preferred easily portable, stringed instruments in the early medieval era. Musical performances had been popular since ancient times, but new melodic innovations expanded possibilities for entertainment.

Musical notation advanced rapidly in the 11th century. Among the many innovations was the development of the musical staff of lines on which notes sat in relation to pitch, still used today.

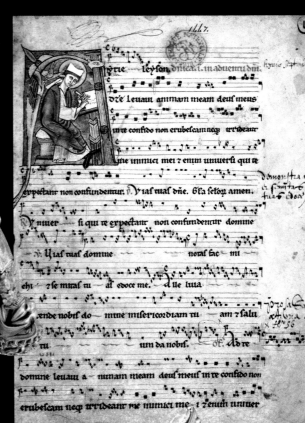

An intricately carved lute from the late 13th century displays the careful ornamentation of the era's stringed instruments.

The harp added a rich texture to the increasingly polyphonic sounds of medieval music. This 15th-century Irish example, with its simple construction, looks much like our modern-day instrument.

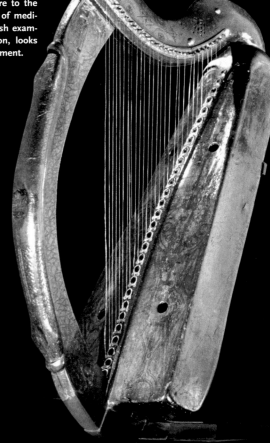

Although secular musical traditions—including music for dance and entertainment—varied from culture to culture, traveling musicians helped to spread these traditions throughout the continent.

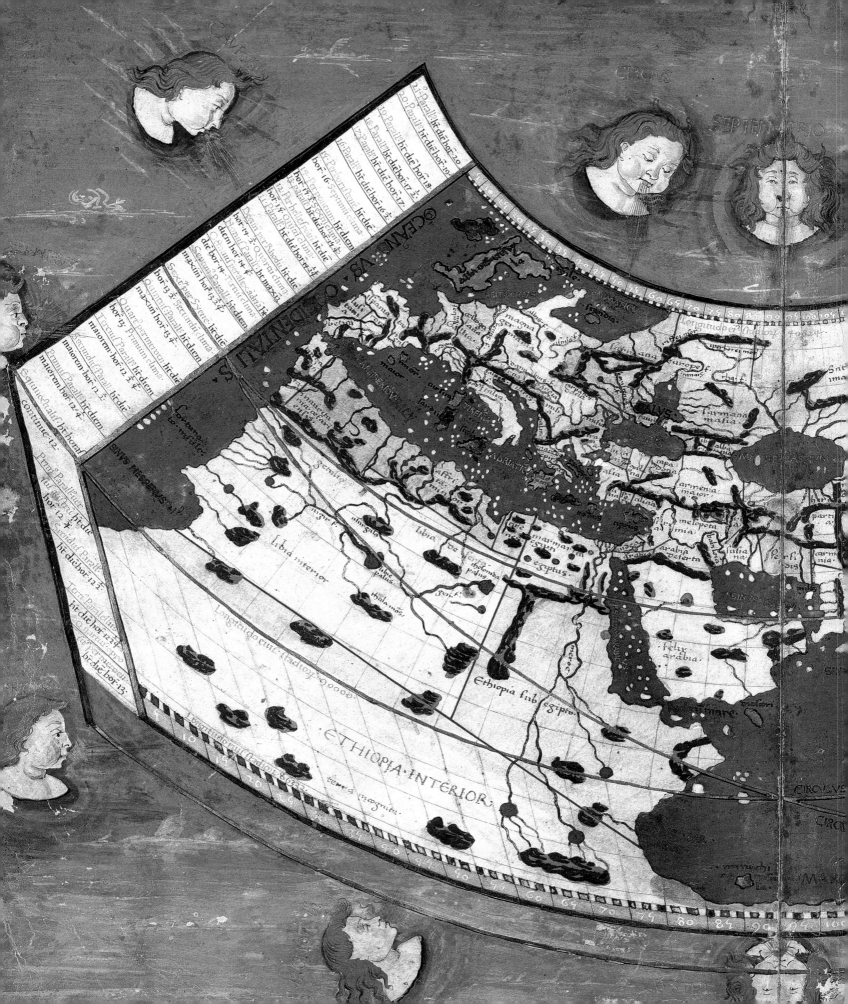

1400 – 1500

AT WHAT POINT DOES THE MEDIEVAL PERIOD END AND THE MODERN AGE BEGIN? THE MAJOR cities of western Europe, particularly in Italy and France, were already seeing a cultural renaissance by the end of the 14th century. Yet the large rural areas continued to live an agrarian, medieval existence until the 17th century and beyond. The industrial revolution of the late 18th century was a long ways off, and new technologies continued to spread slowly—over the course of generations and centuries rather than years. But several significant events had taken place by the year 1500 that marked a turning point for Western civilization. The early 15th century in central Europe was distinguished by a war of ideology known as the Hussite revolt. Sparked by the work and later the execution of Bohemian religious leader Jan Hus, the popular revolt was an attempt by the masses to liberate their church from the demands of the papacy.

Preachers wanted more freedom, and parishioners no longer wanted to pay to support a centralized church bureaucracy they viewed as corrupt. To the north, Poland and Lithuania combined forces to push out the Teutonic Knights, who had occupied the Baltic coast since the early 1300s, finally giving the two countries access to the sea. Royal marriages linked these two countries with each other and with Germany, yet their hemmed-in location and grasping nobility doomed their chances for greatness.

France and England continued to capture the European spotlight in the first half of the century with their drawn-out conflict of the Hundred Years War. Victory seemed to be England's with Henry V's stunning win at Agincourt in 1415. Yet the stubborn French continued trying to rid their land of the English, and with the help of a devoted young visionary named Joan of Arc, King Charles VII of France was able to prevail. The account of this victory describes one of the most amazing events in the Middle Ages.

The story in the East was of the end of the Byzantine Empire. Since the beginning of the 14th century, the Ottoman Turks had been growing stronger, while the Byzantine Empire had been steadily fading. Finally the empire pulled back to protect just its heart, Constantinople, that ancient city of legendary riches. In 1453, a driven Sultan Mehmed II laid siege to Constantinople while Emperor Constantine XI rallied his subjects to a valiant fight to stave off disaster. Constantine XI would turn out to be the last emperor, and the city and its historic buildings would soon be transformed in the spirit of Islam.

The Russian Orthodox Church produced works of Christian art based on Byzantine originals, such as this stylized portrait of Mary and child.
PRECEDING PAGES: The frame of the known world—such as shown in this 15th-century version of Ptolemy's world map, circa A.D. 150—was about to change.

In the second half of the 15th century. England and France were still recovering from the Hundred Years War. France came together under Louis XI; England took a bit longer, the bitter Wars of the Roses occupying the country until Henry VII, the first Tudor king, took over in 1485. Italy was still a fractured land of city-states, now run by ruthless, art-loving bankers such as the Medicis.

Iberia was the unlikely locale from which new world conquerors would arise. Portugal had its face to the Atlantic and its feet practically on the African coast. From here, Prince Henry the Navigator sent voyages of discovery farther and farther south. By the end of the century, Portugal had found a new route to India. Meanwhile Spain, united under Ferdinand and Isabella, had discovered a new world. The colonial era was underway.

SOCIAL AND POLITICAL UNREST

The budding rationalism touched off by John Wycliffe in the English church was tamped down during the 15th century. Not so the similar movement in Bohemia (in today's western Czech Republic). In this part of the Holy Roman Empire, an intellectual ferment was mixing philosophy and religion in new ways.

The leader of this Czech-speaking movement was realist philosopher Jan Hus (ca 1372-1415), a follower of Wycliffe. Born in poverty in southern Bohemia, Hus decided to become a priest in order to enjoy a better quality of life. He frittered away his early teaching years in the pursuit of pleasure but then suddenly took on a serious attitude, or, as he put it, "I discarded from my foolish mind that kind of stupid fun-making." In 1402 he was made rector of Bethlehem Chapel in Prague, which put him in the midst of

This terracotta bust is presumed to be of Joan of Arc, whose religious zeal drove her to military victory—and, ultimately, sainthood—in 15th-century France.

THE FIFTEENTH CENTURY

1431
Joan of Arc is burned at the stake.

1445
King Charles VII establishes the first French standing army.

1453
The Hundred Years War between France and England ends.

1453
Ottomans capture Constantinople and rename it Istanbul; the Byzantine Empire ends.

1455-1485
In England, Wars of the Roses are waged.

1462
Portuguese colonize the Cape Verde Islands.

1473
Construction begins on the Sistine Chapel.

1492
Christopher Columbus sails west from Italy.

1497
Leonardo da Vinci completes *The Last Supper*.

a national reform movement. Services here were conducted in Czech instead of Latin. Hus thrived in the stimulating atmosphere and taught theology.

Wycliffe's writings had just reached Bohemia, and though Hus did not agree with all of them, he and others were excited by their bold freshness. Like Wycliffe, he was disenchanted with the wealth of the clergy. He believed in a Bible-reading laity that could exchange ideas and challenge leaders. Many of the university masters, particularly the Germans, considered this outlook heresy. So did the archbishop of Prague. Bohemian king Wenceslas IV sided with the reformers, his policies leading to an exodus of many German masters in 1409.

Hus then became rector of the university and soon fell out with the archbishop during the papal schism. When ordered by the new pope to give up preaching, Hus flatly refused, for which he was excommunicated. Hus not only went on preaching and teaching; he became more firmly opposed to the papacy. In 1411 he denounced the pope's bull that called for a crusade against Naples, and he spoke vehemently against the sale of indulgences.

Hus lost the king's support over the indulgence issue, because Wenceslas took a cut of the sales. But he had a groundswell of support from the outraged populace, who began staging protests and burning mock papal bulls. The beheading of three protesters only fanned the flames. The pope then placed Prague under interdict. To take the heat off the city, Hus fled to southern Bohemia. For the next couple of years he holed up in friends' castles and rapidly churned out sermons and polemical tracts, as though he knew his years were numbered.

In 1414 Sigismund, king of Germany and Hungary, to gain points for ending the schism, called for a council in southern Germany and promised safe passage for Hus. Reluctantly, Hus set off. For several weeks he went about safely, then a group of enemies lured him to the papal residence and had him imprisoned in a monastery dungeon.

While the council was working out the solution to the papal schism, a commission tried Hus for heresy. Hus declared that he had never believed in transubstantiation. To recant now would be perjury, he declared. He repeatedly asked the commission to show him where he differed from the teachings of the Bible, but they could not. After his final refusal to recant, he was condemned, his soul was committed to the devil, and he was literally defrocked—his priestly vestments torn off him. Turned over to secular law enforcement for execution, he was taken outside the city and burned at the stake. He prayed aloud until he died.

THE HUSSITE MOVEMENT

A Hussite revolt rose up from the flames. Encouraged by Hus's unwavering stand against church corruption, his followers spread his message, and the Bohemian nobility protected them. Wenceslas died in 1419. His half-brother Sigismund became king of Bohemia, and later Holy Roman Emperor, and cracked down on the Hussites. As king of Hungary, Sigismund had been roundly defeated by the Ottomans at the Battle of Nicopolis 23 years earlier. In calling the Council of Constance and healing the papacy, he envisioned leading a new campaign against the Ottomans. But first he had to deal with the troublesome Hussites.

The Hussites quickly gained control of Bohemia and refused to acknowledge Sigismund as their king until he accepted their demands, which included freedom of preaching, clerical poverty, and church divestment. Instead, with the pope's help, Sigismund launched a series of crusades known as the Hussite wars.

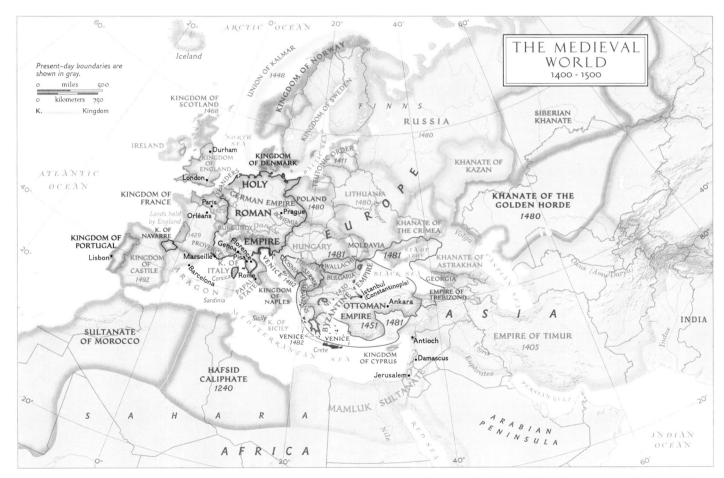

In this century the Ottoman Empire continued to expand, finally seizing Constantinople in 1453 and renaming the city Istanbul. Their conquests continued up and down the Balkan Peninsula. Portugal gained a foothold in Africa by capturing Ceuta, opposite Gibraltar. England lost almost all its lands in France and Ireland by mid-century.

Italian navigator Christopher Columbus unwittingly changed the world when he landed on the Caribbean island of Hispaniola in 1492, though he believed he had reached the East Asian mainland, his goal.

THE TEUTONIC KNIGHTS

In another eastern European theater, the German organization called the Teutonic Knights had gained increasing power along the Baltic Sea in the previous two centuries. It began in the late 12th century as a charitable order in Palestine, then withdrew to Germany after the early Crusades and grew into a military power. In 1237 the Knights conquered Prussia (northern Poland), and by the early 1300s controlled the Baltic coast from Finland to Pomerania (northwestern Poland).

The Knights' occupation of the coast blocked sea access for Poland and Lithuania. The two countries forged a union in 1386 when Jagiello, grand prince of Lithuania, married Jadwiga, heiress of Poland. Jagiello promoted the conversion of his people to Christianity. The Knights lost their excuse for occupation, and the time had come to forcibly remove them.

In 1410 a massive army of 100,000 Poles, Lithuanians, Czechs, Tatars, and Russians destroyed the Teutonic army in the Battle of Grünwald (today's Tannenberg) in northeastern Poland. After ten hours of fierce fighting, the grand master of the Knights was dead, as were most of his commanders and more than 200 knights. The Teutonic Knights began a gradual withdrawal from the region, starting by surrendering most of the Polish castles they held.

The defeat of the Teutonic Knights added to the luster Poland had achieved under the long and peaceful reign of Casimir III (1333-1370). Casimir had expanded the country, founded the University of Krakow, freed the serfs, and codified Polish laws, all while maintaining neighborly relations along his borders. He also supported the immigration of Jews and Germans to Poland,

After many years of fruitless battles, the Catholic Church sought peace in the early 1430s, but negotiations broke down because of the uncooperative Taborites—a group of extremists based in Tabor, south of Prague. A final battle in 1434 quelled them, and two years later a settlement restored peace in Bohemia.

Hus and his followers brought lasting change to the Bohemian church, freeing it from Roman domination and providing an example for the coming Reformation. The Moravian Church would later be founded upon the principles of the Hussites.

Throughout the remainder of the 15th century, state governments continued to score gains over papal power. The papacy's authority in European politics was much diminished.

Scholars have paced the courtyard of the University of Bologna, Italy, for centuries. The school has been drawing students since the 11th century, when it was founded as an academic guild for the licensing of teachers.

THE UNIVERSITY

The Guild of Learners

Medieval universities followed two courses of development. In northern Europe, professors were the guild masters, setting the length of semesters and the academic expectations that students had to meet to receive a degree, with which they could then begin to teach. Within this closed system, competition was fierce, revolutionary thinking was discouraged, and minute points of socially irrelevant matters were discussed ad infinitum.

In Italy, on the other hand, the students controlled the guilds, meaning that they dictated subject matter and terms of study. The resulting flexibility meant that intellectual life could blossom—which is one reason that the Renaissance first bloomed in Italy.

One of Europe's first degree-conferring universities was founded in Bologna, Italy, in the late 11th century, followed by the University of Paris around 1200, which in turn led to imitators and emulators throughout Europe.

Bologna was known for its faculty of law; Paris was known for its faculty of theology. Students flocked from all over to study under their renowned masters.

The universities came to be chartered and funded by popes, emperors, and kings, and although these benefactors occasionally censored activities, the universities and those studying and teaching in them enjoyed relative academic freedom as long as they stayed away from subjects like atheism or heresies.

The student's life in medieval Europe was not an easy one, though. Townspeople often took advantage of students, charging excessive room-and-board rates. Sometimes these circumstances resulted in violent riots. The University of Cambridge was founded in this way in 1209, when a group of dissatisfied students left the University of Oxford to seek better treatment elsewhere.

The architecture of medieval universities such as Oxford, Paris, and Bologna continues to influence the sense of what a college campus should look like: stone constructions with Gothic arches and spires, a clock tower, enclosed courtyards, and covered walkways connecting one building to another. ∎

At the Battle of Neville's Cross near Durham in northeastern England, in October 1347, Edward III's English forces drove off an attack by David II's Scottish forces, masterminded as a distraction by France's Philip VI, who feared an English invasion of his own country. David II was captured, and many Scottish noblemen died.

believing their presence likely to foster industry and trade. Under Casimir, Poland became eastern Europe's center of Jewish culture. His inclination to grant the aristocracy too much privilege, however, hampered the growth of a strong centralized state.

Casimir IV (r. 1447-1492) Poland's leading 15th-century monarch, finished off the Teutonic Knights in the Thirteen Years War, which lasted from 1454 to 1466 and finally gave the landlocked nation a corridor to the sea. When Casimir IV was born in 1427, his father, Jagiello, was over 75. Casimir was just 13 when he was made grand duke of Lithuania, and 20 when he was crowned king of Poland. His marriage seven years later to Elizabeth of Habsburg connected Poland and Lithuania with the German and Austrian nobility. By arranging dynastic marriages for his many children, he kept strong ties with other European nations.

Casimir IV's leadership made Lithuania a more powerful state in eastern Europe, but failing to support Russia militarily, he lost loyal Russian vassals.

He did not respond when the Turkish captured Lithuanian protectorates along the Black Sea. His only real military initiative was the war on the Teutonic Knights, which helped Poland.

> IT WAS THEN THAT THE POLISH KING GAVE A SIGN TO ORDER THE KNIGHTS TO CHASE THE FLEEING ENEMIES, HAVING ADMONISHED THEM TO REFRAIN ABSOLUTELY FROM SLAUGHTER. THE PURSUIT STRETCHED FOR MANY MILES.

FROM THE ANNALS OF JAN DŁUGOSZ
Krakow, Poland, circa 1475

Lithuania would go on to become a pawn between Poland and Russia. As for Poland, it would not be able to achieve the bright future that seemed within its grasp in the late Middle Ages. Its lack of secure borders and its increasingly greedy and selfish nobility made it susceptible to decay from within and without.

The End of a Very Long War

The Hundred Years War remained unresolved at the turn of the 15th century. The conflict entered its final phase, when Henry V (r. 1413-1422) took the throne of England. Henry's father, Henry IV (r. 1399-1413) had seized the throne from his cousin Richard II. He spent much of his reign putting down rebellions. But the energetic, aggressive young Henry V had bigger ideas. He dreamed of not just Aquitaine but also Normandy, as well as other French provinces that England had never possessed.

To that end Henry laid out a plan to invade, conquer, and occupy France. He started by raising taxes, then borrowed more money and gained the backing of the English nobility. He also courted the favor of the duke of Burgundy, a potential ally on French soil.

In France, Charles the Mad was still on the throne. The government was being run by two factions—one controlled by Charles's younger brother, Louis, duke of Orléans; the other by the duke of Burgundy. In 1415 Henry's forces crossed the English Channel in September and captured Harfleur at the mouth of the Seine. Thanks to the diplomacy of Henry V, Burgundy stayed neutral.

In late October Henry retreated from a much larger French force near Crécy, in northern France. Had the French learned anything since the drubbing there 69 years ago? Forced to fight at Agincourt, Henry was about to find out, in what would be the war's most famous battle.

The terrain favored the English, who were more lightly equipped than the heavily armored French. On October 25, Henry's 6,000 longbow archers were assailed by a French army of 20,000 men. For three hours the air thrummed with arrows, swords, spears, and oaths. The French were annihilated—when it was over, 1,500 knights and 4,500 foot soldiers lay dead on their own home soil. Henry's losses were minimal.

The victory gave Henry great renown in Europe. A visit the following year from the Holy Roman Emperor led to a treaty between England and the Holy Roman Empire, which then broke an impasse at the Papal Schism council. Successive, smaller triumphs in France confirmed Henry's military brilliance and resulted in the 1420 Treaty of Troyes, whereby Henry was recognized as the heir to France. His marriage that year to Catherine, daughter of Charles the Mad, sealed the deal. England now seemed sure of its

The city of Orléans, France, had one of the few bridges over the River Loire, making Joan of Arc's breaking of the English siege there a victory of significant strategic importance during the Hundred Years War.

Barcelona looks east, to the Mediterranean—a port with a long history of wealth through commerce.

BARCELONA
HOME PORT OF EXPLORERS

Seaside | Change | Abundance | Outsiders

Recent archaeological evidence suggests that little existed of the seaport city of Barcelona before the Romans settled there, although claims have been made for its having been founded by the Phoenicians, the Carthaginians, and the Greeks. Natural fortifications made it an ideal site for a city—poised on a narrow plain, with rivers flowing to the north and the south, a rocky outcrop to the west, and the blue-green Mediterranean to the southeast.

The city of Barcelona was designed on a grid, as many Roman cities were, with walls defining its outline and farms scattered beyond. It was the only harbor along a vast stretch of coastline, although quite shallow, and the wealth that comes from trade infused the city. With the decline of the empire, the Roman guard was called back to Rome, and outsider armies began encroaching on Iberian cities. By the time of Rome's official fall in 476, the Visigoths were well established as Barcelona's new rulers.

They ruled for the next 300 years, but they remained the minority throughout that time. Poor documentation and the later destruction of Visigoth architecture have left little information about their occupation. Government was probably poorly orchestrated, for they lost control to the first outside challengers, the Moors, who were themselves soon overthrown by the Franks in 801.

The Franks organized the region, making Barcelona its administrative capital, and accomplished some significant building projects, although few traces of them survive today. In 988 Barcelona won its independence from the Franks and settled into a period of prosperity as the capital of Catalonia, the northeastern region of the Iberian Peninsula, a region that still prides itself on its own distinctive identity.

In 1137 a royal marriage linked Catalonia with the kingdom of Aragon, a region directly inland. Economically, the Catalans benefited from the union: The Aragonese defended the country from invaders from the south, west, and north, while the Catalans could focus on commerce and maritime expansion.

The Moors still posed the greatest challenge. With a hold on the Balearics, five islands between North Africa and France,

BARCELONA THROUGH THE MIDDLE AGES

415
Ataulf, Visigoth chieftain, is assassinated.

531-554
The Visigoths make the city their capital: Barcinona.

587
Visigoth King Reccared makes Catholicism the official religion.

717
The Moors defeat the Visigoths, renaming the city Barjelunah.

801
Charlemagne, Carolingian emperor, captures the city.

985
Al Mansur, of Córdoba's Umayyad caliphate, attacks.

988
The County of Barcelona, later Catalonia, wins independence.

they maintained supremacy in the western Mediterranean. In 1227, knowing that jurisdiction over these islands was crucial to his country's economic future, James I of Aragon began a campaign to win them. "It was a fine thing for those on the land and for us to watch," he wrote in his autobiography, "for all the sea seemed white with sails, so great was the fleet." Within a few years he had succeeded, and from that conquest arose the Empire of Aragon, its capital the city of Barcelona.

Over the following years the empire expanded, gaining control of Sardinia, Corsica, Naples, and even Athens for a while, and wielding power throughout the Mediterranean and up into the Black Sea. During this time the Barri Gòtic— "Gothic quarter"—took shape in the city of Barcelona, and it remains to this day one of the most concentrated areas of medieval buildings in all Europe.

Of particular note is the Carrer de Montcada, a street named for a family with wealth and influence during the 12th century. It follows the course of an old Roman road, linking the harbor with the commercial district. Noblemen and rich merchants constructed palaces along this road, at first outside the city walls, but a new fortification wall built in the 13th century incorporated these structures into the city. Five of these medieval palaces, excellent examples of the civic Gothic style of Catalonian architecture, now house the Picasso Museum, celebrating the art of Barcelona's famous native son.

Disasters struck Barcelona, beginning in 1333. The first was the failure of the wheat crop, which resulted in the death of thousands by starvation. Then, before the population could fully recover, trade ships carried the Black Death into the city, which killed thousands more, sparing no one, rich and poor. Tensions between the landholders and peasants erupted into violence and more deaths. Such suffering created a poignant backdrop for the construction of exquisite cathedrals during the 14th century, some still standing today: Santa María del Pí and Santa María del Mar.

Barcelona's power began to wane in 1410, with the death of Martí I, the last of the direct line of court-kings of

Founded in classical times, Barcelona's position on the coast of Spain made it an early trade center.

Barcelona. Not only was he replaced by a Castilian Spaniard, completely ending the rule of the Catalans, but in 1442 the capital of Catalonia moved to Naples, a competing Mediterranean port then rising in power. This shift sped Barcelona's demise, compounded by plagues and a collapsed economy.

The rise of the Habsburg Empire, the discovery of America, and the growing power of the Turkish fleet in the Mediterranean also furthered its decline. When Ferdinand and Isabella gained control, forging the beginnings of modern Spain, Barcelona's political power had faded— and yet the Catalan spirit and identity remain strong, up to the present day.

Barcelona is located on a plateau between the Collserola mountain range and the Mediterranean Sea. Rivers to the north and south form natural defenses.

1018
Gold coins are manufactured in Barcelona and no other European city.

1137
Noble marriage unites Catalonia and Aragon.

1258
James I, King of Aragon and Count of Barcelona, writes maritime law.

1298
Building begins on the Cathedral of Barcelona.

1348
The plague reaches and weakens the city.

1442
Naples replaces Barcelona as capital of the Catalonian-Aragonese kingdom.

1493
The treaty of Barcelona cedes parts of southern France to Spain.

The Cathedral of Notre Dame in Rouen, France, took 400 years to complete. For that reason, various parts of the building represent different phases in the evolution of Gothic church architecture.

above the Meuse. Her father, Jacques d'Arc, was a peasant farmer of some means; her mother was devoutly religious. Small, strong, homely, and persuasive, Joan began hearing the voices of saints when she was about 13—they told her to save Orléans and bring about the coronation of Charles VII.

Donning men's clothing, she set out on horseback with an armed escort to where Charles held court, 300 miles away. She called herself Jeanne la Pucelle—Joan the Maid—and camped out with the soldiers. Her audacity won her an audience with the crown prince. She appeared to have psychic powers—she knew, for instance, what Charles had dreamed. For three weeks clergymen interrogated her, trying to determine if she was sent by God or the devil. Finally, because France was desperate for divine intervention, she was allowed to lead an armed force of several hundred men to reduce the siege.

They set out in April, and she established herself as a leader. One by one the English forts capitulated, and after ten days the English army retreated. Joan was defiant throughout, yelling at the English while around her raged the clang of steel and roar of culverins, muskets that hurled stones. She and the other French commanders decided to press on into British-occupied territory in the north. Her goal was Reims, in the northeast, the traditional city for coronations.

The French won more battles in the Loire Valley, including a major victory at Patay, to the west of Orléans. Joan finally convinced Charles to make the journey to Reims, and on July 17, 1429, he was officially crowned king of France. French morale was at a new high. The army took the fight to Paris, where they were rebuffed and Joan was wounded.

victory, with Henry at the pinnacle of success. A short-lived success, alas—Henry's early death in 1422 at age 35 left his infant son, Henry VI, on the throne. Charles died that same year, and the two nations struggled for direction.

Paris was now under the control of Burgundy, which in turn was in the palm of England. But central and southern France remained free of English power, and the gateway to that large territory was Orléans—an important center of culture and commerce on the Loire River. The French crown prince, Charles's son, Charles VII (1403-1461), was tucked away farther south in Bourges, so the English determined to take Orléans by siege in 1428. After four months of steady punishment, the French were ready to collapse, when a miracle arrived in the form of a teenage girl.

Joan of Arc was born around 1412 in the village of Domrémy, in northeastern France where the Vosges foothills rise

In 1430 Joan headed to Compiègne, a small town north of Paris. In May she was captured by the Burgundians and sold to the English. In Rouen, the capital of Normandy, a church court tried her, accusing her of being "a witch, enchantress, false prophet," "thinking evil in our Catholic faith," and "inciting to war, cruelly thirsting for human blood . . . having utterly and shamelessly abandoned the modesty befitting her sex, and indecently put on the ill-fitting dress . . . of men of arms." Joan answered honestly and directly, though she refused to divulge the contents of her private conversations with Charles. The judges wanted to know about the saints she had heard—whether St. Margaret, for example, spoke in English. "Why should she speak in English?" Joan answered. "She is not on the English side."

After five months of interrogation, Joan was sentenced to death. She was taken to the marketplace on May 30, 1431, and burned at the stake. The executioner later claimed that her heart would not burn; it was thrown into the Seine so that it could not become a sacred relic. Charles, seemingly embarrassed by his debt to a peasant girl, made no effort on her behalf. For a while, the French people forgot about her, but 25 years later, a new trial found her innocent, and she was declared a heroine.

Joan had lifted the spirits of the French people and turned the war into one of patriotism. After Orléans, the tide tipped in favor of the French. In the mid-1430s Burgundy dropped its allegiance to England and joined the French cause. Culverins and other cannons were proving more and more effective against the English longbows, and the French concentrated on winning back English

PERSONAE

JOAN OF ARC

Maiden Warrior

Spurred on by voices in her head she believed to be sent from heaven, Joan of Arc left her father's farm, donned armor, and led the French army against the invading English. The English and their allies controlled large tracts of northern France, including Joan's native village of Domrémy, which had already been abandoned. Joan sought an audience with the French heir, who first had her examined by theologians and then enlisted her.

In 1429, she led a force to successfully break up the English siege of the city of Orléans, then she marched the French regent, Charles of Ponthieu, into Reims, the traditional coronation site for French monarchs.

Joan was ultimately captured and handed over to the pro-English bishop of Paris, who tried her as a heretic, threatened her with torture, and burned her at the stake in 1431. The English were expelled from the Continent within the next two decades, and Joan of Arc has served as a symbol of French nationalism ever since. ■

Joan of Arc, the maid of Orléans, is to this day a national heroine of France for her bravery during the Hundred Years War.

holdings in southwestern France. Starting in 1449, the French took one town after another. They captured Bordeaux in 1451, lost it the next year, then recaptured it in 1453, and with that, the Hundred Years War officially ended.

With the war essentially over, both countries were taxed out, and the French countryside was a wasteland. Yet no treaty was signed, and sporadic fighting continued over Calais until 1475. Not until 1801 did the English king stop laying claim to kingship over France.

THE END OF THE BYZANTINE EMPIRE

With the rise of the Ottomans in the 14th century, the Byzantine Empire had shrunken to little more than Constantinople and Morea, in southern Greece. By the time Ottoman Murad II became sultan in 1421, Byzantine Emperor Manuel II was desperately seeking alliances with Murad's Turkish rivals. Murad focused on shoring up the Balkans. Salonika, in northeastern Greece, was controlled by the Venetians, but in 1430, after a five-year fight, Murad captured this key port. Then, in the 1440s, Murad lost several battles in Bulgaria to a coalition of Germany, Poland, and Albania.

Yet the Ottoman grip on the Balkans was anything but tentative, as Murad was to prove in 1444 by his victory over the Hungarians at Varna, on the Black Sea. Since the fall of Salonika, Manuel's son and successor, John VIII, had been trying to garner European support for the fading Byzantine Empire. He traveled to Italy to propose a reunion of the Greek and Latin churches. The agreement he obtained went down poorly with his people, for it meant submitting to Rome and the pope. Protection from Islam was apparently not as dear to them as

marshaled several thousand soldiers and 26 warships—mere stage dressing in light of what was to come.

THE FALL OF CONSTANTINOPLE

When the Ottoman ruler Murad died, in 1451, his son Mehmed II (1432-1481) was named sultan. In his 30-year reign, Mehmed became a hard-nosed dictator, a brilliant conqueror, and a great patron of the arts. By firmly establishing the Ottoman realm and codifying its laws, he also became known as the true founder of the Ottoman Empire. But first he needed to capture that final prize.

Deciding to take no chances, Mehmed signed peace treaties with Venice and Hungary. Then he built a massive stone fort, Rumili Hisar—New Fortress—on the Asian side of the Bosporus, blocking Constantinople's access to the Black Sea and its corn-rich regions. In support of the blockade and siege, he ordered the construction of the largest cannons ever made, and the building of 31 new galleys to supplement his fleet of several hundred ships. His army consisted of more than 100,000 soldiers, Janissaries, and assorted others—15 Turks for every Greek. All this for a city holding only 50,000 people, its defenders armed with arrows, lances, and catapults.

By 1452 Constantinople was choked off from both land and sea, and former allies deemed it hopeless to try to get through with supplies. People in the city, knowing the end was coming, became more fervently patriotic and religious than ever before.

In April 1453 Mehmed began blasting away at the city walls. After the first

After a two-month siege, Ottoman forces finally took Constantinople in 1453. The Byzantine Empire was toppled, Hagia Sofia was turned from a church into a mosque, and the city received a new name: Istanbul.

freedom to practice their own brand of Christianity. Still, John had a glimmer of hope now, as eastern Europeans began crusading against the Turks. But Murad's forces outnumbered his foes three to one. The Christian army was destroyed at the Battle of Varna and its leader, the king of Hungary and Poland, was killed. Constantinople was on its own now. There would be no further help from the West.

By the late 1440s, Constantinople was an island in a Turkish sea. The thousand-year-old empire of the New Rome, as Byzantium had been called, was facing a spectacular end. Murad advanced on Morea and exacted tribute. John's brother

became Constantine XI, the last of the Byzantine emperors, in 1449. In his four years on the throne, he provided spiritual leadership and made a valiant eleventh-hour effort to stave off disaster—but it was too late.

His pleas for aid from Europeans fell on deaf ears. Failing to find outside assistance, Constantine helped the city hunker down for the coming siege. Food and supplies were stockpiled, and a great chain was slung across the Golden Horn, blocking water access to the city. Defenses were old and crumbling, but the four-mile wall that had protected Constantinople for a millennium still stood. To meet the coming enemy, Constantine

JANISSARIES An elite corps in the Ottoman army, this highly organized mercenary force was begun by Sultan Murad I in the 14th century. The name is Turkish for "new soldier." The force, originally made up of Christian youths from the Balkans, lasted until 1826.

wave of assault was repulsed, he decided to drag some 70 ships by land around the sea chain so that they could enter the Golden Horn. Thousands of laborers, directed by Italian engineers, laid out a seven-mile road. Two weeks later, Turkish ships entered the Golden Horn, alarming the city. The Turks put up a wooden siege tower outside the walls, but the city's defenders burned it down. Mehmed demanded surrender. Constantine responded in a spirit of self-sacrifice: "We will not save our lives."

The people of Constantinople gathered on May 28, 1453, for a final mass at the church of Hagia Sophia. The assault came the next day in three relentless waves, the final one unleashing the disciplined fury of the Janissaries. Some 50 Turks found a breach, then fought like dervishes to hold it. Constantine had by now taken off his imperial insignia and joined the common soldiers. He was last seen in a violent fight to the death near the city gates. Not long after, the

> SHE FURTHER CONFESSED THAT WHEN SHE WAS THIRTEEN YEARS OLD SHE HAD A VOICE FROM GOD TO AID HER IN SELF-DISCIPLINE. AND THE FIRST TIME SHE WAS GREATLY AFRAID.

FROM THE TRIAL OF JOAN OF ARC
Rouen, France, 1431

Ottomans raised their banner above the city walls. For all intents and purposes, the Byzantine Empire was no more.

Mehmed entered the city in triumph. With the stipulation that buildings be left intact, he allowed his soldiers three days of plunder, then rescinded the order. A local historian wrote that the army "evacuated and devastated the whole city, to such an extent that no one could have believed that it had ever contained inhabitants, or

riches, or urban prosperity, or anything else in the way of furnishings or magnificence." "Libraries were burnt, books destroyed," recorded another. "The doctrine and the knowledge of the Greeks, without which no one can call himself learned, went up in the smoke." Some people escaped; the rest had to hope for the mercy of the sultan.

Leaders of the resistance were executed. Mehmed straightaway converted Hagia Sophia into a mosque, and changed the name of the city to Istanbul, which became the new Ottoman capital. Later he brought Greek and Italian scholars to his court and created a personal library of Greek and Latin books, as if to recover some of what had been lost. Mehmed allowed Greeks and Genoese to come back to their homes, and he imported both Christians and Muslims from Anatolia and the Balkans. He also reestablished the Greek Orthodox Church and supported Jewish as well as Muslim institutions. His intention was to create

THE SPANISH INQUISITION

Religious Fervor Taken to Inhumane Extremes

The Catholic Church of the Middle Ages was not just a metaphorical shepherd tending the flock; it was an omnipresent social force that bound Europe into a cohesive society. In this role, the church concerned itself with the whole of human thought and behavior, regulating in detail the lives of its constituents. Heresy, or dissent from church doctrines, was viewed as a threat to the very fabric of society.

In the 13th century, the papacy set forth laws requiring that communities should establish judicial inquisitions in order to identify and convert any heretics among them. The ruling even sanctioned capital punishment for obstinate heretics—and results got out of hand.

The Inquisition became more virulent in 1478, when Spanish King Ferdinand and Queen Isabella took it on as a cause. Medieval Spain, with large populations of Muslims, Jews, and Christians, was historically the only multiracial state in western Europe. Such diversity, we know with hindsight, sparked the development of great Spanish literature, art, architecture, commerce, and education. With the onslaught of the Black Death, Jews faced a more hostile environment than ever: Their wealth was resented, and they were even blamed for the plague itself.

Persecutions, expulsions, and pogroms led to mass conversions, but inherited resentment died hard among the old Christians. Inquisition

activities were often based on accusations from anonymous individuals. Those accused were neither informed of the charge against them nor allowed a lawyer or witnesses. They were presumed guilty and faced torture as a way to force confession. If they confessed, defendants often had their property confiscated by the state. If they refused to confess or recant, defendants were handed over to civil authorities and publicly burned at the stake.

The Inquisition continued in Spain and its colonies for 350 years, and it resulted in the murder of some 5,000 people and the expulsion of more than 160,000 Jews from Spain in the late 15th century. ■

a multinational empire. Though his son Bayezid II (r. 1481-1512) would reverse many globalizing policies, Istanbul was by the early 1500s Europe's largest city.

Ottoman Sultan Murad II expanded Ottoman authority throughout the Balkan peninsula.

Constantinople's downfall came as a shock. The pope proclaimed a new crusade, but after the Hundred Years War and other ravages, Europe was not interested. Instead, the West began the long process of adjusting to the fact that a non-Christian power had taken over part of Europe. It took eight more years for Mehmed to gain control of the final Byzantine outposts—Athens, Morea, and Trebizond, in northeastern Turkey. The Ottoman Empire now stretched from Turkey to Hungary.

NATION-STATES IN TURMOIL

After the Hundred Years War, France was still a fractured nation. The diffident, pleasure-loving Charles VII was uninterested in another conflict. He did manage some financial and military reforms, and his pardon of English towns that had fought against the French army was good postwar policy. Burgundy had made a tenuous peace with France in 1435, but the duchy remained staunchly independent—a problem that his son, Louis XI (1461-1483), had to solve.

Fat, clever, and ruthless, Louis was the right man at the right time to stabilize and strengthen the French government. In 1436, at the age of 13, he was forced into a marriage with the daughter of James I of Scotland for political purposes. He later rebelled against his father and allied with the duke of Burgundy.

Soon after becoming king, however, he found himself the object of a conspiracy led by the Burgundian nobility. After several reversals, and the death of the duke at the Battle of Nancy in 1477, Louis was finally able, near the end of his reign, to conclude a treaty that gave him sovereignty over Burgundy. His firm hand, shrewd diplomacy, and wide network of informants helped establish a strong centralized monarchy in France.

England also degenerated into a period of internecine struggle. The long reign of Henry VI (r. 1422-1461), punctuated with bouts of insanity—inherited through his mother, daughter of Charles the Mad—created a power struggle among the English nobility. Two branches of the royal family, York and Lancaster—their names corresponding to the lands they owned in northern England—began dynastic wars that lasted from 1455 to 1485. The House of York's family badge

was a white rose, that of Lancaster was a red rose—thus the struggle between them was called the Wars of the Roses.

Edward of York deposed Henry VI of Lancaster in 1461, claiming the throne as King Edward IV (1442-1483). The young king made plenty of friends by his charm, yet he was mostly interested in women and carousing, and his enemies forced him out in 1470. He took refuge in the Netherlands, and Henry VI was restored to the throne.

> THE ACT OF GIVING THIS CITY TO YOU IS NOT FOR ME OR FOR ANYONE ELSE AMONG ITS INHABITANTS TO PERFORM, FOR WE ARE ALL GOING TO DIE IN A COMMON DECISION, OF OUR OWN VOLITION, AND WE WILL NOT SAVE OUR LIVES.
>
> CONSTANTINE XI TO MEHMED II
> *Constantinople, 1453*

But early the next year, Edward and his brother, Richard, Duke of Gloucester, stormed back into England determined to take over for good. Two major battles followed, with Edward and the House of York emerging as the clear victor. Henry was murdered, clearing the way for the second part of Edward's reign.

England—or at least the crown—could not let France go. King Edward rekindled ties with Burgundy and launched a cross-channel invasion. Though England probably could not have won, France took no chances and paid Edward to go away—which he

While icons were the center of debate in the early Middle Ages, Russian artists embraced the practice in later centuries.
Andrei Rublev, widely considered one of the greatest medieval Russian artists, painted this iconic portrait of John the Baptist in the early 1400s.

THE WORLD IN THE FIFTEENTH CENTURY

Ottoman Turks seized the city of Constantinople in 1453, and Sultan Mehmed II restored it to its former glory, with a culturally diverse population. The Ottomans settled with the Mamluks, ending six years of war. By 1500 the Ottoman Empire stretched from the Taurus Mountains to the Adriatic Sea.

The decline of the Mongols in the East left Asia relatively stable. China's Ming dynasty fostered a period of peace and prosperity, establishing trade with Japan, relocating the capital to Beijing, and fortifying the Great Wall. The Khmer capital moved from Angkor to Phnom Penh, already a cultural center.

African empires continued to prosper, largely due to the gold trade. Commercial ties to the Islamic world helped maintain prosperity, too, especially in rich cultural centers like Timbuktu, although Portuguese exploration along the continent's west coast—and the resultant slave trade—would plant the seeds of their decline.

The slave trade linked Africa to the Americas, where European exploration was drawing a new generation of transatlantic conquerors. Columbus landed in the Caribbean in 1492, Vespucci explored the coast of South America in 1499, and by the following century, Spanish conquistadores were challenging the Aztec. Tribal confederations of North America and powerful empires in Central and South America thrived well into the 1500s, their civilizations destined to influence their region's cultural traditions forever. ∎

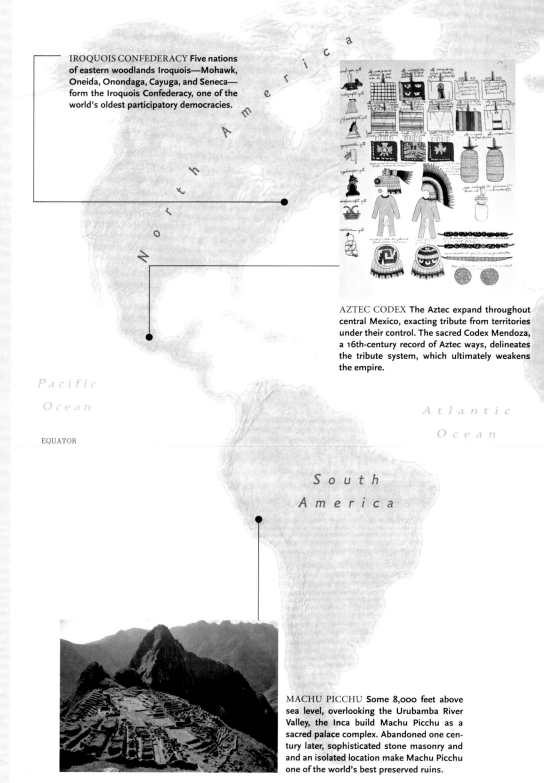

IROQUOIS CONFEDERACY **Five nations of eastern woodlands Iroquois—Mohawk, Oneida, Onondaga, Cayuga, and Seneca— form the Iroquois Confederacy, one of the world's oldest participatory democracies.**

AZTEC CODEX **The Aztec expand throughout central Mexico, exacting tribute from territories under their control. The sacred Codex Mendoza, a 16th-century record of Aztec ways, delineates the tribute system, which ultimately weakens the empire.**

MACHU PICCHU **Some 8,000 feet above sea level, overlooking the Urubamba River Valley, the Inca build Machu Picchu as a sacred palace complex. Abandoned one century later, sophisticated stone masonry and and an isolated location make Machu Picchu one of the world's best preserved ruins.**

Ocean

Europe

Asia

SULTAN MURAD II Ottoman Sultan
Murad II gains control of Byzantium and
expands the Ottoman Empire into the
Balkans. His military campaigns are continued by his son, Mehmed II, who captures Constantinople in 1453—the end of
the Byzantine Empire.

Pacific
Ocean

Africa

SLAVE TRADE Portuguese explorers
sail Africa's west coast and reestablish
a slave trade. The commerce between
West Africa and the Iberian Peninsula
extends to the New World, launching
a commercial enterprise that will ultimately devastate the African continent.

EQUATOR

Indian   Ocean

JAMA MASJID Built in 1438 in Jaunpur, Uttar Pradesh, and commissioned by Hussain Shah of the Sharqi dynasty, Jama Masjid reflects the
blend of Indian and Islamic traditions. Islam grows throughout northern
India, distinguishing this region from the kingdoms of the south.

Naked figures frolic in sensual pleasure in this detail from the second of three paintings making up Hieronymus Bosch's triptych titled *The Garden of Earthly Delights*. The lefthand painting shows the Garden of Eden, the righthand Hell—portraying in total the human condition.

happily did, rich enough now to be independent of Parliament. In his last years he improved government administration and trade relations, and he oversaw the introduction of printing and silk production in England. He apparently did not give up his promiscuous ways, though, for he died at 40, the rumored cause sexual exhaustion.

In 1483 Edward's 12-year-old son became Edward V for two months, until his uncle Richard had him and his little brother confined in the Tower of London, a fortress that was both a royal residence and a prison. The ambitious Richard trumped up a case for illegitimacy, thus depriving Edward V of the throne. The two boys disappeared, likely victims of a murder, although it is possible that an enemy of the family murdered them, hoping that Richard would get the blame. Skeletons discovered in the Tower some 200 years later were thought to be those of the boys.

> OUR GREAT CITY
> OF FLORENCE,
> THE DAUGHTER AND
> CREATION OF ROME,
> WAS ASCENDING
> TO GREATNESS
> WHILE ROME
> WAS DECLINING.
>
> GIOVANNI VILLANI
> *FLORENTINE CHRONICLE*
> **Florence, circa 1330**

Once he became king, Richard III (1452-1485) struggled with his past as an evil uncle. When a Lancastrian rival named Henry Tudor arrived from France in 1485, Richard's supporters vanished. He was defeated at the Battle of Bosworth Field in central England, the last battle of the Wars of the Roses. Thrown from his horse in a bog, Richard died while fighting.

The victor became King Henry VII (1485-1509), the first of the Tudor line, which would last for more than a century.

England under Henry finally settled into prosperity, and national power and unity achieved new heights. Though the first years of his reign were spent in quashing insurrections (partly fueled by rumors that Edward V's brother had survived), Henry was able to establish a firm hold on the monarchy, and his efficiency in extracting revenue from every corner of the country, coupled with the nation's growing economy, put unprecedented wealth in England's royal coffers.

THE MAGNIFICENT MEDICIS

The political and social life of Italy in the 15th century differed from that of England and France. Whereas a landed nobility stood at the head of stratified feudal systems in England and France, Italy featured a developing aristocracy of urban merchants and traders. Without

HIERONYMUS BOSCH

Macabre Visions in the Medieval World

Hieronymus Bosch was a Dutch painter of the 15th century whose work typified in an imaginative and unique way the pessimism and gloom that struck much of Europe in the throes of the Black Death. Hieronymus Bosch was the pen name of Jeroen van Aken, born around 1450 into a family of painters. Little is known of his early life or training, and even the chronology of his art is unclear, since he never dated and rarely signed any of his paintings.

Bosch often depicted scenes of the corruption of humanity, the allure of evil, the temptations of lust, and the inevitability of death and decay. His most famous work, a triptych titled *The Garden of Earthly Delights*, is filled with complex symbolism, graphic detail, and fantastical and apocalyptic creatures.

This work depicts in the left panel an idealized Garden of Eden, still inhabited by birds of the night, such as ravens and owls. The middle panel is filled with slender naked human figures, frolicking licentiously and surrounded by large bird and vegetable forms. The righthand panel depicts Hell, where grotesque, quasi-human figures torture men and women to the tune of some diabolical music. When closed, the triptych reveals a transparent globe, half-filled with some kind of primordial soup, over which floats the tiny distant figure of God.

Many have tried to interpret this work, since Bosch never wrote down his intentions. Some have been convinced that Bosch belonged to a secret heretical sect of the occult arts. Others have viewed the work as representing life on Earth as a false paradise between Eden and Hell. Others see an allegory for the practices of alchemy and the process of distillation, of which Bosch may have had some knowledge.

Whatever the specifics of interpretation, the effect is immediate as one sees the distant God on the outer panel, then opens the triptych to reveal the birth of humans, their delightful devolution, and, left to their own devices, their ultimate damnation. ∎

MATTHEVS REX VNG

King Matthias Corvinus I of Hungary—also known as Matthias the Just—centralized and strengthened the political and military resources of his administration in the face of continual threats of invasion by Turkish forces. He made diplomatic inroads with many European courts.

a central monarchy, powerful families dominated the political landscape, their strength relying on money and enterprise instead of law and inheritance; vendettas were settled by intrigue, bribery, and murder, followed by temporary truces.

Florence was typical of these city-state communes. In the 1430s a banking and mercantile family named Medici strong-armed its way to total control of the city government. By championing guilds and commoners, Giovanni de' Medici basically ruled Florence in the 1420s without any title. His sons Cosimo and Lorenzo became the progenitors of the two powerful branches of the family. Enemies could be destroyed in a number of ways—if taxation, refusal of credit, or outright harassment failed, there was always the well-placed dagger in a dark alley.

Cosimo's grandson, Lorenzo the Magnificent (1449-1492), became the most renowned of the Medicis. Both a tyrant and a patron of the arts, he enriched the cultural life of Florence and helped establish Tuscan as the language of Italy. Among the early Renaissance painters patronized by Lorenzo was Domenico Ghirlandaio (1449-1494), whose church frescoes often cleverly incorporated members of the Medici family.

By forming an alliance with the Sforza family of Milan, Lorenzo maintained a balance of power among the northern Italian city-states. His enemies schemed to stab him at mass, but he foiled the plot. He struggled against the ambitions of a resurgent post-schism papacy. He neglected the operations of the bank and nearly brought the family to financial ruin, yet never were the Medicis as powerful as in the late 15th century.

INNOVATION

PRINTING PRESS

The Beginnings of a Print Culture

In the mid-15th century, the time was ripe for a revolution in communications. Paper and wood-block printing had arrived in Europe from Asia, metalsmithing had achieved a high level of precision and durability, wine and oil presses were in widespread use, and there was demand among the literate populace for a greater quantity of books at more reasonable prices. It fell to German silversmith Johannes Gutenberg to combine all these elements into the world's first mechanical printing press.

Gutenberg began his experiments around 1440 by carving letters into a soft metal die, pouring lead around the die to form a mold, then pouring an alloy into the mold to form a single piece of type. Individual pieces of type were mounted and affixed on a wooden frame, which was covered in ink and pressed onto paper.

The only extant book attributed for certain to Gutenberg is the so-called 42-line Bible printed in 1456, a year after Gutenberg's financier had foreclosed on the business partnership after a lengthy lawsuit. The rights to the business were sold, and Gutenberg's associates became rich off the sale of printed Bibles, while he died in relative obscurity in 1468. ∎

Gutenberg's printing press revolutionized the spread of knowledge in Europe, making printed works available to the masses.

Matthias I, called Corvinus, (r. 1458-1490), was king of Hungary and another significant patron of learning and the arts. Maintaining close ties with Florence and other Italian cities, he became the model of a modern ruler. His skill in battle, bargaining, and finance made him the strongest force in central Europe.

With the Turks annexing lands just south of Hungary, Matthias went to war and prevented them from advancing farther north. He then turned to the north and in the 1460s and '70s successfully took on neighbors Bohemia, Moravia, Silesia, and Lusatia. By the 1480s Matthias was at war with Holy Roman Emperor Frederick III, who claimed title to the Hungarian throne. Matthias captured Vienna, but after his death Hungary lost its conquests and prosperity. Despite his reputation as a heavy taxer, he was a just ruler.

Strong monarchies were crystallizing around Europe, and the populace was growing more educated. The invention of the printing press had an enormous impact on European learning. Movable type had long been known in Asia, but with the large numbers of characters in those languages, the system never evolved. In the 1440s, Johannes Gutenberg and his associates in Mainz, Germany, adapted wine-press mechanics to create the first printing press. Cast metal letters were locked into a metal form hanging above the press bed. The type was then inked, paper placed on the bed, and the form pressed down with a handle-turned screw to imprint evenly on the paper. Gutenberg's press could crank out 300 pages a day. The famous Gutenberg Bible came out in about 1455. By the early 1500s, more than 100 printing presses had produced nine million copies of some 40,000 works.

DIVIDING THE WORLD

The Christian reconquest of Spain was nearly complete by the 14th century, leaving Granada, in the south, Iberia's sole Moorish kingdom. Three kingdoms now occupied the peninsula: Castile in central Spain, Aragon in the northeast, and Portugal in the west. Their interrelationships would partition the globe for centuries to come.

Castile was the largest kingdom, though years of war and natural disasters had reduced its prosperity. The lack of an ingrained feudal structure had allowed the nobility, the church, and the cities to usurp all riches and power, and these three entities controlled the political and social institutions. Peasant rebellions met with little success. The head noble was the king, who extracted taxes from the *cortes*, or estates, and though he could command power this way, he was often limited by his own talent and by the lack of a strong, centralized bureaucracy.

Aragon had united with its eastern neighbor, Catalonia, in the 1100s, giving it a Mediterranean coast up to the French border. This geography inclined Aragon toward a more Continental outlook, and seaside Barcelona grew into a major center of commerce and culture. The cortes in Aragon served to check the power of the monarchy, as in Castile, though Aragon had better luck with strong, capable rulers. The most impressive such ruler, Ferdinand II, was born in 1452, son of an Aragon king with Castilian origins. The reunion of these two kingdoms came about with Ferdinand's marriage to Princess Isabella of Castile in 1469.

A year Ferdinand's senior, Isabella had fair hair, blue eyes, and a penchant for finery, and she proved a formidable ruler in her own right. The couple

Spanish Jews petition Ferdinand and Isabella for mercy in this artist's interpretation of a dramatic moment during the Spanish Inquisition. The mediating prelate holds a cross to symbolize righteous decisions—decisions that led to the execution of thousands of Jews, Muslims, and freethinkers, and the exile of thousands more.

weathered several years of civil war, during which they outmaneuvered various claimants to the Castilian throne. Finally in 1479 they became joint rulers of a united Spain, leaving only Granada and the tiny kingdom of Navarre in the far north independent. Their dominance as leaders into the early 1500s would propel Spain into a world power. What began as a political marriage came to involve real affection, the union resulting in several heirs, though the usual strains of royal marriage inevitably occurred with Ferdinand constantly away on business and lured by the charms of other women.

One of their first objectives was to take Granada, the final Muslim stronghold on the peninsula. Not until 1492 were they able to achieve this, but the effort helped build a national army and strengthen political and economic institutions. Taxes were levied on commercial transactions. As the monarchy rose in power, the nobility, clergy, and cities declined.

Ferdinand and Isabella were also devoutly religious, and their efforts to rid the church of corruption met with much success. But the excesses of reform allowed a notoriously fanatical institution to develop under their auspices. The Inquisition had been around since the early 1200s as a Roman Catholic tribunal for rooting out heretics. The Spanish Inquisition took the system to new levels of torture and terror.

As Christian fervor spread across a newly united Spain, places that had tolerated a mix of religions were suddenly less than tolerant. Many Jews and Muslims often found it wiser to convert than to face bigotry and persecution by the Christian majority. But these new converts were looked on with suspicion as "crypto-Jews" by the "old" Christians, who persuaded Ferdinand and Isabella to set up a court of inquiry in 1478.

The first, and most infamous, grand inquisitor was a Dominican friar named Tomás de Torquemada. His tribunals investigated not just heresy, but also sorcery, sodomy, usury, and other crimes. He authorized the use of torture to extract confessions, his methods so cruel that at one point the pope had to intervene.

Typical sentences were flogging or burning at a public ceremony called an auto-da-fé—act of the faith. Some 2,000 suspected heretics were burned at the stake during Torquemada's tenure. He also was instrumental in the monarchs' decision to expel more than 160,000 Jews from Spain in 1492. The Jews were stripped of their wealth, while Spain was stripped of significant talent.

The Inquisition would continue in Spain and its colonies for more than 300 years, accepted by most as a way to unify the country. Poised to increase its wealth and power, Spain looked west, out to sea.

Portuguese Enterprise

The even smaller country of Portugal had already stolen a march on Spain by exploring Africa's west coast over the preceding few decades. With Italy's hegemony over Mediterranean routes and the Ottomans now controlling trade to the Orient, there was great incentive to

During the Spanish Inquisition, heretical books were considered as dangerous as heretics themselves, and sometimes they met the same fiery end.

find an alternate trade route. Facing the Atlantic just above Africa, Portugal was in the best position to do just that.

Gold and slaves imported from the African coast only whetted the explorers' appetites. One by one, the Portuguese occupied the stepping-stones off the coasts of Portugal and Africa: the Azores, Madeira, the Canary and the Cape Verde Islands. Closest to the coast, the Canaries were inhabited by Stone Age people, and the islands were not completely subdued until the end of the century. In the meantime, though, the explorers' maneuverable, three-masted caravels kept pushing their way south.

The prime mover of Portugal's maritime outreach was Prince Henry the

INQUISITION A tribunal held by the Catholic Church to seek out and suppress heresy by severe questioning. Literally "inquiries," the process evolved into torture and intimidation—and the Spanish Inquisition now symbolizes investigations disrespectful of human rights.

Navigator (1394-1460), founder of a school devoted to navigation and sponsor of expeditions of discovery. Henry began his distinguished career by helping capture the Moroccan port of Ceuta, on the Strait of Gibraltar, in 1415—really a training exercise devised by his father, King John I. A few years later Henry became governor of the Algarve, the southernmost province of Portugal, and began attracting cartographers, shipbuilders, instrument makers, and astronomers. No aspect of seamanship was left unstudied in this explorers' laboratory.

Henry's ultimate aim was to send a voyage around Africa to India for the purposes of trade and missionizing. Expeditions began in the 1420s, and by the 1440s Henry's sailors had rounded Cape Verde, some 1,500 miles away, bravely overcoming superstitions about boiling water and sea monsters. Though Henry himself never sailed on these voyages, he was so keen on financing them that he went into heavy debt.

> IN REGARD TO
> THE DISCOVERY OF
> NEW COUNTRIES,
> I THINK PERMISSION
> SHOULD BE GRANTED
> TO ALL THAT WISH TO GO.
>
> ———————————
>
> CHRISTOPHER COLUMBUS
> TO THE KING AND QUEEN OF SPAIN
> *1494*

With Portugal making headway in the new enterprise of exploration, Spain took notice. So when a Genoese sailor named Christopher Columbus (1451-1506) wanted funding for a trip to Japan and was turned down by the king of Portugal, Ferdinand and Isabella gave the matter some thought.

Columbus's idea of sailing due west to reach the Orient was, if not wholly original, still unusual. It took him nearly a decade to get his plan approved, which included a promise to spread Christianity

abroad. Finally, mostly thanks to Isabella, Columbus's proposed venture was funded and launched.

In October 1492 Columbus's three ships made landfall in the Bahamas, although for the rest of his life he continued to believe that he had in fact landed on the eastern reaches of Asia. He had optimistically underestimated the ocean's width and the size of the Earth, and he had not imagined the presence of the Americas.

It remained for a later navigator, Italian Amerigo Vespucci (1454-1512), to prove that Columbus had bumped into a new world. A publisher of Vespucci's accounts named the new lands "America" in his honor. In 1497 a Venetian named John Cabot, sailing under English patronage, took a northern route across the Atlantic and explored areas of the North American coast that had been discovered by the Vikings nearly 500 years before.

Of much more immediate commercial interest than the early westward

THE MEDICI FAMILY

Patrons of the Coming Renaissance

The Medici family rose from the ranks of merchants and bankers to take control of the government of Florence in the 15th century. A bourgeois family of peasant origins, the Medici built up their wealth, not through landholdings but through trade in textiles. The family weathered an economic depression of the 14th century and then became bankers for the papacy.

In 1434 Cosimo de' Medici, as manager of the family bank, became de facto ruler of Florence. Feudal committees still exercised nominal authority, but they all answered to Cosimo, whose bank controlled taxation and loans and could at will drive any rival into financial ruin.

Cosimo was a generous patron of the arts, subsidizing painters, sculptors, architects, and poets—a personal enthusiasm that inspirited the Italian Renaissance. He also established Europe's first public library since the classical era, spending the equivalent of 20 million dollars on books and manuscripts. Cosimo's grandson, Lorenzo, was even more lavish in his patronage of the arts, commissioning works by Ghirlandaio, Botticelli, and Michelangelo, among others. The Medici family continued to control Florence on and off until the 18th century, producing four popes, two queens, and seven authoritarian dukes—but the golden age of the Medici died with Lorenzo in 1492. ∎

Lorenzo de' Medici and his family financed many works of Italian Renaissance art.

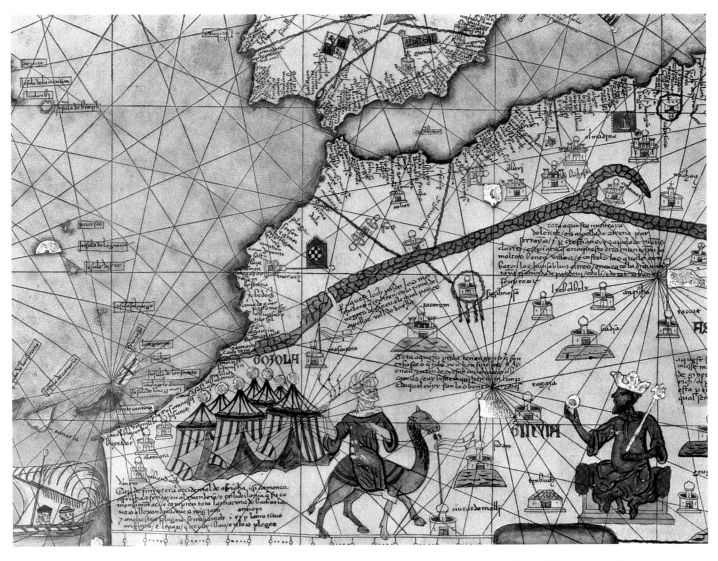

This nautical chart, part of a Catalan atlas of the world produced in Majorca, Spain, in 1375, pictures Mansa Musa, the King of Mali, approached by a Tuareg nomad on camelback. Such information meant that explorers and entrepreneurs from Europe would shortly arrive and change the world of West Africa forever.

expeditions—which yielded no riches in those days—was Vasco da Gama's sensational accomplishment in 1498. He sailed around the Cape of Good Hope, the tip of Africa, and went on to Calicut, on the southwest coast of India. Here finally was the long-hoped-for feat that promised real wealth. Now the jewels, silks, pepper, cloves, and cinnamon of the Far East could flow into western markets without a Mediterranean middleman. The high cost of

spices plummeted by half, and Venice and other established centers of trade saw their monopolies disappear.

Along with the opportunities opened up by world exploration came the abuse of native populations, giving pause to Isabella and other leaders who believed that serving God was their highest duty.

Yet whether under the guise of Christianization or expansion, the new colonial urge overwhelmed any moral qualms. Abuses were problems of the

frontier—back at home, the humanities were flowering like springtime. Leonardo da Vinci, Michelangelo, and other geniuses of the late 1400s and early 1500s were rediscovering the artistry of the classical period and putting their own indelible imprint on European culture. The Middle Ages were coming to an end, and nations with distinct identities and powerful monarchs were opening the curtains on the modern era.

MAPPING THE MEDIEVAL WORLD

Before the age of exploration generated a need for more sophisticated cartography, medieval map-makers, especially in western Europe, produced images of the world that were largely governed by religious beliefs. Jerusalem was often depicted as the center of the world, with the lands east of the city at the top of the map. This kind of projection followed the tradition of Ptolemy and the Greek cartographers, who mapped a spherical world with Greece at the center. Church-sponsored cartographers also typically illustrated their maps with images of Christ, the Virgin Mary, or angels on the Day of Judgment, intimating that the maps provided spiritual guidance as much as geographical information.

Before printing, mapmaking was a highly specialized, tedious craft. Each document had to be individually drafted, illustrated and embossed. On the most decorated of maps, colors were added: blue or green for seas and rivers, red and black for towns and boundaries.

Trade broadened knowledge of the world, and cartographers could produce maps with ever more accurate detail. Arab mapmakers in particular drew on the experience of seafaring traders and advanced the art of mapping the world. Al Idrisi's map of 1154 (below) was commissioned by Roger II, the Norman king of Sicily. The most important of its day, it compiled extensive new information from both historical and contemporary sources. Al Idrisi imagined the world as a sphere at rest in space. He divided it into seven climates, then each of them into ten longitudinal regions. Part of a larger geographical treatise on the known world, his map remains one of our finest insights into the medieval era.

The 1154 world map by Arab cartographer Al Idrisi drew on vast banks of knowledge, both ancient and contemporary. The experience of merchants and seafarers along new trade routes enabled him to add more detail and accuracy to his rendering.

Earlier medieval maps were produced as much for religious contemplation as for orientation while traveling. This 13th-century example, in harmony with the spirit of the Crusades, placed Jerusalem at the center of the world. Colorful Christian icons watch over the city and the land that surrounds it.

The art of mapmaking was a specialized skill, and before the technology of printing developed, each document was carefully drawn, colored, and embossed by hand. A 14th-century map, with Jerusalem at its center, uses various hues to represent waterways and boundaries.

A richly illustrated 14th-century map pictures the world as a globe, albeit a small locale of known residences. Illustrations of castles depict various states of interest, all adding up to a map that has more use as a symbolic and political statement than as a travel-oriented tool.

Glossary

Apocalypse: The cataclysmic end of earthly life, predicted in Judeo-Christian tradition. In this cosmic and irreversible event, God will destroy all evil and elevate all the righteous into heavenly eternity. Millenarians believed it would take place at the turn of the millennium.

Ascetic: A person, often a religious devotee, who chooses to practice self-denial as a discipline, believing that denial of the bodily pleasures represents a path to purity or enlightenment. Many monastic orders with origins in the Middle Ages require vows of asceticism.

Bubonic plague: A highly infectious disease caused by the bacterium Yersinia pestis, carried by fleas on rats and easily transmitted to humans. It is named for the buboes, or swollen lymph nodes, that those stricken with the disease suffer in armpits, groin, and neck.

Caliph: The civil and the religious ruler of the ancient Muslim world, caliph was both a position of honor and authority. The word comes from the Arabic for "successor"; the caliphate was considered a line of succession going back to the Prophet Muhammad himself.

Canon law: A collection of rules established by a council of the church and incorporated into the church's ecclesiastical law. In the Middle Ages, canon law often exerted more power than civil law. Many laws in modern legal systems originated in canon law of the Middle Ages.

Canonization: The declaration by the church of a person as a saint. In the Roman Catholic tradition, a person is canonized if he or she lived a life of heroic virtue and effected or experienced more than one miracle attributable to divine intervention.

Carolingian: A dynasty that included Charlemagne at its peak and ruled western Europe from the middle of the eighth century through most of the ninth century. The term also refers to that period of history or to styles and artifacts from that time.

Chivalry: The system and rules of behavior for knights, comprising bravery, honor, humility, and gallantry, especially toward women. The word comes from the French "cheval," meaning horse, because knights were mounted soldiers.

Crusade: First used in the 12th and 13th century, the term specifically referred to zealous activities furthering the goals of Christianity: The root of the word comes from the Latin word for "cross." It has since broadened to mean any shared effort for a perceived cause.

Dynasty: A dynasty is created by a powerful ruling family that maintains its power and influence over a region or a nation for generations, even centuries; therefore, a dynasty can also mean rulership by leaders who spring from the same line of descent.

Ecumene: Derived from the Greek, the term refers to the entire inhabited world. It can also be applied to all those worldwide within a specified religion: the Islamic ecumene, for example. From this word derives the concept of an ecumenical, or, worldwide church, council.

Excommunication: The formal exclusion of an individual from church membership, based on the judgment of church leaders. In the Roman Catholic tradition, a person who has been excommunicated may not receive communion or be buried in a church cemetery.

Flying buttress: A buttress is a stone prop that supports a wall built to significant height; a flying buttress stands apart from the wall it supports, joined by arches. Flying buttresses were significant architectural developments that allowed vaulted cathedral ceilings.

Foederatus: From the Latin for ally, a foederatus was one of the tribes bound to Rome by treaty. Foederati were not Roman colonies; those who lived in them did not enjoy Roman citizenship, but they were required to serve in the imperial military force if needed.

Freeman: A man who was not a slave—not owned by another—in a society based on slavery, such as ancient Rome, who had full rights of citizenship but did not have the wealth or family title to make him a landowner or aristocrat.

Icon: A painting or a sculpture that depicts a holy figure and is used in religious practice. Those who believe in icon worship use the icons as an aid to prayer, believing that the physical representations serve as intermediaries between them and God.

Illumination: The process of decorating a manuscript. Before printing, books were created by hand. Usually the lettering was made in black ink but often decorated with ornaments in gold and colors. Illuminated manuscripts may include marginal decorations, illustrations, and intricate capital letters.

Imam: A term that originally referred to the line of holy leaders descending from Muhammad through his daughter, Fatima, and considered the true leaders of Islam by Fatimid (or, later, Shiite) Muslims. Today the word is used more generally to mean an Islamic prayer leader.

Inquisition: A tribunal held by the Catholic Church to seek out and suppress heresy by severe questioning. Literally "inquiries," the process evolved into torture and intimidation—and the Spanish Inquisition now symbolizes investigations disrespectful of human rights.

Investiture: The act of placing an individual in a clerical, or church, office. Lay investiture occurs when a layman—someone who does not hold a position within the church—performs it rather than an official of the church. Some feudal lords assumed such a right.

Janissary: An elite corps in the Ottoman army, this highly organized mercenary force was begun by Sultan Murad I in the 14th century. The name is Turkish for "new soldier." The first Janissaries were Christian youths from the Balkans. The force lasted until 1826.

Knight: An armed, mounted warrior in service to a monarch or nobleman. A knight gained this elevated position after time spent in service as a page or squire. Vestiges of this post remain as the honor awarded by the crown for extraordinary service to society.

Longships: Sleek wooden Viking boats up to 100 feet long, powered by square sails and multiple oarsmen. Their tall prows were sometimes adorned with mythological figureheads. Shallow drafts allowed coastal navigation. Some may have reached a speed of ten knots.

Medieval: A term that refers to the time between the fall of the Roman Empire and the age of discovery, roughly 450 to 1500. From the Latin word for "middle," the term was coined by Renaissance historians who saw the period as an interim between the classical age and their own.

Merovingian: The first Frankish dynasty, lasting more than 200 years, was founded in the middle of the fifth century by Merovech, father of Childeric, and is named for him. It ended when Pepin II became king, thus initiating the Carolingian period.

Monasticism: A practice characterized by dedication to the monastery lifestyle, which includes frugality, celibacy, relinquishing of material possessions, and a meditative routine, often including silence, ritual, and prayer. Some monastic orders encourage work in the community; others, isolation.

Paganism: A spiritual practice that envisions multiple deities, especially spirits of nature. In monotheistic religions such as Judaism, Christianity, and Islam, paganism has sometimes been characterized as primitive, dangerous, threatening to social order, and evil.

Papacy: The office and powers held by the pope, the bishop of Rome who also serves as spiritual and administrative leader of the Roman Catholic Church worldwide. This definition originated with Pope Gregory I around A.D. 600. Its interpretation has long provoked debate.

Pogrom: A term that refers to the organized massacre of a minority people, rationalized by religious or intellectual opinions. From the Russian for devastation, the word entered the English language in the 19th century and would not have been used in the Middle Ages.

Relic: A relic originally meant a preserved part of the body of a saint or holy figure and came to mean anything that had been in physical contact with a holy person, like clothing or possessions. Considered sacred, relics were displayed in ornate boxes called reliquaries.

Scriptorium: A room in a monastery where monks copied manuscripts, usually holy books. The work performed by medieval monks in scriptoria is handed down to us in rare illuminated manuscripts covering history and theology and rich with art and calligraphy.

Shire: An administrative subdivision within Britain, established during Anglo-Saxon times as a system of tax collection. Each shire had a fortressed town as its seat. Today's counties evolved from the old shires, as indicated by names such as Lancashire and Leicestershire.

Sultan: A king or leader of a Muslim state. The term originated in the Middle Ages and came into greater use during the Ottoman Empire. Caliphs were religious and spiritual leaders, while sultans were worldly leaders, and therefore expected to be obedient to a caliph.

Vassal: A vassal was a person who vowed loyalty and homage to the lord of the estate on which he lived. In exchange, a vassal usually received a home for his family and land to work for food. The land on which he lived was called a fief. Intricate laws of inheritance evolved.

Zoroastrianism: A monotheistic religion dating to the fifth century B.C., founded by the prophet Zoroaster, who described the struggle between good and chaos or nothingness in the world. Through good work, man can contribute to the ultimate triumph of good.

FURTHER READING

Backman, Clifford R. *The Worlds of Medieval Europe* (Oxford Univ. Press, 2009)

Bartlett, Robert. *Medieval Panorama* (Getty Publications, 2001)

Bitel, Lisa M. *Women in Early Medieval Europe, 400-1100* (Cambridge Univ. Press, 2002)

Bridgeford, Andrew. *1066: The Hidden History in the Bayeux Tapestry* (Walker & Co., 2006)

Cantor, Norman F. *The Civilization of the Middle Ages* (HarperCollins, 1963)

Chaucer, Geoffrey. *The Canterbury Tales* (Norton, 2005)

Dahmus, Joseph. *The Middle Ages: A Popular History* (Doubleday, 1968)

Davies, Norman. *Europe: A History* (Oxford Univ. Press, 1996)

———. *The Isles: A History* (Oxford Univ. Press, 1999)

Davis, R.H.C. *A History of Medieval Europe* (Pearson, 2006)

Fossier, Robert (ed.). *The Cambridge Illustrated History of the Middle Ages* (Cambridge Univ. Press, 1986)

Frugoni, Chiara. *Books, Banks, Buttons: And Other Inventions from the Middle Ages* (Columbia Univ. Press, 2005)

Geoffrey of Monmouth. *The History of the Kings of Britain* (Penguin, 1977)

Gies, Joseph and Francis Gies. *Cathedral, Forge, and Waterwheel* (Harper Perennial, 1995)

Hanawalt, Barbara A. *The Middle Ages: An Illustrated History* (Oxford Univ. Press, 1998)

Hay, Jeff (ed.). *The Early Middle Ages* (Greenhaven, 2001)

Heaney, Seamus (tr.). *Beowulf: A New Verse Translation* (Norton, 2001)

Hicks, Carola. *The Bayeux Tapestry: The Life Story of a Masterpiece* (Random House, 2007)

Hitchcock, Susan Tyler, and John L. Esposito. *Geography of Religion* (National Geographic, 2004)

Holmes, George (ed.). *The Oxford Illustrated History of Medieval Europe* (Oxford Univ. Press, 1988)

Horne, Alistair. *Seven Ages of Paris* (Knopf, 2002)

Howarth, David. *1066: The Year of the Conquest* (Penguin, 1981)

Kotker, Norman (ed.). *The Horizon Book of the Middle Ages* (American Heritage, 1968)

La Fay, Howard. *The Vikings* (National Geographic, 1972)

Leone, Bruno (ed.). *The Middle Ages* (Greenhaven, 2002)

Lewis, David Levering. *God's Crucible: Islam and the Making of Europe, 570-1215* (Norton, 2008)

Mackay, A. with D. Ditchburn. *Atlas of Medieval Europe.* (Routledge, 1997)

Madden, Thomas F. (ed.). *Crusades: The Illustrated History* (Univ. of Michigan Press, 2005)

Malory, Sir Thomas. *Le Morte D'Arthur* (Norton, 2003)

Marie de France. *The Lais of Marie de France* (Penguin Classics, 1993)

Marsden, John. *The Fury of the Northmen: Saints, Shrines, and Sea-Raiders in the Viking Age* (St. Martin's Press, 1993)

McKitterick, Rosamond. *Atlas of the Medieval World* (Oxford Univ. Press, 2004)

The Middle Ages. (National Geographic, 1977)

Miller, David. *Brassey's Book of the Crusades* (Brassey's, 2001)

Pernoud, Regine. *Martins of Tours* (Ignatius Press, 2006)

———. *Those Terrible Middle Ages* (Ignatius Press, 2000)

Rosenwein, Barbara H. *A Short History of the Middle Ages* (Broadview, 2004)

Sekules, Veronica. *Medieval Art* (Oxford Univ. Press, 2001)

Staines, David. *The Complete Romances of Chrétien de Troyes* (Indiana Univ. Press, 1993)

Stalcup, Brenda (ed.). *The 1000s: Headlines in History* (Greenhaven 2001)

Stalley, Roger. *Early Medieval Architecture.* (Oxford Univ. Press, 1999)

Stone, George W. *From Mist and Stone: History and Lore of the Celts and Vikings* (National Geographic, 2005)

About the Contributors

JOHN M. THOMPSON (author of Chapters 2-12) has authored 10 books and contributed to more than 30. His most recent books, both published by National Geographic, are *Dakotas: Where the West Begins* and *An Uncommon History of Common Things,* coauthored with Bethanne Kelly Patrick. He lives with his wife and two children in Charlottesville, Virginia.

DAN O'TOOLE (author of sidebars) graduated from Georgetown University with a degree in Classical Languages. He has written for a number of National Geographic books, including *Concise History of the World: An Illustrated Time Line* and *1000 Events that Shaped the World.* He is also a professional archaeologist and has worked at sites in North America, South America, and Europe.

BETHANNE KELLY PATRICK (author of book outline) is an author and a book critic. Her first book for National Geographic was *An Uncommon History of Common Things,* co-authored with John Thompson. She is currently working on a nonfiction memoir and hosts "The Book Studio" for WETA-PBS. A graduate of Smith College, Patrick received her master's degree in English from the University of Virginia. She lives with her husband and two daughters in Arlington, Virginia.

LAUREN PRUNESKI (author of world maps and thematic spreads) received her B.A. from Wesleyan University and her M.F.A. from the University of Michigan. She has contributed to several other books for National Geographic, including *1000 Events that Shaped the World.* She currently lives in Ann Arbor, Michigan, where she works as a writer and editor.

TIFFIN THOMPSON (author of city spreads) is an editorial assistant for National Geographic Books. She received a B.A. in archaeology from the College of William and Mary. Her interests in ancient history have taken her to Ireland, Scotland, Egypt, Turkey, and Cyprus. She is now pursuing a master's degree in architectural conservation at the University of Pennsylvaniaís School of Design.

RODERICK MARTIN (author of Chapter 1 and consulting historian) holds a Ph.D. in history from the University of Virginia, specializing in medieval and early modern European history, and an M.T.S. from the Boston University School of Theology, specializing in church history and historical theology. He lives with his wife and son in Charlottesville, Virginia, and works at the University of Virginia's Claude Moore Health Sciences Library.

The Medieval World Online

Beowulf: http://greenehamlet.com/beowulf.html
Heilbrunn Timeline of Art History: http://www.metmuseum.org/toah/
Images of Medieval Art and Architecture: http://vrcoll.fa.pitt.edu/medart
The Internet Connection for Medieval Resources: http://www.netserf.org/
Internet Medieval Sourcebook, edited by Paul Hallsall: http://www.fordham.edu/halsall/sbook.html
King Arthur and the Knights of the Round Table: http://www.kingarthursknights.com/
Medieval London: http://www.museumoflondon.org.uk/English/EventsExhibitions/Permanent/medieval/
Medieval Map: http://www.medievalmap.org
Medieval Women, An Interactive Exploration: http://mw.mcmaster.ca/world/
On-line Reference Book for Medieval Studies: http://the-orb.net
The Realms of Medieval Europe: http://www.mnsu.edu/emuseum/history/middleages/index.shtml
Robin Hood: http://www.lib.rochester.edu/camelot/rh/rhhome.htm

THE MEDIEVAL WORLD IN POPULAR CULTURE

THE MEDIEVAL WORLD IN FICTION

The Alchemist by Paulo Coelho

The Clerkenwell Tales by Peter Ackroyd

Eaters of the Dead by Michael Crichton

The Enchantress of Florence by
    Salman Rushdie

Ivanhoe by Sir Walter Scott

The Name of the Rose by Umberto Eco

The Once and Future King by T. H. White

Rashi's Daughters by Maggie Anton

Timeline by Michael Crichton

A Troubadour's Testament: A Novel by
    James Cowan

The White Company by Sir Arthur
    Conan Doyle

THE MEDIEVAL WORLD IN FILM

The Adventures of Robin Hood (1938)

The Agony and the Ecstasy (1965)

Attila (1954)

Becket (1964)

Beowulf (2007)

Braveheart (1995)

El Cid (1961)

The Fall of the Roman Empire (1964)

The Hunchback of Notre Dame (1939)

Ivanhoe (1952)

A Knight's Tale (2001)

The Lion in Winter (1968)

Macbeth (1948)

Mohammad, Messenger of God (1976)

Monty Python and the Holy Grail (1974)

Robin Hood (animated) (1973)

Robin Hood: Men in Tights (1993)

Robin Hood: Prince of Thieves (1991)

Romeo & Juliet (1968)

The Sword in the Stone (animated) (1963)

The 13th Warrior (1999)

The War Lord (1965)

THE MEDIEVAL WORLD ON TELEVISION

The Last Templar, NBC (2009)

Marco Polo, NBC (1982)

Merlin, NBC (2009)

LIST OF MAPS

ILLUSTRATIONS CREDITS

Cover: (Foreground) © The British Library Board. All Rights Reserved. Royal 16 F. II, f.73; (Background) The Ebstorf World Map of 1284, by Gervasius of Tilbury. Largest medieval map, ca. 350 cm. diam. Facsimile (original destroyed in 1945 in Hanover). Inv. 9630. Photo: Ruth Schacht. Manuscript Divison. Staatsbibliothek zu Berlin, Stiftung Preussischer Kulturbesitz, Berlin, Germany/Bildarchiv Preussischer Kulturbesitz/Art Resource, NY.

Front matter
Interior: 1, Facsimile copy of the "Ebstorf Mappamundi," originally made for the convent at Ebstorf, near Luneberg, ca 1339 but destroyed in 1943 (color litho)/British Library, London, UK/© British Library Board. All Rights Reserved/Bridgeman Art Library; 2, MS 58 fol.32v Christ with four angels, introductory page to the Gospel of St. Matthew, from the *Book of Kells,* ca 800 (vellum), Irish School, (9th century)/© The Board of Trinity College, Dublin, Ireland/Bridgeman Art Library

1 The Medieval Worldview 400-1500
10-11, akg-images/British Library; 12, The Pierpont Morgan Library/Art Resource, NY; 14, Helmet, from the Sutton Hoo Ship Burial, ca 625-30 AD (iron & gilt bronze), Anglo-Saxon, (7th century), British Museum, London, UK/Bridgeman Art Library; 15, Hugues I Capet (941-996), the King with a Hat (vellum), French School, (14th century), Bibliothèque Mazarine, Paris, France/Archives Charmet/Bridgeman Art Library; 16, Royal 12 F.IV, f.135v Diagrammatic world map, ca 1175 (vellum)/British Library, London, UK, British Library, London, UK/Bridgeman Art Library; 17, The castle, originally founded in the 10th century by Fernan Gonzalez (photo), Spanish School, (15th century)/Turegano, Castilla y Leon, Spain/Lauros/Giraudon/Bridgeman Art Library; 18, Eric Van Den Brulle/Getty Images; 19, James L. Stanfield; 20, Page from the Theodosian Codex (vellum),/Biblioteca Nazionale, Turin, Italy/Bridgeman Art Library; 21, Philippe Lissac/Godong/CORBIS; 23, Cott Nero D II f.191v Edward I (1239-1307) of England investing his son Edward (1284-1327) as Prince of Wales (later Edward II) in February 1301/ British Library, London, UK/British Library, London, UK/Bridgeman Art Library; 24, Interior of the Great Mosque showing bays of two-tiered horseshoe arches, 785 (photo),/Mezquita (Great Mosque) Cordoba, Spain/Index/Bridgeman Art Library; 26, Bildarchiv Preussischer Kulturbesitz/Art Resource, NY; 27, © The British Library Board. All Rights Reserved. Royal 18 D. II, f.30v; 29, Mappa Mundi, ca 1290 (vellum), Richard of Haldingham (Richard de Bello) (fl. ca 1260-1305)/Hereford Cathedral, Herefordshire, UK/Bridgeman Art Library; 30 (UP), Detail from the south facade (stone), Italian School, (14th century)/Palazzo Ducale, Venice, Italy/Sarah Quill/Bridgeman Art Library; 30 (LO), Medieval minstrels (painted stone), English School/St. Mary's Church, Beverley, East Riding, Yorkshire, UK/Neil Holmes/Bridgeman Art Library; 31 (UP), Plan and elevation of Cluny Abbey (engraving) (b/w photo), Giffart, Pierre (1638-1723)/Bibliothèque Nationale, Paris, France/Lauros/Giraudon/Bridgeman Art Library; 31 (LO), Eric Van Den Brulle/Getty Images

2 The End of an Empire 400-500
32-33, The Saint Prophesizes to Totila King of the Goths, detail from the Life of Saint Benedict (ca 480-c550), in the Sacristy, 1387 (fresco), Spinello or Spinelli, Aretino Luca (ca 1340-1410/San Miniato al Monte, Florence, Italy/Bridgeman Art Library; 34, The Baptism of Christ surrounded by the Apostles, from the vault of the central dome (mosaic), Byzantine, (5th century AD)/Battistero Neoniano, Ravenna, Italy/Lauros/Giraudon/Bridgeman Art Library; 36, Vandal on Horseback, Roman mosaic from Carthage, ca 500 AD, Roman, (6th century AD/British Museum, London, UK/Bridgeman Art Library; 38, St. Geminianus, St. Michael and St. Augustine, ca 1319 (tempera with gold on panel) (details 58834 and 58836), Martini, Simone (1284-1344)/Fitzwilliam Museum, University of Cambridge, UK/Bridgeman Art Library; 39, Ms 250 plate XXIII The Life of St. Radegund (518-87) (vellum), French School, (11th century)/Bibliothèque Municipale, Poitiers, France/Bridgeman Art Library; 41, akg-images; 42, B. Anthony Stewart; 43, Ms 65/1284 f.141v Plan of Rome, from the Tres Riches Heures du Duc de Berry, early 15th century (vellum), Limbourg, Pol de (d.ca 1416)/Musée Conde, Chantilly, France/Bridgeman Art Library; 44, akg-images/Pirozzi; 45, Karl Weatherly/Getty Images; 47, Vase in shape of double head, ca 400 AD (pottery), Roman (5th century AD)/Louvre, Paris, France/Bridgeman Art Library; 48, he Cup of Solomon, bearing a relief cameo of a king, Sassanian Period (226-651) (gold, rock crystal, garnet and green glass), Persian School, (6th century)/Bibliothèque Nationale, Paris, France/Bridgeman Art Library; 50, akg-images; 52 (UP), Head of Serapis (marble),/© Museum of London, UK/Bridgeman Art Library; 52 (LO), View of Temple of the 1000 Columns with the Pyramid of Kuculcan (photo), Mayan/Chichen Itza, Yucatan, Mexico/Ken Welsh/Bridgeman Art Library; 53 (UP), CBL InE 1479 Krishna and his cousin Arjuna Preparing for Battle, from the Bhagavadgita, 18th-19th century (ink, gouache & gold on paper), Indian School/© The Trustees of the Chester Beatty Library, Dublin/Bridgeman Art Library; 53 (LO), Paul Nieuwenhuysen; 54, Christ, or The Good Shepherd (marble), Byzantine, (5th century AD)/Hermitage, St. Petersburg, Russia/Bridgeman Art Library; 55, Chris Hellier/CORBIS; 56, Ms Add 12228 f.202v Merlin tutoring Arthur, from the Roman du Roy Meliadus de Leonnoys, ca 1352 (vellum) (detail of 151840), Italian School, (14th century)/British Library, London, UK/Bridgeman Art Library; 58, St. Jerome Translating the Bible (oil on panel), Netherlandish School, (15th century)/Muse-

um Boymans van Beuningen, Rotterdam, The Netherlands/Bridgeman Art Library; 59, Fol.11r St. Remigius, Bishop of Rheims (ca 438-533) baptising and annointing Clovis I (465-511), King of the Franks, from the Grandes Chroniques de France, 1375-79 (vellum) (detail of 192489), French School, (14th century)/Bibliothèque Municipale, Castres, France/Giraudon/Bridgeman Art Library; 60 (UP), Two floor tiles from the Cistercian monastery in Heilsbronn (fired and glazed clay), German School, (14th century)/Germanisches Nationalmuseum, Nuremberg (Nuernberg), Germany/Bridgeman Art Library; 60 (LO), A Maid Milking a Cow, 1491 (colored woodcut), German School, (15th century)/Private Collection/Archives Charmet/Bridgeman Art Library; 61 (UP), Apocalypse Miniatures: The Dragon Waging War and The Beast of the Sea, ca 1295 (tempera on vellum), French School, (13th century)/The Detroit Institute of Arts, USA/Founders Society purchase, Founders Junior Council and Mr & Mrs Walter B. Ford II Fund/Bridgeman Art Library; 61 (LO), Equestrian portrait of Charles V in armour (1500-58) (color engraving), Liefrinck, Hans (the Elder) (1518-72)/Stedelijk Prentakabinet, Antwerp, Belgium/Lauros/Giraudon/Bridgeman Art Library; 61 (RT), The Lady and the Unicorn: "Sight" (tapestry), French School, (15th century)/Musée National du Moyen Age et des Thermes de Cluny, Paris/Bridgeman Art Library

3 The Post-Roman Landscape 500-600
62-63, Empress Theodora with her court of two ministers and seven women, ca A.D. 547 (mosaic), Byzantine School, (6th century)/San Vitale, Ravenna, Italy/Giraudon/Bridgeman Art Library; 64, Ms 860/401 fol.296 The Execution of Brunhilda (534-613) from the Story of Phocas, from "Cas des Nobles Hommes et Femmes," by Giovanni Boccaccio (1313-75) translated by Laurent de Premierfait, 1465 (vellum), French School, (15th century)/Musée Conde, Chantilly, France/Giraudon/Bridgeman Art Library; 66, Ball (rock crystal) (see also 270522), Merovingian (6th century)/Private Collection/Photo Heini Schneebeli/Bridgeman Art Library; 68, Eagle-shaped brooch (metal and enamel), Merovingian School/Musée National du Moyen Age et des Thermes de Cluny, Paris/Lauros/Giraudon/Bridgeman Art Library; 69, Codex 73 Abbot John offering the manuscript to St. Benedict (ca 480-ca 550), abbot and founder of Montecassino, written by Deacon Paul, Italian, 915, from the "Commentary on the monastic rules of St. Benedict" (vellum)/Abbey of Monte Cassino, Cassino, Italy/Bridgeman Art Library; 70, Ms 869/522 fol.33v Belisarius Received by Emperor Justinian I (482-565) (vellum), French School, (15th century)/Musée Conde, Chantilly, France/Giraudon/Bridgeman Art Library; 71, Erich Lessing/Art Resource, NY; 72, Ms 828 f.33r Siege of Antioch, from the Estoire d'Outremer (vellum), William of Tyre (ca 1130-85)/Bibliothèque Municipale de Lyon, France/Bridgeman Art Library; 73, Francis G. Mayer/CORBIS; 74, akg-images/Gerard Degeorge; 76, Bowl, 6th-7th century AD (gilded & carved silver), Sasanian School/The Detroit Institute of Arts, USA/Founders Society Purchase Sarah Bacon Hill Fund/Bridgeman Art Library; 77, Harvey Lloyd/Getty Images; 79, Emperor Justinian I (483-565) ca 547 AD (mosaic) (detail), Byzantine School, (6th century)/San Vitale, Ravenna, Italy/Giraudon/Bridgeman Art Library; 80, akg-images/Bildarchiv Steffens; 81, By permission of The National Library of Wales; 82 (UP), Richard Stead; 82 (LO), William Albert Allard/NationalGeographicStock.com; 83 (UP), Head of a Smiling Buddha, Greco-Buddhist style, from Hadda, 1st-4th century (stucco), Afghan School/Musée Guimet, Paris, France/Giraudon/Bridgeman Art Library; 83 (LO), Khusrau in front of the Palace of Shirin, from "Khusrau and Shirin" by Elyas Nezami (1140-1209) 1504 (gouache on paper), Islamic School, (16th century)/Private Collection/Giraudon/Bridgeman Art Library; 84, The Visigoth Kings, from the Codex Emilianensis, 992 AD (vellum), Spanish School, (10th century)/Biblioteca Monasterio del Escorial, Madrid, Spain/Flammarion/Bridgeman Art Library; 85, akg-images; 86, St. Martin of Tours, detail from an altar frontal from the Church of Sant Marti in Gia, Ribagorca Workshop (tempera on panel), Spanish School, (13th century)/Museo de arte de Catalunya, Barcelona, Spain/Giraudon/Bridgeman Art Library; 87, akg-images/Rabatti - Domingie; 88, Man and Woman Ploughing a Field, after a miniature from an Anglo-Saxon manuscript, from "Le Moyen Age et La Renaissance" by Paul Lacroix (1806-84) published 1847 (litho), French School, (19th century)/Private Collection/Ken Welsh/Bridgeman Art Library; 89, Jean-Leon Huens; 90 (UP), Game piece 11th or 12th century (wood), English School/© Museum of London, UK/Bridgeman Art Library; 90 (LO), The Pierpont Morgan Library/Art Resource, NY; 91 (UP LE), F. Kellerhoven chromolithograph from *Moeurs, Usages et Costumes Au Moyen Age*, 3rd Ed., 1873, Librairie de Fermin Didot Freres, Fils et Cie; 91 (UP RT), King chess piece, showing an enthroned figure in a curtained alcove with two attendants, Italian, late 11th century (ivory)/Museo Nazionale del Bargello, Florence, Italy/Bridgeman Art Library; 91 (LO), Image copyright © The Metropolitan Museum of Art/Art Resource, NY

4 A New World Religion 600-700
92-93, MS 447 View of Medina and mosque of the Prophet Muhammad (opaque pigments on paper), Ottoman School, (18th century)/© The Trustees of the Chester Beatty Library, Dublin/Bridgeman Art Library; 94, akg-images/Werner Forman; 96, Purse lid, from the Sutton Hoo Ship Burial, ca 625-30 AD (gold, garnets and millefiori glass), Anglo-Saxon, (7th century)/British Museum, London, UK/Photo Boltin Picture Library/Bridgeman Art Library; 98, akg-images/Werner Forman; 100, Schematic View of Mecca, showing the Qua'bah, from a book on Persian ceramics (print), Persian School/Private Collection/The Stapleton Collection/Bridgeman

Art Library; 102, James L. Stanfield; 103, Courtesy of Historic Cities Research Project: http://historic-cities.huji.aca.il, The National Library of Israel , Shapell Family Digitization Project, Eran Laor Cartographic Collection and The Hebrew University of Jerusalem; 104, © The British Library Board. All Rights Reserved. Or. 2936, f.322v; 105, Near East Collections, Library of Congress; 106, akg-images/British Library; 108, The Dome of the Rock, Temple Mount, built AD 692 (photo), Islamic School, (7th century)/Jerusalem, Israel/Bildarchiv Steffens/Bridgeman Art Library; 109, Kufic calligraphy from a Koran manuscript (parchment), Islamic School, (9th century)/Private Collection/Bridgeman Art Library; 110, Ms 722/1196 f.82r St. Bathild (d.680) from Le Miroir Historial, by Vincent de Beauvais (vellum), French School, (15th century)/Musée Conde, Chantilly, France/Giraudon/Bridgeman Art Library; 111, akg-images/Bildarchiv Monheim; 112 (UP), Painted stones (photo), Hohokam/Arizona, USA/Ancient Art and Architecture Collection Ltd./Bridgeman Art Library; 112 (LO), View over Palenque (photo)/Chiapas State, Mexico/Bildarchiv Steffens Henri Stierlin/Bridgeman Art Library; 113 (UP), akg-images/Werner Forman; 113 (LO), From Wikimedia Commons, http://commons.wikimedia.org/wiki/File:Bilal.jpg; 114, Franks Casket, Northumbria (whalebone), English School, (8th century)/British Museum, London, UK/Bridgeman Art Library; 115, Cotton Nero D IV, f.29 Second incipit page to the Gospel of St. Matthew, from the Lindisfarne Gospels, 720-721 (vellum), English School, (8th century)/British Library, London, UK/British Library Board. All Rights Reserved/Bridgeman Art Library; 116, St. Cuthbert's Cross (gold inlaid with garnet), Anglo-Saxon/Dean and Chapter Library, Durham Cathedral, UK/Bridgeman Art Library; 118, akg-images/Herve Champollion; 119, Add 39943 f.24 St. Cuthbert praying in the sea observed by a monk, and having his feet dried by sea otters, from "Life and Miracles of St. Cuthbert" by Bede, Latin (Durham) (vellum), English School, (12th century)/British Library, London, UK/British Library Board. All Rights Reserved/Bridgeman Art Library; 120, Devil pushing a damned person in the fire, from the Last Judgement of the Cathedral of St. Etienne in Bourges (detail) (plaster cast from stone) (b/w photo), French School, (13th century)/Musée des Monuments Francais, Paris, France/Giraudon/Bridgeman Art Library; 121 (UP), Ms 422 f.95v Hell (vellum), French School, (13th century)/Bibliothèque Municipale, Cambrai, France/Giraudon/Bridgeman Art Library; 121 (LE), Ms 9/1695 fol.35v The Story of St. Theophilus, Theophilus and the Devil, and the Repentence of Theophilus, from the "Psautier d'Ingeburg de Danemark," ca 1210 (vellum), French School, (13th century)/Musée Conde, Chantilly, France/Giraudon/Bridgeman Art Library; 121 (RT), Witches Making a Spell, 1489 (engraving) (b&w photo), English School, (15th century)/Private Collection/Bridgeman Art Library

5 Charlemagne's Century 700-800

122-123, The Battle of Poitiers, 25th October 732, won by Charles Martel (688-741) 1837 (oil on canvas), Steuben, Charles Auguste (1788-1856)/Chateau de Versailles, France/Bridgeman Art Library; 124, Bibliothèque Nationale, Paris, France/Index/Bridgeman Art Library; 126, The Hunterston Brooch, early 8th century (gold), Celtic/© National Museums of Scotland/Bridgeman Art Library; 129, Tim Graham/Getty Images; 130, Tomb of Pepin "the Short" (ca 715-768), King of the Franks, detail of the king's head (stone), French School, (13th century)/Basilique Saint-Denis, France/Lauros/Giraudon/Bridgeman Art Library; 131, Pepin "the Short" (ca 715-68) King of the Franks (vellum), French School, (15th century)/Bibliothèque Mazarine, Paris, France/Archives Charmet/Bridgeman Art Library; 132, Walter M. Edwards; 133, Courtesy of Historic Cities Research Project: http://historic-cities.huji.aca il/, The National Library of Israel , Shapell Family Digitization Project, Eran Laor Cartographic Collection and The Hebrew University of Jerusalem; 134, The Venerable Bede (engraving), Cook, J.W. (19th Century)/Private Collection/Ken Welsh/Bridgeman Art Library; 135, Emperor Charlemagne, ca 1511-13 (oil on panel), Durer or Duerer, Albrecht (1471-1528)/Germanisches Nationalmuseum, Nuremberg, Germany/Bridgeman Art Library; 136, f.86v Charles Martel looks after punishment and banishment of two men, from the Grandes Chroniques de France, 1375-79 (vellum), French School, (14th century)/Bibliothèque Municipale, Castres, France/Giraudon/Bridgeman Art Library; 137, Interior of the Great Mosque (photo)/Mezquita (Great Mosque) Cordoba, Spain/Ken Welsh/Bridgeman Art Library; 138, The Ardagh Chalice, early 8th century (silver with silver gilding, enamel, brass and bronze) (see also 228627), Celtic, (8th century)/National Museum of Ireland, Dublin, Ireland/Photo Boltin Picture Library/Bridgeman Art Library; 141, Icon of St. Cyril (826-69) and St. Methodius (ca 815-85) 1862 (panel), Bulgarian School, (19th century)/Museum of History of Sofia, Sofia, Bulgaria/Archives Charmet/Bridgeman Art Library; 142, Roland blows the horn at Roncevaux, illustration from "Le Chanson de Roland," copy of an original manuscript conserved at Saint-Gall in Switzerland (color litho), French School, (13th century) (after)/Private Collection/Archives Charmet/Bridgeman Art Library; 143, Penny of Offa, King of Mercia, 757-96 (obverse) (silver) (for reverse see 168072), English School, (8th century)/Fitzwilliam Museum, University of Cambridge, UK/Bridgeman Art Library; 144 (UP), View of the palace of Qasr el-Mshatta, built ca 743-744 AD (photo)/Amman, Jordan/World Religions Photo Library/Bridgeman Art Library; 144 (LO), Tikal Temple 1 (photo)/Topoxte, Peten, Guatemala/Jean-Pierre Courau/Bridgeman Art Library; 145 (UP), Emperor Hsuan Tsung (712-756 AD) at home, from a history of Chinese emperors (color on silk), Chinese School, (17th century)/Bibliothèque Nationale, Paris, France/Lauros/Giraudon/Bridgeman Art Library; 145 (LO), Detail of the exterior, AD 778-850 (volcanic stone), Indonesian, (9th century)/Temple of Borobudur, Central Java, Indonesia/Bridgeman Art Library; 146, Bell of Clogher, from Ireland (bronze), Celtic, (8th century)/National Museum of Ireland, Dublin, Ireland/Photo Boltin Picture Library/Bridgeman Art Library; 147, The Pala d'Oro, detail of Empress Irene Comnenus (gold & enamel inlaid with precious stones), Byzantine/Basilica di San Marco, Venice, Italy/Cameraphoto Arte Venezia/Bridgeman Art Library; 148, MS 58 fol.114r The Arrest of Christ, Gospel of St. Matthew, from the Book of Kells, ca 800 (vellum), Irish School, (9th century)/© The Board of Trinity College, Dublin, Ireland/Bridgeman Art Library; 149, akg-images/British Library; 150 (UP), Tunic, ca 1020 (embroidered linen), Egyptian/© Ashmolean Museum, University of Oxford, UK/Bridgeman Art Library; 150 (LO), Engraving from *Moeurs, Usages et Costumes Au Moyen Age*, 3rd Ed., 1873, Librairie de Fermin Didot Freres, Fils et Cie; 151 (UP LE), Leather shoes dating from the 13th and 14th centuries (leather), English School/© Museum of London, UK/Bridgeman Art Library; 151 (UP RT), F. Kellerhoven chromolithograph from *Moeurs, Usages et Costumes Au Moyen Age*, 3rd Ed., 1873, Librairie de Fermin Didot Freres, Fils et Cie; 151 (LO), Engraving from *Moeurs, Usages et Costumes Au Moyen Age*, 3rd Ed., 1873, Librairie de Fermin Didot Freres, Fils et Cie

6 A World Divided 800-900

152-153, akg-images/Werner Forman; 154, Cod.22 St. Mark, from the Ada manuscript (vellum), Carolingian School (9th century)/Stadtbibliothek, Trier, Germany/Bridgeman Art Library; 156, Carolingian denarii (silver), Carolingian School/Germanisches Nationalmuseum, Nuremberg, Germany/Bridgeman Art Library; 158, Viking amulet in the shape of a cross with a dragon's head design (silver)/National Museum of Iceland, Reykjavik, Iceland/Bridgeman Art Library; 159, ds Lat 1 fol.423r King Charles II Receiving a Bible from Count Vivian and the Monks of Saint-Martin de Tours, from the First Bible of Charles the Bald, ca 843-51 (vellum), French School, (9th century)/Bibliothèque Nationale, Paris, France/Bridgeman Art Library ; 160, Head of Lothair I (stone) (see also 347302), French School, (13th century)/Musée Saint-Remi, Reims, France/Giraudon/Bridgeman Art Library; 162, Gervais Courtellemont; 163, Courtesy of Historic Cities Research Project: http://historic-cities.huji.aca il; The National Library of Israel, Shapell Family Digitization Project, Eran Laor Cartographic Collection and The Hebrew University of Jerusalem; 165, akg-images; 166, Detail of an animal head carving, from a sledge found with the Oseberg ship (wood), Viking, (9th century)/Viking Ship Museum, Oslo, Norway/Bridgeman Art Library; 169, akg-images; 170, Water jug presented to Charlemagne (742-814) by Harun al-Rashid (ca 766-809) (cloisonne enamel), Byzantine/Treasury of the Abbey of Saint-Maurice, Valais, Switzerland/Lauros/Giraudon/Bridgeman Art Library; 171, The Great Mosque, Aghlabid, 836-875 AD (photo)/Kairouan, Tunisia/Bridgeman Art Library; 172, Anthropomorphic vessel, ca 800 (terracotta) (photo), Pre-Columbian/Museo Nacional de Arqueologia, Mexico City, Mexico/Photo © AISA/Bridgeman Art Library; 173 (UP), The Great Pagoda, Tanjore, plate XXIV from "Oriental Scenery," published 1798 (colored aquatint), Daniell, Thomas (1749-1840)/Private Collection/The Stapleton Collection/Bridgeman Art Library; 173 (RT), Preserved Maori Head/Museum fur Volkerkunde, Basel, Switzerland/Bridgeman Art Library; 173 (LO), Spiral minaret of the Great Mosque (photo)/ Samarra, Iraq/© World Religions Photo Library/Bridgeman Art Library; 174, Bibliothèque Nationale de France; 175, Abbasid period (750-1258) (earthenware), Mesopotamian (9th century)/© Ashmolean Museum, University of Oxford, UK/Gift of Sir Alan Barlow/Bridgeman Art Library; 176, akg-images; 177, Julian Finney/Getty Images; 179, Ms Lat 8850 f.6v The Fountain of Life, from the Court School of Charlemagne (vellum), French School, (9th century)/Bibliothèque Nationale, Paris, France/Topham Picturepoint/Bridgeman Art Library; 180 (UP), Ms H 89 Surgical treatment, from an edition of "Book of Surgery" by Rogier de Salerne (vellum), French School, (14th century)/Musée Atger, Faculte de Medecine, Montpellier, France/Giraudon/Bridgeman Art Library; 180 (LO), Ms 724/1596 Fol.155v An Astrological geocentric Planetary Chart, from "Liber Floridus" by Lambert de Saint-Omer, ca 1448 (vellum), Flemish School, (15th century)/Musée Conde, Chantilly, France/Giraudono/Bridgeman Art Library; 181 (UP), Diagram of a system for pumping water into a basin, from "Treaty on Mechanical Procedures" by Al-Djazari, 1206 (vellum), Islamic School, (13th century)/Topkapi Palace Museum, Istanbul, Turkey/Bridgeman Art Library; 181 (RT), Mortar with Handle in the Shape of a Lizard, ca 1500 (bronze), Leopardi, Alessandro (1450-ca 1523)/Fitzwilliam Museum, University of Cambridge, UK/Bridgeman Art Library; 181 (LO), The Alchemist, from "The Working World" cycle after Giotto, ca 1450 (fresco), Miretto, Nicolo & Stefano da Ferrara (15th century)/Palazzo della Ragione, Padua, Italy/Bridgeman Art Library

7 The Millennium Approaches 900-1000

182-183, The Expulsion of the Danes from Manchester, 920 AD, Brown, Ford Madox (1821-93)/Town Hall, Manchester, UK/Bridgeman Art Library; 184, © The British Library Board. All Rights Reserved. Egerton 3028, f.25; 186, Gjermundbu Viking Helmet (metallic), Viking, (10th century)/Universitetets Oldsamksamling, University of Oslo, Norway/Photo © AISA/Bridgeman Art Library; 188, Two men duelling on horseback, from Old Cairo (Fostat) (vellum), Islamic School/Museum of Islamic Art, Cairo, Egypt/Giraudon/Bridgeman Art Library; 189, Ewer with birds from the Treasury of Saint-Denis, Egyptian, Fatimid Period, late 10th century (rock crystal) (b/w photo), Islamic School, (10th century)/Louvre, Paris, France/Giraudon/Bridgeman Art Library; 190, Abd al-Rahman III (891-961) Receiving the Ambassador, 1885 (oil on canvas), Baixeras-Verdaguer, Dionisio (1862-1943)/University of Barcelona, Spain/Index/Bridgeman Art Library; 192, Andrew Holt/Getty Images; 193, Map showing the ocean that was believed to surround the world, Anglo-Saxon (vellum), English School, (10th century)/British Library, London, UK/© British Library Board. All Rights Reserved/Bridgeman Art Library; 195, © The British Library Board. All Rights Reserved. I.O. Islamic 3540, f.91; 196, Ms 1186 f.1 Astrologer with an astrolabe, a Scribe and a Mathematician, from a Latin psalter from the Psalter of St. Louis and Blanche of Castile, 1225-1250 (vellum), French School, (13th century)/Bibliothèque de L'Arsenal, Paris, France/Flammarion/Bridgeman Art Library; 197, The Imperial Crown made for the coronation of Otto I, "the Great" (912-73) showing one of four enamel plaques representing King Solomon as the symbol of Wisdom, West German, late 10th century with later additions (gold, precious stones, pearls and enamel)/Kunsthistorisches Museum, Vienna, Austria/ Bridgeman Art Library; 199, DEA/W. BUSS/Getty Images; 200, © The British Library Board. All Rights Reserved. Cotton Claudius D. VI f.7v; 201, © The British Library Board. All Rights Reserved. Cotton Augustus.ii, f.45.; 202 (UP), Tlaloc (stone), Toltec/Museo Nacional de Antropologia, Mexico City, Mexico/Photo: Michel Zabe/AZA INAH/Bridgeman Art Library; 203 (UP), Portrait of Li Shengtian, King of Yutian, Five Dynasties, 907-960 (wall painting)/Mogao Caves, Dunhuang, Gansu Province, NW China/Bridgeman Art Library; 203 (RT), Seokgatap Pagoda, Silla Period (photo), Korean School, (8th century)/Bulguksa Temple, Mt. Tohamsan, Gyeongju, South Korea/Bridgeman Art Library; 203 (LO), F.116v The Relationship between the Human Body and the Signs of the Zodiac, from a medical treatise by Abul Qasim Khalaf ibn al-Abbas al-Zahrawi (Abulcasis) (936-1013) translated by Gerard de Cremone (1114-870 (vellum), French School, (14th century)/Bibliothèque Mazarine, Paris, France/Archives Charmet/ Bridgeman Art Library; 204, © The British Library Board. All Rights Reserved. Cotton Claudius B. VI, f.87v; 206, January, February, March and April, from "The Julius Calendar and Hymnal," illustration from "History of the English People" (engraving) (b/w photo), English School/Private Collection/Bridgeman Art Library; 207, Cott Tib B V Part 1 f.56v Rectangular map of the World, ca 1030 (vellum), Anglo-Saxon, (11th century)/British Library, London, UK/© British Library Board. All Rights Reserved/Bridgeman Art Library; 208, © Wolfgang Kaehler/CORBIS; 209, akg-images/Schütze/Rodemann; 210 (UP), Inner face of a Koran case with a thulth inscription on the binding (leather) (see 181735), Islamic School, (16th century)/Islamic Arts Museum, Tehran, Iran/Bridgeman Art Library; 210 (LO), Add 49598 f.9v The Second Coming, from the Benedictional of St. Aethelwold, Winchester, ca 980 (vellum), English School, (10th century)/British Library, London, UK/Peter Willi/Bridgeman Art Library; 211 (UP LE), Cover of the Trier "Codex Aureus," ca 983-991 (gold plate, precious stones, pearls and enamel mounted on oak), German school, (10th century)/Germanisches Nationalmuseum, Nuremberg (Nuernberg), Germany/Bridgeman Art Library; 211 (UP RT), Printing Press of 1498, from a book printed in that year (engraving), German School, (15th century)/Private Collection/Ken Welsh/Bridgeman Art Library; 211 (LO), Two folios from the Gutenberg Bible, printed in the workshop of Johannes Gutenberg, 1455 (parchment), German School, (15th century)/Universitatsbibliothek, Gottingen, Germany/Bildarchiv Steffens/Bridgeman Art Library

8 Postmillennial Changes 1000-1100

212-213, Here they cross the River Couesnon, and get stuck in the quicksand, detail from the Bayeux Tapestry, before 1082 (wool embroidery on linen), French School, (11th century)/ Musée de la Tapisserie, Bayeux, France/With special authorisation of the city of Bayeux/ Giraudon/Bridgeman Art Library; 214, Ms 774 (4)/1632 f.3r The Creation of the World, from "Antiquitates Judaicae" (vellum), Flemish School, (12th century)/Musée Conde, Chantilly, France/Lauros/Giraudon/Bridgeman Art Library; 216, Gospel Cover, Ottonian, Germany, 11th century (gold, enamel and semi-precious stones), German School, (11th century)/Peter Willi/Bridgeman Art Library; 218, MS. 6, fol. 105v Edward the Confessor, from the St Alban's Chronicle (vellum), English School, (15th century)/© Lambeth Palace Library, London, UK/ Bridgeman Art Library; 219, A lord and his vassal, from "Liber Feudorum Major" (vellum), Spanish School, (12th century)/Archivo de la Corona de Aragon, Barcelona, Spain/Photo © AISA/Bridgeman Art Library; 220, Ms Hunter 9 f.36r Dissection, from De Medina Fen I. II, by Avicenna (980-1037) (vellum), Flemish School, (15th century)/© Glasgow University Library, Scotland/Bridgeman Art Library; 221, Ms Lat 17716 fol.91 The Consecration of the Church at Cluny by Pope Urban II (1042-99) in November 1095 (vellum), French School, (12th century)/ Bibliothèque Nationale, Paris, France/Bridgeman Art Library; 222, El Duomo, founded by Walter, Archbishop of Palermo ("Gualatiero Offamiglio") in 1185 (photo)/Palermo, Sicily, Italy/ Peter Willi/Bridgeman Art Library; 223, Map of Palermo, from "Civitates Orbis Terrarum" by Georg Braun (1541-1622) and Frans Hogenberg (1535-90) ca 1572-1617 (colored engraving), Hoefnagel, Joris (1542-1600) (after)/Private Collection/The Stapleton Collection/Bridgeman Art Library; 224, Alexius I Comnenus (1048-1118), Byzantine emperor (1081-1118) (vellum), Byzantine/Vatican Library, Vatican City, Rome, Italy/Giraudon/Bridgeman Art Library; 225, Ms 482/665 f.60v Heloise and Abelard, from Le Roman de la Rose, le testament, by Jean de Meung, ca 1370 (vellum), French School, (14th century)/Musée Conde, Chantilly, France/Giraudon/Bridgeman Art Library; 226, Interior View of St. John's Chapel, Tower of London, 1883 (w/c on paper), Crowther, John (1837-1902)/Guildhall Library, City of London/Bridgeman Art Library; 228, The Battle of Hastings in 1066 (oil on canvas), Debon, Francois Hippolyte (1807-72)/Musée des Beaux-Arts, Caen, France/Giraudon/Bridgeman Art Library; 229, Facsimile copy of The Domesday Book, 1085-86 (vellum), English School, (11th century) (after)/ Alecto Historical Editions, London, UK/Bridgeman Art Library; 230, Duke William exhorts his troops to prepare themselves for the battle against the English army, detail from the Bayeux Tapestry, before 1082 (wool embroidery on linen), French School, (11th century)/Musée de la Tapisserie, Bayeux, France/With special authorisation of the city of Bayeux/Bridgeman Art Library; 232 (UP), akg-images/Werner Forman; 233 (UP), Numismondo.com; 233 (LO), Or Ms 161 fol.16r The Birth of Caesar, from "The Chronology of Ancient Nations" by Al-Biruni, 1307 (gouache on paper), Islamic School, (14th century)/Edinburgh University Library, Scotland/With kind permission of the University of Edinburgh/Bridgeman Art Library; 233 (RT), Hoodo (Phoenix Hall), Byodoin Temple, Uji, near Kyoto, 11th century (photo)/Private Col-

lection/Bridgeman Art Library; 234, Elaborate brickwork at the top of the Semnan Minaret (brick), Islamic School, (11th century)/Semnan Province, Iran/Bridgeman Art Library; 235, Exterior view (photo), English School, (13th century)/Rhuddlan Castle, North Wales, UK/John Bethell/Bridgeman Art Library; 236, Pope Urban II (ca 1035-99) Consecrating the Church of St. Sernin of Toulouse (oil on canvas), Rivalz, Antoine (1667-1735)/Musée des Augustins, Toulouse, France/Lauros/Giraudon/Bridgeman Art Library; 237, Eg 1500 f.45v Peter the Hermit, preacher for the First Crusades, 1095, Histoire Universelle, ca 1286 (detail of 53271)/British Library, London, UK/© British Library Board. All Rights Reserved/Bridgeman Art Library; 238, Hildegard Altarpiece depicting the arrival of Saint Hildegard of Bingen (1098-1179) with her family at the Benedictine Abbey of Disibodenberg, 1898, German School, (19th century)/ Historisches Museum, Bingen, Germany/Bildarchiv Steffens/Bridgeman Art Library; 239, Fortress, built by Baldwin I (ca 1058-1118) (photo)/Aqaba, Jordan/Bridgeman Art Library; 240 (UP), Chalice from Hildesheim, ca 1230 (silver gilt and filigree), German School, (13th century)/Germanisches Nationalmuseum, Nuremberg (Nuernberg), Germany/Bridgeman Art Library; 240 (LO), Nova 2644 fol.80v Preparation of spleen, from "Tacuinum Sanitatis" (vellum), Italian School, (14th century)/Osterreichische Nationalbibliothek, Vienna, Austria/Alinari/ Bridgeman Art Library; 241 (UP), F. Kellerhoven chromolithograph from Moeurs, Usages et Costumes Au Moyen Age, 3rd Ed., 1873,Librairie de Fermin Didot Freres, Fils et Cie; 241 (LO LE), Paten, from Hildesheim, ca 1230 (silver gilt and filigree), German School, (13th century)/ Germanisches Nationalmuseum, Nuremberg (Nuernberg), Germany/Bridgeman Art Library; 241 (LO RT), akg-images/Werner Forman

9 Cultures Clash 1100-1200

242-243, Roy 15 EI f.335 Christians and Saracens fighting, from the "Chronique d'Ernoul et de Bernard le Tresorier," Bruges (vellum), Netherlandish School, (15th century) /British Library, London, UK/© British Library Board. All Rights Reserved/Bridgeman Art Library; 244, Frederick I with his two sons King Henry VI and Duke Frederick, ca 1180 (vellum), German School, (12th century)/Private Collection/Bridgeman Art Library; 246, Reliquary bust of Frederick I (ca 1123-1190) made in Aachen, 1155-71 (gilded bronze), German School, (12th century)/Church of St. Johannes, Cappenberg, Germany/Bridgeman Art Library; 248, The Krak des Chevaliers, reconstruction (engraving) (b/w photo), Sauvageot, Claude (1832-85)/Private Collection/Giraudon/Bridgeman Art Library; 249, Group of Troubadours, illustration from "Cantigas de Santa Maria," made under the direction of Alfonso X ("The Wise") King of Castille and Leon (1221-84) (vellum) (see also 56625), Spanish School, (13th century)/Biblioteca Monasterio del Escorial, Madrid, Spain/Bridgeman Art Library; 250, Roy 15 E I f.321v Baldwin II visits Manuel Comnenus, from Estoire d'Outremer (vellum), Flemish School, (15th century)/ British Library, London, UK/© British Library Board. All Rights Reserved/Bridgeman Art Library; 252, Bruce Dale; 253, Map of Paris from "Civitates orbis terrarrum" by Georg Braun (1541-1622) and Franz Hogenbergh (1540-92), French, 1572-1617, Braun, Georg (1541-1622) and Hogenberg, Franz (1535-90)/Bibliothèque Nationale, Paris, France/Lauros/Giraudon/ Bridgeman Art Library; 254, Guido Cozzi/Atlantide Phototravel/CORBIS; 255, Pilgrim badge of St. Thomas Becket (pewter), English School, (14th century)/© Museum of London, UK/ Bridgeman Art Library; 256, MS. 6, fol.136v Murder of St Thomas a Becket, from the St Alban's Chronicle (vellum), English School, (15th century)/© Lambeth Palace Library, London, UK/ Bridgeman Art Library; 257, Parable of the Fig Tree, 12th Century (stained glass), English School, (12th century)/Private Collection/Bridgeman Art Library; 259, Three scenes from "Parsifal" by Wolfram von Eschenbach (d.ca 1230) facsimile from a 13th century manuscript (color litho), German School, (19th century)/Bibliothèque des Arts Decoratifs, Paris, France/ Archives Charmet/Bridgeman Art Library; 260, Copy of a fresco depicting Queen Thamar (1184-1213) and her father King Grigori III (1156-1184) (color litho), Georgian School, (12th century) (after)/Bibliothèque des Arts Decoratifs, Paris, France/Archives Charmet/Bridgeman Art Library; 261, View of the castle surrounded by trees (photo)/Dunster Castle, Somerset, UK/National Trust Photographic Library/Magnus Rew/Bridgeman Art Library; 262 (UP), Chimu Deathmask, 12th-15th century (gold), Peruvian School/Museo del Oro, Lima, Peru/ Bildarchiv Steffens Henri Stierlin/Bridgeman Art Library; 262 (LO), Monolithic Statues at Rano Raraku Quarry, ca 1000-1600 (photo)/Easter Island, Polynesia/Ken Welsh/Bridgeman Art Library; 263 (UP), akg-images; 263 (LO), Angkor Vat Temple, Cambodia (photo)/Angkor Wat, Cambodia/© Dirk Radzinski/Bridgeman Art Library; 264, St. Bernard of Clairvaux (1090-1153) and William X (1099-1137) Duke of Aquitaine (oil on canvas), Pepyn or Pepin, Martin (1575-1642)/Musée des Beaux-Arts, Valenciennes, France/Giraudon/Bridgeman Art Library; 266, Ms. 400-2000: Miniature from Gratian's Decretum showing a bishop preaching to a congregation, ca 1325-30 (vellum), Italian School, (14th century)/Fitzwilliam Museum, University of Cambridge, UK/Bridgeman Art Library; 267, iew of the West facade, begun ca 1135 (photo), French School, (12th century)/Basilique Saint-Denis, France/Peter Willi/ Bridgeman Art Library; 268, Richard Thompson; 270 (UP), Ms 645-647/315-317 t.III Tristan in Battle, from the Roman de Tristan (vellum), French School, (15th century)/Musée Conde, Chantilly, France/Lauros/Giraudon/Bridgeman Art Library; 270 (LO), Ms 139/1363 fol.44v An angel carrying two coats of arms, from "Le Miroir de l'Humaine Salvation" (vellum), Flemish School, (15th century)/Musée Conde, Chantilly, France/Lauros/Giraudon/Bridgeman Art Library; 271 (UP), F. Kellerhoven chromolithograph from Science and Literature in The Middle Ages, 1878, Bickers and Son; 271 (LO LE), akg-images/Electa; 271 (LO RT), Suit of armour and matching horse armour, English School, (15th century)/Private Collection/Photo © Boltin Picture Library/Bridgeman Art Library

10 The Rise of Commerce 1200-1300

272-273, The Birth of the Virgin (fresco), Astrapas and Eutychios (13th-14th century)/Church of Sveti Kliment, Ohrid, Macedonia/Bridgeman Art Library; 274, Map of England, Scotland and Wales, Ms Royal 14.C VII, fol 5 v, 1250 (vellum), Paris, Matthew (ca 1200-59)/British Library, London, UK/The Stapleton Collection/Bridgeman Art Library; 276, The crown of St. Louis, 13th century (silver-gilt inlaid with precious stones), French School, (13th century)/Louvre, Paris, France/Bridgeman Art Library; 278, Cott Vitt A XIII f.6 Henry III being Crowned, from the "Decrees of Kings of Anglo-Saxon and Norman England" (vellum), English School, (14th century)/British Library, London, UK/© British Library Board. All Rights Reserved/Bridgeman Art Library; 279, Lebrecht Music & Arts/CORBIS; 280, The Magna Carta of Liberties, Third Version issued in 1225 by Henry III (vellum), English School, (13th century)/Dept. of the Environment, London, UK/Bridgeman Art Library; 281, Bettmann/CORBIS; 282, Simon Russell/Getty Images; 283, Map of London, from "Civitates Orbis Terrarum," by Georg Braun (1542-1622) and Frans Hogenburg (1635-90),ca 1572 (colored engraving), Hoefnagel, Joris (1542-1600) (after)/Guildhall Library, City of London/Bridgeman Art Library; 284, Scala/Art Resource, NY; 285, Pair of wooden tally sticks, Gloucester, England, 13th century/© Jewish Museum London; 286, Ciborium, made in Limoges by G. Alpais for the Abbey at Montmajour, 13th century (gold, enamel and precious stones)/Louvre, Paris, France/Peter Willi/Bridgeman Art Library; 287, Hulton-Deutsch Collection/CORBIS; 289, Map of Rostock, from "Civitates Orbis TeRrarum" by Georg Braun (1541-1622) and Frans Hogenberg (1535-90) ca 1572-1617 (colored engraving), Hoefnagel, Joris (1542-1600) (after)/Private Collection/The Stapleton Collection/Bridgeman Art Library; 290, akg-images; 291, © National Gallery, London/Art Resource, NY; 292, The Temple of Warriors and the Hall of 1000 Columns, built 10th-12th century (photo), Mayan/Chichen Itza, Yucatan, Mexico/Bildarchiv Steffens Henri Stierlin/Bridgeman Art Library; 293 (UP), Stapleton Collection/CORBIS; 293 (LO), akg-images/Werner Forman; 293 (RT), akg-images/Rainer Hackenberg; 294, Ms 129 f.32 A Lesson in Theology at the Sorbonne, from Postilles sur le Pentateuch, illustration to text written by Nicolas de Lyre (vellum), French School, (15th century)/Bibliothèque Municipale, Troyes, France/Bridgeman Art Library; 297, akg-images; 298, Alinari Archives/CORBIS; 299, Rose and lancet windows from the north wall (stained glass), French School, (13th century)/Chartres Cathedral, Chartres, France/Giraudon/Bridgeman Art Library; 300, Wolfgang Kaehler/CORBIS; 301 (UP), Puku/Grand Tour/CORBIS; 301 (LO LE), The Castle Water Clock, Mamluk period, 1354 (ink, opaque w/e & gold on paper), Egyptian, (14th century)/Museum of Fine Arts, Boston, Massachusetts, USA/Francis Bartlett Donation of 1912 and Picture Fund/Bridgeman Art Library; 301 (LO RT), Oldest European Astrolabe, 1326 (brass), English School, (14th century)/British Museum, London, UK/Photo © Boltin Picture Library/Bridgeman Art Library

11 Out of the Ashes 1300-1400

302-303, akg-images/Jérôme da Cunha; 304, Chaucer (ca 1343-1400) reading his poems to the Court of Richard II of England (1367-1400) (vellum)/Corpus Christi College, Cambridge, UK/Bridgeman Art Library; 306, Green glazed jug with a man's bearded face (pottery), English School, (14th century)/© Museum of London, UK/Bridgeman Art Library; 308, Statue of Pope Boniface VIII (1235-1303) 1301 (bronze), Manno di Bandino (fl.1301-12)/Museo Civico Medievale, Bologna, Italy/Lauros/Giraudon/Bridgeman Art Library; 310, Dante, Virgil and the Plague-stricken, from "The Divine Comedy" by Dante Alighieri (1265-1321) (vellum), Italian School, (14th century)/Biblioteca Marciana, Venice, Italy/Bridgeman Art Library; 311, Giovanni Boccaccio (1313-1375) (engraving), English School, (19th century)/Private Collection/Ken Welsh/Bridgeman Art Library; 312, James L. Amos; 313, The "Carta della Catena" showing a panorama of Florence, 1490 (detail of 161573), Italian School, (15th century)/Museo de Firenze Com'era, Florence, Italy/Alinari/Bridgeman Art Library; 314, Roy 18 D 11 f.148 Lydgate and the Canterbury Pilgrims leaving Canterbury from "Troy Book and the Siege of Thebes' by John Lydgate (ca 1370-ca 1451) 1412-22 (vellum), English School, (15th century)/British Library, London, UK/© British Library Board. All Rights Reserved/Bridgeman Art Library; 316, akg-images; 317, John Wycliffe reading his translation of the Bible to John of Gaunt, 1847-48, Brown, Ford Madox (1821-93)/© Bradford Art Galleries and Museums, West Yorkshire, UK/Bridgeman Art Library; 318, Battle of Poitiers, depicting the Prince of Wales and King Jean of France, 1367, from Froissart's Chronicle, late 15th century (vellum), French School, (15th century)/Bibliothèque de L'Arsenal, Paris, France/Index/Bridgeman Art Library; 319, Portrait of Sir William Wallace, ca 1870 (ca 1272-1305) (oil on canvas), Scottish School (19th century)/Smith Art Gallery and Museum, Stirling, Scotland/Bridgeman Art Library; 320, Seal of Robert VIII Bruce, 1326 (stone), Scottish School, (14th century)/Centre Historique des Archives Nationales, Paris, France/Giraudon/Bridgeman Art Library; 321, akg-images/Jost Schilgen; 322 (UP), Koran Page, Mamluk, ca 1400 (ink, gold & color on paper), Egyptian, (15th century)/Museum of Fine Arts, Boston, Massachusetts, USA/Denman Waldo Ross Collection/Bridgeman Art Library; 322 (LO), The Casa Grande Ruins Reservation, built early 14th century (photo), Hohokam/Gila Valley, Arizona, USA/Ancient Art and Architecture Collection Ltd./Bridgeman Art Library; 323 (UP), Comical Mask, Noh Theatre (painted wood), Japanese School, (19th century)/American Museum of Natural History, New York, USA/Photo © Boltin Picture Library/Bridgeman Art Library; 323 (LO), Othman (Osman) I (1259-1326), founder of the Ottoman empire, Sultan 1299-1326, from "A Series of Portraits of the Emperors of Turkey," 1808 (w/c), Young, John (1755-1825)/Private Collection/The Stapleton Collection/Bridgeman Art Library; 324, Ms 624/1596, fol.17r, Compass Rose, from "Liber Floridus" by Lambert de Saint-Omer, ca 1448 (vellum), Flemish School, (15th century)/Musée Conde, Chantilly, France/Bridgeman Art Library; 325, Cott Nero E II pt2 fol.100v The Templars before Philippe IV (1268-1314) and Pope Clement V (ca 1260-1320), from "The Chronicles of France" (vellum), Boucicaut Master, (fl.1390-1430) (and workshop)/British Library, London, UK/Bridgeman Art Library; 326, View of the Dome, Timurid period, ca 1403 (photo)/Gur-i-Amir Mausoleum, Samarkand, Uzbekistan/Bridgeman Art Library; 327, Mosque lamp with enamelled decoration inscribed with three quotations from the Koran and dedicated to Beybars II, early 14th century (glass), Syrian School, (14th century)/Victoria & Albert Museum, London, UK/Bridgeman Art Library; 328, Harl 4431 fol.3 Christine de Pisan presenting her book to Queen Isabella of Bavaria (1371-1435), from the poems of Christine de Pisan, ca 1410-15 (vellum) (detail of 53284), Master of the Cite des Dames (15th century)/British Library, London, UK/© British Library Board. All Rights Reserved/Bridgeman Art Library; 329, Roy 20 C VII f.48 Jacques de Molay, last leader of the Knights Templar, burned at the stake for heresy in 1314 (manuscript), French School, (14th century)/British Library, London, UK/© British Library Board. All Rights Reserved/Bridgeman Art Library; 330, A Musician, from "De Musica" by Boethius (480-524) (vellum), Italian School, (14th century)/Biblioteca Nazionale, Naples, Italy/Giraudon/Bridgeman Art Library; 331 (UP LE), Citole, ca 1280-1330 (carved wood), English School/British Museum, London, UK/Photo © Boltin Picture Library/Bridgeman Art Library; 331 (UP RT), akg-images; 331 (LO LE), F.86 Two Men Dancing, from the Beatus Apocalypse from Santo Domingo de Silos, 1109 (vellum), Spanish School, (12th century)/British Library, London, UK/© British Library Board. All Rights Reserved/Bridgeman Art Library; 331 (LO RT), Harp (wood with brass & silver), Celtic, (15th century)/National Museum of Ireland, Dublin, Ireland/Photo © Boltin Picture Library/Bridgeman Art Library

12 The Dawn of a New Age 1400-1500

332-333, Biblioteca Estsense Universitaria, Modena; 334, Virgin Hodegetria Icon of Smolensk, ca 1450 (tempera on fabric, gesso, and wood), Russian School, (15th century)/Tretyakov Gallery, Moscow, Russia/Bridgeman Art Library; 336, Head presumed to be of Joan of Arc (1412-31) (terracotta), French School, (15th century)/Musée des Beaux-Arts, Orleans, France/Archives Charmet/Bridgeman Art Library; 338, Christopher Columbus (oil on panel), Piombo, Sebastiano del (S. Luciani) (ca 1485-1547)/Metropolitan Museum of Art, New York, USA/Peter Newark Pictures/Bridgeman Art Library; 339, Stephanie Maze/CORBIS; 340, Fr 2643 f.97v Battle of Neville's Cross from the Hundred Years War in 1341, from Froissart's Chronicle (vellum), French School, (15th century)/Bibliothèque Nationale, Paris, France/Bridgeman Art Library; 341, Ric Ergenbright/CORBIS; 342, Image Source/Getty Images; 343, Map of Barcelona, from "Civitates Orbis Terrarum" by Georg Braun (1541-1622) and Frans Hogenberg (1535-90), 1567 (colored engraving), Hoefnagel, Joris (1542-1600) (after)/Private Collection/The Stapleton Collection/Bridgeman Art Library; 344, Vanni/Art Resource, NY; 345, Historiated Initial depicting Joan of Arc (1412-31), 15th century (vellum), French School, (15th century)/Centre Historique des Archives Nationales, Paris, France/Archives Charmet/Bridgeman Art Library; 346, akg-images; 348, Amurath (Murad) II (1404-51) Sultan 1421-51, from "A Series of Portraits of the Emperors of Turkey," 1808 (w/c), Young, John (1755-1825)/Private Collection/The Stapleton Collection/Bridgeman Art Library; 349, Icon of St. John the Baptist (tempera on panel), Rublev, Andrei (ca 1370-1430)/Andrei Rublev Museum, Moscow, Russia/Bridgeman Art Library; 350 (UP), Page from a copy of the Codex Mendoza, showing information about towns giving tribute of warriors' clothing, dried chillies and bags of feathers/British Museum, London, UK/Bridgeman Art Library; 350 (LO), Bates Littlehales; 351 (UP), Set of anklets, from West Africa (iron), African, (19th century)/Private Collection/© Michael Graham-Stewart/Bridgeman Art Library; 351 (LO), The Jummah Musjed, Delhi, plate XXIII from "Oriental Scenery," published 1797 (colored aquatint), Daniell, Thomas (1749-1840)/Private Collection/The Stapleton Collection/Bridgeman Art Library; 352, The Garden of Earthly Delights: Allegory of Luxury, detail of the central panel, ca 1500 (oil on panel), Bosch, Hieronymus (ca 1450-1516)/Prado, Madrid, Spain/Bridgeman Art Library; 354, Matthias I, Hunyadi (oil on paper)/Kunsthistorisches Museum, Vienna, Austria/Bridgeman Art Library; 355, Portrait of Johannes Gutenberg (ca 1400-68) (engraving) (later coloration), Mentz, Albrecht (15th century) (after)/Bibliothèque Nationale, Paris, France/Bridgeman Art Library; 356, Image Asset Management Ltd./SuperStock; 357, Autodafe of Books in the Middle Ages, illustration from the "Nuremberg Chronicle" by Hartmann Schedel (1440-1514) 1493 (colored woodcut), Wolgemuth, M. (1434-1519) & Pleydenwurff, W. (d.1494)/Bibliothèque Sainte-Genevieve, Paris, France/Archives Charmet/Bridgeman Art Library; 358, Portrait of Lorenzo de' Medici "the Magnificent" (1449-92) (panel), Italian School, (15th century)/Palazzo Medici-Riccardi, Florence, Italy/Bridgeman Art Library; 359, Detail from the Catalan Atlas, 1375 (vellum), Cresques, Abraham (1325-87)/Bibliothèque Nationale, Paris, France/Bridgeman Art Library; 360, © The British Library Board. All Rights Reserved. Maps.856.(6), lower centre; 361, Additional Ms 28681, f.9: World Map (vellum), English School, (13th century)/British Library, London, UK/© British Library Board. All Rights Reserved/Bridgeman Art Library; 362, Roy.Ms.14 CA f.1 1v-2r Map of the World with Jerusalem as the Centre, Polychronicon, ca 1380, Higden, Ranulf (d.1364)/British Library, London, UK/© British Library Board. All Rights Reserved/Bridgeman Art Library; 363, Ms 782 fol.16v. Map of the world in the form of a globe, miniature from "Grandes Chroniques de Philippe le Hardi" (vellum), French School, (14th century)/Bibliothèque Sainte-Genevieve, Paris, France/Archives Charmet/Bridgeman Art Library

INDEX

Boldface indicates illustrations. *Italic* indicates time line entry.

The Medieval World: An Illustrated Atlas
John M. Thompson

Published by the National Geographic Society
John M. Fahey, Jr., President and Chief Executive Officer
Gilbert M. Grosvenor, Chairman of the Board
Tim T. Kelly, President, Global Media Group
John Q. Griffin, Executive Vice President; President, Publishing
Nina D. Hoffman, Executive Vice President;
 President, Book Publishing Group

Prepared by the Book Division
Barbara Brownell Grogan, Vice President and Editor in Chief
Marianne R. Koszorus, Director of Design
Carl Mehler, Director of Maps
R. Gary Colbert, Production Director
Jennifer A. Thornton, Managing Editor
Meredith C. Wilcox, Administrative Director, Illustrations

Staff for This Book
Susan Tyler Hitchcock, Editor
Karin Kinney, Text Editor
Adrian Coakley, Illustrations Editor
Carol Norton, Art Director
Sanaa Akkach, Senior Designer
Roderick Martin, Consulting Historian
Sven M. Dolling, Principal Cartographer
Matt Chwastyk, Michael McNey, Nicholas P. Rosenbach, Gregory Ugiansky,
 Contributing Cartographers
Dan O'Toole, Bethanne Patrick, Lauren Pruneski, Tiffin Thompson,
 Contributing Writers
Mike Horenstein, Production Project Manager
Robert Waymouth, Illustrations Specialist
Al Morrow, Design Assistant

Manufacturing and Quality Management
Christopher A. Liedel, Chief Financial Officer
Phillip L. Schlosser, Vice President
Chris Brown, Technical Director
Nicole Elliott, Manager
Rachel Faulise, Manager

The National Geographic Society is one of the world's largest nonprofit scientific and educational organizations. Founded in 1888 to "increase and diffuse geographic knowledge," the Society works to inspire people to care about the planet. It reaches more than 325 million people worldwide each month through its official journal, *National Geographic,* and other magazines; National Geographic Channel; television documentaries; music; radio; films; books; DVDs; maps; exhibitions; school publishing programs; interactive media; and merchandise. National Geographic has funded more than 9,000 scientific research, conservation and exploration projects and supports an education program combating geographic illiteracy. For more information, visit nationalgeographic.com.

For more information, please call 1-800-NGS LINE (647-5463) or write to the following address:

National Geographic Society
1145 17th Street N.W.
Washington, D.C. 20036-4688 U.S.A.

Visit us online at www.nationalgeographic.com

For information about special discounts for bulk purchases, please contact National Geographic Books Special Sales: ngspecsales@ngs.org

For rights or permissions inquiries, please contact National Geographic Books Subsidiary Rights: ngbookrights@ngs.org

Library of Congress Cataloging-in-Publication Data

National Geographic Society (U.S.)
 The medieval world : an illustrated atlas.
  p. cm.
 Includes index.
 ISBN 978-1-4262-0533-0 (regular ed.) -- ISBN 978-1-4262-0534-7 (deluxe ed.)
 1. Civilization, Medieval--Maps. 2. Europe--Historical geography--Maps. I. Title.
 G1791.N2 2009
 911.09'02--dc22
                                        2009029741

ISBN: 978-1-4262-0533-0
        978-1-4262-0534-7 Deluxe

Printed in U.S.A.

09/RRDW/1